SHACKLETON ON
THE LAW AND PRACTICE OF MEETINGS

AUSTRALIA
Law Book Co
Sydney

CANADA and USA
Carswell
Toronto

HONG KONG
Sweet & Maxwell Asia

NEW ZEALAND
Brookers
Auckland

SINGAPORE and MALAYSIA
Sweet & Maxwell Asia
Singapore and Kuala Lumpur

SHACKLETON

ON THE
LAW AND PRACTICE
OF MEETINGS

TENTH EDITION

By

MADELEINE CORDES, LLB, FCIS
JOHN PUGH-SMITH, MA (Oxon), FSA
ALEX RUCK KEENE, MA (Oxon), MA (Johns Hopkins)
JAMES BURTON
GERALDINE CAULFIELD, ACIS
ROBIN WAGHORN, LLB, ACIS

LONDON
SWEET & MAXWELL
2006

First Edition (1934)
Second Edition (1948)
Third Edition (1951)
Fourth Edition (1958)
Second Impression (1960)
Fifth Edition (1967)
Sixth Edition (1977)
Seventh Edition (1983)
Eighth Edition (1991)
Ninth Edition (1997)
Tenth Edition (2006)

Published in 2006 by Sweet and Maxwell Limited
100 Avenue Road
London NW3 3PF
(http://www.sweetandmaxwell.co.uk)

Computerset by Interactive Sciences Limited, Gloucester
Printed and bound in Great Britain by Athenaeum Press Ltd., Gateshead.

No natural forests were destroyed to make this product;
only farmed timber was used and re-planted.

ISBN 042192200

A CIP catalogue record for this book is available
from the British Library.

PREFACE

Shackleton has been acknowledged, for many years, as the authoritative source of information on the law and practice of meetings. This Tenth Edition contains, like previous editions, a complete statement of the law with detailed practical guidance. It draws the reader's attention to recent legislative changes arising from the Human Rights Act 1998, Anti-social Behaviour Act 2003, Terrorism Act 2000, Electronic Communications Order 2000, the Combined Code on Corporate Governance published in 2003, changes in the Listing Rules, Community Interest Companies, Societas Europaea, Local Government Act 2000, and the Enterprise Act 2002.

As a public law practitioner, specialising in environmental, planning and related administrative law, I have always found *Shackleton* an extremely useful reference source; and it was an enquiry to Sweet & Maxwell, my own publishers, last year as to the likelihood of a new edition which led to my personal involvement in this project, as general editor of the public law chapters and now the author of this Preface. My personal thanks go to my 39 Essex Street colleagues, James Burton and Alex Ruck Keene, who actually took up the challenge of updating those particular Chapters (10, 28 and 29) and graciously took on board my modest suggestions.

With a work embracing so many diverse areas of law and practice, due recognition should also go to Madeleine Cordes (Chapters 1–9, 18–23, 30), Geraldine Caulfield (Chapters 11–17, 25–27) and Robin Waghorn (Chapter 24) without whose labours the copy would never have reached Sweet & Maxwell by the deadline. Our collective thanks also go to the staff of Kent University's Law Library.

To all involved in the practice of meetings we hope that you will find this Tenth Edition of particular help.

John Pugh-Smith
39 Essex Street Chambers
36–39 Essex Street
London
WC2R 3AT

ABOUT THE AUTHORS

Madeleine Cordes, LLB, FCIS, has 20 years' experience as a Chartered Secretary in industry. She was Company Secretary of Carpetright, a FTSE 250 company from 1993 to 1999 and worked on the flotation of Orange on the Paris Stock Exchange in 2001. Her recent role as a Senior Manager in Ernst & Young's Company Secretarial Group involved compliance and corporate governance support for FTSE 250 companies, large private companies and companies preparing to float. In January 2005 Madeleine joined Capita Registrars as Director of their fast growing Company Secretarial Services division which provides company secretarial outsourced and support services to The Capita Group plc and a portfolio of clients ranging from AIM companies to investment trusts. Madeleine is a regular speaker at conferences and is also Executive Editor of Gee's Company Secretary's Factbook.

John Pugh-Smith MA (Oxon), FSA is a barrister and CEDR accreditated mediator practising from 39 Essex Street Chambers. He has been instructed by many developers and local authorities for a number of years on Planning, Environmental and related Local Government work and is highly regarded as a leading and experienced junior in these fields. He has been the originating author, editor and contributor to a range of titles, from *Neighbours and the Law* (4th Edition, 2006), *Archaeology in Law* (1996), to OUP's *Environmental Law* (2000), the Planning, Property & Compensation Reports ("P&CR"), the Journal of Planning & Environment Law and the Landscape Design Journal. He is a Fellow of the Society of Antiquaries, member of UKELA and ELF and on the committee of PEBA. He regularly lectures at seminars on both planning and environment law and practice, including Sweet & Maxwell's Annual *Planning Law Conference*.

Alex Ruck Keene came to the Bar via History at Oxford and International Relations at Johns Hopkins. He is a tenant at 39 Essex Street, where his areas of speciality include local government and environment and planning. In 2004–5, he spent 9 months on secondment one day a week to Buckinghamshire County Council, where he advised on matters ranging from highways to hire cars, and acted in environmental and educational prosecutions; for the Council he also conducted a three month inquiry into how allegations of child abuse were handled at a maintained school in the 1980s. He is the 2005 Pegasus Scholar at the European Court of Human Rights.

James Burton was called to the Bar in October 2001 and is a tenant at 39 Essex Street. He has a broad practice that includes a range of local government work, in respect of which James has the benefit of experience gained during a year-long weekly secondment with Buckinghamshire County Council. James has advised local authorities on matters ranging from waste trading schemes to ASBOs to highway-obstructing Christmas trees. He appears at inquiries into planning appeals, enforcement proceedings and definitive map modification orders. James also conducts environmental prosecutions and enjoys a full range of common law work, from negligence actions through to representation in the employment tribunals. He advises on and appears in judicial review proceedings and has carried out statutory drafting work for the ODPM. Presently James is assisting the FSA in connection with the capital adequacy directive.

CONTENTS

CHAPTER 1
THE LEGAL RIGHT

CHAPTER 2
BREACH OF THE PEACE AND OTHER ASPECTS OF THE CRIMINAL LAW

CHAPTER 3
THE MAINTENANCE OF ORDER

CHAPTER 4
A PUBLIC MEETING

CONTENTS

CHAPTER 5
CONVENING THE MEETING

CHAPTER 6
CONSTITUTION AND ADJOURNMENT OF THE MEETING

CONTENTS

CHAPTER 7
THE CONDUCT OF THE MEETING

CHAPTER 8
MINUTES

CHAPTER 9
THE COMMITTEE SYSTEM

CHAPTER 10
THE PRINCIPLES OF NATURAL JUSTICE

CHAPTER 11
APPLICABLE LAW AND OTHERS MATTERS

CHAPTER 12
MEMBERS' MEETINGS: STATUS AND CONVENTION

CHAPTER 13
CONSTITUTING A MEMBERS' MEETING

CHAPTER 14
MEMBERS' MEETINGS: ATTENDANCE AND VOTING

CHAPTER 15
MEMBERS' MEETINGS: RESOLUTIONS

CHAPTER 16
MEMBERS' MEETINGS: MINUTES

CHAPTER 17
CLASS MEETINGS

CHAPTER 18
MEETINGS UNDER SECTION 425
(COMPROMISES AND ARRANGEMENTS)

CHAPTER 19
MEETINGS OF MEMBERS OF COMPANIES: EXAMPLES IN PRACTICE

CHAPTER 20
POWERS AND DUTIES OF DIRECTORS

CHAPTER 21
APPOINTMENT TO AND DEPARTURE FROM OFFICE

CHAPTER 22
CONSTITUTION AND CONDUCT OF DIRECTORS' MEETINGS

CHAPTER 23
BOARD MEETINGS: EXAMPLES IN PRACTICE

CHAPTER 24
MEETINGS IN INSOLVENCY SITUATIONS, SHORT OF WINDING UP

CHAPTER 25
MEETINGS IN INSOLVENCY SITUATIONS—WINDING UP

CHAPTER 26
PROXIES AND COMPANY REPRESENTATION
IN AN INSOLVENCY

CHAPTER 27
MEMBERS' VOLUNTARY WINDING UP

CHAPTER 28
MEETINGS OF LOCAL AUTHORITIES

CHAPTER 29
LOCAL AUTHORITIES AND OTHER BODIES—ACCESS TO MEETINGS AND INFORMATION

CONTENTS

CHAPTER 30
DEFAMATORY STATEMENTS

TABLE OF CASES

[References throughout these tables are to paragraph numbers]

TABLE OF STATUTES

1

TABLE OF STATUTORY INSTRUMENTS

CHAPTER 1

THE LEGAL RIGHT

1 AN HISTORICAL VIEW

Wills J., in a case in 1888 relating to a meeting in Trafalgar Square, said that the **1–01**
right of public meeting "has long passed out of the region of discussion or doubt."[1]
The right rests on the fundamental assumption in our law that a citizen is free to
do something unless restrained by the common law, including the law of contract,
or by statute.[2] The state has a positive obligation to enable lawful demonstrations
to proceed in a peaceful manner.[3] The point is put as follows in Dicey's *Introduction
to the Study of the Law of the Constitution*:

> "No better instance can be found of the way in which in England the
> constitution is built up upon individual rights than our rules as to public
> assemblies. The right of assembling is nothing more than a result of the view
> taken by the courts as to individual liberty of a person and individual liberty
> of speech."[4]

On this view, the liberty to meet with others in a public place is an individual, **1–02**
rather than a collective right.

In *Hirst and Agu v. Chief Constable of West Yorkshire*[5] Otton J. said that the rights
to demonstrate and protest on matters of public concern are rights which it is in
the public interest that individuals should possess and exercise without impedi-
ment, as long as no wrongful act is done and there is no obstruction to traffic.

The White Paper, *Review of Public Order Law* (1985), used positive language:

> "The rights of peaceful protest and assembly are amongst our fundamental
> freedoms: they are numbered among the touchstones which distinguish a free
> society from a totalitarian one."[6]

The same concept finds expression in Article 11 of the European Convention on
Human Rights, to which the United Kingdom is a signatory and which has now
been incorporated into domestic law by the Human Rights Act 1998 which came
into force in October 2000:

---

[1] *Ex p. Lewis* (1888) 21 Q.B.D. 191, 196.
[2] *A.-G. v. Guardian Newspapers Ltd (No. 2)* [1988] 3 All E.R. 545, 596.
[3] Halsbury's Laws (4th ed.) Vol. 8(2) (Re-issue) para.160.
[4] (10th ed., 1959), p. 271.
[5] [1987] Crim.L.R. 330.
[6] Cmnd. 9510 (1985), para.1.7. This will be referred to below as the "White Paper."

"(1) Everyone has the right to freedom of peaceful assembly and to freedom of association with others, including the right to form and to join trade unions for the protection of his interests.

(2) No restrictions shall be placed on the exercise of these rights other than such as are prescribed by law and are necessary in a democratic society in the interests of national security or public safety, for the prevention of disorder or crime, for the protection of health or morals or for the protection of the rights and freedoms of others. This Article shall not prevent the imposition of lawful restrictions on the exercise of these rights by members of the armed forces, or the police, or of the administration of the State."

The right to freedom of assembly covers peaceful protests and demonstrations. Public and private meetings are protected under this Article and may be limited mainly on the grounds of public order. The right to freedom of association guarantees the capacity of all persons to join with others to attain a particular objective.

Article 10(1) and (2) of the Convention provides that everyone has the right to freedom of expression. This right shall include freedom to hold opinions and to receive and impart information and ideas without interference by public authority and regardless of frontiers . . . The exercise of these freedoms, since it carries with it duties and responsibilities, may be subject to such formalities, conditions, restrictions or penalties as are prescribed by law and are necessary in a democratic society, in the interests of national security, territorial integrity or public safety, for the prevention of disorder or crime, for the protection of health or morals, for the protection of the reputation or rights of others, for preventing the disclosure of information received in confidence, or for maintaining the authority and impartiality of the judiciary".

Primary and secondary legislation and the common law can be made the subject of an action under the Human Rights Act, in addition to decisions and actions of public authorities. Section 6 of the Act makes it unlawful for public authorities to act in a way which is incompatible with the rights in the Convention.

The important qualification which exists in relation to public assemblies is that the participants must not commit a breach of civil or criminal law, for example by trespassing on private property, committing a nuisance or infringing the provisions of the Public Order Act 1986, as amended and added to by the Criminal Justice and Public Order Act 1994.[7] These limitations are discussed in greater detail below.

2   ASSEMBLIES

Public Order Act 1986, s.14 (Imposing Conditions on Public Assemblies)

1–03   The Public Order Act 1986 introduced into English law a general statutory right for the police to impose conditions on public assemblies. Some statutory control

---

[7] See Halsbury's *Statutes* (4th ed.) Vol. 12 (Re-issue) 1060 and current Statutes Service.

had previously existed in relation to processions,[8] but static meetings had been subject to control only through the general obligation of the police to prevent disorder and to preserve the peace.[9]

An important distinction between the two types of event is that there is no requirement on the organisers of a public meeting to notify the police in advance, whereas in relation to processions, prior notice has in certain circumstances to be given.[10]

Section 14(1) of the Act provides as follows:

> "(1) If the senior police officer, having regard to the time or place at which and the circumstances in which any public assembly is being held or is intended to be held, reasonably believes that—
> (a) it may result in serious public disorder, serious damage to property or serious disruption to the life of the community; or
> (b) the purpose of the persons organising it is the intimidation of others with a view to compelling them not to do an act they have a right to do, or to do an act they have a right not to do,
> he may give directions imposing on the persons organising or taking part in the assembly such conditions as to the place at which the assembly may be (or continue to be) held, its maximum duration, or the maximum number of persons who may constitute it, as appear to him necessary to prevent such disorder, damage, disruption or intimidation."

A number of definitions should be noted. "Public assembly" means "an assembly of 2 or more persons in a public place which is wholly or partly open to the air."[11] It should be noted that prior to this amendment made to the Public Order Act by the Anti-social Behaviour Act 2003, public assembly meant an assembly of "20" or more persons. "Public place" in turn is defined as any highway or any place to which at the material time the public or any section of the public has access, on payment or otherwise, as of right by virtue of express or implied permission.[12]

"The senior police officer" for the purposes of the section means, in relation to an assembly being held, the most senior in rank of the police officers present at the scene, and in relation to an assembly intended to be held, the chief officer of police.[13] Powers of delegation exist.[14]

Directions under section 14(1) are only valid if the time and place of the proposed assembly are sufficiently certain; it is not clear whether an offence under the section can be committed before the public assembly has taken place.[15]

A direction given in relation to an assembly which is intended to be held must be given in writing.[16]

---

[8] See para. 1–08.

[9] See para. 2–02.

[10] See para. 1–09.

[11] Public Order Act 1986, s.16, as amended by Anti-social Behaviour Act 2003, s.57.

[12] *ibid.*

[13] *ibid.*, s.14(2).

[14] *ibid.*, s.15.

[15] *D.P.P. v. Baillie* [1995] Crim.L.R. 426, D.C.

[16] *ibid.*, s.14(3). The distinction may be important in relation to the remedy of judicial review.

1–04   From the above it will be seen that the powers of the police in relation to the larger, open-air type of meeting are extensive although they are confined (under this section) to matters of venue, duration and number of participants. The Act does not in itself give the police any additional powers in relation to meetings in closed premises; if, however, an indoor meeting provokes a counter-demonstration outside the hall, this will itself be subject to the right of the police to impose controls under section 14.[17]

Further, it will be apparent from the reference to "serious disruption to the life of the community" in section 14 (1)(a) that the powers of the police will operate in relation even to meetings which are peaceful in intent, but which may cause, for example, severe traffic congestion.[18]

The powers exist when the senior police officer "reasonably believes" that the conditions defined in subsection (a) or (b) may be present. A case decided before the passing of the Act suggests that the courts may be reluctant to challenge the judgment of a chief officer of police who has had to bear the burden of dealing with events as they unfolded, particularly in cases of potential disorder.[19]

There must, however, be relevant evidence on which the chief of police forms his judgment:

> The defendant was charged with knowingly failing to comply with a condition imposed on a public assembly. The senior officer who had imposed the condition gave evidence that he defined "intimidation" (within the meaning of s.14(1)(b)) as "putting people in fear or discomfort". Held, that the question was whether the demonstrators acted with a view to "compelling" visitors not to go into South Africa House or merely with the intention of making them feel uncomfortable; the latter was not intimidation. The officer had not claimed in evidence that he believed the organisers acted with a view to compelling. Accordingly, he had had no ground for imposing the condition and the case was dismissed.[20]

The Anti-social Behaviour Act 2003 gives improved powers to deal with public assemblies and aggravated trespass, in particular the powers to disperse groups of two or more in designated areas suffering persistent and serious anti-social behaviour (s 30).

Public Order Act 1986, s.14A (Prohibiting Trespassory Assemblies)

1–05   This section, and sections 14B and 14C, were inserted into the Public Order Act 1986 by sections 70 and 71 of the Criminal Justice and Public Order Act 1994. These latter sections are contained in Part V of the 1994 Act, which includes provisions aimed at squatters, participants in raves and hunt saboteurs.

Section 14A(1) of the Act provides as follows:

---

[17] See also para. 2–02.
[18] See, for example, White Paper, para. 5.9.
[19] *Kent v. Metropolitan Police Commissioner, The Times*, May 15, 1981 C.A. See also *Thomas and others v. NUM (South Wales Area) and others* [1985] I.R.L.R. 136.
[20] *Police v. Reid (Lorna)* [1987] Crim.L.R. 702.

"(1) If at any time the chief officer of police reasonably believes that an assembly is intended to be held in any district on land to which the public has no right of access or only a limited right of access and that the assembly—

(a) is likely to be held without the permission of the occupier of the land or to conduct itself in such a way as to exceed the limits of any permission of his or the limits of the public's right of access, and

(b) may result—

(i) in serious disruption to the life of the community, or

(ii) where the land, or a building or monument on it, is of historical, archaeological or scientific importance, in significant damage to the land, building or monument,

he may apply to the council of the district for an order prohibiting for a specified period the holding of all trespassory assemblies in the district or a part of it, as specified."

Again, some definitions should be noted. "Assembly" means an assembly of two or more persons; "land" means land in the open air; "limited", in relation to a right of access by the public to land, means that their use of it is restricted to use for a particular purpose (as in the case of a highway or road) or is subject to other restrictions; "occupier" means the person entitled to possession of the land by virtue of an estate or interest held by him, and includes the person reasonably believed by the authority applying for or making the order to be the occupier; and "public" includes a section of the public.[21]

Section 14A(1) does not apply to the City of London or the metropolitan police district, but for these areas similar provisions are contained in section 14A(4).

An order prohibiting the holding of trespassory assemblies operates to prohibit any assembly which (a) is held on land to which the public has no right of access or only a limited right of access, and (b) takes place without the permission of the occupier of the land or so as to exceed the limits of any permission of his or the limits of the public's right of access.[22]

No order under the section shall prohibit the holding of assemblies for a period exceeding four days or in an area exceeding an area represented by a circle with a radius of five miles from a specified centre.[23]

The order may be made either in the terms of the application or in a modified form.[24]

Public Order Act 1986, s.14C (Stopping Persons from Proceeding to Trespassory Assemblies)

This section provides that if a constable in uniform reasonably believes that a **1–06** person is on his way to a prohibited assembly, he may stop him and direct him not to proceed in the direction of the assembly.

[21] Public Order Act 1986, s.14A(9).
[22] *ibid.*, s.14A(5).
[23] *ibid.*, s.14A(6).
[24] *ibid.*, s.14A(2).

Local Variations

1–07   Several local and particular enactments were repealed by the Public Order Act 1986 (for example the Seditious Meetings Act 1817, which related to meetings within a mile of Westminster Hall), but the following remain in force:

(a) Trafalgar Square: under the Trafalgar Square Regulations 1952,[25] wilfully interfering with the comfort of any person in the square is a prohibited act; the written permission of the Department of Culture (at 2–4 Cockspur Street, London SW1Y 5DH) is required for organising, conducting or taking part in any assembly, parade or procession, for making or giving a public speech or address, and for the use of sound amplifying equipment. The Department only accepts bookings for the square within three calendar months of the proposed meeting, so as to avoid block bookings and to allow for meetings of a topical nature. The Department has regard to such matters as the convenience of the public and the likelihood of traffic congestion. Under section 52 of the Metropolitan Police Act 1839 the commissioner of police is empowered to prevent obstruction in this area.

(b) Hyde Park: This park also comes within the jurisdiction of the Department of Culture (at Royal Parks Agency, Old Police House, Hyde Park, London W2 2UH). There are only two places where meetings are allowed : one is at Speakers' Corner and the other, for large gatherings, is at the Reformers' Tree area. Where large numbers are involved, the Department will arrange a meeting with the organisers to which the Metropolitan Police and any other interested parties are invited. Detailed instructions governing the use of the Park for the particular meeting are then issued by the Department.

The Royal Parks and Gardens generally are governed by the Parks Regulation Acts 1872 to 1977.[26]

(c) Defence establishments: processions and demonstrations on or near such establishments may need to take account of the Official Secrets Act 1911 (under which it is an offence, for a purpose prejudicial to the safety or interests of the State, to approach or enter a "prohibited place") and section 14 of the Military Lands Act 1892. Byelaws made in any year under the latter Act, which are local in character, are listed in the Classified List of Local Statutory Instruments (under Class 7) at the end of the annual volumes of S.R. O. and S.I. since 1924.[27]

(d) Universities etc.: section 43 of the Education (No.2) Act, 1986 (as amended by the Further and Higher Education Act 1992) provides that governing bodies of universities and other institutions within the higher and further education sectors are obliged to ensure freedom of speech for members, students and employees, and for visiting speakers, and have to maintain in force a code of practice to be followed in connection with the

---

[25] S.I. 1952 No. 776.

[26] See S.I.1977 No. 217 (The Royal and Other Parks and Gardens Regulations). The Department of Culture has prepared a list of the standard conditions under which organisations are allowed to assemble and/or hold a rally in Hyde Park.

[27] See also *D.P.P. v. Hutchinson* [1990] 3 W.L.R. 196, H.L.

organisation of meetings. The jurisdiction of the university or other body extends to its own premises; in considering whether to allow a meeting to be held, when there is a threat of disorder, it is not entitled to take into account threats of trouble outside its own precincts—that is a matter for the police.[28] Conditions restricting publicity and admission to the meeting, and relating to a charge for the provision of security, can be imposed where considered necessary in the interests of free speech and good order.[29]

3 PROCESSIONS AND MARCHES

Up to 1987 processions were regulated by a combination of the general powers of the police in relation to public order, a number of local authority enactments calling for advance notice,[30] and the general power under the Public Order Act 1936 permitting the re-routeing and banning of processions which in the view of a chief officer of police were likely to cause serious public disorder.[31]   **1–08**

These laws were in substance re-enacted, and new provisions were introduced by the Public Order Act 1986. These have since been extended by the Criminal Justice and Public Order Act 1994, the Crime and Disorder Act 1998 and recently amended by the Anti-social Behaviour Act 2003. Another significant statute is the Police and Criminal Evidence Act 1984 as amended by the rash of new measures post 2000, which give the police powers to arrest and detain people suspected of committing criminal offences. Even after these major pieces of recent legislation, public order law is far from unified. This is because, as well as their powers under these statutes, the police retain some historic common law powers such as the power to take action to prevent a breach of the peace (discussed in Chapter 2). Other legislation sometimes regulates the right to demonstrate, for instance picketing during industrial disputes is regulated by employment laws.

Set out below is a general summary of those provisions which may be most relevant where, for example, a meeting or rally is to be accompanied by a protest march.

Advance Notice

Section 11(1) of the Public Order Act 1986 requires advance written notice to be given of any proposal to hold a public procession intended: **1–09**

    (a) to demonstrate support for or opposition to the views or actions of any person or body of persons,

    (b) to publicise a cause or campaign, or

    (c) to mark or commemorate an event

---

[28] R. v. University of Liverpool, ex p. Caesar-Gordon [1991] 1 Q.B. 124.

[29] ibid.

[30] For example, the West Midlands County Council Act which required, in general, 72 hours' advance notice of processions to be given.

[31] Public Order Act 1936, s.3.

unless it is not reasonably practicable to give advance notice of the procession.[32] "Public procession" means a procession in a public place.[32]

The advance notice requirement does not apply where the procession is one which is commonly or customarily held in the relevant police area.[33]

The notice must specify the date when it is intended to hold the procession, the time when it is intended to start it, its proposed route, and the name and address of the person (or one of the persons) proposing to organise it.[34]

Notice must be delivered to a police station in the police area in which it is proposed the procession will start.[35] Normally six clear[36] days' notice has to be given. The exception arises where (as noted above) it is not "reasonably practicable" to give any advance notice. This provision was inserted in the Act to cover the situation where it is likely (indeed may be desirable) that a march is arranged rapidly to deal with an urgent issue. The words "reasonably practicable" are not defined and still await the interpretation of the courts. Organisers of rallies, however, must, where notice can be given before the procession, give it to the police as soon as delivery is reasonably practicable, and, however late it is given, the police have power to impose conditions under section 12 (see below). Notice should normally be given by hand, but provided six clear days' notice can be given, the recorded delivery service can be used.[37]

Imposing Conditions on Processions

1–10   Under section 12(1) of the Public Order Act 1986, if the senior police officer, having regard to the time or place at which and the circumstances in which any public procession is being held or is intended to be held and to its route or proposed route, reasonably believes that:

  (a) it may result in serious public disorder, serious damage to property or serious disruption to the life of the community, or
  (b) the purpose of the persons organising it is the intimidation of others with a view to compelling them not to do an act they have a right to do, or to do an act they have a right not to do,

he may give directions imposing on the persons organising or taking part in the procession such conditions as appear to him to be necessary. The conditions can cover the route of the procession and can prohibit it from entering any public place specified in the directions.[38] It is to be noted, however, that the conditions which may be imposed are not limited to those stated, but can include, for example, a direction as to the timing of the procession and the numbers of marchers who are

---

[32] Public Order Act 1986, s.16. See also *Flockhart v. Robinson* [1950] 2 K.B. 498, where it was said that a procession was more than "a mere body of persons; it is a body of persons who are moving along a route." See para.1–03 for definition of "public place."

[33] *ibid.*, s.11(2).

[34] *ibid.*, s.11(3).

[35] *ibid.*, s.11(4)(a).

[36] See para. 5–10.

[37] *ibid.*, s.11(5) and (6).

[38] For definition of "public place", see para. 1–03.

8

permitted to go on it, provided these restraints arise from the needs of public order.

Prohibiting Processions

Section 13 of the Public Order Act 1986 permits the police authorities to seek **1–11** to have processions banned if they reasonably believe that their powers under section 12 will not be sufficient to prevent serious public disorder. Application may be made to the district council for an order prohibiting for a specific period not exceeding three months the holding of all public processions in the area concerned. As under the previous law, there is no power to ban specific marches, as opposed to classes of marches or all marches.

The council may, with the consent of the Home Secretary, make an order either in the terms of the application or with such modifications as may be approved by the Home Secretary.[39] In London, the relevant police commissioner may himself, with the permission of the Home Secretary, make a similar banning order.[40]

4 THE ORGANISER'S POSITION UNDER THE PUBLIC ORDER ACT

Sections 11–14 of the Public Order Act 1986 contain provisions dealing specifically **1–12** with the position of persons who organise public assemblies (section 14), trespassory assemblies (section 14A) and processions (sections 11–13). An "organiser" is not defined, but it will be noted that under section 11, an advance notice of processions has to state the name of at least one of the organisers[41]; but others who participate in the preparation or supervision of the arrangements, for example stewards, could also fall within the definition. The offences of which an organiser may be guilty are:

(a) In relation to assemblies, organising a public assembly, and knowingly failing to comply with a condition imposed. There is a defence where the failure arose from circumstances beyond the organiser's control.[42] This places the burden of proof on the organiser, who has to establish his innocence on a balance of probabilities.[43]

(b) In relation to trespassory assemblies, organising an assembly the holding of which the organiser knows is prohibited, or taking part in such an assembly,[44] or failing to comply with a direction by a constable not to proceed in the direction of a trespassory assembly.[45]

---

[39] Public Order Act 1986, s.13(2).
[40] *ibid.*, s.13(4).
[41] *ibid.*, s.11(3). Some discussion of the meaning of "organiser" is found in *Flockhart v Robinson* [1950] 2 K.B. 498. Diverting people towards a meeting place can be part of the organisation of the event: *D.P.P. v. Baillie* (see n. 17 above).
[42] *ibid.*, s.14(4).
[43] Magistrates' Courts Act 1980, s.101. See also [1987] Crim.L.R. 154–5.
[44] Public Order Act 1986, s.14B (1),(2).
[45] *ibid.*, s.14(C)(3).

(c) In relation to processions, organising a public procession when the requirements as to notice have not been complied with, or organising a procession that differs from that for which the notice has been given,[46] or organising a procession which does not comply with the conditions imposed[47] or organising a banned procession.[48] Again there is a defence where the failure arose from circumstances beyond the organiser's control.[49]

The sections also contain provisions making it a criminal offence to incite others to participate in the prohibited acts.[50]

The sections contain a number of defences, based on absence of relevant knowledge,[51] that the events complained of were beyond the defendant's control,[52] or, in one case, that the events were the subject of an agreement with the police.[53]

Apart from those defences, it will be open to the organiser to show, for example, that the police were acting outside the powers conferred by the relevant section.[54] It is clear, too, that decisions made by the police are subject to judicial review.[55] The latter remedy was the subject of considerable mention in the White Paper, with emphasis being laid on it as a way of ensuring the "demonstrators have an effective means of challenging any decision by the police to impose conditions which is not justified by a real risk of serious disorder, disruption or coercion."[56]

5   USE AND ABUSE OF THE HIGHWAY

1–13   The primary object for which a highway exists is passage and a person using it for other purposes is, theoretically at least, a trespasser.[57] Streets are public, but they are public for passage and there is no common law right to hold meetings in the street.[58] It should not, however, be inferred that all meetings held on the highway are unlawful.[59] Two aspects must be considered: whether what is going on in the street is likely to interfere with the right of passage, and whether the meeting is likely to lead to a public nuisance. In practice too, as in all matters relating to public assemblies, the possibility of a breach of the peace has to be considered.[60]

---

[46] ibid., s.11(7)
[47] ibid., s.12(4).
[48] ibid., s.13(7).
[49] ibid., s.12(4).
[50] ibid., ss.12(6), 13(9), 14(6), 14B(3).
[51] ibid., s.11(8).
[52] ibid., s.11(9), 12(5), 14(4),(5).
[53] ibid., s.11(9).
[54] See, e.g. Police v. Reid (Lorna), n. 22 above.
[55] Mohammed-Holgate v. Duke [1984] A.C. 437.
[56] White Paper, para. 4.25.
[57] Harrison v. Duke of Rutland [1893] 1 Q.B. 142.
[58] R. v. Cunninghame, Graham and Burns (1888) 4 T.L.R. 212.
[59] See Burden v. Rigler [1911] 1 K.B. 337.
[60] See para. 2–01.

A further aspect, arising out of the above principles, is whether an order is in force under section 14A of the Public Order Act 1986 which prohibits trespassory assemblies.[61] In an area covered by such an order, a meeting cannot lawfully be held on the highway:

> A peaceful demonstration took place on part of the public highway near Stonehenge. An order under section 14A was in force for the area. Police officers asked the demonstrators to disperse, but they refused and were arrested. Their convictions were upheld on the ground that the rights of the public were limited to using the highway for the purpose of passing and re-passing and ancillary purposes which were usual and reasonable. The holding of a demonstration on the highway had nothing to do with the right of passage; the assembly near Stonehenge therefore exceeded the public's right of access and an offence had been committed under the section.[62]

Obstruction of the Highway

Section 137(1) of the Highways Act 1980 provides that it is an offence in any way wilfully to obstruct the free passage along a highway,[63] without lawful authority or excuse.   **1–14**

The offence lies in the obstruction; if this is proved, it is no defence that no inconvenience had in fact been caused to others.[64] On the other hand the requirement for a conviction that the obstruction was "without lawful authority or excuse" offers the defendant a chance to claim that his conduct falls within the principles laid down in *Nagy v. Weston*:

> "It depends on all the circumstances, including the length of time the obstruction continues, the place where it occurs, the purpose for which it was done, and of course whether it does in fact cause an actual obstruction as opposed to a partial obstruction."[65]

This approach was re-affirmed in an animal rights case, where conviction was quashed because the trial court had failed to consider whether the protesters' use of the highway (in fact, a spacious pedestrian precinct) was reasonable or unreasonable.[66] This case is also authority for the proposition that one of the factors to be taken into account in determining reasonableness is the legitimate exercise of rights of assembly and demonstration.[67]

---

[61] *D.P.P. v. Jones and another, The Times,* January 27, 1997.

[62] *ibid.*

[63] "Highway" is defined in s.328 of the Highways Act 1980 as meaning the whole or part of a highway other than a ferry or waterway; where a highway passes over a bridge or through a tunnel, that bridge or tunnel is to be taken for the purposes of the Act to be a part of the highway. For the common law meaning of "highway", see Halsbury's Laws (4th ed.) vol. 21, para.1. See also two recent cases relevant to the status of a car park as a highway: *Cutter v. Eagle Star Insurance Co. Ltd, The Times,* December 3, 1996, and *Clarke v. Kato, The Times,* December 11, 1996.

[64] *Read v. Perrett* (1876) 1 Ex.D 349.

[65] *Nagy v. Weston* [1965] 1 W.L.R. 280, per Lord Parker C.J. at 284.

[66] *Hirst v. Chief Constable of West Yorkshire Police* [1987] Crim.L.R. 330.

[67] *ibid., per* Otton J.

Public Nuisance

1–15   In relation to conduct on a highway, the common law offence of public nuisance has been defined as:

> " . . . any wrongful act or omission upon or near a highway, whereby the public are prevented from freely, safely and conveniently passing along the the highway".[68]

Prosecutions for this offence are rare; instances of obstruction are usually dealt with under the Highways Act. The offence is, however, available in reserve and might be used in cases of severe disruption.

6   PROVISIONS RELATING TO ELECTION MEETINGS

Parliamentary Elections

1–16   The Representation of the People Act 1983 (as amended) confers a specific right to use certain schools and halls for meetings at parliamentary and local government elections.

Section 95 provides that a candidate at a parliamentary election shall be entitled, for the purpose of holding public meetings in furtherance of his candidature, to the use, free of charge, at reasonable times between the receipt of the writ for the election and the day preceding the date of the poll, of—

(a) a suitable room in the premises of a school to which the section applies;

(b) any meeting room to which the section applies.

The section applies, in England and Wales, to county schools,[69] voluntary schools and grant-maintained schools, of which the premises are situated in the constituency or an adjoining constituency, but a candidate is not entitled to the use of a room in school premises outside the constituency if there is a suitable room in other school premises in the constituency which are reasonably accessible from the same parts of the constituency as those outside.

The section also applies to meeting rooms situated in the constituency, the expense of maintaining which is payable wholly or mainly out of public funds or out of any rate, or by a body whose expenses are so payable.

Where a room is used, under the provisions of the section, the person by whom or on whose behalf the meeting is convened shall defray expenses incurred in preparing, warming, lighting and cleaning the room and providing attendance for the meeting and restoring it to its usual condition. He has also to pay the cost of

---

[68] *Jacobs v. LCC* [1950] A.C. 361 at 375.

[69] Primary and secondary schools maintained by a local education authority (Education Act 1944, s.9(2)).

any damage done to the room or the premises, or to the furniture, fittings or apparatus in the room or premises.

A candidate has to give reasonable notice if he wishes to take advantage of these rights. The section does not authorise any interference with the hours during which a room in school premises is used for educational purposes, or with the use of a meeting room either for the purposes of the person maintaining it or under a prior agreement for its letting.

The Fifth Schedule relates to the detailed arrangements which are mainly concerned with the preparation of lists of available rooms by local education authorities, district councils and London borough councils.

The expression "meeting room" means any room which it is the practice to let for public meetings; and "room" includes a hall, gallery or gymnasium. For the purposes of the section, the premises of a school shall not be taken to include a private dwelling house.

A local authority may not refuse the use of a room, even if the candidate's views are offensive to many.[70]

Local Government Elections

Section 96 of the Representation of the People Act 1983 provides that a **1–17** candidate at a local government election shall be entitled, for the purpose of holding public meetings in furtherance of his candidature, to use free of charge, at reasonable times, any suitable room in the premises of a county,[71] voluntary or grant-maintained school situated in the electoral area for which he is a candidate, (or, if there is no such school in the area, in any such school in an adjacent electoral area), or in a parish or community in part comprised in that electoral area. The right extends to a meeting room situated in the electoral area for which the candidate is standing, or in a parish or community, as the case may be, in part comprised in that electoral area, the expense of maintaining which is payable wholly or mainly out of public funds or out of any rate, or by a body whose expenses are so payable. The right applies during the period between the last day on which the notice of the election may be published and the day preceding election day.

Similar arrangements as to expenses, the making good of damage, and the giving of notice, apply as in relation to the use of rooms for parliamentary elections.[72]

Once it is established that the applicant for a room is a duly nominated candidate, his right under the section is a private law right enforceable by way of action against the local authority.[73]

Election Expenses

Section 75 of the Representation of the People Act 1983 provides that no **1–18** expenses shall, with a view to promoting or procuring the election of a candidate at an election, be incurred by any person other than the candidate, his election

[70] See *Webster v. Southwark London Borough Council* [1983] 2 W.L.R. 217.
[71] See n. 67, above.
[72] In relation to disturbances at election meetings, see para. 2–17.
[73] *Ettridge v. Morrell* (1987) 85 L.G.R. 100, C.A. The same principle would appear to apply under s.95.

agent and persons authorised in writing by the election agent, on account of a number of specified matters. One of these is the holding of a public meeting. Incurring expenditure without the stated authority is a "corrupt practice" and is punishable by fine or imprisonment or both.

If the authority is given, the candidate concerned takes on responsibility for the expenditure, and it has to be included in his return of election expenses.

An alternative course, which has been used by church groups and other voluntary organisations, is to organise a meeting which does not have the aim of "promoting or procuring the election" of any of the candidates. Here the important factors are likely to be:

1. Is the intention of the meeting, overtly or otherwise, to improve the electoral chances of one candidate over the others, or to disparage one or more candidates?
2. Is the structure and organisation of the meeting such as to exclude one or more candidates from participation?

If both questions can be answered in the negative, the meeting can safely be held and the voluntary group can meet the expense. An important factor, obviously, is that all the candidates should be invited to attend. If any are unable to be present, it should be made clear to the public present at the meeting that all candidates were invited. If an absent candidate wishes to have a statement of his views read out at the meeting, this should be done.

7 MEETING ROOMS PROVIDED BY A LOCAL AUTHORITY

1–19 Where a local authority makes available a meeting facility for public use it should, in principle, make the facility available to all and not apply irrelevant factors in turning down the applicant.[74] Reasons for refusal should always be given.[75]

---

[74] *Wheeler v. Leicester City Council* [1985] 3 W.L.R. 335 H.L. (applicant's failure to support Council's policy on South Africa).
[75] See *Administrator*, Vol. 10, No. 9 (September 1991).

CHAPTER 2

BREACH OF THE PEACE AND OTHER
ASPECTS OF THE CRIMINAL LAW

1 BREACH OF THE PEACE

The provisions of the Public Order Act 1986 relating to processions and assemblies **2–01** were described in the previous chapter. Section 40(4) of that Act makes it clear that nothing therein affects the common law powers to deal with or prevent a breach of the peace. These powers go far back into history.

No statutory definition of what amounts to a breach of the peace exists, in spite of its importance in the field of public order law. The omission may be in part deliberate, because of the view that some flexibility will bring advantages.[1]

A tendency has been to place emphasis on menace to person or property rather than noise or other unseemly behaviour. Thus in *R. v. Howell*[2] the Court of Appeal took the following view:

> "We are emboldened to say that there is a breach of the peace whenever harm is actually done or is likely to be done to a person or in his presence to his property or a person is in fear of being so harmed through an assault, an affray, a riot, unlawful assembly or other disturbance. It is for this breach of the peace when done in his presence or the reasonable apprehension of it taking place that a constable, or anyone else, may arrest an offender without warrant."[3]

A long-standing example of conduct *not* amounting to a breach of the peace is *Wooding v. Oxley*:

> At a meeting at which a person had caused considerable annoyance by crying "hear, hear" and putting questions and observations, the chairman summoned the police and had the offender arrested. It was held that in the circumstances this action was wrongful.[4]

The words used by speakers at public meetings can lead to a breach of the peace; the conflict between the need to preserve public order and the right of free speech is deferred to a later point in this chapter[5] as it will be convenient to consider first the position of the police in relation to public order.

---

[1] See White Paper, para. 6.13.
[2] *R. v. Howell* [1982] Q.B. 416.
[3] *ibid.*, at 427.
[4] *Wooding v. Oxley* (1839) 9 C. P. 1.
[5] See para. 2–04.

2   DUTIES AND POWERS OF THE POLICE

2–02   A police constable has a duty to preserve the peace. Again, the obligation is a well-established one.[6] There are two important pre-conditions to the exercise of any of their powers in this area.

First, there must be a real and not a remote possibility of a breach of the peace. The mere statement by a constable that he anticipated a breach is not enough: there must be proven facts from which he could reasonably have anticipated a breach.[7] The point was put in the following way in *Moss v. McLachlan*[8]:

"The situation has to be assessed by the senior police officers present. Provided they honestly and reasonably form the opinion that there is a real risk of a breach of the peace in the sense that it is in close proximity both in place and time, then the conditions exist for reasonable preventive action . . ."[9]

Secondly, the police must act impartially, as was emphasised in the Green Paper[10]:

"The role of the police is and must continue to be confined to maintaining order. Under our law every citizen is under a duty to preserve the 'Queen's Peace', that is, the normal peaceful and orderly state of society. A police officer has a special duty in that respect, which he accepts when he assumes the office of constable. The law already gives him a number of powers which he must use when disorder occurs or is reasonably anticipated. But it is no part of the policeman's task to judge between opposing factions in the street. . . . His duty is simply to preserve order and prevent offences and to enforce the law, no more and no less."

When a breach of the peace is threatened, a constable has very wide powers. He has the right to take reasonable steps to make the person who is breaking or threatening the peace refrain from doing so; and those reasonable steps in appropriate cases will include detaining him against his will, *i.e.* arresting him.[11] The powers of the constable extend to situations where a breach of the peace has been committed and he has reasonable grounds to believe it will be renewed.[12] In practice, the constable will (or at least, he should) suggest a practical means by which the breach of the peace can be averted: for example, by changing the location of the assembly,[13] by persuading those causing an obstruction to stop

---

[6] See *Duncan v. Jones* [1936] 1 K.B. 218 at 223 (*per* Humphreys J.).
[7] *Piddington v. Bates* [1961] 1 W.L.R. 162.
[8] [1985] I.R.L.R. 76.
[9] *ibid.*, at 78.
[10] At para. 14. See Chap. 1, n. 7.
[11] *Albert v. Lavin* [1982] A.C. 546, *per* Lord Diplock.
[12] *R. v. Howell* (n. 2 above). But not where there is no reason to suppose this will happen: *Baynes v. Brewster* (1841) 2 Q.B. 375.
[13] *Duncan v. Jones* (n. 6 above).

doing so,[14] or by attempting to disperse the meeting.[15] In a case arising out of the National Coal Board dispute the police stopped vehicles on the highway and requested the drivers to turn back, away from the demonstration.[16] There are, in fact, no fixed categories: the police must do what they reasonably consider to be necessary to avoid a breach of the peace.

It is well established that the police may enter private premises to prevent a breach of the peace from occurring.[17] This common law right has been preserved by the Police and Criminal Evidence Act 1984; the Act abolished all other common law rules under which a constable had power to enter premises without a warrant.[18]

In addition to the general powers referred to above, the police have specific **2–03** rights of arrest without warrant under the provisions of the Police and Criminal Evidence Act 1984 and the Public Order Act 1986. Under section 25 of the 1984 Act (the section which deals with the "general arrest conditions"), where a constable has reasonable grounds for suspecting that any offence which is not an arrestable offence (an "arrestable offence" is defined in section 24—generally, the more serious type of criminal offence) has been or is being committed or attempted, he may arrest the offender if it appears to him that service of a summons is impracticable or inappropriate because one of the general arrest conditions is satisfied. These conditions (paraphrased) are:

1. The name of the offender is unknown to and cannot be readily ascertained by the constable.
2. The constable has reasonable grounds for doubting whether the offender has given his real name.
3. The offender has not given a satisfactory address for service.
4. The constable has reasonable grounds for believing that arrest is necessary to prevent the offender from causing physical harm to himself or any other person,[19] suffering physical injury, causing loss of or damage to property, committing an offence against public decency or causing an unlawful highway obstruction.
5. A child or other vulnerable person is at risk.

Under the Public Order Act 1986 a constable *in uniform* has power to arrest persons (including organisers) whom he reasonably suspects are committing offences under the sections relating to the imposing of conditions on public processions (section 12), the prohibition of public processions (section 13) the imposing of conditions on public assemblies (section 14), offences in connection

---

[14] *Chief Constable of Devon and Cornwall ex p. C.E.G.B.* [1981] 3 All E.R. 826, *per* Lawton L.J. at 834.

[15] See Green Paper, para. 81 and White Paper, para. 6.15. The powers of the police under s.14 of the Public Order Act and the new sections introduced into that Act by the Criminal Justice and Public Order Act 1994 will in practice, supersede some of these common law powers: see para. 1–06.

[16] *Moss v. McLachlan* (n. 8 above). See, however, Police and Criminal Evidence Act, 1984, s.4 (power to operate "road checks").

[17] *Thomas v. Sawkins* [1935] 2 K.B. 249. See also *McConnell v. Chief Constable of Greater Manchester Police* [1990] 1 All E.R. 423 (Court of Appeal) and *McLeod v. Metropolitan Police Commissioner* [1994] 4 All E.R. 553.

[18] Police and Criminal Evidence Act 1984, s.17(5) and (6).

[19] Here, the offender could be arrested for threatening a breach of the peace.

with trespassory assemblies (section 14B) and stopping persons from proceeding to trespassory assemblies.[20] Constables also have the power to arrest without warrant persons committing an offence under sections 4, 4A and 5 of the Public Order Act 1986 (see paras 2–12 to 2–14 below).

Essentially, the powers of arrest are preventative in nature; where no offence has been committed, for example because the police acted in time to prevent it, the offender may be brought before the court and bound over to keep the peace and/ or to be of good behaviour. A refusal can lead to imprisonment for a term of up to six months.[21]

In the context of police powers, it is necessary to note the provisions of section 51 of the Police Act 1964. Under section 51(1) any person who assaults a constable in the execution of his duty or a person assisting a constable in the execution of his duty, is guilty of an offence. Under section 51(3), an offence is committed by any person who resists or wilfully obstructs a constable in the execution of his duty, or anyone so assisting him. Since a constable's duty includes the preservation of the peace, these offences are clearly relevant to public order law, but it is very doubtful whether, in the absence of a breach of the peace, section 51(3) provides the constable with a power of arrest.[22]

There are, finally, other powers which the police may only be able to exercise at the request or with the co-operation of private citizens. An example is the ejection of trespassers. In the absence of an actual or threatened breach of the peace, the police have no powers to remove trespassers from private land. They may, however, at the request of the occupiers of the premises or the promoters of the meeting assist in removing them. In that situation, if they agree to help, they are acting, in effect, as private citizens and possess no rights not possessed by any other citizen in similar circumstances.[23]

The police may also come to an arrangement with the promoters or organisers of a meeting under which special police services are provided in return for payment. This practice is sanctioned by section 25 of the Police Act 1996. "Special police services" is not defined in that Act, but the following guidelines have been suggested[24]:

1 The fact that the police do not generally have access to private premises suggests their presence on them would involve special police services.
2 If violence has occurred or is imminent, it is unlikely that the services would be regarded as special.
3 A regular event causing a strain on police resources might be more likely to require special police services.
4 If the police had to deploy a large number of officers who would otherwise be off-duty, this again might be an indication of special police services.

---

[20] See relevant paras. in Chap. 1.
[21] Magistrates' Courts Act 1980, s.115(3). The binding over powers are conferred by the Justices of the Peace Act 1361. See also Justices of the Peace Act 1968, s.1(7): *Hughes v. Holley* (1988) 86 Cr.App.R. 130.
[22] See *Gelberg v. Miller* [1961] 1 All E.R. 291 and *Wershof v. M.P.C.* [1978] 3 All E.R. 540.
[23] See also para. 3–05.
[24] *Harris v. Sheffield United Football Club Ltd* [1987] 2 All E.R. 838.

3 FREEDOM OF SPEECH

It will be clear from the above paragraphs that there is a potential conflict between **2–04** the freedom of citizens to assemble and express their views, and the needs of public order. *Duncan v. Jones* supported the view that it is the duty of the police to take such steps as they think necessary in the circumstances, regardless of whether or not the consequence is to bring to an end the assembly, and with it the chance of hearing the views of the speakers:

> On 30 July 1934 a meeting was convened in Nynehead Street, New Cross to "defend the right of free speech and public meeting." The appellant was about to address a number of people when a police officer forbade her to do so. She persisted in trying to hold the meeting and was arrested. The conviction was upheld because of the police officer's fear of a breach of the peace.[25]

No suggestion was made in that case that any alternative course of action might have been followed by the chief inspector. In *Piddington v Bates*[26] the comment was made by Lord Parker C.J. that a police officer charged with the duty of preserving the peace must be left to take such steps as he thinks are proper, given the evidence before him. It is now more generally accepted (perhaps because of the influence of Article 11 of the European Convention on Human Rights) that the steps to be taken by the police should reflect the need to permit free assembly and expression of opinion.[27] In principle, too, the police would attempt to defend the rights of the meeting organisers to carry on (bearing in mind the need of the police to be impartial[28]) in spite of possible disruption by opponents: otherwise it is, in effect, the mob which is setting the agenda.

4 OTHER OFFENCES REGULATED BY STATUTE

Disruption—Public Meeting Act 1908

Section 1 of the Act provides that any person who at a lawful public meeting acts **2–05** in a disorderly manner for the purpose of preventing the transaction of the business for which the meeting was called together shall be guilty of an offence. A person who incites others to commit such an offence shall also be guilty. If a constable reasonably suspects any person of committing such an offence, he may if requested by the chairman of the meeting require that person to give his name and address and, if he refuses or gives a false name and address, he shall be guilty of an offence.[29]

---

[25] *Duncan v. Jones* [1936] 1 K.B. 218.
[26] [1961] 1 W.L.R. 162.
[27] See for example, Home Office Circular No. 11/87, para. 11.
[28] See para. 2–02.
[29] The section does not apply as respects meetings to which s. 97 of the Representation of the People Act 1983 applies. See para. 2–17.

Definitions are lacking in the Act itself, but can probably be taken from section 9 of the Public Order Act 1936 as amended by the Criminal Justice Act 1972:

"Meeting" means a meeting held for the purpose of discussion of matters of public interest or for the purpose of expression of views on such matters.

"Public meeting" includes any meeting in a public place and any meeting which the public or any section thereof are permitted to attend, whether on payment or otherwise. "Public place" includes any highway and any other premises or place to which at the material time the public have or are permitted to have access, whether on payment or otherwise.

Uniforms—Public Order Act 1936

2–06   By section 1, an offence is committed by any person who in any public place or at any public meeting (see definitions above) wears uniform signifying his association with any political organisation, or with the promotion of any political object. In certain circumstances, a chief officer of police may permit an exception where he is satisfied that the wearing of uniform on any ceremony, anniversary, or other special occasion will not be likely to involve risk of public disorder.[30]

Section 2 of the Act prohibits quasi-military activities, including the equipping of persons to be employed in usurping the functions of the police, but expressly excepts the appointment of stewards "to assist in the preservation of order at any public meeting held on private premises or the making of arrangements for that purpose or the instruction of the persons to be so employed in their lawful duties as such stewards or their being furnished with badges or other distinguishing signs." It should be emphasised however that nothing in the Act gives stewards at public meetings any special right, not possessed by any other civilian, to use force.

Proscribed Organisations—Terrorism Act 2000

2–07   A person who displays support for a proscribed organisation (amongst others, the Irish Republican Army and the Irish National Liberation Army), by wearing in a public place of any items of dress or carrying any article in such a way or in such circumstances as to arouse reasonable apprehension that he is a member or supporter of such an organisation, is guilty of an offence under section 13 of the Act.

It is an offence under section to arrange or assist in arranging or to address a meeting of three or more persons (whether or not one to which the public are admitted) known by the defendant to be a meeting to support a proscribed organisation, to further the activities of such an organisation or to be addressed by a person belonging or professing to belong to such an organisation.

Police Powers of Stop and Search—Terrorism Act 2000

2–08   There is a general power to search for evidence of terrorism, defined very broadly in section 1 of the Act, Areas may be designated in which officers can stop

---

[30] Conditions may be imposed on the wearing of the uniform.

vehicles and search the driver or anyone else inside. The power also covers pedestrians.

Offences Related to Violence—Public Order Act 1986

The Act created the offences of riot, violent disorder and affray. The first and **2–09** third of these existed in the common law, but the Act made some changes. The second is a new offence. A fourth offence, provoking violence or inducing fear of it, replaces section 5 of the Public Order Act 1936. A new offence, causing harassment, was introduced by section 5 of the Act. These statutory offences are briefly described below. The Criminal Justice and Police Act 2001 ss 12–16 make provision for combating alcohol-related disorder in designated public places and the Anti-social Behaviour Act 2003 ss 30–36 make provision for dispersing groups causing intimidation, alarm or distress in public places.

Riot—section 1

If a meeting ends in a riot, it can in general terms be said to be a failure, since **2–10** those responsible face imprisonment for up to ten years. The offence is as follows:

(1) Where 12 or more persons who are present together use or threaten unlawful violence for a common purpose and the conduct of them (taken together) is such as would cause a person of reasonable firmness present at the scene to fear for his personal safety, each of the persons using unlawful violence for the common purpose is guilty of riot.
(2) It is immaterial whether or not the 12 or more use or threaten unlawful violence simultaneously.
(3) The common purpose may be inferred from conduct.
(4) No person of reasonable firmness need actually be, or be likely to be, present at the scene.
(5) Riot may be committed in private as well as in public places.

A person is guilty of riot only if he intends to use violence or is aware that his conduct may be violent.[31]

Under the Riot (Damages) Act 1886 the local police authority is required to compensate for damage to property caused during a riot. This is, in effect, a means of providing some self-insurance to local people out of the police fund. In assessing the compensation to be awarded, regard must be had to the precautions taken by the claimant, or as respects his being a party or accessory to the "riotous, or tumultuous assembly, or as regards any provocation offered to the persons assembled or otherwise.[32]

Violent Disorder—section 2

This is the offence relating to group violence which was introduced by the 1986 **2–11** Act and its definition is as follows:

---

[31] s.6.(1), Public Order Act 1986.
[32] See also Public Order Act 1986, s.10(1). See also [1989] L.S. Gaz. 18.

(1) Where three or more persons who are present together use or threaten unlawful violence and the conduct of them (taken together) is such as would cause a person of reasonable firmness present at the scene to fear for his personal safety, each of the persons using or threatening unlawful violence is guilty of violent disorder.

(2) It is immaterial whether or not the three or more use or threaten unlawful violence simultaneously.

(3) No person of reasonable firmness need actually be, or be likely to be, present at the scene.

(4) Violent disorder may be committed in private as well as in public places.

A person is guilty of violent disorder only if he intends to use or threaten violence or is aware that his conduct may be violent or threaten violence.[33]

Affray—section 3

2–12   Affray is essentially an offence against the person, and its public order connotations have, in practice, been lost. A person is guilty of an affray if he uses or threatens unlawful violence towards another and his conduct is such as would cause a person of reasonable firmness present at the scene to fear for his personal safety.

Provoking Violence or Inducing a Fear of it—section 4

2–13   This section replaces the old "conduct likely to cause a breach of the peace" offence contained in section 5 of the Public Order Act 1936. The wording of the relevant parts of section 4 of the 1986 Act is as follows:

(1) A person is guilty of an offence if he—
  (a) uses towards another person threatening, abusive or insulting words or behaviour, or
  (b) distributes or displays to another person any writing, sign or other visible representation which is threatening, abusive or insulting,
  with intent to cause that person to believe that immediate unlawful violence will be used against him or another by any person, or to provoke the immediate use of unlawful violence by that person or another, or whereby that person is likely[34] to believe that such violence will be used or it is likely that such violence will be provoked.

(2) An offence under this section may be committed in a public or a private place, except that no offence is committed where the words or behaviour are used, or the writing, sign or other visible representation is distributed or displayed, by a person inside a dwelling and the other person is also inside that or another dwelling.

---

[33] s.6(2), Public Order Act 1986.
[34] See a case under the 1936 Act, *Parkin v. Norman* [1983] 1 Q.B. 92 for a discussion of the difference between "liable" and "likely", in this kind of situation.

(3) A constable may arrest without warrant anyone he reasonably suspects is committing an offence under this section.

A person is guilty under this section only if he intends his words or behaviour, or the writing, sign or other visible representation, to be threatening, abusive or insulting, or is aware that it may be so; or if he intends his behaviour to be disorderly or is aware that it may be so.[35]

A person is guilty of an offence under the Crime and Disorder Act 1998 s.31 if he commits an offence under s.4 of the Public Order Act 1986 which is racially or religiously aggravated for these purposes.

Causing Harassment, Alarm or Distress—section 5

Section 5 of the 1986 Act makes it an offence to use threatening, abusive or insulting words or behaviour, or disorderly behaviour,[36] or to display any writing, sign or other visible representation which is threatening, abusive or insulting within the hearing or sight of a person likely to be caused harassment,[37] alarm or distress thereby.

2–14

A person is guilty of an offence under the Crime and Disorder Act 1998 s.31 if he commits an offence under s.5 of the Public Order Act 1986 which is racially aggravated for these purposes.

Intentional Harassment, Alarm or Distress—section 4A

This new section was introduced into the Public Order Act 1986 by section 154 of the Criminal Justice and Public Order Act 1994. It is aimed essentially at cases of persistent harassment, especially those with a racial element. It is necessary to prove that a person actually be caused harassment. The penalties on conviction are more substantial than those under section 5. Further prohibitions against harassment were introduced by the Protection from Harassment Act 1997.

2–15

5   RACIAL HATRED OFFENCES

The law relating to the stirring up of racial hatred is now mainly to be found in Part III of the Public Order Act 1986. Racial hatred is defined as "hatred against a group of persons in Great Britain defined by reference to colour, race, nationality (including citizenship) or ethnic or national origins.[38] In relation to meetings, the most important sections are 18, 19 and 23. The consent of the Attorney-General to prosecution is required[39]—a significant disincentive.

2–16

---

[35] s.6(3), Public Order Act 1986.

[36] These two words are not defined in the Act. They are to be given their "normal meaning": *Chambers and Edwards v. D.P.P.* (1988) 89 Cr.App.R. 82.

[37] No element of apprehension about one's personal safety is necessary for there to be harassment: *Chambers and Edwards v. D.P.P.* (1988) 89 Cr.App.R. 82.

[38] Public Order Act 1986, s.17.

[39] *ibid.*, s.27(1).

Use of Words or Behaviour or Display of Written Material—section 18

2–17   A person who uses threatening, abusive or insulting words or behaviour, or displays any written material which is threatening, abusive or insulting, is guilty of an offence if (a) he intends thereby to stir up racial hatred, or, (b) having regard to all the circumstances racial hatred is likely to be stirred up thereby.[40] "Written material" includes any sign or other visible representation.[41] An offence may be committed in a public or private place, but there is an exception relating to activities taking place inside a dwelling.[42] A constable has power of arrest.[43] A person who is not shown to have intended to stir up racial hatred is not guilty of an offence if he did not intend his words or behaviour, or the written material, to be, and was not aware that it might be, threatening, abusive or insulting.[44]

Publishing or Distributing Written Material—section 19

2–18   A person who publishes or distributes written material which is threatening, abusive or insulting is guilty of an offence if (a) he intends thereby to stir up racial hatred, or, (b) having regard to all the circumstances racial hatred is likely to be stirred up thereby.[45] References to the publication or distribution of written material are to its publication or distribution to the public or a section of the public.[46] Publication to a "section of the public" has been held not to include leaving pamphlets in the porch of a Member of Parliament's house, for him and his family to read[47] but distribution of racially inflammatory material at a public meeting would clearly be an offence. There is a defence if the defendant is unaware of the contents of the material he has published or distributed[48] and did not suspect and had no reason to suspect that it was threatening, abusive or insulting.

Possession of Racially Inflammatory Material—section 23

2–19   This section in effect, extends section 19 to the mere possession of racially inflammatory material. Again, it is necessary to show that the material is threatening, abusive or insulting, and in the case of written material, that its possession is with a view to its being displayed, published, distributed or broadcast. An offence is committed if the intention is thereby to stir up racial hatred.[49]

6   DISTURBANCES AT ELECTION MEETINGS

2–20   Section 97 of the Representation of the People Act 1983 (as amended) provides that any person who, at a lawful public meeting to which the section applies, acts

---

[40] *ibid.*, s.18(1).
[41] *ibid.*, s.29.
[42] *ibid.*, s.18(2).
[43] *ibid.*, s.18(3).
[44] *ibid.*, s.18(5).
[45] *ibid.*, s.19(1).
[46] *ibid.*, s.19(3).
[47] *R. v. Britton* [1967] 2 Q.B. 51.
[48] Public Order Act 1986, s.19(2).
[49] *ibid.*, s.23(1).

or incites others to act in a disorderly manner for the purpose of preventing the transaction of the business for which the meeting was called together shall be guilty of an illegal practice.

The section applies to:

(a) a political meeting held in any constituency between the date of the issue of a writ for the return of a member of Parliament for the constituency and the date at which a return to the writ is made;

(b) a meeting held with reference to a local government election in the electoral area for that election in the period beginning with the last date on which notice of the election may be published and ending with the day of election.

If a constable reasonably suspects any person of committing an offence under this section, he may, if requested so to do by the chairman of the meeting, require that person to declare to him immediately his name and address, and if that person refuses or fails so to declare his name and address or gives a false name and address he shall be liable on summary conviction to a fine.

As will be seen, the offence is in many respects similar to that contained in section 1 of the Public Meeting Act 1908.[50]

---

[50] See para. 2–05.

CHAPTER 3

THE MAINTENANCE OF ORDER

1 THE ROLE OF THE CHAIRMAN

3–01 Responsibility for the conduct of a meeting rests particularly on the chairman. He will call the speakers, regulate the length of the speeches, deal with points of order, put motions to the meeting to enable the wish or decisions of the meeting to be ascertained and control the arrangements for any vote that may be taken.

If there is heckling, it will be for the chairman to decide to what extent to allow the speaker himself to deal with interruptions and whether or not to intervene from the chair. Heckling adds to the enjoyment of public meetings, and is part of the right of free speech, but the chairman should try to ensure that each speaker is allowed a fair hearing; in this, he will usually be supported by the majority of the audience. Heckling can perhaps be regarded as a spontaneous commentary by individuals; a chairman will be on more difficult ground if he has to deal with organised interruption by groups, whose purpose may be to ruin the meeting or at least to attract damaging publicity. Here, the chairman should, if he has the chance, prepare his response carefully. He may attempt to position the disruptive elements where they are more isolated, and the stewards should be forewarned of possible trouble and given clear instructions. Control of the microphone, and its accompanying decibels, is an important factor. The chairman must combine fairness with tact. An element of humour may assist in avoiding matters getting out of hand—particularly if the disruption takes the form of an attempt to provoke an intemperate response. There can be a certain amount of disorder provided the business of the meeting can still be transacted and voting intentions are still clear.

Other powers and duties of the chairman of a meeting are discussed in greater detail in the remainder of this chapter and in Chapter 6 (paras. 6–07 to 6–13).

2 EJECTION

3–02 Where public meetings are held on private premises (including premises which are available to the public for hire) there may be a right of ejection. This depends on whether or not payment has been made for admission. If admission is free, any person who attends does so with the licence of the promoters. He can be asked to leave the meeting at any time, regardless of whether or not he has been guilty of misbehaviour. In practice, however, this right would not usually be exercised without good reason.[1]

Where payment has been made for admission, the participant is deemed to have entered into a contract for valuable consideration with the promoters. He is entitled to remain so long as he behaves himself and abides by the rules governing the meeting.[2]

In any situation where a person is asked, with legal justification, to leave a meeting and he refuses, he can be forcibly ejected, although only reasonable force should be applied.[3]

Expulsion should only be used as a last resort. If the conduct of a person is such that the business of the meeting is seriously interfered with and if after repeated requests from the chair the offender still persists in his obstructive methods, it would be desirable for the chairman to warn him of the consequences of his actions. Should the interrupter continue in defiance of these warnings, he should be given an opportunity of leaving the meeting voluntarily, and if he refuses to leave of his own accord reasonable force should then be used to expel him. It would be desirable to secure the support of the majority of the meeting on this matter if this is at all practicable but, once decided upon, whether by the meeting or by the chairman on his own authority (or perhaps on the authority of standing orders), the expulsion should be effected expeditiously. The removal should be carried out by the stewards or by attendants employed by the owners of the meeting hall. Beware, too, of the risk of the person ejected bursting back into the meeting.[4]

An illustration of a case where ejection was justified is *Marshall v. Tinnelly*:

> At a meeting of a committee of an urban district council a member was asked to quit the council chamber owing to his disorderly conduct. The member refused to do so, whereupon he was removed. Upon his bringing an action for assault, it was held that when the chairman, acting in pursuance of a resolution carried by the committee and under power given in the standing orders, ordered the member to withdraw, upon his refusing to do so he became a trespasser. In these circumstances the chairman was entitled to order the member's ejection, and it was found as a fact that what had been done was done as gently as the circumstances permitted.[5]

If unnecessary force is used in effecting the expulsion, the person removed will have a cause of action for assault against the persons responsible; these may include the chairman and the stewards.[6] On the other hand, in *Lucas v. Mason* the chairman escaped responsibility:

[1] The rule that a licence to attend for which no payment has been made can be revoked at any time rests on an old case which was not concerned with a meeting: *R. v. Horndon-on-the-Hill Inhabitants* (1816) 4 M. S. 562. There are remarks of the Court in *Hurst v. Picture Theatres* (see n. 2) which suggests that if a person attending a free public meeting were to be turned out, against his will, without good reason, the organisers could expect little sympathy from the Court.

[2] *Hurst v. Picture Theatres* [1915] 1 K.B. 1.

[3] *Collins v. Renison* (1754) 1 Sayer 138.

[4] *Re British Union for the Abolition of Vivisection* [1995] 2 BCLC 1 (see para 12–16 below).

[5] (1937) 81 S.J. 902.

[6] *Doyle v. Falconer* (1866) L.R. 1 P.C. 328; *Hawkins v. Muff* (1911) 2 Glen's Local Government Case Law 151.

At a certain meeting there was considerable disturbance in the gallery and the chairman said: "I shall be obliged to bring those men to the front who are making the disturbance; bring those men to the front." A person was seized by the stewards and injured in the process of removal, although he was not the person actually making the disturbance. He took proceedings against the chairman for assault but failed on the ground that the words uttered by the chairman did not authorise the stewards to act upon their own judgment as to who were the persons making the disturbance.[7]

In addition, the aggrieved person may, if the ejection is wrongful, bring an action for breach of contract (although the damages awarded are unlikely to be more than nominal).[8]

3 EXCLUSION

3–03 As stated above, where payment is made for admission, there will be a contract between the promoters and those members of the public who wish to attend. The contractual terms may limit the right of admission; although a right of exclusion as opposed to expulsion, directed against particular individuals, may be difficult to operate in practice. It would be necessary to display the terms of admission prominently near the kiosk or other place where the tickets were sold, or to have them printed on the back of the ticket in the case of advance sales. Refusal of admission would have to be carried through with a decisive show of authority and with a clear statement of the reasons. The organisers would be obliged to weigh the advantages to be gained against the possibility of disorder taking place before the meeting had even started. There is always the risk that the meeting might be rushed by a crowd of disgruntled ticketholders.

The above remarks are somewhat conjectural, since the topic has rarely come before the courts. One example (not however based on contract, but on administrative law) is *R. v. Brent Health Authority ex p. Francis and Another*:

Meetings of the Brent Health Authority had been repeatedly disrupted by organised rowdy behaviour and stamping feet, accompanied by other acts of intimidation and even, in one instance, by an attempt to storm the tables where the authority members were seated. The authority decided that, as matters stood, it would not succeed in dealing with the business before it, and the authority's chairman accordingly decided to hold a meeting from which members of the public were excluded. The validity of the meeting was challenged in the courts. It was held that a public body had a common law power to prevent members of the public entering a meeting if the public body had reasonable grounds for believing that they would disrupt the meeting by disorderly conduct and make it impossible for the public body to conduct its business properly. Furthermore, such a power could in urgent cases be

---

[7] (1875) 10 L.R. Ex. 251.
[8] *Wood v. Leadbitter* (1845) 13 M W 838. See also *Salmond Heuston on the Law of Torts* (21st ed.), pp. 76–80.

exercised by the chairman of the public body (not necessarily the same person as the chairman of the meeting) in advance of any meeting, provided it was exercised *bona fide*, since otherwise the power would be useless.[9]

It will be noted that the above case relates to the meetings of a local authority. There is no precedent for the application of the principle to privately convened meetings. Equally, however, there would seem to be no overriding reason why the *bona fide* decision of the organisers of a meeting to exclude a section of the public on the grounds of feared disruption should not be upheld.

4 ADJOURNMENT

In cases of disorder the chairman may, of his own volition, adjourn the meeting. **3–04** In the case of *John v. Rees* it was made clear that, if the disorder is severe, the chairman has a duty to effect an adjournment. The principles to be applied are as follows.

The first duty of the chairman of a meeting is to keep order if he can. If there is disorder, his duty is to make earnest and sustained efforts to restore order, e.g. by summoning others to assist. If all his efforts are in vain, he should endeavour to put into operation whatever provisions for adjournment there are in the rules, as by obtaining a resolution to adjourn. If this proves impossible, he should exercise his inherent power to adjourn the meeting for a short while, taking due steps to ensure so far as possible that all present know of this adjournment. If instead of mere disorder there is violence he should take similar steps, save that the greater the violence the less prolonged should be his efforts to restore order before adjourning. He has not merely a power but a duty to adjourn in this way, in the interests of those who fear for their safety. The power and the duty must be exercised *bona fide* for the purpose of forwarding and facilitating the meeting, and not for the purpose of interruption or procrastination. The adjournment must be for no longer than the necessities appear to dictate.[10]

5 ASSISTANCE FROM AND TO THE POLICE

As has been noted, the police have no power to enter upon private premises, **3–05** except by leave of the occupiers of the premises or the promoters of the meeting, unless a breach of the peace is being committed there or they have reasonable grounds for believing that a breach of the peace is likely to be committed.[11]

Organisers would therefore be well advised to arrange matters with the police in advance, if they think there is the need for extra help and that the presence of the

---

[9] [1985] Q.B. 869. See also Chap. 29.
[10] *John v. Rees* [1969] 2 W.L.R. 1294, 1317.
[11] See paras. 2–02 and 2–03.

police would not be provocative. It must be borne in mind that stewards, as such, have no special right not possessed by any other civilian to use force.[12]

In the case of a breach of the peace, or threatened breach of the peace, the police should be called and they have power to arrest without warrant such persons as they have reason to believe are responsible.[13] To this end, they may call for help from the stewards of the meeting or any other person present. There is no statutory authority for this, but the right has been established by judges in several old cases. The dictum of Alderson B. in the leading case on the subject is of interest:

> "Whether the aid of the defendant, if given, would have proved sufficient or useful is not the question or the criterion. Every man might make that excuse and say that his individual aid would have done no good, but the defendant's refusal, may have been, and perhaps was, the cause of that of many others. Every man is bound to set a good example to others by doing his duty in preserving the public peace."[14]

A constable present at a meeting in a private capacity would be failing in his duty as a constable if he did not intervene in a case of a breach of the peace.

It will be recalled, too, that the police may require a person present at a meeting to give his name and address, under the Public Meeting Act 1908.[15]

---

[12] See para. 1–03 in relation to assemblies where serious public disorder is anticipated. See also para. 2–03 in relation to the provision of special services by the police.

[13] *R. v. Howell* [1982] Q.B. 416 at 426.

[14] *R. v. Brown* (1841) Car. M. 314.

[15] See para. 2–05.

CHAPTER 4

A PUBLIC MEETING

EXAMPLE IN PRACTICE—CHECKLIST

There follows a checklist of points. It is assumed that the body proposing to hold the meeting wishes to consult the public, but at the same time has its own views which it wishes to put forward.

Agenda

The chairman or the main speaker must ensure that the public understand the **4–01** purpose of the meeting. For example, if the meeting has been called to discuss a planning proposal, discussion on the subject of the rents for market traders' stalls will not be permitted. In any but single-topic meetings, a written agenda will be helpful.

Attendance Sheets

These can be useful for follow-up. They can be placed at the door or at a **4–02** registration desk, and the stewards invite members of the public to sign them. They can cover different categories among the expected audience.

Audience

It is important for the target audience to be identified so that in planning the **4–03** meeting everyone concentrates on the right objective.

Background Papers

These should be available for, say, two weeks before the meeting and the **4–04** publicity material should indicate where they can be inspected. Maps, models and other visual displays are useful. A summary of any background reports which will be referred to should be conspicuously available at the meeting. Members of the public dislike the feeling that they do not have a copy of something which others have.

Budget

The preparation of a budget covering available resources in terms of manpower **4–05** and money, is a necessary first step.

Chairman

The choice is important. He or she should be well-known, impartial and used **4–06** to handling the big occasion. It is for consideration whether to choose someone who comes from outside the area mainly affected by the proposals (for a greater appearance of impartiality) or within it (for greater knowledge). Perhaps the organisers should seek a well-known local figure, for example the chairman of the residents' association.

4–07   The chairman must be able to devote sufficient time to preparation—particularly his own briefing on the procedural points involved.

Chairs

4–08   Make sure there are enough chairs. Hiring of extra chairs should be done in good time.

Comments Sheet

4–09   A simple comments sheet can be left on each chair, or be available at the back of the hall. Members of the public can complete them and leave them with an organiser. (They can include a brief summary of the proposals, as well.)

Confidentiality

4–10   Some questions by members of the public might, if answered, cause an area of confidentiality to be infringed (for example, "how much is the council proposing to pay for that piece of land?"). The chairman should be briefed on these in advance.

Crèche

4–11   The necessity of a crèche should be considered. If pre-meeting notices are being sent out, recipients can be asked to telephone the office if they will need child-minding facilities.

Disabilities

4–12   Physical mobility—make sure access is easy for those with wheelchairs, and that there are not too many steps to negotiate.

Sight problems—written material should be clearly legible; use large print. Avoid red and green combinations on leaflets (which would be difficult for colour-blind people). For large meetings prepare a cassette of the main proposals.

Hearing—check the acoustics carefully; at most meetings a PA system will be needed, even for those with good hearing. If the venue does not have an acoustic loop, a signer might be considered: this would be expensive, and therefore it would be necessary to try and judge the extent of the demand for one by enquiring in any pre-meeting notice.

Disorder

4–13   The points set out elsewhere in this book (see, in particular, Chapter 3) cover most eventualities.

Enquiries

If possible, publicity about the meeting should indicate where to telephone for further information. Obviously, the recipient of those calls should have available all necessary information.

4–14

Equipment

By this is meant: microphones (fixed and roving), audio-visual equipment, loudspeakers, projectors, screens, flipcharts, etc. Order, instal and test these in good time.

4–15

Fire Alarm

Usually, this matter will be in the hands of the owners of the venue. The organisers should be fully prepared, and it may be necessary to inform the meeting, at the outset, of what happens in the event of fire.

4–16

First Aid

Facilities should be available.

4–17

Insurance

Check your own insurance policy for the adequacy of public liability cover or raise the topic with the hirer of the hall.

4–18

Language

In some areas it may be necessary to hold repeat meetings in different languages. Background material, etc. should be available in English and such other languages as are appropriate, with a telephone contact point.

4–19

Minutes

A good note-taker should attend the meeting. Action points must be noted and followed up. To assist, a tape recording of the meeting can be made. The people at the hall can be informed that a summary of the meeting will be made, of which copies will be available and from whom.

4–20

Number

One good central meeting is better than a number of poorly-supported events in different parts of the town.

4–21

Organiser

The organisation of the meeting should be vested, and be known by all to be vested, in a single person who has a safe pair of hands and sufficient authority to get the job done well.

4–22

Platform

4–23   The platform should be at such a level that the platform party, when seated, is visible from all parts of the hall. The table should be well-lit and covered with an appropriate cloth going to ground level in front. A gavel, water, notepaper and glasses should be provided.

Platform Party

4–24   There can be a temptation to put up everyone who might be asked a question. It is best to keep the party small: it is quite possible to contribute effectively from the floor of the hall.

4–25   The chairman should introduce everyone by name, office and responsibility. Anyone arriving late should also be introduced. Name cards on the table and large lapel badges (to be seen when the platform party member circulates afterwards) are a help.

Police

4–26   There should be no need for a police presence, but the police should be informed if an exceptional amount of traffic is expected.

Presentations

4–27   These should be carefully planned and co-ordinated in advance to ensure:

    (1) consistency (with each other);
    (2) appropriate message;
    (3) short length;
    (4) some colour and humour.

Press/TV/radio

4–28   The press, local television and radio can be important factors in ensuring publicity about the date and place of the meeting and about the message itself (see Publicity, below). The aim should be to have the meeting treated as a news item. Facilities for the press should be made available at the meeting, and care taken in the choice of spokespersons.

Publicity

4–29   Notices about the meeting should be published about 10–14 days in advance. They can be accompanied by a press release. Notices and posters can be put up in local community locations. Make them colourful and eye-catching. Use different languages in multi-cultural areas. Provide a telephone contact for more information. Include a map showing the venue and the location of car parks.

4–30   Direct invitations can be sent to groups such as local councillors, religious leaders, community and residents' associations, and any people who might be particularly involved in the matter which will be under discussion at the meeting. A display advertisement in local newspapers will be helpful.

Punctuality

The meeting should start on time, and the chairman should indicate how long **4–31** it is expected to take. At the time appointed for the end of the meeting, the chairman must bring matters to a conclusion, unless there is a clear consensus on the floor of the hall in favour of going on a short while longer. During the meeting he should issue an occasional reminder of the need for brevity.

Refreshments

Light refreshments are a courtesy to those who have taken the trouble to attend. **4–32** They might have a small favourable effect on the numbers who come if advertised in advance. At least the people on the top table should have a cup of tea before the meeting starts.

Security

It should be clear in advance who is to provide security at the meeting. In most **4–33** cases a few stewards provided by the organisers may be sufficient. Alternatively, they may be part of the facilities provided by the hirers of the hall.

Signs

Within the building and in the surrounding area if necessary, use plenty of large **4–34** and clear signs giving directions to the hall. Is more than one language required?

Speeches (from the floor)

Everyone who wishes to speak should begin by giving his name and any **4–35** organisation he represents. The chairman may have said, at the outset, that contributions from the floor will be limited in time (say three minutes each) in return for the chairman attempting to allow all points of view to have their say.

Anyone who begins by saying he wishes to make two or three points should be asked to choose one question and then raise the remainder later when others have had their turn.

The chairman should try to select all points of view, in turn if possible. In a public meeting, seniority is not relevant. "Insiders" to the topic usually make the longest and most boring contributions. Ideas to ensure good order include:

— use of a roving microphone with a steward;

— a system whereby those wishing to ask a question have to queue behind a steward who looks after the microphone;

— a system of those wishing to ask a question holding up cards and the Chairman dividing the room into sections (eg I will take three questions from this side of the hall, and then three questions from the other side); or

— a timer giving so many minutes to each person wishing to pose questions.

Stewards

4–36   Ensure that there are enough stewards to deal with enquiries, direct attendees to their seats for the start of the meeting, provide general assistance eg with refreshments and distribution of any papers.

Timing

4–37   This should be fixed by reference to the expected audience and the locality. If more than one meeting in a series is being held at different locations, the start time at each place can differ.

Venue

4–38   A number of points are obviously crucial:

(1) Size.
(2) Accommodation (seating, entrances, toilets, etc.).
(3) Car parking availability (preferably manned, or at least overlooked).
(4) Access by public transport.
(5) Heating.
(6) Lighting.
(7) Platform and dais suitability.
(8) Licence to use (check the small print).
(9) Cost.

Other points will be relevant:

(a) The organisers should bear in mind the religious and other convictions of those who may attend. For example, it is best to avoid premises belonging to a particular religious denomination, and licensed premises.
(b) The period for which the hall is booked should allow plenty of preparation/rehearsal time and post-meeting debrief and clearing up.
(c) Think about the atmosphere in the hall: perhaps display the insignia of the sponsoring organisation and/or consider the use of plants and flowers.

Vote

4–39   The meeting may wish to pass a resolution. This can only be declaratory of the opinions of those present. The chairman should ensure that any discussion on a motion is orderly, and follows the rules of debate. He can point out that a record of the meeting is being kept which will show that everyone's views have been taken into account, whether or not a resolution is passed. If the top table wishes to sponsor a resolution, selecting the proposer and seconder and choosing the timing of its introduction are advisable steps.

CHAPTER 5

CONVENING THE MEETING

1 GENERAL

In this chapter, and in the immediately following ones, we shall be concerned with the legal framework of meetings of a private, rather than a public kind: meetings which transact business and which are regulated by the rules of the body (even though that body may be concerned with social or recreational matters) under whose auspices they are held. The discussion will cover the essential aspects of such a meeting: its convention, constitution and conduct.

5–01

Convening means "cause to come together". In relation to the convening of a meeting, two aspects will be considered: the notice, and the business proposed to be carried through (the agenda).

2 NOTICE

Essentials of a valid notice

To be valid a notice must:

5–02

    (1) State the date, time and place of meeting.
    (2) State with sufficient fullness the purpose of the meeting.
    (3) Give notice of any special business to be conducted at the meeting.
    (4) Comply with any statutory and legal obligations.
    (5) Be clear, honest, unambiguous and definite.
    (6) Be issued on good authority.
    (7) Be given in the prescribed manner (hand, post, advertisement or other means).
    (8) Allow the appropriate length of time between service and the date of meeting.
    (9) Be sent to every person entitled to receive it.
    (10) Comply in all respects with the regulations, rules or byelaws of the body issuing it.

These requirements are dealt with in detail below.

(1) Date, time and place

It is self-evident that the notice should give accurate information as to the date and time of the meeting, and its venue. The only exception might be where

5–03

custom and practice has established, for example, that a monthly board meeting is always held at the registered office at say 10.15 a.m.; in that case the accidental omission to give the standard details in the notice would not invalidate it. On the other hand, departure from normal arrangements clearly requires specific mention.[1]

A meeting date will usually be fixed to accord with the convenience of participants. Where the directors of a company deliberately attempted to convene an annual general meeting on a date which prevented certain shareholders from exercising their voting powers, they were restrained from doing so.[2]

As regards venue, in a case where the general meeting of an insurance company fell to be held at such place "as may be determined by the directors" the court refused to interfere upon the decision being made to transfer the venue from London to Liverpool even though there were matters of moment to be discussed at the meeting and the majority of shareholders would find London more convenient. It would have been different if fraud had been alleged.[3]

(2) The purpose to be stated

5–04　A notice, to be valid, must clearly state the business to be transacted at the meeting and give all material information to enable it to be fully understood. Examples are as follows:

> Following an incident, the name of a member of a club was removed from the list of members. The notice for the committee meeting, at which it had been decided to remove her name, did not state the fact that there was an intention to expel her. This omission was deemed to be a defect in the notice.[4]
>
> A notice convened an extraordinary meeting for the purpose of altering the articles of a company. The new articles contained, among other things, clauses enabling the board to pay a retiring managing director a pension, increasing the directors' remuneration, appointing three directors for life, relieving the directors from liability for loss and extending the board's borrowing limit. *Held*, that the notice was insufficient, because the nature of the alterations was not specified therein, and that as the meeting was irregularly convened the resolutions were invalid. It made no difference that the new articles were available for inspection.[5]

The above cases[6] are examples of where the notice was too general to cover the particular. A case where the notice was too particular to cover the general is as follows:

> At a vestry meeting a resolution was passed authorising the churchwardens to borrow money on the security of the church rates in order that damage caused by a fire might be repaired. A second resolution authorised the levying

---

[1] See *Moore v. Hammond* (1827) 6 B. C. 456.
[2] *Cannon v. Trask* (1875) 20 Eq. 669. This case is referred to at para.12–04
[3] *Martin v. Walker and Others* (1918) 145 L.T. Jo. 377.
[4] *Young v. Ladies Imperial Club* [1920] 2 K.B. 523.
[5] *Normandy v. Ind Coope Co.* [1908] 1 Ch. 84.
[6] See also *Kaye v. Croydon Tramways Co.* [1898] 1 Ch. 358 (para. 5–07 below).

of a rate to pay for the first instalment of the loan and "for making a rate for necessary and incidental expenses of the church". The levying of a rate for purposes other than the restoration work was not covered by the notice. It was held that the rate was invalid.[7]

The court does not scrutinise notices with a view to exercising criticism, or to find out defects, but it looks at them fairly. In the words of Chitty J. in *Henderson v. Bank of Australasia*:

"I think the question may be put in this form: What is the meaning which this notice would fairly carry to ordinary minds? That, I think, is a reasonable test. Another matter of very considerable importance in dealing with this as a practical question, is, how did the meeting itself understand the notice?"[8]

In another case, a vestry meeting was called "for making of a church rate and other purposes". A new church building had recently been consecrated, and the meeting resolved to levy a rate of one shilling in the pound to meet the expenses of opening the new church. It was alleged that insufficient notice had been given. The judge agreed that no specification of the exact purposes to which the rate was to be applied had been given in the notice, but said it was hypercritical to require every particular circumstance and object to be stated in the notice: no one could have been taken by surprise.[9]

Whether a notice is sufficient must be decided on the facts of each case. A crucial test is whether it contains enough information to enable the recipient to decide for himself whether he should attend, or appoint a proxy on his behalf, or whether he is content to let matters take their course at the meeting: to enable him "to decide for himself whether he should do any more."[10]

(3) Special business

The regulations of the body concerned may provide that certain items of **5–05** business shall be "special business." In that event, the notice requirements of the regulations must be strictly observed. A well-known example comes from the field of company law: since at least 1862 the Table A attached to the company statute of the time has provided for all items taken at an annual general meeting to be deemed to be special business, with the exception of regular items such as the declaring of a dividend, the receipt of accounts and reports and the election of directors.[11]

An illustration from outside the field of company law is as follows:

The Oxford and Cambridge University Club was governed by rules. The subscription had been raised in 1832, 1867 and 1881 without exception being taken; but in 1902 a member opposed an increase. The rules provided for special business as follows:

[7] *Smith v. Deighton* (1852) 8 Moore P.C. 179.
[8] (1890) 45 Ch.D. 330, 337.
[9] *Warner Gater* (1839) 2 Curt. 315.
[10] *Normandy v. Ind. Coope Co.* (see n. 5 above).
[11] See para. 13–14.

"If any measure not connected with the affairs of the club for the past
year shall be intended to be proposed at the annual general meeting, 21
days' notice shall be given of the same . . . "

(In the event, the special business covering the 1902 increase was held invalid
by the court because although the correct notice had been given, the amount
of the subscription was enshrined in another of the club rules and the rules
contained no provision for amendment.)[12]

It is implicit in the concept of special business that no particular mention is
required of other (ordinary) business is to be conducted at the meeting; when he
gets his notice the member is deemed to have knowledge of the regulations of the
body concerned and, therefore, of the agenda items.[13] He will have the advantage,
too, that at the meeting he will be able to propose amendments to the ordinary
business being transacted without giving prior notice to the other members. So far
as company meetings are concerned, it is now universal practice for notices of
company general meetings to state the main items of the agenda and therefore the
distinction, in that area, between special and ordinary business has tended to
diminish.

It is sufficient to give a general indication of the nature of the special business,
and, usually, conveners of a meeting are under no obligation to state the precise
terms of the resolutions to be proposed:

A notice of an annual general meeting of a company stated that such meeting
was called for the purpose of considering and, if thought fit, passing certain
resolutions "with such amendments as shall be determined upon at such
meeting." One of the resolutions was that three persons named in the notice
should be appointed directors. They were duly proposed at the meeting, but
an amendment was carried that in addition to the three persons originally
nominated two additional named directors should be appointed. It was held
that the appointment of the additional directors was within the scope of the
special business indicated in the notice.[14]

Of course, if a notice of meeting is less precise, it offers greater opportunity for
resolutions to be amended:

An AGM notice stated that one of the purposes of the meeting was "to elect
directors." It also stated that in accordance with the articles Mr. C. retired and
offered himself for re-election. At the meeting, he was proposed for election,
but an amendment was moved that three other persons be elected directors.
It was held that the chairman was wrong in rejecting the amendment, as the
notice sufficiently specified, within the meaning of the company's articles, the
general nature of the (special) business before the meeting and it was therefore
within the competence of the meeting to elect directors up to the number
permitted by the articles.[15]

---

[12] *Harington v. Sendall* [1903] 1 Ch. 921.
[13] *Choppington Collieries v. Johnson and Others* [1944] 1 All E.R. 762.
[14] *Betts Co. Limited v. Macnaghten* [1910] 1 Ch. 430.
[15] *Choppington Collieries Limited v. Johnson* (see n. 13 above); and see paras 19–12 and 19–27 below.

Although a notice may be adequate if it states the nature of the special business, it is nevertheless desirable, where the business is of great importance, to supplement the notice with an explanatory statement or circular.[16]

Somewhat different rules apply to meetings of company boards and management bodies. It has been held that company directors may at their meetings transact business, whether of an ordinary or special nature, and notice of special business is not necessary. Any other rule would be most inconvenient in view of the urgency of much business with which directors have to deal.[17]

The same has been held to apply to acts done by the executive council of a trade union.[18]

(4) Statutory and legal obligations

The form of a notice must comply with any statutory or other legal obliga-   **5–06**
tions.

For example, Schedule 2, paragraph 24(4) of the Building Societies Act 1986 provides that in every notice calling a meeting of a building society there shall appear with reasonable prominence a statement (a) that a member entitled to attend and vote may appoint a proxy (or, where it is allowed, one or more proxies) to attend and vote at the meeting instead of him; (b) that the proxy need not be a member of the society; and (c) that the member may direct the proxy how to vote at the meeting.[19] By paragraph 3 of Schedule 2, the rules must provide for the calling and holding of meetings, and in particular[20] for the form of notice for the convening of a meeting, and the manner of its service.

(5) Clear, honest, unambiguous and definite

A notice must be clear, open and free from trickiness, and must be in language   **5–07**
understood by ordinary people.

These requirements were held to be absent in a case where a meeting had been convened for the purpose of authorising the sale of the undertaking of one company to another, but nothing had been said in the notice of the fact that substantial compensation was to be paid to the directors of the selling company as compensation for loss of office.[21]

A notice must be definite, as contingent notice is not a sufficient notice:

The notice for an extraordinary general meeting of shareholders to be held on July 12, 1889 for the passing of certain resolutions concluded that "should

---

[16] *Young v. South African and Australian Exploration and Development Syndicate* [1896] 2 Ch. 268. See para. 13–15.
[17] *La Compagnie de Mayville v. Whitley* [1896] 1 Ch. 788. See further as to directors' meetings at para. 22–04.
[18] *Cotter v. National Union of Seamen* [1929] 2 Ch. 58, 77.
[19] See Companies Act 1985, s.372 for a similar provision; at para. 13–12.
[20] See "Table of Matters to be covered by the Rules" in para. 3 of Sched. 2.
[21] *Kaye v. Croydon Tramways Co.* [1898] 1 Ch. 358.

such resolutions be duly passed the same will be submitted for confirmation . . . to a subsequent extraordinary general meeting which will be held on Monday 29 July 1889. . . . " It was held that the notice of the second meeting was conditional and was therefore bad when sent: nor could the validity of the second meeting be saved by the shareholders acquiring extraneous information that the resolutions had in fact been passed at the first meeting.[22]

On the other hand, where a single notice convened two meetings, but included the words "Should the resolution not be passed by the requisite majority at [the first meeting] due notice will be given to the shareholders that [the second meeting] will not be held," the notice convening the second meeting was valid.[23]

It is of course quite frequent for the business to be transacted at the meeting to be dependent on some prior event. In these circumstances, the right course is for normal and due notice of the meeting to be given, but the resolution proposed will read along the following lines:

> "That subject to and conditionally upon [the prior event occurring] [then follow details of the proposed resolution to be passed by the meeting]."

If the prior event does not occur the meeting must still be held, but the chairman should explain the facts and state that in the circumstances there is no point in putting the resolution before members; the meeting can then be closed.

In relation to ambiguity, it seems clear that a notice convening a meeting for, say, Monday, July 4 will be bad if in that year July 4 falls on a Tuesday.

(6) Authority

5–08   If a meeting is summoned without authority, it will be invalid.

It is customary for a notice to indicate clearly on whose authority it is issued, and for it to be issued over the name of an authorised official. The first requirement is fundamental, but the second is more a matter of form and is perhaps not indispensable, provided the notice is in other respects good.[24]

Most meetings of company shareholders are convened by and over the name of the company secretary, but where a meeting is convened by shareholders themselves, for example, under section 368 of the Companies Act 1985, it is appropriate for the notice to be issued over the names of the shareholders. Under section 371, a meeting may be called on the authority of the court. These provisions of the Companies Act are discussed in more detail.[25]

A notice issued without authority is good if subsequently ratified:

> The secretary of a company, on the requisition of shareholders, summoned an extraordinary meeting for the purpose of removing one of the directors of the company from office. The plaintiff commenced proceedings for an injunction

---

[22] *Alexander v. Simpson* [1890] 43 Ch. 139.
[23] *Re Espuela Land Cattle Co.* (1900) 48 W.R. 684.
[24] See *Re Brick and Stone Company* [1878] W.N. 140.
[25] Chap. 12, below.

to prevent the meeting being held on the ground that it had not been lawfully summoned, but before the date of the meeting the directors met and ratified the action of the secretary. *Held*, that the notice was good, on the basis that the ratification by a principal of an act purporting to be done by an agent dates back to the performance of the act.[26]

Where there is no such ratification the invalidity of the notice cannot be cured:

A requisition was sent to the directors of a company requesting them to convene a meeting to pass an extraordinary resolution for voluntary winding up, and the secretary of the company, acting on his own authority, summoned an extraordinary meeting of the members for this purpose. The validity of the winding-up was challenged on the ground that the meeting was convened without the authority of the board, and such irregular act had not been ratified. The resolution was held to be invalid.[27]

(7) Prescribed manner

The regulations of the body on whose behalf notice is being given usually prescribe the method to be followed.   **5–09**

The rules of a club, for example, may provide that notices of meetings shall be posted at the club house and a copy sent to every member.[28] Where no club rule prescribes a mode, it is within the general functions of the committee of a club to say how notices should be given on each particular occasion.[29] The greater the importance of the matter to be discussed, for example where the expulsion of a club member is to be considered or rules are to be altered, the more the need to send a copy of the notice to each member rather than merely affixing it to the club notice board. On the other hand, in matters affecting clubs the courts eschew a meticulous examination of the rules: reasonableness and fairness are given more weight than a rigid interpretation. In the words of Megarry V.C., "allowance must be made for some play in the joints."[30]

In general, if there are no specific provisions, and subject to custom and practice—for example, the following of similar previous arrangements—notice may be given by advertisement: a notice in newspapers convening a meeting of debenture holders under a trust deed has been held good.[31]

Where a particular form of service is provided for in the regulations, no other form is permitted; thus, where service by post is stipulated, delivery by dropping the notice into the letter box personally or by handing it to a clerk would not be in order.

---

[26] *Hooper v. Kerr, Stuart and Co.* (1900) 83 L.T. 729.

[27] *Re State of Wyoming Syndicate* [1901] 2 Ch. 431.

[28] *Encyclopaedia of Forms and Precedents* (5th ed.), Vol. 7, para. [3215].

[29] *Labouchere v. Earl of Wharncliffe* (1879) 13 Ch.D 346 at 352.

[30] *Re GKN Sports and Social Club* [1982] 1 W.L.R. 774, 776. See also *Hamlet v. General Municipal Boilermakers and Allied Trades Union* [1987] 1 All E.R. 631 where Harman J. pointed out that the rules of trade unions, too, should not be construed as if they were statutes but should be considered in a "more benign and loose way of reading."

[31] *Mercantile Investment and General Trust Co. v. International Company of Mexico* [1893] 1 Ch. 484n.

It has been held that "post" includes registered post,[32] and, so far as documents which are required or authorised by any enactment to be sent by registered post are concerned, sending can be effected by the recorded delivery service.[33] Where an important notice is concerned, the use of recorded delivery can provide proof that it has been received; but the use of this service or registered post for notice of meetings is rare.

Where the regulations of the body concerned provide for notice to be sent by post, it is normally the responsibility of the member to keep up to date the record of his address in that body's records.[34]

(8) Length of notice

5–10   It is clear where the regulations provide for a stated period of notice to be given, this requirement must be met or the meeting will be invalid.[35]

The following paragraphs relate to calculation of the time during which the notice period runs.

The articles of companies incorporated under the Companies Acts will often contain a clause regulating when notice is deemed to be served: the 1985 Table A provides that a notice shall be deemed to be given at the expiration of 48 hours after the envelope containing it was posted.[36]

Under section 7 of the Interpretation Act 1978, where an Act authorises or requires any document to be served by post then, unless the contrary intention appears, the service is deemed to be effected by properly addressing, prepaying and posting a letter containing the document and, unless the contrary is proved, to have been effected at the time at which the letter would have been delivered in the ordinary course of post. The provisions of this section can probably be relied upon by analogy where the regulations are silent as to when a notice sent by post is deemed to have been delivered. In relation to first-class post, it can usually be assumed that delivery will be made within 48 hours, but if the second-class mail is used the conveners of the meeting should bear in mind that delivery can take a week or more.

Under many regulations affecting the service of notices it is provided that "clear days" must be given, that is to say that the notice shall be exclusive of the day on which it is served, and of the meeting. It is established that, even in the absence of specific provision, "days" means clear days, since it has been held that the words "at least 14 days before the date" of a meeting means 14 clear days between the date of the advertisement or notice calling the meeting and the day of the meeting,[37] and an interval of "not less than fourteen days" between two meetings, means an interval of 14 clear days, exclusive of the respective days of meeting.[38]

---

[32] *T. O. Supplies (London) Limited v. Jerry Creighton Limited* [1951] 2 All E.R. 992.

[33] Recorded Delivery Service Act 1962, s.1.

[34] *James v. Institute of Chartered Accountants* (1907) 98 L.T. 225.

[35] *Woolf v. East Niger Gold Mining Co., Limited* (1905) 2 T.L.R. 660.

[36] See further at para. 13–18.

[37] *Mercantile Investment and General Trust Co. v. International Company of Mexico* [1893] 1 Ch. 484. See also *R. v. Herefordshire Justices* (1820) 3 B. A. 581.

[38] *Re Railway Sleepers Supply Company* (1885) 29 Ch.D. 204. See also *Re Hector Whaling Limited* [1936] Ch. 208. See also para. 13–19.

It frequently occurs that those responsible for convening a general meeting of an organisation find that no mention is made in the rules of the period of notice required to be given. Here, the organisers should err on the safe side and give as much notice as is practicable. A rough rule of thumb might be 21 clear days' notice for an annual general meeting and 14 clear days' notice for any other general meeting, but much will depend on how important and exceptional is the business to be discussed. In such a situation, the officers of the organisation should take an early opportunity to take steps to amend the rules so that the notice requirements are clearly covered.

(9) Sent to everyone entitled

Notice should be sent to all those entitled under the rules or regulations of the **5–11** body concerned to receive a notice, or the meeting will generally be invalid. The following cases, some of them of considerable antiquity, illustrate this point:

> The custom of a borough was that every resident burgess was to be served personally with notice of a meeting. One of the burgesses informed an official of the corporation that he need not trouble to send him notices as he was often away, and these instructions were acted upon. At a meeting at which the same burgess was absent, which he could have attended had he received notice, a mayor was elected, but, as notice had not been served on the absent burgess, the proceedings were held to be void. The judge remarked that "the notice is served not for the personal benefit of the recipient but as an admonition to him to perform a public duty, and a person undertaking a public office cannot exempt himself from these admonitions."[39]
>
> In an election of burgesses, it was held to be essential that notice of the meeting and of the business to be transacted should have been given to all persons resident within the limits of the borough who were entitled to vote; the notice should have been reasonable and the time should also have been reasonable.[40]
>
> At a meeting of a constituency Labour Party there was strong disagreement, a good deal of noise, and some minor violence, and the chairman and those who supported him left the meeting. Those who remained proceeded with the meeting and passed a resolution of disaffiliation from the national Labour Party. The national agent then convened a meeting of the local branch but did not send notice of the meeting to the rebels. It was held that since notice of the second meeting was not sent to the plaintiffs (the rebels) the meeting was not properly constituted.[41]

Relief is sometimes available where the failure to give notice was accidental. In relation to companies, for example, regulation 39 of the 1985 Table A provides that the accidental omission to give notice of a meeting to, or the non-receipt of notice of a meeting by, any person entitled to receive notice shall not invalidate the

[39] *R. v. Langhorn* (1836) 4 A E. 538.
[40] *R. v. Hill* (1825) 4 Barn. Cress. 426.
[41] *John v. Rees; Martin v. Davies; Rees v. John* [1969] 2 W.L.R. 1294.

proceedings at that meeting.[42] Relief of this type would however probably not be available where, for example, a notice should under the rules be sent to all members of a society but it is sent only to, say, voting members. In practice, it would then be difficult to show that the omission was accidental.[43]

Illness may be another ground for not sending a member notice of a meeting; but the court has expressed the view that the illness would need to be extremely serious, because the sick member may either write to ask for an adjournment of the meeting or express his views in writing to the convening body.[44]

Should an absent member be abroad, it is desirable to send him notices, unless advised to the contrary, as by so doing he is kept informed of what is taking place at meetings of the body of which he is a member. It is relevant to point out that the vastly increased speed of travel today has the consequence that there are few spots on the earth's surface from which return is not possible in emergency within two or three days. The assumption that a person is not within summoning distance cannot therefore be lightly made.

In relation to the sending of notices to shareholders outside the United Kingdom, see below.[45]

(10) Comply with the rules

5–12   It is plain that a notice must comply in all respects with the regulations, rules or bye-laws of the body on whose behalf is it issued. Most of the relevant heads have been dealt with in the analysis above, but the general rule is stated in conclusion to emphasise the underlying authority against which procedural matters must be tested. The courts, however, have the final say when disputes arise relating to the interpretation of the rules of any organisation, and their jurisdiction cannot be ousted by a clause which provides, for example, that a central committee shall have the sole right to interpret the rules.[46]

Validation of irregular notice

5–13   As a practical matter, it may be possible to put right an invalid notice by sending out a letter or notice of amendment: for example, where the original notice had omitted to state the hour at which the meeting was to be held. Such an amending note, however, should be sent within the time limit prescribed for the giving of the original notice. If this is not possible, there may be little alternative but to cancel the arrangements for the first meeting and start again. If, however, the notice is arguably good (for example, there is some dispute as to whether sufficient details have been given on an agenda item) the conveners may prefer to let the arrangements stand and await a challenge to the resolutions passed by the meeting. Alternatively, the proceedings may be saved by the application of the principle that if all the members of a particular body are present and waive the formality of notice a resolution passed by the meeting will be good even though the meeting was not

---

[42] See para. 13–10.
[43] See *Royal Mutual Benefit Building Society v. Sharman* [1963] 1 W.L.R. 581.
[44] *Young v. Ladies Imperial Club Ltd* [1920] 2. K.B. 523, 536.
[45] See para. 13–06.
[46] *Baker v. Jones* [1954] 1 W.L.R. 1005.

assembled for that particular purpose.[47] Examples are as follows (but it should be noted that in relation to company meetings the specific provisions of section 369 of the Companies Act 1985 will now apply):

> All the members of a company (five in number) met as directors in board meeting and afterwards, in their capacity as shareholders, passed a resolution to issue debentures without any notice of the general meeting having been given to the shareholders. It was held that, as the resolution was in a matter *intra vires* the members of the company, and there was no fraud, the shareholders could waive all formalities as regards notice, and the resolution was just as valid as if there had been a requisite notice.[48]

> Two shareholders, the only members of the company, met and agreed that it was desirable to wind up the company, and a minute to that effect drawn up by a solicitor was signed by the two shareholders although no notice of the intention to propose the resolution as an extraordinary resolution had been given. *Held*, that it was competent for the shareholders of the company acting together to waive the formalities required by the Acts as to notice, and that as all the shareholders had met and passed the resolution to wind up the company the resolution was valid as an extraordinary resolution.[49]

It might occur that a resolution is passed but it is subsequently discovered that the notice was insufficient, for example because an explanatory note had failed to disclose all the financial information which might have been material in enabling members to decide how to vote. In such an instance, the sponsoring body might decide to present a confirmatory resolution, which could be on the following lines (and the notice of that resolution would have to be sent to all the current members of the body concerned):

> "THAT, for the avoidance of doubt, this meeting hereby confirms, with effect from [date of original resolution], the resolution passed at the meeting of . . . held on [date] and all action taken in pursuance thereof."

There can, however, be no validation of an irregular notice if the object of the meeting is *ultra vires*.[50]

Challenge to the validity of a notice

Those who seek to challenge the validity of a notice must act with promptness[51] and the courts will not interfere on the basis of minor irregularities: **5–14**

> In *Southern Counties Deposit Bank Limited v. Rider Kirkwood* a notice summoning a general meeting to wind up the company was issued on the authority of a board meeting at which only two directors were present. The quorum for

---

[47] *Machell v. Nevinson* (1809) 11 East 84n: and *R. v. Theodorick* (1807) 8 East 543.
[48] *Re Express Engineering Works* [1920] 1 Ch. 466.
[49] *Re Oxted Motor Co.* [1921] 3 K.B. 32.
[50] *Re Vale of Neath South Wales Brewery Joint Stock Co.* (1852) 1 De G.M. G. 421. Validation can be implicit: see *Longfield Parish Council v. Wright* (1919) 88 L.J. 119.
[51] *Re Bailey, Hay Co. Ltd* [1971] 1 W.L.R. 1357.

board meetings had for six years been regarded as two directors, but it was discovered that the resolution altering the quorum from three to two had not been validly passed in 1889. The resolution to wind up was passed in January 1895, but in July 1895 application to the court was made to declare it invalid. The court refused the application, saying it would not interfere "for the purpose of forcing companies to conduct their business according to the strictest rules, where the irregularity complained of can be set right at any moment."[52]

A person who is present and who takes an active part in the meeting will not be entitled to challenge an invalidity in the notice.[53]

Further, if the court takes the view that the irregularity in the notice could be quite simply cured by the issuing of another notice, and it is clear to the court that the majority of members supports the resolution passed at the meeting, the court will not grant an injunction restraining other parties from acting on the resolution.[54]

Adjourned meetings: notice

5–15   An adjournment, if *bona fide*, is only a continuation of the meeting and the notice that was given for the first meeting holds good for and includes all the other meetings following upon it.[55] If however the meeting is adjourned without a date for the adjourned meeting having been fixed, a fresh notice must be given.

No new business can be introduced unless notice of such new business is given.[56] This topic is further discussed in paragraphs 6–17 and 14–29.

3   AGENDA

5–16   The function of the agenda is to disseminate information relating to the business to be discussed at the meeting. As we have seen, the notice of the meeting should state in sufficient detail the purpose of the meeting. If a full and complete agenda is sent with the notice, or forms part of the same document, then this requirement is observed. The law relating to this aspect of meetings has been discussed earlier in the chapter and this section is largely procedural.

Basically, an agenda consists of a list of items, but preferably there will be included a brief note of guidance or a briefing paper as to what precisely the meeting is intended to discuss and form decisions upon. If a formal resolution has been submitted for discussion, the full text should be given, especially when there will be legal consequences flowing from the passing of the resolution.

The standing orders or rules of the body concerned may prescribe what is to be included in the agenda; otherwise, the responsibility for determining the contents of the agenda will rest with the governing committee of the body sponsoring the

---

[52] (1895) 11 T.L.R. 563.
[53] *Re British Sugar Refining Co.* (1857) 3 K. J. 408.
[54] *Bentley-Stevens v. Jones and Others* [1974] 2 All E.R. 653.
[55] *Kerr v. Wilkie* (1860) 1 L.T. 501.
[56] *R. v. Grimshaw* (1847) 11 Jur. 965.

meeting, or its chairman. The secretary frequently acts on his own initiative in preparing the agenda, with such consultation as is necessary, in particular with the Chairman, to ensure that no item of business has been overlooked. If there is a dispute as to whether an item should be included in the agenda or not, the secretary should err on the side of the inclusion, leaving the matter for the ultimate decision of the meeting itself. In order to preserve impartiality, the secretary should, at the request of a member, include any matter which can be regarded as the proper business of the meeting.

The secretary will usually keep a temporary file of matters for inclusion in the agenda, and a register of items that have been deferred for further consideration. He will generally keep a forward diary for matters of more distant watch.

It is good practice for matters which are brought forward to have their own separate agenda item number, for example:

> "6. Affiliation Fees.
> To receive the report of the treasurer (see no. 13 in the minutes of the meeting held on . . .)."

This would be better practice than to leave the question of affiliation fees to be raised under "matters arising from previous minutes"—an item which often gets grossly overloaded.

Items of special importance should be set out prominently, and should preferably be accompanied by a note of explanation.

The names of those persons who will be attending the meeting in an advisory or consultative capacity should be given in the agenda.

It is usual to include in the agenda the item "Any other business." This might more correctly read "Any other business which can properly be put before the meeting", as only matters of an informal or unimportant nature can be transacted under this heading. The chairman should not permit a matter of major importance to be raised under this item unless it is urgent. In such an event, if the matter is of significance, it should be placed before another meeting of which due notice, with details of the relevant item, has been given. If this is not practicable, the action taken should be ratified by the next ordinary meeting of the body concerned; this should be done by a specific resolution or confirmation, and not just by approving the minutes of the earlier meeting. The chairman should be vigilant to ensure that those whose main interest lies in the passing of resolutions do not use "other business" to bounce a resolution through a meeting.

The order of agenda items

The traditional order of business is on the following lines:　　　　　　**5–17**

(1) Introduction of new members.
(2) Apologies for absence.
(3) Minutes of the previous meeting.
(4) Correspondence.
(5) Reports.
(6) Important items of business of a non–recurring nature.
(7) Date of next meeting.
(8) Any other business.

It is quite customary for the chairman to wish to rearrange the agenda items into a different sequence. He should explain his reasons to the meeting, which can object: the order of the agenda will then itself become a topic for debate and subject to motions from the floor. Usually, and preferably, the subject is one which is dealt with by the informal agreement of those present.

4   Precedent of Notice Combined with Agenda

5–18   A simple form of notice and agenda of an unincorporated association is set out below. Details will, of course, need to follow the requirements of the rules of the association. It is assumed that matters will be dealt with at the meeting by a show of hands or voting papers circulated at the time (see paras 7–19 to 7–23), and no mention is made of proxy voting or a postal vote.

THE WORK-RATE ASSOCIATION
[Address]

NOTICE is hereby given that the annual general meeting of the Association will be held at on........[year] at [time am/pm] for the following purpose: To transact the business on the agenda set out hereunder.

By order of the Committee.

..........................Secretary.

..........................[year][57]

AGENDA

Item 1   MINUTES: to approve the minutes of the previous annual general meeting, held on........ [year].[58]

2   ELECTION OF COMMITTEE MEMBERS: to elect members to the committee of the Association.[59]

---

[57] Proper length of notice must be given: see para. 5–10.
[58] These can, for example, be circulated with the agenda, or be made available at the meeting, or read out by the secretary at the meeting.
[59] The standing orders or rules might provide for the sending out of a nomination paper (see para. 5–19). If the list of candidates is complete, further details of them can be given in the agenda. In more complex instances, the agenda can be accompanied by a note which gives C.V.s of the candidates (perhaps in random order) with a note of those who are standing respectively for re-election and election. The agenda may state that the chairman will announce the election procedure at the meeting (see also para. 7–17).

3   REPORT AND ACCOUNTS: to consider the adoption of the annual report and accounts for the period to...... [year].[60]

4   AUDITORS: to consider the appointment of..... Co., of........ as auditors for the ensuing year.[61]

5   SPECIAL BUSINESS: to consider the resolution submitted by...members under rule...... of the rules of the Association.[62]

6   Any other business which can properly be put before the meeting.[63]

With reference to item 2 in the agenda set out in para. 5–18, the following (para. 5–19, see over) is an example of a nomination paper:

THE WORK-RATE ASSOCIATION

NOMINATION OF CANDIDATE FOR ELECTION TO THE COMMITTEE

Name of Candidate: **5–19**
Sponsoring Company/Body:
Address:

Telephone:
Fax:

Proposer:
(signature)
Name:
Address:

Seconder:
(signature)
Name:
Address:

I confirm that I am willing to serve on the Committee if elected.
....
(Signature of Candidate)

Return to

by not later than

---

[60] Often, reports on the year's activities will be given orally at the meeting by the principal officers. At least an abbreviated version of the accounts should be sent out with the agenda; if this is not done, the agenda should state where the accounts can be inspected and that copies will be distributed at the meeting.

[61] The auditors' report should be part of, or accompany, the accounts.

[62] The standing orders or rules must be followed with particular care in relation to this item.

[63] See para. 5–16.

CHAPTER 6

CONSTITUTION AND ADJOURNMENT OF THE MEETING

6–01 A meeting will be properly constituted when, at an adequate venue, sufficient members are present to form a quorum and someone to control the meeting (*i.e.* a chairman) has been duly appointed. A meeting may be adjourned; in law, the adjourned meeting will form part of the originally convened meeting.

1   VENUE

The fact that a venue is cold, gloomy and uncomfortable will not prevent a valid meeting being held there. The minimum requirements are that it is of adequate size for the number attending (the practical effects of which are discussed in more detail in the section on companies),[1] and that it enables all those present to hear and be heard and to see and be seen.[2]

2   QUORUM

Definition

6–02 The word quorum denotes the number of members of any body of persons whose presence at a meeting is requisite in order that business may be validly transacted. (Conversely, the mere fact that a number of members, sufficient to form a quorum, may meet casually, does not constitute a meeting where the other requisites, such as due notice, are absent.)

The word is the Latin for "of whom" and derives from the wording of commissions by which persons were, from at least the fifteenth century, designated as members of a body by the words "quorum vos . . . unum esse volumus," *i.e.* "of whom it is our wish that you . . . shall be one."

In this chapter the word is taken to refer to both (1) the concept that a "meeting" must usually consist of more than one person and (2) the necessity, imposed by the regulations of the body concerned, that a minimum number of members must be present. The latter is a matter for the rules of that body. It is quite possible for example to have a quorum consisting of, say, "any three members of whom one shall be the secretary"— or as may be required.

---

[1] See paras 19–03 and 19–20 below.
[2] *Byng v. London Life Association* [1989] 2 W.L.R. 738.

Minimum number

In general, two persons is the minimum number for a meeting to be properly **6–03** constituted, since the term "meeting" prima facie means a coming together of more than one person. This rule was applied in the following cases:

Only one shareholder was present at a general meeting of a mining company. although the secretary was in attendance. This shareholder took the chair, approved a resolution making a call, approved the accounts and changed the bank mandate; then he passed a vote of thanks to himself as chairman. The secretary, in the name of the company, instituted an action to enforce the call, but it was held that as there was only one person present at the meeting, he could not constitute a meeting, and the call was therefore invalid.[3]

This principle was followed in a similar case where a shareholder, present by himself but holding proxies for the other shareholders, approved of a resolution to wind up the company voluntarily. The resolution was set aside.[4]

With the passing of time, there has been an increase in the number of circumstances where the rule will not apply, as where one person holds all of a class of shares,[5] where one creditor attends a creditors' meeting in an insolvency,[6] where there is a committee of one,[7] or where the articles of a company provide for a quorum of one director at board meetings,[8] or where under section 367 or section 371 of the Companies Act 1985 a meeting is called by the Department of Trade and Industry or the court.[9] By regulations made in 1992, single-member companies (and therefore single-member meetings) are now permitted.[10] This type of exception, however, is generally unknown in local government practice.

Counting the quorum

The number of persons necessary for a quorum must be present in person unless the regulations provide for proxies to be counted in determining the required number.

A representative of a corporation which is a shareholder may be counted in ascertaining whether or not there is a quorum.[11]

Where, at a meeting of directors for which the quorum fixed was two directors and two of the three directors were disqualified from voting under the company's articles, there was no quorum present; to form part of a quorum the participants must be competent to transact and vote on the business before the meeting.[12]

A quorum is as necessary at an adjourned meeting as at the original meeting.

---

[3] *Sharp v. Dawes* (1876) 2 Q.B.D. 26.
[4] *Re Sanitary Carbon Co.* [1877] W.N. 223. See also paras. 13–32 and 13–33.
[5] *East v. Bennett Bros. Limited.* [1911] 1 Ch. 163. See also para. 17–04.
[6] See para. 25–24.
[7] See para. 9–01.
[8] See para. 22–06.
[9] See paras. 12–04 and 12–15.
[10] See para. 11–05.
[11] See *Re Kelantan Coconut Estates Limited and Reduced* (1920) 64 S.J. 700.
[12] *Re Greymouth Point Elizabeth Railway and Coal Company, Limited* [1904] 1 Ch. 32.

The question of the fixing and maintenance of a quorum at company meetings is considered later.[13]

Where no quorum prescribed

6–04   In the unlikely event of no quorum being prescribed in the regulations, the number in the case of a non-trading corporation would be the major part of the corporators. "The acts of a corporation are those of the major part of the corporators corporately assembled . . . in the absence of special custom, the major part must be present at the meeting, and of that major part there must be a majority in favour of the act or resolution."[14] The same rule appears to apply to an informal association such as a club.[15]

Where the articles of association of a company do not prescribe the number of directors required to constitute a quorum (an unlikely event in modern circumstances), the number who usually act in conducting the business of the company will constitute a quorum.[16]

In another old case, however, the articles stated that "the board shall mean the directors for the time being or, as the case may be, a quorum of such directors assembled at a meeting thereof." A quorum was never in fact appointed by the directors, and in the circumstances the quorum was declared to be the majority of the directors present at the meeting.[17]

Where a board of directors delegates its powers to a committee, without any provision as to the committee acting by a quorum, all acts of the committee must be done in the presence of all the members of the committee.[18]

Effect where a quorum is not present

6–05   It is a generally accepted principle that business transacted at a meeting at which a quorum is not present is invalid. This principle, however, will not apply to a contract entered into with third parties who are not acquainted with any defect in the constitution of the authority creating the instrument:

> The directors of a joint stock company had power under their articles to fix the number of the directors which should form a quorum, and by resolution they fixed three. A meeting of directors at which only two were present authorised the secretary to affix the company's seal to a mortgage which was accordingly done by the secretary in the presence of the same two directors. It was held that as between the company and the mortgagees, who had no notice of the irregularity, the execution of the deed was valid; outsiders are

---

[13] See paras. 13–31 to 13–33.
[14] *Mayor, Constables and Company of Merchants of the Staple of England v. Governor and Company of the Bank of England* (1887) 21 Q.B.D. 160, 165.
[15] *McColl v. Horne and Young* (1888) 6 N.Z.L.R. 590; but see para. 7–27, in relation to changes in the rules of a club.
[16] *Re Tavistock Iron Works Co., Lyster's Case* (1867) L.R. 4 Eq. 233.
[17] *York Tramways Co. v. Willows* (1882) 8 Q.B.D. 685.
[18] *Re Liverpool Household Stores Association, Limited* (1890) 59 L.J. Ch. 616.

not expected to search the company's minutes as to the internal regulations and they are to presume that the document is, on the face of it, in order.[19]

This rule would not apply where the company had never had the minimum number of directors prescribed by the articles since this would not be just a matter of internal regulation.[20]

Where during the course of the meeting the number of members present falls below that required for a quorum, the meeting is "inquorate" and should be adjourned, since it can no longer validly conduct business:

> One of two shareholders called a meeting to appoint a liquidator. One of the shareholders proposed himself as liquidator but the other left the room before a vote, thus reducing the meeting to one, although a quorum of two was prescribed in the articles. The remaining shareholder then appointed himself as liquidator by the convincing margin of one vote to nil. The appointment was a nullity.[21]

It should be noted, however, that the regulations may provide that the meeting merely has to be quorate at the start of the meeting.[22]

If an inquorate meeting decides to have an informal discussion about the topics for which it has been convened, the chairman should make it clear at the outset that no decision can be made by those present. The minutes should simply record that as no quorum was present no business had been transacted.

Lapse of time

If the validity of proceedings at a meeting is to be challenged because of the absence of a quorum, appropriate action must be taken within a reasonable time. If a meeting has reached decisions which are acted upon and treated as valid by all concerned, it is not within the competence of a person not concerned at the time to seek to invalidate the proceedings because of the lack of a quorum: **6–06**

> In 1894 the court made an order confirming the reduction of the nominal value of the ordinary shares of a company, part of a scheme under which the dividend on the preference shares was reduced. In 1966 it was noticed that the resolutions of each class of shareholder, required by the company's articles before the scheme could be implemented, had in fact been passed without the necessary quorum. It was held that no contention based on that fact could be sustained since the scheme had been acted on for 70 years.[23]

---

[19] *County of Gloucester Bank v. Rudry Merthyr Steam and House Coal Colliery Co. Ltd* [1895] 1 Ch. 629.

[20] *Re Sly Spink and Co.* [1911] 2 Ch. 430.

[21] *Re London Flats* [1969] 1 W.L.R. 711.

[22] See, for example, article 53 of Table A, Part I of the Companies Act 1948 (the corresponding provision in the 1985 Table A, articles 40 and 41, is differently worded; see para. 13–31, below).

[23] *Re Plymouth Breweries, Plymouth Breweries v. Penwill* (1967) 111 S.J. 715.

3 THE CHAIRMAN

Qualities required

6–07   The qualifications required in a chairman are hard to define. A pleasing presence, a good voice, while desirable, are not essential, but self-confidence, fair-
mindedness and the ability to arrive at correct decisions on the spur of the moment
are absolutely necessary. While he should possess the power to express with facility
and discretion the mind of the meeting on the particular question under discussion,
he must avoid both garrulousness and secretiveness. As the representative of the
meeting itself, chosen or appointed to preside, while he must be ready to guide it
into decisions that will make for a successful result, he must at the same time be
careful to subordinate his own views to those of the meeting, both of the majority
and the minority.

Careful preparation for each meeting and a full understanding of the relevant
procedural rules are essential requirements. As Sir Walter Citrine has written:

> "You wouldn't want to get into a mess and find yourself being put right
> by some of the deadheads who have firmly declined to be pressed into
> service."[24]

Appointment

6–08   In general, where there is no chairman and there are no regulations providing for
his appointment, he is appointed by those present at the meeting. This might arise
where people meet as a group for the first time. It is then usual for the person
responsible for convening the meeting to call for nominations. If there is more than
one the matter should be put to the vote. The motion to elect a chairman need not
be in writing. Alternatively, the meeting may—usually on an informal basis and
without opposition—appoint a temporary chairman to run the meeting until the
chairman proper is elected

The above rules will not operate where the rules of the body concerned
determine who is to be the chairman at meetings of that body or its committees,
or provide a method for his election or re-election. For example, under the
regulations governing meetings of the National Trust, the chairman or the deputy
chairman of the National Trust will, if present, take the chair at a general meeting.
Only if neither were present would the members attending the meeting elect a
chairman.[25] This rule is typical of many.

The regulations of many bodies provide for the appointment of a deputy
chairman to act in cases where the chairman is absent through illness or other
causes. Should the chairman be late at a meeting, his deputy, if already in the chair,
would probably vacate it in favour of the chairman, but there is no obligation on
him to do so.

---

[24] *ABC of Chairmanship*, (1945), p.5. The fourth edition (reprinted 1994) of this book is available from
NCLC Publishing Society Ltd at 11 Dartmouth Street, London SW1H 9BN. It contains a full
analysis of the rules of debate (see Chap. 7, below).

[25] National Trust Act 1971, Sched. 2.

Any objection to the appointment of a chairman should be made immediately as any irregularity in the nomination may be cured by acquiescence.[26]

The appointment of a chairman at company meetings is dealt with in Chapter 13.[27]

At public meetings the chairman is usually a person invited by the conveners to preside.

Basic duties: summary

In an old case Jervis C.J. remarked that where a number of persons assemble and put a man in the chair, they devolve upon him by agreement the conduct of that body. "They attorn to him, as it were, and give him the whole power of regulating themselves individually. The chairman collects his authority from the meeting."[28] This authority comprises the following elements: **6–09**

> (1) to preserve order;
> (2) to ensure that the proceedings are properly conducted according to law and according to the standing orders or rules of the body concerned;
> (3) to ensure that all shades of opinion are given a fair hearing so far as practicable; and,
> (4) to ensure that the sense of the meeting is accurately ascertained and recorded.

Preservation of order

By "order," in this context, is meant the absence of disruption. The chairman's powers in relation, for example, to adjourning the meeting in the event of disorder have been discussed in Part I[29]; the same powers apply to the serious disruption which can equally occur at private meetings, for instance meetings of shareholders.   **6–10**

In relation to a private meeting, a person who has no right to be present is an intruder and is committing the tort of trespass, and the chairman can order him to be removed by force, though using only the minimum force necessary.[30]

The proper conduct of the meeting

The chairman has a number of specific duties: **6–11**

(1) *Time-keeping.* The chairman should ensure that the meeting starts and finishes on time. To do this he will have to keep an eye on the clock at each stage of the agenda.

(2) *Regulation of speakers.* The standing orders or rules will often provide for the period allowed for speakers. The chairman must see that the rules are followed. He

---

[26] *Cornwall v. Woods* (1846) 4 Not. Cas. 555.
[27] At para. 13–30.
[28] *Taylor v. Nesfield* (1855), *Wills on Parish Vestries* 29n.
[29] In Chap. 3.
[30] See para. 3–02.

should ensure that all speeches are addressed to the chair and receive a fair hearing. If the speaker wanders into material irrelevant to the motion before the meeting, or is offensive, the chairman should stop him. Everyone who wishes to speak should be given a chance to do so, subject to the rules of debate.[31]

(3) *Points of order.* The chairman will rule on questions relating to procedure.[32] If his decision is challenged the proceedings must be regulated by the majority of those present.[33] The chairman must disallow "points of order" which attempt to bring up points of substance in disguise.

(4) *Impartiality.* The chairman has a duty to remain impartial. If, in a formal debate, he wishes to address the meeting himself, he should leave the chair for the purpose. An exception to this rule is made where the chairman is not merely the chairman of the meeting but also head of the organisation concerned. Here he is, by convention, allowed considerable latitude, at least to the extent of replying on behalf of the organisation to questions from the members.

(5) *Adjournment.* It has recently been stated that the chairman has a residual common law power to adjourn a meeting so as to give all persons entitled a reasonable opportunity of voting and speaking at the meeting.[34]

Sense of the meeting

6–12   A chairman must exercise his powers and discretions in good faith and carry out the purpose for which the meeting is convened (*Second Consolidated Trust Ltd v. Ceylon Amalgamated Tea and Rubber Estates Ltd* [1943] 2 All E.R. 567). A meeting should reach a conclusion on each of the matters before it, which should be clear to those present. This end is achieved by adhering to the agenda (except where variations are agreed by the meeting), and ensuring that the meeting always has a motion, amendment or other specific subject-matter before it. The chairman should sum up clearly: if his interpretation of the result is challenged, he should confirm or amend it. In more formal matters there will be a motion before the meeting which will be voted on: it is helpful if the chairman at the conclusion of the debate asks the secretary to read out the motion on which members are about to vote. It is the responsibility of the chairman to see that resolutions are correctly embodied in the minutes before he signs them, usually at the next meeting.

A declaration by the chairman that a motion has been carried or lost is sufficient evidence without his having to state the number of votes for or against the motion. In other words, the chairman has a duty to obtain the sense of the meeting and his declaration of the result is good prima facie evidence which will be valid in the absence of fraud, an intention to mislead, or error. Instances of the latter arise where the chairman has improperly closed the meeting:

An ordinary general meeting of a society was called for the purpose of passing the accounts, considering reports, and electing auditors. The chairman moved

---

[31] See Chap. 7.
[32] *Re Indian Zoedone Co.* (1884) 26 Ch.D. 70. See para. 9–05 below.
[33] *Wandsworth and Putney Gas Light Co. v. Wright* (1870) 22 L.T. 404.
[34] See para. 6–16.

the formal motion: "That the report and accounts be received." This was seconded by another member, but several members wished to move an amendment that a committee of investigation be appointed. The chairman mistakenly refused to admit this amendment. He thereupon put the former motion to the vote, and on this being lost declared the result and closed the meeting. The members remaining elected another chairman to transact the business left unfinished, and at an adjourned meeting the appointment of a committee of investigation was approved. *Held*, that the chairman in leaving the meeting at his own will and pleasure was not acting within his power, and the meeting by itself could resolve to go on with the business for which it had been convened and appoint a chairman to conduct the business which the other chairman had tried to stop.[35]

A general meeting of a company was called for the transaction of ordinary business, but owing to considerable opposition among the members present, the meeting was adjourned, the only item of business transacted being the appointment of a committee of five shareholders to investigate the affairs of the company. At the adjourned meeting there was much hostility towards the chairman who purported to declare the meeting closed and who then left when important business remained to be transacted. Those remaining thereupon continued the business of the meeting and elected two directors in the place of two who should have retired. It was held that the appointment of the two new directors was valid.[36]

Removal of chairman

It is clear that a chairman who has been elected by the meeting can be removed **6–13** by the meeting.[37] The usual procedure would be for a member to propose a vote of no confidence in the chair, and for this to be seconded. In such event, the chairman would normally have a right of reply; if he loses the vote he should relinquish the chair. If the chairman holds his place as chairman by reason of a wider appointment in the organisation, it may be that he cannot be removed in the absence of bad faith.

Regulations of the body concerned may govern the point and may also provide for a challenge to be made to a ruling of the chairman, short of an attempt to force him from office.[38]

4 ADJOURNMENT

Definition

Adjournment is the act of postponing a meeting of any private or public body **6–14** or any business until another time, or indefinitely, in which case it is an adjournment *sine die*. The word applies also to the period during which the meeting or

---

[35] *National Dwellings Society v. Sykes* [1894] 3 Ch. 159.
[36] *Catesby v. Burnett* [1916] 2 Ch. 325.
[37] *Booth v. Arnold* [1895] 1 Q.B. 571.
[38] See also para. 7–06.

business stands adjourned. It is often necessary to adjourn a meeting *e.g.* because a quorum was not present or because of insufficient time to complete proposed business. An adjournment may be:

(1) For an interval expiring on the day of the adjournment.
(2) For an interval expiring on some later date.
(3) For an indefinite time (*i.e. sine die*).
(4) Until a fixed time and date.
(5) To another place.

It may be brought about by:

(1) Resolution of the meeting.
(2) Action of the chairman.

Adjournment by resolution of the meeting

6–15   A right to adjourn is, at common law, vested in the meeting itself.[39] In the following case the assembly chose not to adjourn, contrary to the chairman's wishes:

> A vestry meeting was held for the election of churchwardens, at which the vicar presided. Before the election was completed the vicar adjourned the meeting against the wish of many present. The latter remained behind and completed the poll, which resulted in the plaintiff's favour. The next day, the vicar and his supporters met and continued the poll with a different result. *Held*, that the right of adjournment was in the parish at large and the power arose from "the common right, which is in the whole assembly, where all are upon an equal foot," and the plaintiff was therefore duly elected.[40]

The rights exercised by the remaining members in circumstances similar to those referred to in the above case will apply where the chairman, neglectful of his duties, has taken a course contrary to the interests of the general assembly. These cases should be contrasted with the following:

> A meeting was regularly convened for the purpose of nominating and electing a new mayor, and the existing mayor presided over the meeting. He declared that the voting for the persons nominated was equal and he thereupon dissolved the meeting. Nobody objected at the time, but after allowing the mayor and many freemen to depart the rest remained and proceeded to complete the election. *Held*, that such election was void under statute as a surprise and fraud on the other electors.[41]

In relation to the power of adjournment vested in the meeting, the vote of the majority will decide whether or not that power is to be exercised.

[39] *Kerr v. Wilkie* (1860) 1 L.T. 501.
[40] *Stoughton v. Reynolds* (1736) 2 Strange 1044.
[41] *R. v. Gaborian* (1809) 11 East 90.

Adjournment by the chairman

It does seem clear that a chairman cannot capriciously adjourn meetings—if he **6–16** does so, a new chairman may be appointed to continue the meeting (*National Dwellings Society Ltd v. Sykes* [1894] 3 Ch. 159; and *John v. Rees* [1969] 2 W.L.R. 1294).

However, instances where the chairman has the right to adjourn the meeting are as follows:

(1) A power of adjournment is often vested in the chairman by the regulations of the body under whose auspices the meeting is held. This power is usually discretionary: it has been held that where articles provide that the chairman may adjourn a meeting "with the consent of the members present," he is not bound to effect any adjournment, even though a majority of those present desire one.[42]

(2) The chairman may adjourn on his own authority, in order to facilitate the business of the meeting, *e.g.* to take a poll.[43]

(3) In the case of persistent disorder, the chairman is empowered to adjourn the meeting; sometimes a short adjournment—for, say, 15 minutes—has the desired effect.[44]

(4) Where a quorum is not present, the chairman may adjourn the meeting to another date (or as may be prescribed by the rules of the body concerned).

As an extension to the above principles the Court of Appeal has indicated that the chairman has a common law power to adjourn so as to give all persons entitled a reasonable opportunity of speaking and voting at the meeting:

An extraordinary general meeting was convened at Cinema 1, the Barbican, London on October 19, 1988. Cinema 1 proved too small to accommodate all members wishing to be present. Members were diverted to overflow rooms and the foyer but the audio–visual link with the overflow rooms was deficient. The chairman adjourned the "meeting" and directed that it be resumed in the afternoon at the Café Royal. After a vote at the Café Royal and a poll, the resolution was passed. It was held that the power in the Company's articles for the chairman to adjourn with the consent of a quorate meeting could not be exercised where it was not possible properly to ascertain the views of the majority of those present. In such circumstances, however, the chairman had a residual power at common law to adjourn so as to give all persons entitled a reasonable opportunity to vote and speak. The impact of the proposed adjournment on those seeking to attend the original meeting and the other members must be a central factor in considering the validity of the chairman's decision to adjourn. His decision, in that case, had failed to take account of the fact that the matter was not of such urgency as to require a decision on the same day, or that those who could not be at the Café Royal would not only

---

[42] *Salisbury Gold Mining Co. v. Hathorn* [1897] A.C. 268; see para. 14–29.
[43] *R. v. D'Oyly* (1840) 12 A. E. 139.
[44] See para. 3–04.

be unable to speak but would, under the company's articles, be unable to vote by proxy. It was not enough that he had acted in good faith. The proceedings conducted at the meeting at the Café Royal were therefore invalid and of no effect.[45]

Procedure in relation to adjournment

6–17   In a situation where (as is usual) a meeting has the power under the rules of the body concerned to determine its own procedure and to adjourn, the chairman must put before the meeting a motion for the adjournment which is properly proposed and seconded. If he does not, any subsequent business transacted by the meeting will be of no effect.[46]

A motion for adjournment of the meeting may be moved or seconded by any person who has not hitherto spoken in the debate; this is to prevent those who have had their say from attempting to stifle discussion. If seconded, it supersedes the motion or amendment before the meeting and constitutes a new question upon which any person may speak. If however its purpose is to terminate discussion on the main question, it should be put to the meeting with the minimum of debate. A motion for adjournment may be amended, but only as to the time, date and place of the adjourned meeting or debate. The motion cannot be moved during the election of a chairman.

An adjourned meeting is deemed to be a continuation of the former meeting and no new notice is necessary:

> Where at a vestry meeting a rate was proposed and the meeting was adjourned four times the notice on the church door for the assembly of the first meeting was deemed to be notice of all the adjourned meetings as all such meetings were, in effect, a continuation of the first meeting.[47]

Exceptions to this rule are:

> (a) where the regulations of the body concerned provide that notice of an adjourned meeting should be given; and
> (b) where the meeting has been adjourned *sine die*—here, clearly, the date and place of the reconvened meeting will need to be advised to members.

At an adjourned meeting only the adjourned business should be taken. This usually takes the form of the original motion again being moved and debate taking place on it.

A quorum must (subject to any provision in the regulations of the body concerned) be present at the adjourned meeting.

Companies

6–18   Adjournment of meetings of companies is discussed in detail below.[48]

---

[45] *Byng v. London Life Association Limited* [1989] 1 All E.R. 560, C.A.
[46] *Mulholland v. St. Peter, Roydon, Parochial Church Council* [1969] 1 W.L.R. 1842.
[47] *Scadding v. Lorant* (1851) 3 H.L. Cas. 418; *Kerr v. Wilkie* (1860) 1 L.T. 501.
[48] At paras. 14–24 and 14–29.

CHAPTER 7

THE CONDUCT OF THE MEETING

The conduct of a meeting is largely in the hands of the chairman, but as was stated **7–01** in the previous chapter he derives his authority from the meeting. The point is amplified in *Carruth v. ICI*:

"There are many matters relating to the conduct of a meeting which lie entirely in the hands of those persons who are present and constitute the meeting. Thus it rests with the meeting to decide whether notices, resolutions, minutes, accounts and such-like shall be read to the meeting or be taken as read; whether representatives of the Press, or any other persons not qualified to be summoned to the meeting, shall be permitted to be present, or if present shall be permitted to remain; whether and when discussion shall be terminated and a vote taken; whether the meeting shall be adjourned. In all these matters, and they are only instances, the meeting decides, and, if necessary, a vote must be taken to ascertain the wishes of the majority. If no objection is taken by any constituent of the meeting, the meeting must be taken to be assenting to the course adopted."[1]

1   RULES OF DEBATE

The rules of debate are the rules which have been proved by experience to be conducive to the efficient transaction of business and exchange of views. They are based on custom and practice. It is highly desirable for any assembly in which debate is likely to take place to have its own standing orders, and the larger the assembly the more important it is for such standing orders to be observed. In a small meeting it is often convenient for proceedings to be informal, but this ought always to be recognised as being at the discretion of the chairman who has the right to call members to order and to insist upon observance of proper procedural rules. Subject to this comment, an attempt is made below to outline what may be regarded as normal procedure.

Motions

The term "motion" is here used in the sense of a proposition submitted for **7–02** debate as opposed to the term "resolution" used in the Companies Acts. Strictly speaking, a motion does not become a resolution until it has been adopted by the meeting as such.

---

[1] [1937] A.C. 707 at 761.

A motion should propose definite action, and not be framed in the negative (although the motion "that no action be taken" is, in practice, often accepted). If possible, "notice of motion" should be given to the secretary so that the motion can be included in the agenda sent out to members; such prior notice is obligatory in the case of local authority meetings, except for certain procedural motions. After such notice of motion has been given it should not be amended except in minor details or with the consent of the meeting.

It often happens that a motion arises spontaneously out of discussion. If such a procedure is permitted by standing orders, the motion should be reduced to writing by the person proposing it so that there can be no doubt as to what precisely is being moved. Motions are often accepted on an oral basis by the chairman, but the secretary should record it, read it out so that it can be approved and then signed by the mover (and seconder if appropriate). In practice, the chairman of the meeting should, if he feels an inconsequential discussion is taking place, call for a motion to be put before the meeting, which can then be voted on.

It is customary for a motion or amendment to be accepted for discussion only after it has been moved and seconded, and if no seconder is found the motion or amendment will fail, although this rule is not adhered to strictly in small committee meetings. There is, in fact, no common law rule to require a motion to be seconded and if a chairman does allow discussion on, and put to the vote, a motion which is not seconded, there is no way of challenging his action in the courts unless it is in violation of the standing orders of the body concerned. "There is no law of the land which says that a motion cannot be put without a seconder, and the objection that the motion was not seconded cannot prevail."[2] It is commonly accepted that a motion put from the chair does not need a seconder. It is, however, the general practice at local authority meetings which follow model standing orders to require a seconder for a motion or amendment. Conversely, as absence of a seconder usually indicates lack of support, the chairman has it within his discretion to refuse to put a motion that is not seconded.

A motion can be withdrawn by the mover only with the unanimous consent of the members present and before the question has been put to the meeting for decision; if an amendment has been proposed to the motion, the consent of the proposer and seconder of the amendment to the withdrawal of the motion will first be required.

No motion may be moved which in effect is the same as a motion already passed or negatived.

If the motion is not of a contentious nature and there appears to be unanimity in the meeting, the chairman will put it to the vote and, if approved, will declare the motion carried. It then becomes the resolution of the meeting.

If there is not immediate unanimous agreement on the motion, debate will take place on it.

It is here that the role of the chairman is crucial. If the motion is one which has been placed on the agenda and is known to be contentious, it is good practice for the chairman to try to find out, before the beginning of the debate, who wishes

---

[2] *Re Horbury Bridge Coal Co.* (1879) 11 Ch.D. 109. The same applies to an amendment to a motion, but it is customary for the chairman to call for a seconder (see para. 7–03).

to speak; he will try to call upon all the speakers, alternating various points of view so far as practicable.

All speakers should address the chair and preferably be asked by the chairman to stand. Everyone else should remain quiet. Everything said should be relevant to the issue. Observance of these rules is fundamental to the proper and prompt despatch of the business before the meeting. No member should be allowed to speak more than once on any motion until every other member has had an opportunity of speaking, and then only with the permission of the chair. On occasion the chairman will take note of informal signals by persons present that they wish to speak and will inform the meeting of the names of the next few speakers; the chairman may also indicate, if he feels the debate has run its course and other business presses, that he will limit the number of further speakers. If two or more speakers rise simultaneously the chairman may name the one to speak (being the one first noticed by him).

The mover and seconder of any motion are regarded as having spoken, unless in the seconder's case, he clearly reserves the right to speak later in the debate, when seconding.

The mover (but not usually the seconder) will have a right of reply at the end of the debate; it is intended to give the mover the opportunity of rebutting matters raised in debate and in this he should therefore not introduce any new matter. If amendments have been moved, the mover of the original motion should be allowed his right of reply either at the close of the debate on the first amendment or after all the amendments have been moved. No person is permitted to address the meeting after the question has finally been put to the vote. The vote will then be taken.

After a motion has been passed by the requisite majority it becomes the resolution of the meeting, and the persons present can then take no step which has the effect of rescinding, negating or destroying it.[3]

Amendments

An amendment is a proposed alteration in the terms of a motion (or of an   **7–03** amendment already before the meeting) by those whose views would not be met by either the acceptance or rejection of the motion or amendment as moved. An amendment is a rewording of a motion so that its line of approach, but not its objective, is altered. An example would be a motion "That the secretary be instructed to write to the management demanding that canteen facilities be provided for the workers in this factory" amended to read "That the management be requested to receive a deputation in order to discuss the provision of canteen facilities for the workers in this factory."[4] An amendment should take the form of omitting, substituting or inserting certain words in the original motion (or amendment). The alteration should not be such as to constitute a direct negative of the motion, for the same result could be achieved by an adverse vote; neither should it be beyond the scope of the original motion.[5]

---

[3] See para. 7–32 below.

[4] From *A Handy Guide to Procedure at Meetings*, in the pocket diary of the Transport and General Workers' Union.

[5] *Clinch v. Financial Corporation* (1868) L.R.5 Eq.481. For a discussion of amendments to ordinary resolutions proposed at company meetings, see paras 15–09 and 19–24.

It should not be irrelevant or obstructive, neither should it attempt to re-open previously settled business.

If a motion is so mutilated by a proposed amendment that only the initial word "That" and a few skeletal remains of the original motion are retained it becomes necessary for the chairman to decide whether the motion as amended is so far from the intention of the original motion that it should be disallowed as a direct negative or as not being within the scope of the original motion. An amendment which rejects the proposal contained in the original motion but which proposes an alternative is acceptable.

If in doubt, the chairman should accept the amendment, because if he improperly fails to do so the unamended resolution may be set aside by the court.[6]

When an amendment is moved it takes priority over the original motion and must be voted upon before the original motion can be put. No notice is necessary unless standing orders so provide. Amendments should be handed in writing (signed by the mover and seconder) to the chairman, if possible. The chairman, having put the amendment to the meeting in the form proposed, will, if a seconder is forthcoming, invite discussion on it. Procedure in relation to the amendment is the same as on the original motion. The discussion must be strictly relevant to the amendment. Should there be several amendments, they must be considered in the order in which they affect the original motion, and each must be disposed of separately. If the amendment be lost, the original motion is revived, and this is subject to further amendment until such time as all the amendments have been disposed of.

An amendment may not be proposed to any motion already accepted by the meeting, *i.e.* after the "question has been put" (see para. 7–04).

A person may move only one amendment unless the regulations otherwise provide, but there is nothing to prevent his speaking on an amendment to the same question moved by another person. If he has previously spoken on the motion he may not move or second an amendment to it, although he can speak on any amendment which may be moved by another person.

The mover of the original motion has a right of reply to the debate on an amendment, but the mover of an amendment has no such right.

An amendment cannot be withdrawn without the unanimous consent of the meeting.

An amendment to an amendment may be proposed (but it is not good practice, as it can cause confusion) and the meeting will then have to vote on whether the first amendment should be so amended. If accepted, the first amendment as so amended is then debated.

Should there be an equality of voting on an amendment, and the chairman does not exercise his casting vote, the amendment is lost.

Putting the main question

7–04   When amendments have been disposed of they are, if passed, incorporated in the original motion in the form of a substantive motion (or motion as amended) and this must be put to the vote. It may happen that an amendment has been approved, but when the motion is put to the meeting in the form of a substantive motion it

---

[6] *Henderson v. Bank of Australasia* (1890) 45 Ch.D. 330.

is lost. Similarly, if the amendment has been lost, the original motion, as it stood before the proposed amendment, must be put to the meeting and voted upon. The effect of such procedure is to dispose of the whole question under discussion.

The above general rules may be relaxed in the case of small bodies or committees. Further, they would not apply to shareholders' or similar meetings where it is usual to allow a fair amount of latitude to members in the raising of questions, but where freedom to make amendments to resolutions is very limited because of the statutory requirement of notice.

Motion with amendment: example

The following is offered as an illustration of the handling of a motion to which **7–05** a number of amendments have been tabled:

Moved by Mr .... and seconded by Mr ....

"That tenders be invited for the provision of a new swimming bath on the site of the existing bath at the Rectory Field, Muddleham."

Notice has been received of the following amendments:

(1) To insert the words "from local builders" after the word "invited".
(2) To add before the word "swimming" in line two the word "heated".
(3) To insert the following words after "Muddleham": "and that such tenders be referred to the surveyor for approval."
(4) To insert after the word "That" the following words: "the matter of the proposed new swimming bath at Muddleham be remitted to the General Purposes Committee for further consideration."
(5) To insert the word "no" after the word "That".

The amendments will not be put in the order submitted, but in the order in which they affect the original motion. (An important and sometimes controversial point arises here. Strictly, when an amendment to the latter part of a motion has been put to the vote and carried, nobody is allowed to move an amendment to any earlier part of the motion. Vigilance may therefore be required to see that (a) notice of a proposed amendment is given early enough for it to be debated and (b) the chairman takes the amendments in the correct order.)

First, the chairman should ensure that no further amendments are proposed; considerable confusion can result if fresh amendments are added in the course of debate on the first-proposed amendments. (A good idea, derived from local authority practice, is for standing orders to provide (or for the chairman simply to rule) that no further amendments will be allowed after a vote has been taken on the first amendment to be considered by the meeting. This prevents interest-groups from waiting to see how things go and then introducing a fresh proposal.)

The chairman rejects amendment 5 as being a direct negative of the resolution. He then informs the meeting of the order in which the other amendments will be debated. Number 4 has been selected to be debated first. This is proposed, seconded, debated and put to the meeting; it is lost. (If amendment number 4 had been carried, the chairman would have been correct in not putting any of the other amendments to the meeting because they would be inconsistent with what had then become a new substantive motion, *i.e.* "That the matter of the proposed new swimming bath at Muddleham be remitted to the General Purposes Committee for further consideration.") The chairman then calls amendment number 1. This is carried. He then calls amendment number 2, which is lost. Finally, amendment number 3 is carried. The chairman then puts the substantive motion to the meeting in the following form:

> "That tenders be invited from local builders for the provision of a new swimming bath on the site of the existing bath at the Rectory Field, Muddleham, and that such tenders be referred to the surveyor for approval."

The substantive motion is then voted upon. This is an important step, as it allows those who are opposed root-and-branch to the whole swimming bath idea to vote against it in principle.[7]

Chairman's ruling

7–06   The chairman should give any required ruling fairly and promptly and with authority. If he does this, he will be surprised at the degree of acceptance by the meeting. A fatal step would be to get to bogged down in the niceties described in the previous pages: these should be mastered (at any rate in principle) before the meeting starts.

Speakers, and indeed everyone else present at a meeting, should observe the ruling of the chairman on any matter. Standing orders or rules of the body often prescribe that his ruling shall be final, particularly in relation to points of order; in respect of other matters, the rules might provide that a ruling from the chair can be challenged by a minimum number of persons present, and that if this be done a vote shall then be taken. The chairman should vacate the chair while the vote is taken; it is not a matter on which there should be speeches.

Termination of debate

7–07   A debate may be terminated by the introduction of one of a number of formal devices which have become recognised practice. The standing orders or rules may define, regulate and determine the admissibility of these devices, but in general terms they are as follows:

(1) *The "closure."*
(2) *The previous question*
(3) *"Next business."*
(4) *That a matter "lie on the table."*
(5) *Reference back.*
(6) *Adjournment of the debate.*
(7) *Adjournment of the meeting.*

---

[7] For articles on amendments, in local authority practice, see *Administrator* August 1991, p.18, October 1991, p.32, December 1991, p.24 and July 1992, p.26. For voting procedure on amendments in the European Parliament, see O.J., December 7, 1995, Vol. 38, 293/36—r. 115 of Rules of Procedure.

(1) The closure

To move the closure means to move "that the question be now put," *i.e.* that **7–08** discussion shall end and the vote on the matter being considered be taken without delay ("to apply the gag"). If moved, seconded and approved (and assuming that the procedure is permitted under standing orders), it has the effect of ending discussion and getting a decision. It can be moved only by a person who has, until then, not spoken in the debate. No discussion should be allowed on the motion for the closure: the original motion under debate should be put to the meeting, but the mover is first allowed the chance to reply to the debate. A closure motion can in the same way be applied to discussion on an amendment. If carried, the motion before the meeting must be put immediately. Discussion on the motion may continue as before.

The chairman should not allow a closure motion to be put if he feels its objective is to stifle proper discussion.

If a motion for closure is lost, the chairman should not permit it to be raised again for a reasonable period.

(2) The previous question

This means to move "that the question be now not put, *i.e.* to avoid a vote being **7–08a** taken on a motion before the meeting. This can only be moved on a motion. Discussion on the motion is allowed but the mover has no right of reply. If carried, the motion cannot be brought forward again at that meeting. If lost, the original motion should be put to the meeting immediately without further discussion or amendment, after allowing the mover of the original motion his right of reply.

(3) Proceed to the next business

To move that "the meeting proceed to the next business" is the usual way in **7–09** which a subject is shelved, often indefinitely. If moved and passed, it has the effect that discussion is abandoned, and any motions before the meeting in connection with it are never put to the meeting; in this respect it differs from a closure motion. If moved and carried when an amendment is under discussion, it will, under most standing orders, cause the meeting to abandon discussion of the amendment and to return to discussion of the motion in its original form.

The motion is put in the form "that the meeting now proceeds to the next business," and, although in this it is subject to standing orders which usually provide that there shall be no debate on a procedural motion of this type, there is a convention that it should be proposed and seconded by persons who have not previously spoken in the debate. If the motion is passed, the meeting will immediately proceed as directed. If it is not passed, it is customary to allow a reasonable lapse of time (which may be specified in standing orders) before a similar motion is accepted again.

Standing orders often provide that a "next business" motion should not be taken until the mover and the seconder of a motion have been heard. If carried, discussion ends and the meeting proceeds to next business. If lost, discussion resumes. If carried in relation to an amendment, discussion returns to the main motion.

(4) That a matter lie on the table

7–10   The effect of this formal motion is in practice the same as a motion to proceed to the next business. Its use is usually limited to occasions when a document is before the meeting which either calls for no discussion or with which those present do not care to deal. It may indicate that a subject is thought to be irrelevant or unimportant. No amendment is permitted and the mover has no right of reply.

The meeting may later vote to take the matter from the table, but this is unlikely: if there is any proposal that it should be raised at a later date a more meaningful motion will usually be passed—for example, to defer discussion until a fixed date, or until the matter be raised again by the officers of the body concerned.

(5) Reference back

7–11   Another means by which discussion can be suspended is by referring a matter back to a committee. A variety of causes may give rise to a motion of this sort. It may happen that new circumstances have arisen that require a further examination by the committee, or it may be that the parent body disagrees with the recommendation of the committee, in which case it would have the same effect as negativing the motion. In a sense, this is a substantive rather than a procedural motion.

(6) Adjournment of the debate

7–12   Another method of deferring discussion is by moving an adjournment of the debate; it may be either for a fixed time or for an indefinite time. An adjournment of the debate, unlike an adjournment of the meeting, does not interfere with the continuance of the meeting for the transaction of business other than that for which the debate was adjourned. The motion to adjourn the debate should not be moved until the conclusion of a speech. The mover of the original motion is allowed to speak against the motion to adjourn. The person who moves the motion for the adjournment usually has the right of reply if there is debate on the motion, and of reopening the debate when it is resumed. If carried, the matter before the meeting is adjourned to a fixed date or indefinitely and the meeting proceeds to the next item. If lost, discussion continues to a fixed time or indefinitely.

(7) Adjournment of the meeting

7–13   A more radical alternative is a motion that the meeting be adjourned. The motion should be put immediately to the vote, and, if carried, disposes of the question under discussion at the meeting. When the meeting reconvenes, it would be open for any motion which was under discussion at the time of the adjournment to be again moved and debated. If the motion for the adjournment of the meeting fails, the chairman should not permit a similar motion to be heard until the debate has proceeded for some time. If carried, the meeting is adjourned to a specified date or indefinitely. If lost, the meeting continues. See also Chapter 6 in relation to adjournment generally.

(8) Chairman vacate the chair

The motion is put in the form "That the chairman leave the chair" with the **7–14** intention that the meeting is adjourned until the next ordinary meeting. This does not involve the election of a new chairman nor is it the proper motion if a new chairman is desired. The motion cannot be amended and may be moved at any time. If successful, the meeting is adjourned to the next ordinary meeting.

Points of order

A "point of order" is raised when, in the opinion of a member, the rules or **7–15** regulations governing a meeting are being broken, or when a member has a genuine doubt as to the correctness of the procedure being followed. This might include any non-observance of standing orders, any defect in the procedure of the meeting, *e.g.* the absence of a quorum, the use of offensive or abusive language, the fact that the motion under discussion is not within the scope of the notice, or any other informality or irregularity. Contradiction of and requests for explanation from the person speaking in the debate are not points of order, and it is an abuse to try to interpose them as such.

The person raising a point of order should do so by putting a briefly-worded question to the chairman stating that he wishes to speak on a point of order. He may raise the point of order when a person is speaking, but, as this is an obvious way of spoiling the speaker's train of thought, bogus points of order should be suppressed. The person speaking at the time should sit down; once the person taking the point of order has finished he too should sit down. The chairman's ruling on the point of order is final, but others present should be given an opportunity of speaking upon it if they so desire.

Points of order must be raised immediately the alleged breach of order has occurred.

2 Voting—Methods

The common law method of determining votes is by show of hands, and this **7–16** method applies where there are no regulations or enactments to the contrary. Other methods of voting are provided for by statute, or by the regulations of the organisation concerned.

The following are recognised forms of voting:

(1) *Acclamation or voices.*
(2) *Ballot.*
(3) *Division.*
(4) *Show of hands.*
(5) *Poll.*

(1) Acclamation or voices

7–17   The term is derived from a Latin word meaning "a shouting," and it is used to signify a spontaneous shout of approval or praise; "acclamation" is therefore usually used to adopt a resolution or pass a vote of confidence by loud approval in contrast to a ballot or division. The chairman may ask all those in favour to say "aye" and all those against to say "no".

It would be unlikely for this method to be used where any formal business is to be transacted:

> In a New Zealand case, it was held that "voting by voice" was an inappropriate method of deciding whether a majority present at a meeting of borough electors had voted in favour of a resolution as to whether or not a street should be closed.[8]

Whenever there is the smallest chance of uncertainty, the chairman should ask for a show of hands (see (4) below).

(2) Ballot

7–18   The word "ballot" derives from the Italian word "*ballotta*," a round bullet, and originally described the small ball placed in a box on a secret vote; then it was applied to a ticket or voting slip. The expression is applied here to an election of candidates to an office.

In this country the system was not known until the time of Charles II, and it was not until the passing of the Ballot Act in 1872 that the system was generally adopted for parliamentary elections. Under it a paper is used on which the names of the candidates are printed in alphabetical order, the voter putting an X against the candidate of his choice.

The use of a ballot assists secrecy, and is clear and easy to operate. It is useful for all types of election where the voter has to choose from a number of candidates, or has more than one vote.

The following is an example of the voting procedure to be followed in the election of a candidate to an office:

(1) A check is made of those present at the meeting who are entitled to vote.
(2) A check is made that the candidates' nomination papers are in order.
(3) The chairman introduces the candidates.
(4) A draw is made for the order in which the candidates are to address the meeting.
(5) The candidates withdraw.
(6) The candidates are each then invited to address the meeting, in the order of the draw (the other candidates remaining outside the meeting).
(7) Motion from the chair: "That the meeting proceeds to ballot."
(8) If the motion is defeated, the meeting closes. If it is passed, scrutineers are appointed.

---

[8] *Stratford Borough v. Wilkinson* [1951] 9 N.Z.L.R. 814, C.A.

(9) The ballot proceeds. If the rules provide that the winning candidate must have an overall majority of the votes cast, the candidate with the smallest number of votes will be eliminated and the ballot repeated —and so on until the requisite majority is achieved.

(10) The chairman declares the result of the ballot.

(11) The chairman goes to the waiting room and informs the candidates of the result.

(12) The successful candidate is offered the opportunity to address the meeting.

(3) Division

Another method by which a vote may be taken is that known as the division, *i.e.* **7–19** by the separation of members into separate groups, those in favour of the motion passing into one lobby or room, and those against passing into another lobby or room.

This method of voting is hallowed practice in the Houses of Parliament.

(4) Show of hands

On a show of hands, each member present has one vote without regard to other **7–20** factors, such as the number of shares held by him in the organisation[9] or the fact that he may be attending both in his own right and as a proxy holder.[10] The chairman asks those present to indicate their vote by holding up their hands. The formula is: "All those in favour of the motion please show." The chairman counts these votes. The chairman then says "All those against the motion please show." He counts these votes. He should order a second vote if there is any doubt about the result. He then says: "I declare the motion carried" or "I declare the motion lost." If the chairman's declaration is challenged, this must be done promptly and it usually takes the form of an immediate demand for a poll. In fact, a show of hands had been described as "only a rude and imperfect declaration of the sentiments of the electors."[11] However, a declaration by the chairman that a resolution has, on a show of hands, been carried unanimously or by a particular majority (or lost) in the absence of fraud or obvious mistake, together with an entry in the minute book, is conclusive evidence of the fact. No proof of numbers or of proportion of the votes recorded for and against is required in those circumstances. A show of hands will be sufficient where a poll might have been, but was not, demanded:

> At a meeting of parishioners at which a rate was fixed, objections were made that the rate was invalid because the chairman had declared the resolution carried when, from evidence submitted, a majority was against the resolution. An objection was made to the chairman's declaration at the time, but it was not followed through by a demand for a division or a poll. In the absence of this, the validity of the rate was upheld.[12]

[9] *Re Horbury Bridge Coal, Iron Waggon Co.* (1879) 11 Ch.D. 109.
[10] *Ernest v. Loma Gold Mines Limited* [1897] 1 Ch. 1.
[11] *Anthony v. Seger* (1789) 1 Hagg. Con. 9.
[12] *Cornwall v. Woods* (1846) 4 Not. of Cas. 555.

There is no objection to the chairman ordering a second vote should he be uncertain of the result of voting at the first count:

> Under the articles of a company it was necessary to have 12 voting in favour to 4 against before a resolution could be carried, and 11 voted in favour and 4 against; in this situation the chairman was justified in ordering a recount, and on the recount 14 voted in favour and 4 against. The resolution was held to be valid. If the chairman had said that the motion was carried but was in doubt as to whether he was right or wrong, he was entitled immediately to have the votes counted again.[13]

In a meeting at which a large number of people are present it is sometimes difficult to assess whether a motion has been carried or lost, and even when it may be clear to the chairman and others on the platform it may be doubtful to those on the floor. In such a case, it is wise for the chairman to call in the aid of scrutineers to count the votes. Ideally, scrutineers should be drawn equally from those known to support and those known to oppose the motion; and should work in pairs, checking each other's count. In very contentious situations, the scrutineers should be appointed by the meeting.

(5) Poll

7–21 The original meaning of the word "poll" was "the head". The most familiar derivative uses are those connected with parliamentary or other elections; thus, "to poll" is to secure a number of "heads," and "the poll" is the voting, the number of votes cast, or the time during which voting takes place.

In relation to meetings, the purpose of a poll is to ensure that the votes cast are recorded in writing and counted in an accurate way, for example, by the filling in of voting papers or the recording of the names of those voting on voting lists—or perhaps simply by a roll being called and the vote marked against the member's name by the secretary.

The significance of a poll is:

(a) to correct the imperfections of a vote on a show of hands; or
(b) to extend the poll to a wider franchise (for example, to allow the introduction of proxy votes, or to permit voting by parishioners who had not attended the parish meeting); or
(c) to allow for weighted voting, in relation, for example, to the number of shares held by a member in the body concerned.

The right for any member entitled to vote to demand a poll exists by the common law and electors cannot be deprived of this right unless by express provision[14]:

> At a parish meeting two churchwardens were elected on a vote by show of hands but, on a poll being demanded by a ratepayer, two other churchwardens

---

[13] *Hickman v. Kent and Romney Marsh Sheepbreeders' Association* (1920) 37 T.L.R. 163 C.A.
[14] *R. v. Wimbledon Local Board* (1882) 8 Q.B.D. 459.

were elected in their places. No poll had ever been held in the parish in the past and the question arose as to whether the election was effectual. *Held*, that the right to demand a poll is a necessary incident to the mode of election by show of hands unless it is by special custom excluded; where the body of electors is large in number, recourse to a poll is the only effective method of ascertaining the number of those who vote on each side, and one person may demand a poll.[15]

At a meeting to elect churchwardens a poll was duly demanded after voting by show of hands, and those qualified to vote recorded their votes, but it was contended that several qualified inhabitants who were not present at the meeting had been locked out of the poll. *Held*, that even though such persons were not present at the voting by show of hands, they had a right to be admitted to record their vote. In the words of Denman, C.J., "if a poll be demanded it should be kept open for all qualified persons."[16]

In addition to this common law right, the regulations of the body concerned may enable a given minimum number of members to demand a poll, or accord the same right to the chairman.

Once a demand has been validly made, the result of the voting by show of hands ceases to have any effect:

A candidate was elected on a show of hands. Then a poll was demanded. Next, the candidate withdrew his consent to nomination, so that the poll was not proceeded with. Later, the chairman said that in circumstances the candidate, in spite of his unwillingness, had been elected on the show of hands vote. *Held*, there had been no such appointment in view of the demand for a poll.[17]

It is no objection to the proceedings that the chairman directed a poll without first taking a show of hands, even though a poll was not demanded but was opposed.[18]

As a general principle, the demand for a poll should be made immediately after the declaration by the chairman of the result of a show of hands. If it is not so made, the chairman's declaration will stand:

In the case of elections relating to 11 townships, the elections were made in each case by a show of hands. After all the elections had been made, an elector demanded a poll in relation to the elections for the third and fourth townships. It was held that such demand should have been made immediately after the declaration of the show of hands, and the elections on the show of hands were therefore valid.[19]

It is doubtful if a demand for a poll can be withdrawn (unless the regulations or articles permit it):

[15] *Campbell v. Maund* (1836) 5 A. E. 865.
[16] *R. v. St Mary, Lambeth, Rector of* (1838) 8 A. E. 356.
[17] *R. v. Cooper* (1870) L.R. 5 Q.B. 457.
[18] *R. v. Birmingham, Rector of* (1837) 7 A. E. 254.
[19] *R. v. Vicar of St Asaph* (1883) 52 L.J.Q.B. 671.

At an election a member demanded a poll, and this was seconded by another person. The town clerk said that the demand was sufficient without a seconder, but after a lapse of six days the original proposer withdrew his demand. The question arose as to whether the proposed seconder who wished to be associated with the poll still had a right to demand it. Judgment was given in his favour as there was in substance a demand for a poll within the meaning of the relevant statute.[20]

Arrangements for the poll

7–22   The responsibility for declaring that a poll will take place rests with the chairman of the meeting. It is also his task to determine the arrangements for the poll, acting within the standing orders, and he should announce the details to the meeting.

In the absence of other business, the poll should be taken immediately; if time does not permit that, there should be an adjournment.[21] It is the task of the chairman to give everyone a chance to vote, and the detailed arrangements should be directed to that end.

A simple method is for each voter to record his vote on voting lists. There will be a list for those in favour and a list for those against: the voter will record his name, the number of votes he is casting, and add his signature.

If voting papers are used, there must be a system to ensure that each voter is issued the papers, and only the papers, to which he is entitled. A system which has been used is for voting papers to be prepared for each item on the agenda (preferably each in a different colour), and for these to be issued to members arriving at the meeting upon production of a membership card or other evidence of identity.

An example of a simple voting paper is as follows:

THE WORK-RATE ASSOCIATION
ANNUAL GENERAL MEETING

........[year]
VOTING PAPER for the adoption of the Report and Accounts—Agenda item
no. 3

FOR/AGAINST
Delete which is not preferred

There is no common law requirement that polls should be confidential; those who organise a poll vote are entitled to know how people voted so that the validity of the votes can be scrutinised.[22]

---

[20] *R. v. Mayor of Dover* [1903] 1 K.B. 668.
[21] *R. v. D'Oyly* (1840) 12 A. E. 139.
[22] *Haarhaus Co. v. Law Debenture Trust Corporation* [1988] BCLC 640; but see para. 14–13.

Proxy voting on a poll

The word proxy is used variously to describe: **7–23**

1. writing authorising a person to vote instead of another at a meeting
2. a person appointed to act instead of another.

Accordingly, the term "proxy" refers either to the instrument of appointment or to the person appointed by it. There is no common law right to vote by proxy.[23] Attending and voting have to be in person but it has become normal practice that the duties of attendance and voting at a meeting can be undertaken by an agent or proxy. Such a right is frequently conferred by the regulations of the body concerned; and by section 372 of the Companies Act 1985 any member of a company entitled to attend and vote at a meeting of it is entitled to appoint another person (whether a member or not) as his proxy to attend and vote instead of him on a poll.

A person who has voted by proxy may attend and vote in person, but his proxy vote must then be taken out of the records. Arrangements should also be made to ensure that members present who have been named as proxies on behalf of other voters (the proxy forms having usually been delivered to the office, under the regulations, some days before the meeting) are aware of the fact, so that they may vote on behalf of the absent members: this information should be conveyed to them immediately before the meeting begins.

It is not good practice for the provisional voting figures shown by the proxies lodged at the office to be read out before the vote is taken, still less before the commencement of the debate. This is seen as unfair on those who wish to press a minority point of view.[24]

In relation to organisations with a large number of individual members, some difficulties have been experienced with proxy voting:

(1) Expense. A proxy card has to be printed and sent to each member, regardless of whether or not the resolutions are likely to be contentious and hence result in a demand for a poll. Arrangements have to be made for the cards to be checked, sorted and counted. If professional scrutineers are required, their fees may be substantial.

(2) Cumbersomeness. The usual system of allowing the member to nominate a person of his own choice to act as his proxy can cause severe administrative difficulties if used on a large scale (particularly if the system allows the appointment of alternative proxy-holders in the event of failure of the first proxy-holder to vote). Where a member votes in person, any proxies lodged on his behalf have to be taken out of the calculation. Some disruption to the meeting is inevitable while voting cards are collected and the votes counted.

(3) Unresponsiveness. A proxy-voting system is less able to accommodate amendments to the text of resolutions which are made at the meeting, often with the consent of the proposer, or after a debate when most

[23] *Harben v. Phillips* (1883) 23 Ch.D. 14.
[24] See also para. 19–28.

points of view have been heard and taken into account. On an amendment being passed, the original proxy may become invalid unless the point is dealt with specifically in the proxy (see form in para. 14–20). This difficulty particularly affects the chairman, who in accordance with usual arrangements will be holding proxies on behalf of large numbers of for and against votes. In such cases the proxy-holder should vote in accordance with what he believes to be the wishes of his principal.

Postal voting on a poll

7–24   Some of the disadvantages in voting by proxy can be removed if, instead, a system of postal voting is used, assuming the standing orders allow this method. Here, the general meeting can be allowed to proceed and vote (on a show of hands) after full debate and the airing of divergent views. The resolution can then be the subject of a motion to proceed to postal vote, for which a prescribed majority of those present at the meeting, or a prescribed number of affirmative votes, would be required. The chairman could be given discretion to direct the taking of a postal vote. It may be desirable also to permit a demand for a postal vote to be made after the meeting, provided that this is done within a reasonably brief period (to reduce uncertainty) and that the demand is, again, made by a minimum number of members.

There is some indication that postal voting produces a greater response than proxy voting and may therefore be more democratic. Its disadvantage is that it may favour those whose location makes it easier to attend the meeting in person and thus dominate the discussion of whether or not a postal vote (which might assist the more distant members) should be taken. Alternatively, and perhaps preferably, proxy voting can be retained alongside a procedure which allows a postal vote on the resolutions adopted at the meeting.[25] Scrutineers should be appointed.

3 Voting—Other Procedural Matters

Recount

7–25   It is within the discretion of the chairman to order a recount in any situation (including a vote which has been the subject of a ballot) where he feels an uncertainty as to the true result still persists.

Declaration of result

7–26   After the voting, the result will be declared by the chairman who will invariably give the voting figures. There is nothing to prevent him, if he wishes, giving separate figures for the votes of those physically present at the meeting, as well as total figures including votes cast by way of proxy for absent members.

---

[25] See Law Society, Final Report of the Bye-Laws Revision Committee [1985] L.S. Gaz. 1607; [1988] L.S. Gaz. 2710; [1986] L.S. Gaz. 356; [1986] L.S. Gaz. 826.

Casting vote

A "casting vote" is a second vote exercisable by the chairman of a meeting in **7–27** addition to his own vote as a member. There is no common law right to a casting vote[26]; if it is not granted by the regulations governing the meeting, the chairman can exercise his own vote but not a casting vote. Where a committee is presided over by a chairman who is not a voting member of that committee, he cannot as chairman assume the right to a casting vote in the event of an equality of votes.[27]

Where the chairman, in the event of an equal division of votes, declares that the motion is not carried, that is not, unless he expressly states it to be, an exercise of his casting vote.

If the chairman, in the event of an equality of votes, declines to exercise his casting vote, the motion is "not carried". If he exercises his casting vote against the motion it will be "lost". The distinction may be valid under standing orders in relation to when the motion can again be raised before the body concerned (see para. 7–32). The chairman may give a contingent casting vote:

> In a case under the Municipal Corporations Act 1882, 15 votes were recorded in favour of the election of a person as mayor and 16 for another candidate, but the chairman, thinking that one of the 16 votes might be invalid (as it was later proved to be), gave a casting vote contingent upon the disputed vote being disallowed. It was held that equality of votes meant equality of valid votes; furthermore, there is no objection to the chairman giving a casting vote to take effect if the valid votes are equal.[28]

If the chairman has two votes, one as a member and the other a casting vote, he should not exercise them together: he should use his own vote at the same time as the other members vote and then, only if the voting is level, exercise his casting vote.

There is a tradition that the chairman of a meeting, who has a duty to maintain impartiality, will use his casting vote to preserve the status quo, to keep a proposal alive, and to allow further discussion. (Indeed, it is common for the chairman of a meeting to abstain from using his first vote, *i.e.* his vote as a member of the body concerned, in order to maintain his non-partisan role.) The legal basis of this tradition has been questioned:

> The members of Bradford Metropolitan Council voted 57–57 on a number of contentious issues, the chairman on each occasion voting with the proponents of the resolution. He then exercised his casting vote in favour of the resolution. This procedure was challenged. The court held that, while it was clear that a casting vote should be exercised with great circumspection, its purpose was primarily to prevent deadlock and the chairman was under no legal obligation to use his casting vote to preserve the status quo. The chairman's actions were therefore upheld.[29]

[26] *Nell v. Longbottom* [1894] 1 Q.B. 767.
[27] *Weakley v. Amalgamated Union of Engineering Workers, The Times,* June 12, 1975.
[28] *Bland v. Buchanan* [1901] 2 K.B. 75.
[29] *R. v. Bradford Metropolitan Council, ex p. Wilson* [1989] 3 All E.R. 140.

4 MAJORITY

Definition

7–28   Majority is a term signifying the greater number. In legislative and deliberative assemblies, it is usual to decide questions by a majority of those present and voting. This is sometimes expressed as a "simple" majority, which means that a motion is carried by the mere fact that more votes are cast for than against, as distinct from a "special" majority where the size of the majority is critical.

The principle has long been established that the will of a corporation or body can only be expressed by the whole or a majority of its members, and the act of a majority is regarded as the act of the whole.

> Twelve persons were incorporated to elect a chaplain for a church, and by arrangement three of the 12 were permitted to make the choice subject to the consent of the major part of the inhabitants of the parish. At a meeting, two out of the three, with the assent of the major part of the inhabitants, agreed to a proposal but the third objected. In confirming the appointment, Lord Chancellor Hardwicke said: "It cannot be disputed, that whenever a certain number are incorporated, a major part of them may do any corporate act; so if all are summoned, and part appear, a major part of those that appear may do a corporate act, though nothing be mentioned in the charter of the major part."[30]

The above decision was followed in *Grindley v. Barker*[31] where it was held that if a power of a public nature be committed to several people, who all meet for the purpose of executing it, the act of the majority will bind the minority.

It has been held that the same rule will not apply where no duty of a public nature is involved; thus, where articles of a company provided that "the governing directors" would have power to appoint additional directors, it was held that in the exercise of that power they could not act by majority vote.[32]

Similarly, in the case of other private associations such as clubs, because the rights of the members among themselves rest on an implied contract between all of them, there cannot be a majority vote, for example to change the rules, still less to alter the fundamental nature of the club.[33]

A majority vote binds the minority

7–29   Unless there is some provision to the contrary in the instrument by which a corporation is formed, the resolution of the majority, upon any question, is binding on the minority and the corporation, but the rules must be followed:

---

[30] *Att.-Gen. v. Davy* (1741) 2 Atk. 212.
[31] (1798) 1 Bos. P. 229.
[32] *Perrott and Perrott Limited v. Stephenson* [1934] 1 Ch. 171.
[33] See 62 L.S. Gaz. 91; *Harington v. Sendall* [1903] 1 Ch. 921 (see para. 5–05 n. 12). Section 191 of the Licensing Act 1964 sets out a procedure for amending certain rules of clubs established before August 3, 1961. However, the unanimity principle has been doubted: see *Abbatt v. Treasury Solicitor* [1969] 1 W.S.L.R. 1575 (where club rules were changed by a majority vote to which no objection was made by any member) and *Reel v. Holder* [1979] 3 All E.R. 1041 and [1981] 3 All E.R. 321, C.A.; and [1970] L.Q.R. 18.

The rules of a trade union provided that "regular contributions of employed members shall be as per tables . . . and no alteration to same shall be made until a ballot vote of the members has been taken and two–thirds majority obtained." A delegate meeting of the union, without taking any ballot, passed a resolution increasing the amount of the contributions of employed members. The plaintiffs, two members of the union, obtained against the union a declaration that the alteration adopted at the delegate meeting was invalid.[34]

In forming the majority, the vote of a person who is personally interested in the proposed contract may be counted, provided that he is not acting in a manner which is fraudulent or oppressive to the other members:

A contract for the purchase of a steamship, fair in its terms and within the powers of the company, had been entered into by the directors with one of their number who owned the vessel. It was held that the vendor, who controlled a majority of the shares, which had been acquired in a proper manner, was entitled to exercise his voting power as a shareholder in general meeting to ratify such contract; his doing so could not be deemed oppressive.[35]

Where, however, the majority propose to benefit themselves at the expense of the minority, the court will interfere to protect the minority.[36]

The owner of certain mines worth not more than £4,000 agreed with a partner to promote a company to purchase the mines at £7,000. The company was then formed in pursuance of a fraudulent prospectus. A majority of shareholders refused to take steps to get the contract set aside, but such majority was due to the votes of the owner in respect of shares allotted to him as consideration for the purchase. A decree was made cancelling the agreement, with a declaration that the company ought to be wound up.[37]

The courts will not, however, allow a minority to behave in such a way that the business for which the meeting is convened is impeded:

A chairman had closed a debate on a subject which, in the opinion of the meeting, had been sufficiently discussed. This was held not to be oppressive or an undue interference with the rights of the minority, as in this particular case the minority had had a fair opportunity of placing its case before the shareholders. Were there not some power to bring discussion to an end a minority would be able to hold up the business of the meeting by persisting to agitate indefinitely.[38]

---

[34] *Edwards v. Halliwell* [1950] 2 All E.R. 1064.
[35] *North-West Transportation Co. v. Beatty* (1887) 12 App. Cas. 589.
[36] *Menier v. Hooper's Telegraph Works* (1874) 9 Ch. App. 350.
[37] *Atwool v. Merryweather* (1867) 5 L.R. Eq. 464n.
[38] *Wall v. London and Northern Assets Corporation* [1898] 2 Ch. 469.

It should be noted that in relation to companies the rights of minorities have been clearly defined and protected by statute.[39]

Special majorities

7–30   In cases where special majorities are prescribed, the provisions of the relevant statute or rules must be carefully observed. Thus, where under an old Act a motion was to be "determined by a majority consisting of two-thirds of the votes of the ratepayers present" at a meeting, and 37 were present, the votes of 20 ratepayers in favour of the motion (the remainder abstaining) were deemed to be insufficient to comply with the statute.[40]

> Under the rules of a club, the committee had power to call upon a member to resign, and if he refused to resign the votes of two-thirds of those present at a general meeting were necessary to expel him. A meeting was called at which 117 members were present. (Two-thirds of 117 is 78.) Seventy-seven voted for expulsion and 38 against; the plaintiff and another did not vote. The chairman declared the resolution carried, but the court held that the result was improperly declared as 77 was not the necessary two-thirds majority of those present under the rules. The expulsion was for this and other reasons deemed to be irregular.[41]

> The bye-laws of a society could only be altered by the majority of the fellows entitled to vote in person or by proxy. There were over 7,000 fellows of whom 3,034 were present at a meeting in person or by proxy. The resolution was supported by 1,788 and opposed by 1,227 fellows, with 18 abstentions and one disallowed vote. Did the majority mean the whole "electorate," whether they voted or not? The words were held to mean a majority of those fellows who, not being disqualified from voting, were present or represented at the meeting and were, therefore, entitled to vote on the proposal. The resolution was accordingly valid.[42]

> Under a local Act it was provided that the vestry at their meetings, "or the major part of them as shall be assembled at such meetings," might do what could be done by an ordinary vestry. A vestry consisted of 80 persons and 35 attended a meeting, of whom 16 voted for, and 11 against a motion. It was held that through the motion was carried by a majority of those voting, yet not being carried by a majority of those present and assembled, it was not carried by the requisite majority, as those who were present and declined to vote were not considered in point of law as being absent.[43]

It will be seen from the above that where a special majority is required, those who abstain from voting are not, as they might think, remaining neutral but may be assisting in the defeat of the resolution.

[39] See, for example, Companies Act 1985, s.459.
[40] *Re Eynsham* (1849) 18 L.J.Q.B. 210.
[41] *Labouchere v. Wharncliffe* (1879) 13 Ch.D. 346.
[42] *Knowles v. Zoological Society of London* [1959] 1 W.L.R. 823.
[43] *R. v. Christchurch, Overseers of* (1857) 7 E. B. 409.

An example of where the rules were construed in a less rigid manner is as follows:

> A union's rules provided that they could not be changed to abrogate any of the principal benefits of the union unless 40 per cent of the members affected by the benefit voted in favour of abrogation. The executive council resolved that the rules be amended by deleting the 40 per cent rule and that the provisions relating to unemployment and sickness benefit be replaced by new provisions which abrogated those benefits. The rules revision committee approved the changes and decided that there should be no new entrants to the superannuation fund. *Held,* that the rules of a trade union were not to be construed literally; instead, the court would give the rules a reasonable interpretation which accorded with what the court considered they must have been intended to mean, bearing in mind their authorship, their purpose and those who would have to read and use them. Accordingly, since it was *implicit* in the rules that the requirement of a 40 per cent vote of affected members could not be abolished without such a vote, the abrogation of the unemployment and sickness benefits was void. However, in relation to the decision to restrict entry to the superannuation fund such a policy did not "affect" existing members (except perhaps beneficially) and accordingly did not require a 40 per cent vote of affected members.[44]

For special majorities required under the Companies Act 1985, see Chapter 15.

The "ultra vires" rule

No matter what the size of the majority, a meeting cannot validly transact business which is outside its powers. **7–31**

A directors' meeting or other management committee must also have regard to the rules and constitution of the organisation under whose auspices it exists:

> A resolution by a meeting of a divisional Labour Party purporting to disaffiliate the divisional party from the national Labour Party was invalid because such separation would require an alteration in the rules binding a divisional party to the Labour Party.[45]

5   RESCISSION OF A RESOLUTION

Once a motion has been voted upon and has achieved the requisite majority, it becomes a resolution of the meeting. It can be rescinded only by a subsequent resolution of the same body passed at a later, duly convened meeting. Frequently however the regulations of the body concerned will provide that no motion to rescind any resolution passed within, say, the previous six months, and no motion **7–32**

[44] *Jacques v. Amalgamated Union of Engineering Workers* [1987] 1 All E.R. 621.
[45] *John v. Rees, Martin v. Davies, Rees v. John* [1969] 2 W.L.R. 1294.

or amendment to the same effect as one which has been negatived during the same period, shall be proposed unless a stated minimum number of members shall raise the matter in writing. The same rule would be applied to the motion for rescission itself.

Alternatively, the regulations may provide for a special period of notice to be given in respect of any proposal to alter or rescind a resolution.[46]

[46] See, for example, *Mayer v. Burslem Local Board* (1875) 39 J.P.N. 437.

84

CHAPTER 8

MINUTES

1 INTRODUCTION

Minutes are often seen as mundane, routine and bureaucratic but they should play
a fundamental part in any organisation's system of good governance. The keeping
of minutes reflects and fosters the principle that members of an organisation are
collectively delegated the authority of running that organisation. Minutes should
show a healthy, open debate and airing of all issues, leading to the organisation as
a whole reaching a consensus.

Accurate minutes act as an audit trail of actions taken, particularly important
where criticism is levelled at an organisation or litigation is threatened. Without
minutes, important decisions may be made outside meetings by individual members or small groups of members, taken at an inappropriate level within the
organisation or indeed completely overlooked, which could lead to surprises later
on and a breakdown in the governance policies of the organisation. A failure to
maintain accurate, meaningful minutes may be interpreted as being symptomatic of
more serious underlying problems with the organisation and, at worst, a deliberate
attempt to conceal those problems.

2 DIFFERENCE BETWEEN MINUTES AND REPORTS

A clear distinction should be made between minutes and reports. Minutes con-   **8–01**
stitute the formal record of proceedings at a meeting and can be submitted in court
as evidence. The function of preparing minutes moved one commentator to
describe the situation as follows:

> "And so whilst the Great Ones repair to the dinner, The Secretary sits,
> growing thinner and thinner, Racking his brains to record and report, What
> he thinks that they think that they ought to have thought".[1]

Reports are generally prepared for purposes other than formal record and unless
incorporated or identified in some way in the minutes do not have the same legal
significance. Minutes, as a rule, show only the decisions recorded at a meeting,
preceded possibly by a short narration dealing with the essential points leading up

---

[1] Quoted by J. Martin Richie at the Annual Dinner of the UK Institute of Secretaries at the Guildhall,
London, 9 December 1969; see "The Chartered Secretary", February 1970.

to the decision. If reports are submitted to the meeting (reports of committees, etc.), it is not usual to set out the full report: a reference in the minute by which the report can be identified will usually suffice.

3   OBLIGATION TO KEEP

Companies registered under the Companies Acts are required to keep minutes of members' and directors' meetings[2] but other bodies and organisations may or may not be required to keep minutes of proceedings of their meetings. It is essential to check the constitution of the organisation *e.g.* rules and any relevant legislation applying to the organisation.

4   AN AID TO BUSINESS

Even if not required, minutes serve as a useful record of decision-making and of the historical life of the organisation for reference in the future. They are also very useful in reminding individual members of action which they have agreed to take, *e.g.* implementing a decision following a proposal which has been presented or preparing a paper for the next meeting. Whoever is tasked with taking the minutes, can also play a key role in following up with members between meetings including providing any additional assistance required to ensure the smooth progress of business. When a new member joins the organisation, part of the induction process should be to read the minutes of past meetings as this will provide him/her with useful background information, a feel of how the meetings are conducted, how business is carried out, and provide the historical context. The member will then be able to attend his/her first meeting with a basic level of knowledge which can then be built upon in order to make an effective contribution to the organisation as quickly as possible. The minutes also create a link between meetings, looking towards the future and the next meeting. A review of minutes at any "away days" the organisation may hold when good and bad business decisions might be analysed, can be helpful to reflect on how decisions on particular topics were made over a number of meetings.

5   ESSENTIAL POINTS IN DRAFTING MINUTES

8–02   Minutes should commence with the name of the body concerned and give the type of meeting (*e.g.* executive committee). They should state the date, time and place of the meeting and the time the meeting finished (at the end of the minutes). They should also contain a record of the names of the members present and "in attendance," and whether present for all or part of the meeting or a note of the list,

---

[2] s.382(1) Companies Act 1985.

attendance sheets or other document where their names may be found. They should also record the name of the member taking the chair. Minutes should:

(a) be taken by the person best placed to do so. Independence, discretion and a good understanding of the business of the organisation are key here. It is recommended that a member who is required to make a significant contribution to be meeting does not also take the minutes;

(b) be accurate—if there are any especially complex or technical areas recorded in the minutes, it is good practice to double check these with the relevant member to ensure complete accuracy, whilst preparing the draft minutes. The Chairman of the meeting should be given the opportunity to comment on the first draft before they are circulated to all members;

(c) be clear and unambiguous—minutes must be easily understood; not just by the members but by others who may need to glean a good understanding of the company's business and decision-making eg auditors. Avoid too many acronyms and technical language—refer instead to the papers for the detail if the reader requires this;

(d) be well structured—a good minute taker will be able to omit the recording of discussions which strayed away from the agenda items and were not relevant. He should also re-order the minutes to tie in with the agenda if the meeting was not well chaired and the meeting did not strictly follow the agenda order;

(e) be concise—not too long or too short, dependent of course on the culture and style of the organisation and the personal preferences of the Chairman;

(f) record the essential elements of the discussion on each item, *i.e.* narration which is vital to an understanding of the proceedings. This will encourage members to speak up next time and also helps remind the organisation why they made a particular decision and how they came to it. The full text of all resolutions should be recorded;

(g) avoid comment and expressions of opinion unless an essential part of the decision-making process;

(h) be produced in a timely fashion—minutes should ideally be produced within 48 hours of the meeting to ensure accuracy. The minute taker should agree with the Chairman a sensible time period for distribution of the minutes to members after the meeting, taking into account any annual programme of meetings and the period of time between each. He/she should also agree whether any attendees at the meeting are entitled to receive copies of the minutes.

The past tense should be used to record events at the meeting, *e.g.* "It was reported that," and the past perfect tense for events prior to the meeting, *e.g.* "Mr. X reported that he had completed his survey."

The following are examples of minutes with suggested improvements:

Mr. X reported that we had secured a further contract on satisfactory terms from the Z Co. Ltd.

The use of the word "we" instead of "the company", is a common mistake. In addition, the minute omits important particulars. The following is suggested as a more useful record:

1A Mr. X reported the signature on behalf of the company of a contract dated .... with the Z. Co. Ltd. for the purchase of a further 1,000 tonnes of coal of the same quality as that previously supplied, at £ .... per tonne, to be delivered to the company's Birmingham factory, delivery as required July/December [year]. The previous contract was at £ .... per tonne. The approval of the contract was ratified.

From a directors' meeting:

2 Resolved that transfers of 1,000 Ordinary shares produced be approved and passed.

The minute should read:

2A It was resolved that transfers nos. .... to .... inclusive, produced to the meeting, details of transferor and transferee below, elating to 1,000 ordinary shares in the company, be and they are hereby approved for registration and that the common seal of the company be affixed to certificates nos. .... to .... relating thereto.

From the meeting of a charity:

3 Mr Jones said that before we move on to normal business there is a petition which is being presented by the St. Albans branch for the relief of VAT on charities. There are petition forms here tonight and we hope that if possible you will all sign before you leave.

An improved version:

3A The treasurer drew attention to a petition which was being presented by the St Albans branch for the relief of VAT on charities and invited members to sign it at the conclusion of the meeting.

From the minutes of a management meeting:

4 Radios, cabs, yard and general housekeeping were extremely poor. GENERAL COMMENT: "A DISGRACE"!

This might be better written as:

4A The attendees felt that the standard of housekeeping, particularly in respect of the radios, cabs and yard, was extremely poor and indeed disgraceful—and it was agreed that .... (action to be taken, by whom and in what timescale.)

Within a single paragraph it may not be necessary to introduce every sentence with words which imply reported speech. For example, the minutes of a meeting of the council of an association could (quite correctly) read as follows:

> 5 The chairman expressed disappointment at the figures for 1996. She stressed the need for urgent action, to avoid exhaustion of the reserves. She said that, with additional expenditure on the awards, pressure on resources would be acute. She pointed out that part of the problem resulted from the decision of previous councils not to increase subscription rates.

This could be better reported as follows:

> 5A The chairman expressed disappointment at the figures for 1996. With additional expenditure on the awards, and because previous councils had decided not to increase subscription rates, urgent action was necessary to avoid exhaustion of the reserves.

The names of the proposers and seconders of motions are usually shown, but there is no need to record details of voting. Motions which are not seconded need not be recorded although it can be useful in understanding the collective will of members.

6 CONFIRMATION OF THE MINUTES

Decisions once arrived at do not need confirmation: 8–03

At a vestry meeting it was the usual procedure to read over at the next meeting the resolutions of the preceding one. At the second of two meetings there was considerable diversity of opinion as to the votes admitted at the first meeting, but judgment was to the effect that there was no necessity for the confirmation by the second vestry of what was legally done at the first. If the first was a legal vestry meeting the election thereat was legal.[3]

However, confirmation of the minutes as an accurate *record* of the decisions made at the previous meeting is usually obtained by submitting them to the chairman of the next meeting for signature. If they have not been previously circulated he will ask the secretary to read them, and, if the meeting confirms (usually on a show of hands) that they are a correct record, he will sign them. If they have previously been circulated, he will sign them without their being read out if the meeting so agrees.

The chairman who signs the minutes at the next meeting need not necessarily have been the chairman of the previous meeting or indeed even present at the meeting of which the minutes are a record. His action in signing them is merely to record that they are a correct record of the business transacted.

There may however be occasions where the chairman, although having no reason to question the accuracy of the record, refuses to sign the minutes. In such

---

[3] *Mawley v. Barbet* (1803) 2 Esp. 687.

89

cases a record should be made in the minutes to the effect that the minutes of the previous meeting were correct.

If there is a considerable interval between meetings, the chairman can sign the minutes as soon as they have been prepared: this power is useful too when the minutes are needed to confirm to third parties that a particular decision has been made.

7   AMENDMENT TO MINUTES

8–04   If, when the minutes are before the meeting for signature by the chairman, it is noted that they are an inaccurate record of the previous meeting, they should be rectified at the time and the alteration initialled if the amendments are minor. Clerical errors, too, can be put right in this way. If the errors are more substantial, the company secretary should make the required amendments and send the corrected version to the chairman for signature after the meeting. Should there be something recorded in relation to an earlier meeting the substance (as opposed to the form) of which is not acceptable to a later meeting, the correct procedure is to pass a resolution rescinding or amending the previous decision. The former minute should not, in these circumstances, be deleted or amended at the later meeting as all that that meeting is being asked to do is to certify the correctness of the record of the proceedings at the previous meeting.

A discovery, after minutes have been signed, that they are inaccurate should, again, be the subject of a separate, later resolution: signed minutes should never be amended. The same prohibition would apply to the addition of vital details which had not been before the meeting:

> A meeting was held at which a call on shares was made, but no dates were fixed for the calls. After the minutes were signed the secretary on his own account filled in dates of calls, with the result that the minute had the appearance of forming part of the original record. Commenting on the effect of this alteration, Esher M.R. said: "I trust I shall never again see or hear of the secretary of a company altering minutes of meetings, either by striking out anything or adding anything."[4]

The position would be different if a meeting decided to leave to the secretary the duty of completing certain formal details, but even then it is best that the delegation be referred to specifically in the minutes. The details of the subsequent action taken by the secretary can be referred to in a note at the foot of the minutes or in a paper which itself can be approved at the next meeting, preferably as a separate item on the agenda.

8   MINUTES AS EVIDENCE

8–05   In general, minutes form evidence of the matters to which they refer, which can be relied on in civil proceedings:

[4] *Re Cawley Co.* (1889) 42 Ch.D. 209, 226.

In an action against one of several members of the Gosport and Forton Water Works Company for the value of lead pipes supplied by the plaintiffs to the company, after the defendant had been proved to be a partner in the company, the entries in a book containing a record of the proceedings of the society produced at its meetings, and open to the inspection of all members, were admissible in evidence against the defendant; the minutes showed that the order had been authorised by the society.[5]

When minutes are signed by the chairman of the meeting, or the next succeeding meeting, they are prima facie evidence of the proceedings, and decisions recorded therein are deemed to be valid until the contrary is proved. In practice, certified copies of minutes are frequently provided to third parties as evidence of the matters decided upon at the meeting.

The chairman of a meeting has authority to determine all incidental questions which arise at the meeting, and an entry by him in the minute book of the result of a poll, or of his decision on such questions, is prima facie evidence of that result, and the onus of displacing that evidence is thrown on those who impeach the entry:

Where the chairman made an entry in the minute book that a resolution had been confirmed, the court, in the absence of evidence that votes were improperly disallowed, declined to question the decision of the chairman.[6]

Articles of companies and other bodies sometimes provide that minutes shall be conclusive evidence of the proceedings. By "conclusive" is meant conclusive in the absence of evidence of fraud or serious bad faith.[7]

The existence of a formal record, or minutes, of a meeting may be some evidence that the parties intended to be legally bound by what was decided at the meeting, but this is capable of being negated.[8]

The failure to record opposition to a resolution does not invalidate the minutes of a meeting.[9]

9   RIGHT OF INSPECTION OF MINUTES

Minutes are usually open to the inspection of any member on request. It has been held however that beneficiaries under a trust settlement are not entitled to inspect minutes of meetings of trustees nor the agenda prepared for such meetings.[10]

A search on the internet under "minutes" brings up thousands of organisations which make their minutes available for public viewing, either because this is a

---

[5] *Alderson v. Clay* (1816) 1 Stark. 405. It is usually necessary to show that the person against whom the minutes are adduced has had an opportunity of testing or challenging their accuracy (see *Phipson on Evidence* (14th ed.) para. 26–12).
[6] *Re Indian Zoedone Co.* (1884) 26 Ch.D. 70.
[7] See para. 16–02.
[8] *Orion Insurance Co. plc v. Sphere Drake Insurance plc* [1992] 1 Lloyd's Rep. 239 C.A.
[9] *Re Hockerill Athletic Club* [1990] BCLC 921.
[10] *Re Londonderry's Settlement, Peat v. Welsh* [1965] Ch. 918.

legislative requirement in their area of business, or because this forms a key part of the organisation's culture and governance policies. Making minutes of meetings publicly available allows interested parties to gain an insight into how the organisation is directed and strategy implemented. However, careful thought should be given before adopting this practice, as there is often confidential information contained in minutes.

10 MINUTES: FORM AND SAFEKEEPING

8–06 At one time it was customary for minutes to be written by hand in the minute book but this practice is now rare. Usually, minutes are typed and the record signed copy is placed in a loose-leaf book or, where an old book is in use, pasted in. Before this is done, limited copies can be taken for additional needs. If the person who signs the minutes also initials each page, there is usually no objection to the loose-leaf system. Minutes should be kept in chronological order. It is good practice to number each item in the minutes; this aids cross-referencing and the preparation of an index, and assists security.

Minutes and supporting documents to which they refer should be kept in safe custody, ideally in a fireproof safe, by a responsible person and access for inspection only on site should be limited to agreed persons *e.g.* auditors. Any copying of minutes should be kept to a minimum as this may affect the ability to keep minutes confidential. A policy should be agreed on when old minutes are archived and where they should be kept, bearing in mind any document retention policy which applies under relevant legislation.

11 MINUTES OF COMPANIES

8–07 For regulations as to minutes of companies registered under the Companies Acts, see Chapters 16 (members' meetings), 22 and 23 (directors' meetings).

CHAPTER 9

THE COMMITTEE SYSTEM

1 GENERAL PRINCIPLES

A "committee" is a body of persons to whom something is "committed" or **9–01** entrusted. Although a committee can consist of one person, this is unusual, and is not found in local authority practice.[1] The more common meaning of the term is a plurality of persons elected or appointed to consider and deal with certain matters of business specially or generally referred to it.

In the absence of express statutory or other conferred authority, a committee, being a body endowed merely with delegated powers, is bound by the maxim "delegatus non potest delegare" and therefore cannot exceed the powers and duties entrusted to it, or delegate its duties to others even among members of the committee:

> The Deeping Fen Drainage Board appointed a committee of three to act in case of emergency. The three members of the committee agreed among themselves a portion of the Soak Dyke over which each should keep watch. One of the committee acted on his own initiative to ensure the carrying off of flood water, causing the plaintiff to allege he had suffered damage. It was held that the powers conferred on the committee must be exercised by them acting in concert and it was not competent to the committee to apportion among themselves the duties so delegated to them. Judgment was given for the plaintiff.[2]

> The education committee of Liverpool City Council authorised its chairman to make a recommendation on its behalf. It was held that the committee had no power to give such authority.[3]

The scope and terms of a committee are usually contained in the resolution **9–02** appointing it, and care must therefore be taken that the terms of such reference are clear so that the committee may know the limits of its duties and powers. In practice, however, this state of affairs is not always achieved, and there have been court decisions which may assist in clarification:

> (i) A committee can be given the power to decide on matters of fact (an example might be, whether or not a proposed member of a tenants'

---

[1] See para. 28–03.
[2] *Cook v. Ward* (1877) 2 C.P.D. 255.
[3] *R. v. Liverpool City Council, ex p. Professional Association of Teachers, The Times,* March 22, 1984. See also *R. v. Secretary of State for the Environment ex p. Hillingdon LBC* [1986] 1 W.L.R. 192 and 807 (para. 28–05, below).

association has attained a sufficient residence qualification). In matters of law, although the committee may deal with matters before it, the jurisdiction of the courts cannot be ousted (for example, by a rule which says that the committee has the sole right to interpret the rules). In considering whether a committee is acting within its powers, regard must be paid to the purposes of the body concerned.[4]

    (ii) A committee does not usually have the power to act outside those areas which have customarily fallen within its business remit: for example, a cornporters' committee had no power to remove a member from the register of overside cornporters because of an assault which had taken place on a committee member following the termination of a previous meeting.[5]

    (iii) Where a committee has power to do a certain act, it will normally be entitled to carry out matters reasonably incidental thereto. For example, a club rule provided that its arrangements for management should be conducted by a committee who should have all needful powers for its government and the election of new members and additional committee members, and should be empowered to publish bye-laws; it was held that the passing of a bye-law that retired members might be re-admitted on payment of back subscriptions and the subsequent readmission of retired members not only without the usual entrance fee but without the other formalities prescribed by the rules, were valid actions by the committee.[6]

    (iv) A committee cannot extend its jurisdiction by giving a wrong interpretation to the rules, however honest may be the actions of the committee.[7]

9–03   The relationship between delegating authority and committee is basically one of principal and agent. A principal is entitled to revoke the authority of his agent, and therefore the authority conferred on a committee can be revoked. This can extend to revoking the authority of individual members of that committee:

> A standing order of Brighton Corporation provided that standing committees were to be appointed annually in May "for the ensuing year to perform such duties as shall then be delegated to them by council." The plaintiff was, in May 1950, appointed to serve on three standing committees, but in March 1951 the full council acted to remove him from them. He sought an injunction restraining the council. *Held*, (1) that the words "shall be appointed for the ensuing year" provided a limit to the holding of the appointment: they did not mean that in all circumstances the plaintiff should continue in office for the full year, only that in normal circumstances he would do so; and (2) that the corporation, as a delegating authority, could at any time resume its own authority, with which it had never parted; that there was power to revoke the

---

[4] *Baker v. Jones* [1954] 1 W.L.R. 1005.
[5] *Abbott v. Sullivan* [1952] 1 K.B. 189.
[6] *Lambert v. Addison* (1882) 46 L.T. 20.
[7] *Lee v. Showmen's Guild of Great Britain* [1952] 2 Q.B. 329, C.A.

authority of a committee as a whole and to revoke that of a a single member of it. Injunction refused.[8]

A member of Newham London Borough Council declined to provide personal details in a declaration, as required by standing orders. *Held*, the authority had the right to establish its own criteria for appointing members to its committees, and by parity of reasoning had the power to remove those persons failing to satisfy the criteria.[9]

2   KINDS OF COMMITTEES

The following are the main types of committee: 9–04

   (a) A general or executive committee.
   (b) A standing committee.
   (c) A special committee, or working party.
   (d) A sub-committee.
   (e) A joint committee.

  (**a**) General or executive committees are those appointed by bodies such as clubs and associations to manage their affairs and to deal with all matters which it would not be appropriate to deal with in general meeting, and are similar to boards of directors of companies. Executive committees of companies tend to deal with the day-to-day running of the business, department heads often being members of such committees, with the board of the company dealing with more strategic matters. Having been appointed as a governing body and generally given full powers to deal with all matters delegated to them, their decisions cannot, in the absence of special provision in the constitution, be varied or set aside by a general meeting of the parent body.[10]

  (**b**) Standing committees are those appointed on a permanent basis to handle one or more aspects of the parent body's business. The social services committee of a local authority or the audit committee of the board of a company are examples of such committees.

  (**c**) Special committees, as their name implies, are appointed for special purposes, and usually dissolve automatically when their purpose has been accomplished. An example might be a committee set up to examine whether the rules of an organisation should be amended, and to report to the general meeting. If appointed to deal with a particular task of this kind, such a committee is sometimes known as an ad hoc committee, or, in plainer language, a "working party." A special committee is seldom given executive powers and, if it is, those powers are limited.

---

[8] *Manton v. Brighton Corporation* [1951] 2 K.B. 393; *R. v. Greenwich London Borough Council ex p. Lovelace* [1991] 1 W.L.R. 506, C.A. (see para. 28–05, below).
[9] *R. v. Newham London Borough Council, ex p. Haggerty* (1987) 85 L.G.R. 48.
[10] *Battelley v. Finsbury Borough Council* (1958) 56 L.G.R. 165; and see *Goddard v. Minister of Housing and Local Government* [1958] 3 All E.R. 482. But the parent body can take back its powers; see *Huth v. Clarke*, below, and *Manton v. Brighton Corporation*, above.

(d) Sub-committees may be either standing or special. They are appointed by a full committee to deal with matters which may be more conveniently handled by a few persons, such as drawing up a report or interviewing a person, and must report back to the full committee. In practice, a sub-committee often undertakes a great deal of research and detailed work on behalf of its main committee. The system is widely used in local government practice.[11]

A sub-committee derives its origin from the main committee and can only act within the powers conferred by that body. By such delegation the appointing committee does not divest itself of its powers but merely confers on the smaller body duties that it would otherwise perform itself, and these powers can be resumed:

> Under the Contagious Diseases (Animals) Act 1878 the executive committee of a county council delegated to local sub-committees its powers under the Rabies Order 1887. Subsequently, without expressly revoking the delegation, the executive committee issued certain regulations under the Rabies Order as to the muzzling of dogs and keeping them under control; no such regulations had been issued by the local sub-committee. *Held*, that the delegation was not equivalent to a resignation by the executive committee of its own powers, that the delegated authority was subject to resumption at any time, and that the regulations were therefore valid.[12]

It is expressly provided by section 101(4) of the Local Government Act 1972 that any arrangement made by a local authority for the discharge of any functions by a committee or sub-committee shall not prevent the authority or committee by whom the arrangements are made from exercising those functions.

The relationship of the sub-committee to the committee is the same as that of the committee to the general meeting, and the sub-committee will have to present reports to the committee in the same manner as the committee does to its authoritative meeting.

(e) Joint committees are those constituted by and between two or more bodies. For example, section 102 of the Local Government Act 1972 authorises the appointment of joint committees to deal with functions shared between two or more authorities. There will often be arrangements for each sponsoring body to have equal representation on the joint committee and for a rotating chairmanship.

3 PROCEDURE

9–05 Committee meetings are convened by notice and are controlled by their agenda in the ordinary way, although in practice the proceedings of committees, and particularly sub-committees, tend to be less formal.

---

[11] See para. 28–05.
[12] *Huth v. Clarke* (1890) 25 Q.B.D. 391.

Should no quorum be fixed by the parent body or under byelaws or standing orders, all acts of a committee must be done in the presence of all the members of the committee, though they do not have to act with unanimity.[13]

In the absence of any stipulation to the contrary in its constitution, a committee should follow the practice of its main body in relation to voting, including the chairman's casting vote, and should act by majority.[14]

Sometimes a committee is given powers to co-opt additional people, who may or may not be members of the main organisation. Co-opted members are not normally given the right to vote, unless the committee or sub-committee is a purely advisory one, without executive powers.

A committee may not shelve the business delegated to it by carrying a resolution to suspend proceedings or to dissolve itself. Its duty to the main body must be performed.

The result of the committee's deliberations should be placed before the body appointing it. This can be done by the circulation of minutes of the committee's meetings, or by the presentation of a report to the main body. Unless the committee has executive powers on the matter or matters delegated to it, such report or minutes are inoperative until adopted by the main body, which may amend or refer back the report or minutes for further consideration.

If there is any marked difference of opinion when it comes to the preparation of a report, the names of those respectively supporting or opposing the conclusions of the report may be appended, but a minority report may not be presented unless specifically authorised.

Important or doubtful points of order on which a decision might clash with a ruling by the chairman of the main body should, if possible, first be submitted to him for guidance, to avoid creating an embarrassing precedent.

4   COMMITTEES IN COMPANY MATTERS

9–06 Committees of directors play an important role in the work of boards of companies and directors' ability to delegate their authority is discussed in para. 20–04.

For committees in winding-up proceedings, such as liquidation committees, reference is made to paras. 25–05 and 25–16.

---

[13] *Re The Liverpool Household Stores Association Limited* (1890) 59 L.J. Ch. 616.
[14] *Picea Holdings v. London Rent Assessment Board* [1971] 2 Q.B. 216.

CHAPTER 10

THE PRINCIPLES OF NATURAL JUSTICE

10–01 We conclude Part II with a brief look at one particular branch of administrative law; natural justice, or what might, in the United States, be termed due process. The concept is considered because of its practical importance to the mechanics of many meetings. It is aimed at ensuring basic procedural fairness, as opposed to guarding against more esoteric dangers such as the fettering of discretion, and so should form the framework around which the meeting process is shaped. It will be seen that whilst "natural justice" is a convenient peg upon which to hang this Chapter "procedural fairness" would do equally as well; for both embrace the same set of principles.

As these are of such general application, and the circumstances in which they impact upon the law of meetings so many and varied, only a brief summary is attempted.[1] It is important to bear in mind that this is an area that has been significantly affected by the coming into force of the Human Rights Act 1998 ("HRA").[2] This is especially so in relation to the meetings of public authorities. Such authorities, and the definition is a broad one, must now act so as to comply with the European Convention on Human Rights ("ECHR").[3] The fair trial rights set out by Article 6 ECHR, for instance, provide safeguards that bolster those previously offered by the common law and have, in some respects, prompted change.

The first task, then, is to identify the principles of natural justice. As to which it is clear that the courts themselves have seen fit both to recognise and to enforce two key pillars:

(1) A person has a dual right to sufficient notice of a meeting that affects his interests and also to an opportunity to make representations; and
(2) The affected person has a right to an unbiased tribunal.

Until recently both these principles, sometimes referred to as the "rules" of natural justice, were clothed in legal Latin. The first by the phrase *audi alteram partem* (hear both sides), the second by *nemo judex in causa sua* (no man shall be judge in his own cause). To the two pillars can be added a third, complementary, strut—the requirement that the proper procedural requirements must be followed. This is necessary because it will sometimes be the case that the procedural framework governing a meeting in fact goes further than the two core pillars might alone strictly require. Yet a person affected still has the right to expect that the acknowledged framework will be followed.

---

[1] For a comprehensive work on the subject the reader is referred to *Craig's Administrative Law* (5th ed. 2003) or *English Publish Law* (1st ed., Feldman, 2004).
[2] Since October 2, 2000
[3] Section 6, HRA

As far as the concept's history is concerned its principles were, unsurprisingly, **10–02** first applied to the ordinary civil and criminal courts; and so to functions that were classically judicial in nature. Inevitably, protection of those whose rights and interests are threatened either by private suit or public prosecution, the latter in particular, remains the key objective to this day; one need only consider the wording of ECHR Article 6. However such hearings are now so fiercely regulated with a view to ensuring natural justice is achieved that the risk of a breach is mercifully low.

What is important is that over the centuries the concept spread its wings to embrace other quasi-judicial decision-makers and, eventually, meetings. That expansion was prompted in large part by, and paralleled, the inexorable growth of the state as, from the eighteenth century onwards, the administration came to play an ever increasing role in the lives of the population, not only through the conference of benefit but also by regulation of existing interests. As a result the courts were forced to decide whether that safeguard of natural justice which they set around their own activity should be widened to embrace other, administrative yet quasi-judicial, decision-makers. Gradually, they came to the view that it should.

For example:

> A building was erected in contravention of the byelaws of a local board of health. It was held that the board did not have the power under section 158 of the Public Health Act 1875 to pull down the building without giving the owner an opportunity of showing cause why it should not be pulled down.[4]

Having thus settled upon the notion of a "judicial" element to the decision-maker the debate for many years turned upon whether that word was to be given a narrow meaning, generally excluding it from the workings of the administration, or a more flexible, inclusive, one. That debate, though, is now long cold. Since the early 1960s it has been clear that a yet more flexible approach is to be followed.[5] The result, in fact, is that there is now no true requirement that the decision-making person or body be even quasi-judicial in order for the principles of natural justice to apply. Rather, whenever a body has statutory authority to make a decision affecting a person's rights or obligations that body is amenable to review by the courts and, potentially, an order quashing its decision. One of the grounds for which can be that it has disregarded one or other of the fundamental rights protected by the principles of natural justice.[6]

So framed, the concept can be seen to align with the ancient power to correct an action of a corporation not supported by charter or prescription:

> In 1615, James Bagg, a burgess of Plymouth, was removed from his office by the mayor and corporation because he called the mayor a "cozening knave"

---

[4] *Hopkins v. Smethwick Local Board of Health* (1890) 24 Q.B.D. 712, C.A.
[5] *Ridge v. Baldwin* [1964] A.C. 40.
[6] *O'Reilly v. Mackman* [1983] 2 A.C. 237; and see Halsbury's *Laws of England* (4th ed.), vol. 1, para. 64, and Cumulative Supplement.

and threatened to crack his neck. The Court of King's Bench, presided over by Lord Coke, held that the removal was invalid.[7]

The only qualification that should be made is that whilst it is well-established that the "hear both sides" pillar applies to administrative as well as judicial and quasi-judicial decisions the position as regards the rule against bias is less clear. Put simply it has only recently been held that this second pillar extends as far as the first.

10–03   The upshot of this broadening of the application of the principles of natural justice is that there have been many occasions during recent years where decisions taken by meetings of committees, tribunals, and the like have been successfully challenged on the basis that natural justice has not been followed. Such meetings may have been properly constituted and carried through, in the sense that due notice had been given, a quorum achieved, votes cast and decisions reached. Yet someone felt that justice had not been done, that there had been a lack of "common fairness"[8] and, unable to shake that nagging sense of grievance, went to law for redress. Predictably this happened, for the most part, when some tangible legal right was affected. In particular when, as a result of a meeting's decision, an aggrieved party found himself expelled from such as a professional association or a trade union[9] or where a conflict between interests was determined at such as a planning meeting.[10] To put the matter the other way around it is when a person's livelihood or legal status is in question that the need to act in accordance with the principles of natural justice is felt most acutely and becomes most pressing.

The categories of tangible interests, if at stake, that may excite the courts' interest are neither closed nor narrowly defined. So concepts such as "livelihood" will not be construed so as to encompass only earnings in the present day. For instance, a tribunal deciding whether or not to expel a pupil from a school, where such expulsion would be at least as much of a blot on his record as being sent down from university, is required to observe the rules of natural justice.[11] As is a meeting the outcome of which will affect a person's reputation.[12] For these reasons although much of the case law inevitably concerns decisions taken by the organs of local government or similar authorities, its application goes far beyond such creatures of statute.

Thus, whilst the activities of bodies deriving jurisdiction from contract are not amendable to judicial review[13] it is still quite possible that they might be required to observe a substantive principle of public law such as natural justice. This applies

---

[7] *Bagg's* case (1615) 11 Co. Rep. 936.

[8] See *R. v. Aston University Senate, ex p. Roffey* [1969] 2 Q.B. 538, 554.

[9] See *Edwards v. Society of Graphical and Allied Trades* [1971] Ch. 354; trade union could not expel member without a hearing.

[10] See *e.g. R. (Tromans) v. Cannock Chase DC* [2004] EWCA Civ 1036 where the issue concerned a dispute over the number of votes counted at a planning committee meeting.

[11] *R. v. Board of Governors of London Oratory School* (*The Times*, 17/02/1988) *per* McCullough J.

[12] *R. (P) v. Wandsworth LBC* (1988) 87 L.G.R. 370; *R. (M) v. Norfolk CC Social Services Department* [1989] Q.B. 619.

[13] See *Law v. National Greyhound Racing Club* [1983] 1 W.L.R. 1302, where the Court of Appeal held that a challenge to a decision of the club, a company limited by guarantee whose sole jurisdiction over individuals derived from their agreement to be bound by the club's rules, was a matter of private law and not suitable for judicial review, and also *R. (Aga Khan) v. Disciplinary Committee of the Jockey Club* [1993] 1 W.L.R. 909, confirming that bodies who acquire jurisdiction over individuals by contract are excluded from the ambit of judicial review.

not only to the traditional trade union/professional-type bodies mentioned above but also in the sporting field.[14] Take, for instance, a recent example involving the athlete Diane Modahl and her case against the British Athletic Federation arising out of suspected "doping".[15] There, it was held that an individual subject to the Federation's disciplinary procedures was entitled to a fair hearing, including an unbiased tribunal, but that on the facts the Federation's procedures, importantly including its appeal procedures, ensured a fair hearing overall. As in the *Modahl* case the need to observe the principles of natural justice will often be found to arise via an implied term in a contract between the parties.[16]

The individual elements of the concept and the core principles that comprise it, as identified above, are considered below.

(a) Hear both sides/No person shall be condemned unheard

As noted this principle applies where a body acts in the discharge of a duty that   **10–04** involves such as a matter of discipline, livelihood, legal status, competing interests or some other substantial matter. In which event the body is obliged to act fairly. In the words of Lord Denning M.R. if a man:

> "has some right or interest, or some legitimate expectation of which it would not be fair to deprive him without a hearing or reasons given, then these should be afforded him, according as the case may demand"[17]

Thus, the person who will be affected by the decision must be given adequate and proper notice of the case that he has to meet and be allowed an opportunity to make representations in response. The following are illustrations:

> Famously a Watch Committee was required to give to a chief constable notice of charges and an opportunity to be heard before dismissing him from office under the provisions of s.191(4) of the Municipal Corporations Act 1882. The charges related to negligence in the discharge of duty, so a serious matter, but the Watch Committee was not entitled to act forthwith on criticisms of the chief constable expressed in the course of a criminal trial.[18]

> A member of a trade union was told by his branch committee that it intended to recommend his expulsion. The rules, however, provided that in such a case; the charge should be formulated, preferably in writing; the investigation should take place in the presence of the member once he had been granted an opportunity to consider and prepare an answer to the charge; and that, if the charge was found proven, the member should be told of his right of appeal to the executive council. This procedure had not been followed yet the

---

[14] See *Wright v. Jockey Club* (*The Times* 16/06/1995) and also *Jones v. Welsh Rugby Football Union* (*The Times* 06/03/1997); interlocutory injunction to restrain suspension from rugby football where suspected breach of natural justice.

[15] *Modahl v. British Athletic Federation Ltd* [2002] 1 W.L.R. 1192

[16] See also *R. (Lavelle) v. British Broadcasting Corporation* [1983] 1 W.L.R. 23 and *Mclaren v. Home Office* [1990] I.C.R. 824

[17] *Breen v. Amalgamated Engineering Union* [1971] 2 Q.B. 175 at 191.

[18] *Ridge v. Baldwin* (supra).

executive council nevertheless accepted the committee's recommendation. It was held that the expulsion was a nullity.[19]

A member of a trade union was summoned before a management committee to answer a charge of having acted in a manner contrary to the decisions of the union's governing bodies. He defended himself and, by a majority, the committee found the charge not proven. One member of the committee disagreed with the majority. Purporting to act under a rule which gave a member aggrieved with the decision of the management committee the right to appeal to the executive council, the aggrieved committee member made such an appeal. On appeal the executive council reversed the decision of the management committee and expelled the exonerated member without giving him notice or an opportunity to be heard. It was held that the right of appeal could be exercised only by the person accused. Given the committee's decision such a right had never arisen and the so-called appeal was a nullity. Further, and more pertinently, it was contrary to natural justice to hear the appeal without allowing the accused an opportunity to be heard. It was also noted that where natural justice is involved the court will interfere with the decision of a domestic tribunal even where its rules have been complied with.[20]

Bodies may also wish to consider that a failure to observe natural justice may amount to "unfairness" for the purposes of the well known test for unfair dismissal, and hence the right to claim statutory compensation laid down by the Employment Rights Act 1996.[21]

10–05   By way of contrast to the examples given above it should be noted that the public interest and a clear statutory framework can, and often do, override the right to make representations. An example increasingly encountered is that a person has no right to comment on allegations made in an Enhanced Criminal Record Certificate under s.115 of the Police Act 1997 prior to its disclosure by a chief constable. Here, the chief constable is under a duty to disclose this if the information might be relevant unless there is a good reason for not doing so. This is in accordance with the policy of legislation aimed at protecting children and vulnerable adults.[22] Nor, equally, will the courts be quick to find a legitimate expectation that a hearing will be afforded where the activity concerned is itself unlawful. For all that there may be a practice of non-enforcement and the effect on livelihood will be severe.[23]

It is also clear that the principle that a decision-maker must "hear both sides" does not mean a person is necessarily entitled to present his case orally, provided it

---

[19] *Santer v. National Graphical Association* [1973] I.C.R. 60.

[20] *Miles v. Amalgamated Society of Woodworkers* [1968] Ch. 440.

[21] *Earl v. Slater & Wheeler (Airlyne) Ltd* [1973] 1 W.L.R. 51, a point driven home by the financial penalty provisions for failure to follow procedure now imposed by the Employment Act 2002.

[22] *R. (X) v. Chief Constable West Midlands Police* [2005] 1 W.L.R. 65, C.A., overturning the judge at first instance; [2004] 1 W.L.R. 1518. The Court of Appeal noted that the affected person has an opportunity to correct the certificate under s.117 of the Act and/or to explain the position to his prospective employer; no doubt cold comfort for some.

[23] *R (Dinev and others) v. Westminster Council* (unreported, 24/10/2000); street traders (portrait artists) had no legitimate expectation to be consulted about the introduction of a temporary licensing scheme notwithstanding the effect on their livelihoods.

is put fairly by other means,[24] still less cross-examine witnesses.[25] Nor does it mean that he can insist upon being legally represented unless the circumstances are exceptional and justice so requires.[26] During the course of the meeting a person affected by the decision of the tribunal or other body should be told the main points of the case against him and given a sense for the "impression" the tribunal has formed. However, he need not be informed of the source of the evidence.[27]

So far as the reasons for a decision are concerned in principle natural justice does not require that these should be given.[28] However, the courts have shown an increasing willingness to hold that, where an important interest is at stake, fairness demands that they should.[29] For instance, where an applicant had been found unfairly dismissed he was entitled to know the reasons for the tribunal's decision as to the particular sum it decided to award as compensation.[30] The test, then, is one that calls for consideration of the particular circumstances; where they are "appropriate" fairness may require reasons to be given.[31]

In *McInnes v. Onslow-Fane*[32]—a useful case involving a refusal to grant a boxing manager's licence that includes a review of the law relating to the right to a hearing—Megarry V.C. suggested a three-tier categorisation of cases in which the court might consider intervention. In descending order of gravity:

(a) *"Forfeiture"* : Cases where there is a decision which takes away some right or position. As where a member of an organisation is expelled or a licence is revoked;

(b) *"Expectation"*: Cases where the applicant has a legitimate expectation that his application will be granted. For example where an existing licence-holder applies for renewal of his licence; and

(c) *"Application"*: Cases where the decision merely refuses to grant the applicant the right or position that he seeks, *e.g.* membership of an organisation.[33]

In respect of the third the Vice-Chancellor was clear that there could be no question of a requirement that a person be granted an opportunity to be heard. However even in application cases the decision-making body concerned is at least under a duty to reach an honest conclusion, without bias, and not in pursuance of

---

[24] *Local Government Board v. Arlidge* [1915] A.C. 120; *Lloyd v. McMahon* [1987] A.C. 625

[25] *R. (Cottrell & Rothon) v. Commission for Racial Equality* [1981] A.C. 75.

[26] *Pett v. Greyhound Racing Association (No. 2)* [1970] 1 Q.B. 45; *Enderby Town Football Club v. Football Association* [1971] Ch. 591.

[27] *R. v. Gaming Board, ex p. Benaim and Khaida* [1970] 2 Q.B. 417.

[28] *ibid. Payne v. Lord Harris of Greenwich* [1981] 1 W.L.R. 754; *R (Connolly) v. Secretary of State for Social Services* [1986] 1 W.L.R. 421; no basic requirement of natural justice that a Social Security Commissioner give reasons for requiring leave to appeal from a determination of an attendance allowance board.

[29] See, for example, *R. v. London Borough of Lambeth, ex p. Walters, The Times,* October 6, 1993.

[30] *R. (Cunningham) v. Civil Service Appeal Board* [1991] 4 All E.R. 310, C.A.

[31] *R. (Doody) v. Secretary of State for the Home Department* [1994] A.C. 531; where the House of Lords confirmed that it was unfair for a mandatory life sentence prisoner not to be given reasons for any departure by the Secretary of State from the judge's recommendations regarding the penal element of his sentence.

[32] [1978] 1 W.L.R. 1520.

[33] *ibid.* at 1528.

any capricious policy. It is fair to note that the three-tier *Onslow-Fane* categorisation has had its critics,[34] and particularly so as regards its effect on application cases. It does, though, remain a useful rule of thumb and, in any event, was never intended to be exhaustive. The reality is that the content of the "hear both sides" principle has long been held to vary according to the context.[35] Thus the courts will not be too tightly regulated by precedent, or rather too slow to distinguish previous authorities, but will look carefully to the facts of each individual case.[36]

(b) No person shall be judge in his own cause

10–05a   Within this principle there are two distinct elements. The first is that no member of the tribunal or other body concerned with the matter should have a pecuniary or other interest in the result. The second is that there should be an absence of bias. As noted there remains a live issue as to whether or not this part of the principle applies to administrative as well as judicial and quasi-judicial decisions. At High Court level it has been held that it does[37] and that, for now, is where the matter stands.

The first element, that no man should decide a matter affecting the interests of another where he himself has a direct stake in the result, is obvious and requires little explanation. For example:

> Application was made to Hendon Rural District Council for permission to develop The Old Brewery Stables, Great Stanmore. Local residents objected. Councillor Cross, a member of the Planning and Highways Committee, was an estate agent and acting for the vendor in negotiations for a sale of the property; the sale being subject to council consent to the development. At the council meeting at which the application was considered Councillor Cross took no part in the matter. Instead the resolution was; (a) proposed and seconded (b) not spoken to by any member; and (c) carried unanimously. It was held that Councillor Cross had such an interest in the matter as to disqualify him from taking part or voting and the council decision was quashed.[38]

Where a person has a direct pecuniary interest his disqualification is automatic. This is treated as a rule and one that must be "held sacred",[39] even if the interest is small in amount.[40] Note even if disqualification is not automatic the interest may

---

[34] See, for example, Cane, *An Introduction to Administrative Law*, pp. 110–113.

[35] *Russell v. Duke of Norfolk* [1949] 1 All E.R. 109, *per* Tucker L.J. at 118.

[36] For an "application" case where procedural standards have been imposed, due to the impact on livelihood, see *R. (Cowan) v. Huntingdon DC* [1984] 1 W.L.R. 501; applicant for entertainment licence to be given an opportunity to make representations in respect of objections.

[37] *R. (Kirkstall Valley Campaign) v. Secretary of State for the Environment* [1996] 3 All E.R. 304; *R. (Cummins) v. Camden LBC* [2001] EWHC 1116 (Admin), Ouseley J.; *Bovis Homes Ltd v. New Forest DC* [2002] EWHC 483 (Admin), Ouseley J.

[38] *R. v. Hendon Rural District Council, ex p. Chorley* [1933] 2 K.B. 696. On the subject of conflict of interest in local authority matters, see paras. 28–10 to 28–12.

[39] *Dimes v. Grand Junction Canal Proprietors* (1852) 3 HL Cas 759, 793 *per* Lord Campbell; judge holding shares in company party to litigation.

[40] *Serjeant v. Dale* (1877) 2 Q.B.D. 558 at 566–567, albeit now subject to a *de minimis* rule; *Weatherill v. Lloyds TSB Bank plc* [2000] C.P.L.R. 584—judge's shareholding 570 out of a total of 5.5 billion issued.

still give rise to a real possibility of bias. A test that it has been suggested would have been better applied to the facts in the celebrated *Pinochet*[41] case, involving Lord Hoffman's interest in Amnesty International, an intervening party, through his position within Amnesty International Charity Ltd, where such an interest was held to be a further ground for automatic disqualification.[42] Perhaps, fortunately, this part of the automatic disqualification "rule" appears to apply only to the judiciary.

It is in relation to the second element, the need for an absence of bias, that this branch of natural justice becomes complex and potentially confusing; for it necessarily extends to situations beyond a simple clash of interests and, indeed, beyond actual bias itself. The notion that a person frankly and obviously biased on any objective view should not be party to a decision affecting another's rights is uncontroversial. No one should act as both prosecutor and judge, or have a personal relationship with any of the parties, or take any part in proceedings when he has previously held strong views on the matters in issue. By way of example:

> In a fair rent case under the Rent Act 1965 the decision of a rent assessment committee was quashed on the ground of bias because the chairman of the committee lived with his father who was a tenant of an associated company of the landlords, and had advised his father about the fair rent for his flat.[43]

The difficulty comes because in this area of the law appearance is, truly, everything. It is not a question of whether or not the decision maker potentially influenced by the interest or matter giving rise to an appearance of bias was, in fact, so influenced; there is no need to prove actual bias. Rather whether the objective appearance is that justice has been done or not. It is here that the HRA and, in particular, the introduction into English law of Article 6 ECHR has had a considerable impact. The wording of the core of the Article perhaps merits consideration:

> "1 In the determination of his civil rights and obligations or of any criminal charge against him, everyone is entitled to a fair and public hearing within a reasonable time by an independent and impartial tribunal established by law."

Prior to the implementation of the HRA the courts had alternated between two tests. One that demanded no "reasonable suspicion of bias" and another that asked for no "real likelihood of bias". In the early 1990s the House of Lords held in favour of the latter test.[44] Albeit expressed in terms of the need for there to be no "real danger of bias" in the sense that the relevant member of the tribunal or other body might unfairly regard with favour, or disfavour, the case of a party to the issue under consideration by him.[45] Even before the advent of the HRA the courts were moving back towards an "appearance of bias" test. Now, though, real emphasis is placed on the need to avoid such an appearance[46] and the position has shifted back

[41] R. (Pinochet Ugarte) v. Bow Street Metropolitan Stipendiary Magistrate (No. 2) [2000] 1 A.C. 199.
[42] English Public Law cited supra. at page 815, para. 15.77.
[43] Metropolitan Properties Co. (F.G.C.) Limited v. Lannon [1969] 1 Q.B. 577.
[44] R. v. Gough [1993] A.C. 646; [1993] 2 W.L.R. 883.
[45] R. v. Gough supra.
[46] R v. Spear (John) [2003] 1 A.C. 734.

to a "real possibility of bias" test.[47] As a result the famous words of Lord Hewart C.J., spoken in *R. v. Sussex JJ. ex parte McCarthy*,[48] remain true today:

"It is of fundamental importance that justice should not only be done, but should manifestly and undoubtedly be seen to be done."

As noted the circumstances which may give rise to such risk are many and varied. They include friendship with or enmity towards a party, familial connection, close acquaintance or prior expression of an objectively unbalanced view. The courts, though, will not intervene where the suspicion of bias is unreasonable or amounts, for example, to a general "class prejudice".[49] Finally it is, of course, open to an affected party to waive the apparent bias even where the test is met.

(c) The proper procedural requirements shall be followed

10–06   Put simply the proceedings of the tribunal or other body should be properly conducted in accordance with its rules. Again there is a requirement that justice should be seen to be done and several of the cases relate to instances where the procedure followed has given rise to a legitimate suspicion:

A person who is not a member of a tribunal should not retire for consideration of the case with the members, because it might give rise to a suspicion that he was party to the deliberation when not entitled to be.[50]

At a meeting of a committee charged with hearing a contested application for removal of a licence under the Betting, Gaming and Lotteries Act 1963 the chairman twice announced that he was ready to give his decision before counsel had completed cross-examination and appeared to reach a decision without consulting his colleagues who were sitting 12 feet away from him. It was held that justice had not been seen to be done and that the decision should be quashed.[51]

It must be borne in mind, though, that the courts will only intervene where the procedural step omitted was a *mandatory* or *imperative* requirement. Omission of a purely *directory* procedural step will not render the decision reached *ultra vires*. Parliament will rarely see fit to indicate the consequences that will flow from failure to follow a requirement,[52] hence it will frequently be necessary to fall back on the rather vague judicial guidance available. In essence a requirement is likely to be

---

[47] *Porter v. Magill* [2002] 1 All E.R. 465 at paras. 95 to 105 *per* Lord Hope. For two recent examples in the field of planning: see *R. (Georgiou) v. Enfield LBC* [2004] 2 P&CR 26, where the issue was closed minds and a lack of impartiality; and *R. (Ghadami) v. Harlow DC* [2004] EWHC 1982 (Admin), where the planning committee chairman was found to be too personally involved in "behind the scenes" negotiations affecting a town centre redevelopment scheme.

[48] [1924] 1 K.B. 256.

[49] *Williams v. Beesley* [1973] 1 W.L.R. 1295.

[50] *Ward v. Bradford Corporation* (1972) 70 L.G.R. 27.

[51] *Ex p. Ladbroke Group* (1969) 119 N.L.J. 225.

[52] For a rare exception see s.82 of the Local Government Act 1972: "The acts and proceedings of any person elected to an office under this Act and acting in that office shall, notwithstanding his disqualification or want of qualification, be as valid and effectual as if he had been qualified".

mandatory where it relates to the exercise of a right or power as opposed to the performance of a duty[53] or provides an important safeguard to individual interests in accordance with the principles of natural justice. For instance, the requirement to give prior notice of a decision or to hold a hearing,[54] at which a "real and not illusory opportunity to make representations" must be afforded,[55] or to give notice of rights of appeal.[56] The nineteenth century words of Lord Penzance remain a useful rule of thumb:

> "I believe, as far as any rule is concerned, you cannot safely go further than that in each case you must look to the subject-matter; consider the importance of the provision that has been disregarded, and the relation of that provision to the general object intended to be secured by the Act; and upon a review of the case in that aspect decide whether the matter is what is called imperative or only directory."[57]

By way of further example a statutory requirement to consult appropriate bodies is very likely to be considered mandatory.[58] This may be important by way of contrast with cases where the duty to consult arises only from a legitimate expectation as part of the "hear both sides" limb of natural justice. If a duty to consult is imposed by statute then failure to do so will amount to procedural impropriety giving rise to an entitlement to judicial review.[59] By contrast if it arises only through natural justice then, as noted, it will more likely be capable of remedy by a later decision-making process.[60]

As regards which and rights of appeal it is also important to remember that the courts will not generally intervene where such a right exists. The applicant should follow the procedure through to the appellate body.[61] This will offer the decision-making body an opportunity to correct any procedural unfairness below. This principle has been repeatedly affirmed since the implementation of the HRA both in the context of the availability of an appeal procedure and, in circumstances where the facts are uncontroversial, judicial review.

It goes without saying that, where an appeal is made, the appeal hearing too must follow the principles of natural justice.[62] Note, though, that the natural justice does not dictate that a member of a body which had sat at first instance is thereby debarred from sitting on appeal or equivalent hearings; this is particularly so when

---

[53] See *Montreal Street Railway Co v. Normandin* [1917] A.C. 170 at 175.

[54] See *Bradbury v. Enfield LBC* [1967] 1 W.L.R. 1311 concerning a requirement to give public notice when a local education authority "ceased to maintain" a school; the context being the reorganisation of Enfield's schools along comprehensive lines.

[55] Per Donaldson J. in *Lee v. Department of Education and Science* (1967) 66 L.G.R. 211.

[56] *Rayner v. Stepney Corporation* [1911] 2 Ch. 312.

[57] *Howard v. Bodington* (1877) 2 P.D. 203 at 211.

[58] *Agricultural, Horticultural and Forestry Industry Training Board v. Aylesbury Mushrooms Ltd* [1972] 1 W.L.R. 190 and following cases.

[59] *R. (Bryant) v. Gwent County Council* (*The Independent*, 19/04/1988) per Hodgson J.

[60] *R. (South Glamorgan County Council) v. Secretary of State for Wales* (*The Times*, 25/06/1988).

[61] *Hamlet v. General Municipal Boilermakers and Allied Trades Union* [1987] 1 All E.R. 631. See *R (K) v. (1) Governors of W School (2) West Sussex County Council* (2001) E.L.R. 311, Hidden J., for an example of a case where it was acceptable to proceed directly to judicial review without following the appeal procedure.

[62] *Leary v. National Union of Vehicle Builders* [1971] Ch. 34.

the rules provide for it to happen.[63] The principle that militates against bias, though, will of course apply in appropriate circumstances. For instance, the court prohibited a named doctor from determining whether or not a chief inspector was permanently disabled; the doctor had been involved in the case previously and might not be seen to be impartial.[64] Generally, though, the more ready a body is to offer a right of appeal the more likely it is that the courts will look kindly upon it and, perhaps more importantly, the greater the chance that the person aggrieved will accept whatever its decision is.

---

[63] See *Hamlet*, above.
[64] *R. (Golden) v. Kent Police Authority* [1971] 2 Q.B. 662.

CHAPTER 11

APPLICABLE LAW AND OTHER MATTERS

Part III deals with meetings of members of companies, meetings of directors, and **11–01** meetings associated with insolvency and winding-up proceedings. This introductory chapter contains a brief note on the law applicable to companies and their classification and regulation and a short explanation of two rules (*ultra vires* and "*Foss v. Harbottle*") which are of relevance to what follows. The *ultra vires* rule has already been encountered in connection with business meetings.

This chapter, finally, contains a description of the "elective regime" introduced by the Companies Act 1989.

1 APPLICABLE LAW: CLASSIFICATION AND REGULATION OF COMPANIES

A substantial part of the company law of the United Kingdom is contained in the **11–02** Companies Act 1985. This was a consolidating Act, but most of its provisions which related to receivers and managers and winding up (ss.488–650 and 659–674) were repealed and reconsolidated in the Insolvency Act 1986 with further changes introduced in Enterprise Act 2002. The Companies Act 1989 introduced changes relating to company accounts, and a number of administrative reforms, including changes to the *ultra vires* rule and the introduction of the "elective regime" for private companies.

In the whole of Part III the above Acts will be referred to as the "1985 Act" the "1986 Act" and the "1989 Act." "Companies Acts" and "the Acts" refer to the three Acts.

2 CLASSIFICATION

Under the Companies Acts, companies may be registered in a number of forms, which may be summarised as follows:

A company limited by shares: this is defined as "a company having the **11–03** liability of its members limited by the memorandum to the amount, if any, unpaid on the shares respectively held by them."[1] The company limited by shares is the most common form of registered company and has, since at least the mid-nineteenth century, constituted the means through which much of the nation's business has been conducted.

---

[1] 1985 Act, s.1(2)(a).

11–04   **A company limited by guarantee:** this is defined as "a company having the liability of its members limited by the memorandum to such amount as the members may respectively thereby undertake to contribute to the assets of the company in the event of its being wound up."[2]

Companies limited by guarantee are mostly associations formed for the protection of trade, for educational or professional purposes, or to give corporate form to voluntary associations. They are usually organizations in which it is not intended to make a profit. It is common for such a company to take advantage of section 30 of the 1985 Act and dispense with the word "limited" in its name.

11–05   **An unlimited company:** this is defined as "a company not having any limit on the liability of its members."[3] This type of incorporation is, in practice, confined to those bodies which wish to take advantage of section 241(4) of the 1985 Act, (replaced, as section 254, by the 1989 Act), which can exempt an unlimited company from the obligation to file accounts.

Community Interest Companies

11–06   The Community Interest Company was created by the Companies (Audit, Investigations and Community Enterprise) Act 2004 and have been capable of incorporation since July 2005. Such companies must have community interest as their main objective and the assets and profits will be locked in the companies for use in pursuance of these objectives.

Societas Europaea

11–07   Since 8 October 2004 it has been possible to incorporate the Societas Europara (SE) which is a company capable of operating in any European Union country, irrespective of which country it has been incorporated in.

Public and Private Companies

11–07a   A further classification is between public and private companies. "Public company" means a company the memorandum of which states that the company is to be a public company, and in relation to which the provisions of the Acts as to the registration or re-registration of a company as a public company have been complied with. "Private company" means a company that is not a public company.[4] A public company has to have a minimum share capital of £50,000.[5] A private company commits an offence if it offers its shares or debentures to the public.[6]

The minimum number of members for a public company is two. Limited liability may be lost if a public company carries on business for more than six months with only one member.[7]

---

[2] *ibid.*, s.1(2)(b).
[3] *ibid.*, s.1(2)(c).
[4] *ibid.*, s.1(3)
[5] *ibid.*, s.118.
[6] *ibid.*, s.81.
[7] *ibid.*, s.24.

By virtue of subsection 3A of the 1985 Act, inserted by the Companies (Single Member Private Companies) Regulations 1992 (S.I. 1992 No. 1699), one person alone may form a private company limited by shares or by guarantee. Paragraph 15–08 below deals with the way in which decisions of the single member have to be recorded.

3 REGULATION

The internal government of a company is regulated by its articles of association, or its statute in the case of an SE, and it is to these that reference must be made for the provisions applicable to meetings of shareholders and directors. The articles will usually incorporate those sections of the Acts which are mandatory in relation to company procedure, and must be read subject to numerous decided cases. It is the purpose of the succeeding chapters to examine the interrelationship between these three elements: the articles, the Acts and case law.   **11–08**

It will be necessary too to mention the Registrar of Companies. The work of this official (who is referred to as "the Registrar") has grown considerably in recent years and few formal steps can be carried out without seeking a certificate from or sending a return to the Registrar.[8] His main responsibilities are to incorporate and dissolve companies, to examine and record documents submitted to the Registry, and to make this information available for public inspection.

Section 8 of the 1985 Act provided for the making of regulations prescribing specimen sets of articles of association. These regulations are the Companies (Tables A to F) Regulations 1985 (S.I. 1985 No. 805 and S.I. 1985 No. 1052). The tables are the successors to those which first saw the light of day in the Companies Act 1862 (described by Sir Francis Palmer as the "*magna carta* of co–operative enterprise"). The important set is Table A (Regulations for Management of a Company Limited by Shares).

In the case of an SE no format for the statutes has been set out and in the few SEs which have been incorporated to date, the memorandum and articles of association of a limited company have been used as the basis of the statutes.

In the case of a Community Interest Company (CIC) no default memorandum and articles is provided for and a full set must be provided on incorporation. The contents of the M&A are set out in the schedules to the Community Interest Company Regulations 2005.

Table A is, by the Acts, caused to apply if no other articles are filed, but companies are given freedom in the matter and often adopt articles departing widely from Table A. It should be noted that companies registered under earlier statutes and adopting the Table A of that statute continue to be regulated thereby; they do not automatically adopt the Table A of a later statute. Thus a large number of companies will continue to be governed by Table A of the Companies Act 1948 (as amended), and of earlier statutes.   **11–09**

---

[8] At Companies House, which is now an executive agency of the Department of Trade and Industry. Companies House has three main offices in Cardiff, London and Edinburgh and satellite offices in Birmingham, Manchester, Leeds and Glasgow. All these offices receive documents for registration. The address of the main office at Cardiff is: Crown Way, Cardiff CF4 3UZ (telephone for central enquires: 01222 380801).

In the succeeding chapters, where the relevant articles of Table A (the 1985 version) are quoted, they are quoted in full: these extracts are indented in the text. Elsewhere, a certain amount of paraphrasing of the Acts and articles of Table A has been employed to avoid too turgid a narrative. There, the footnotes will enable the reader to refer to the statute for the detailed wording.

Finally, it should be borne in mind that those companies whose securities are listed on the Stock Exchange must comply with the listing rules made under Part IV of the Financial Services Act 1986. In this Part, these rules, which are contained in the Stock Exchange's Yellow Book, will be referred to as the Listing Rules.

4 THE *ULTRA VIRES* RULE

11-10 The basic rule (now subject to the statutory qualifications referred to below) is that the powers of a company are set out in its memorandum. To the extent that a purported action is outside the scope of the objects of the company as set forth in the objects clause of its memorandum, or is not incidental to the attainment of those objects, or capable of being so incidental, it is null and void. An act of the board which is *ultra vires* the company is not capable of being ratified by shareholders in general meeting, even if their vote is unanimous.[9]

If a contract is *ultra vires*, neither the company nor any third party can sue on it; this however is subject to sections 35A and 35B of the 1985 Act. The sections provide that in favour of a person dealing with a company in good faith, the power of the directors to bind the company, or authorise others to do so, is deemed to be free of limitation under the company's constitution; and a party to a transaction with a company is not bound to enquire as to whether it is permitted by the company's memorandum or as to any such limitation on the powers of the directors to bind the company or authorise others to do so. The third party shall be presumed to have acted in good faith unless the contrary is proved.[10]

Under section 35 of the 1985 Act, the validity of an act done by a company shall not be called into question on the ground of lack of capacity by reason of anything in the company's memorandum.

11-11 While these provisions help third parties, directors will remain liable to shareholders if they act, or attempt to act, in a way which exceeds either the powers of the company or their own capacity as directors. In the case of a breach of the objects clauses in the memorandum, the transgression can be restrained by injunction before any legal commitment to a third party is entered into. If the directors act outside their powers as defined in the company's memorandum, and then seek to have the matter ratified by the company in general meeting, a special resolution will be required.

5 THE RULE IN *FOSS v. HARBOTTLE*

11-12 The court will not interfere in the internal affairs of a company when the irregularity complained of can be rectified by the company itself:

[9] *Ashbury Carriage Company v. Riche* (1875) 7 L.R. 653, H.L.; and see *Precision Dippings v. Precision Dippings Marketing* [1985] 3 W.L.R. 812, C.A.
[10] *T.C.B. v. Gray* [1986] 1 All E.R. 587.

In the leading case of *Foss v. Harbottle*, the directors had been charged with transactions whereby the property of the company had been misapplied, but when the matter was discussed at a general meeting the majority decided to take no action. An application by a dissentient shareholder was made to the court for the appointment of a receiver to take over the property of the company. It was held that, as the acts of the board were capable of confirmation by the members, the court would not interfere; there was nothing to prevent the company from obtaining redress, in its corporate capacity, for the wrongs done to it.[11]

The matter is one of procedure and jurisdiction; the court will not do what it is for the company itself to do according to the provisions of its articles. If a general meeting is wanted, the directors have power to call it, but the court cannot, in general, compel directors to do something they determine is not in the interests of the company. If the directors do not call a meeting, it is left for the shareholders to call it as provided in the articles, and if the shareholders do not wish to do so the court has no power to take the management out of the hands of the directors.[12]
Exceptions to the rule in *Foss v. Harbottle* are:

1. Where the right alleged to have been infringed is a personal right vested in the individual shareholder.
2. Where the act complained of is illegal.
3. Where there has been a fraud on the company and those against whom fraud is alleged either control the company, or are in a position to manipulate matters so that the majority do not allow a claim to be brought for the alleged wrong:

   B and L were directors of two companies, Newman and TPG. B and TPG were shareholders in Newman, but did not hold a majority of the shares. B and L also held all the shares of a company which held a substantial shareholding in TPG. TPG was in serious financial difficulties and B drew up a plan to sell, *inter alia*, TPG's assets to Newman. Valuation of assets in the plan was based on deliberately misleading information, and by deceit B and L induced the Newman board to accept it. There followed a general meeting at which a resolution approving the plan was passed. The plaintiff, a minority shareholder in Newman, brought an action claiming damages on behalf of all shareholders. B contended that the court had no jurisdiction as the defendants did not have voting control of Newman. It was held that the action should be allowed, since otherwise the interests of justice would be defeated.[13]

4. Where a specified majority is required (*e.g.* for a special resolution) and this has not been obtained.

As stated, the rule in *Foss v. Harbottle* applies to corporate membership rights and **11–13** does not apply where the right being infringed is that of an individual shareholder.

[11] *Foss v. Harbottle* (1843) 2 Hare 461. See also *Pavlides v. Jensen* [1956] Ch. 565.
[12] *MacDougall v. Gardiner* (1875) 1 Ch.D. 13.
[13] *Prudential Assurance Co. v. Newman Industries (No. 2)* [1982] Ch. 204.

For example, an individual shareholder has a right not to be forced to subscribe for shares in the company or to have his liability increased. He has the right to petition for a compulsory winding up, and to complain to the Department of Trade and Industry where there has been default in holding an annual general meeting. A further example would be a shareholder's right under the company's articles to have his vote accepted at a general meeting of the company.[14] In general, he has individual rights where his position as a shareholder is affected and where he has not, by the contract between himself, the company and the other shareholders arising from his status as a shareholder, impliedly left the matter to the decision of the majority of shareholders in general meeting—when he has corporate membership rights as opposed to individual membership rights.

The application of the rule in *Foss v. Harbottle* has not been consistent. In some cases, the court has chosen not to intervene (usually on the ground that it would serve no useful purpose to do so) where the rule has not been cited. In others, relief has been granted but the rule has not been raised in defence.[15]

While therefore the rule should be noted by those who seek to defend the propriety of procedure followed at a meeting from attacks by members, there is no certainty that it will be applied. In addition, section 459 of the 1985 Act strengthens the hand of a shareholder who can prove that the affairs of the company are being, or have been conducted, in a manner which is unfairly prejudicial to the interests of its members generally or of some part of the members (including at least himself) or that any actual or proposed act or omission of the company (including an act or omission on its behalf) is or would be so prejudicial. Among other things, the court may authorise civil proceedings to be brought in the name of the company (the procedural mechanism which *Foss v. Harbottle* requires).[16]

6 THE ELECTIVE REGIME

11–14   Prior to the 1989 Act, deregulatory proposals had been put forward by the Institute of Directors. These were designed to simplify certain of the administrative requirements of companies; it was intended particularly to help owner-managed companies.

The arrangements are now embodied in section 379A of the 1985 Act (as introduced by section 116 of the 1989 Act) under which private companies will be able, by means of an Elective Resolution:

(1) to extend the authority of directors to allot shares without the approval of a general meeting (1985 Act, s.80A);

---

[14] *Pender v. Lushington* (1877) 6 Ch.D. 70.

[15] See [1976] J.B.L. 323.

[16] 1985 Act, s.461(2)(c). For examples of s.459 in practice, see *Re London School of Electronics* [1986] 1 Ch. 211; *Re Cumana Ltd* [1986] B.C.L.C. 430, C.A.; and *Lowe v. Fahey* [1996] 1 B.C.L.C. 262. On the other hand, in *Re Saul D. Harrison Sons plc* [1995] 1 B.C.L.C. 14, the s.459 remedy was refused, considerable importance being attached in that case to the contract between the company and its shareholders constituted by the company's articles of association. The whole topic of shareholder remedies is under review: see the Law Commission's Consultation Paper, "Shareholder Remedies", published in mid-1996. The paper covers, among other things, *Foss v. Harbottle* and ss.459–461 of the 1985 Act.

(2) to dispense with the holding of an annual general meeting (1985 Act, s.366A);

(3) to reduce the existing level of percentage consent required for holding a shareholders' meeting at short notice (1985 Act, s.369(4) or 378(3);

(4) to dispense with the laying of accounts and reports before a general meeting (1985 Act, s.252); and

(5) to avoid the need for the annual appointment of auditors (1985 Act, s.386).

An Elective Resolution is not effective for any of the above purposes unless:

(a) at least 21 days' notice in writing is given of the meeting, stating that an Elective Resolution is to be proposed and stating the terms of the resolution, and

(b) the resolution is agreed to at the meeting, in person or by proxy, by all the members entitled to attend and vote at the meeting.[17]

However, an Elective Resolution is effective notwithstanding the fact that less than 21 days' notice in writing of the meeting is given if all the members entitled to attend and vote at the meeting so agree.[18]

The company may revoke an Elective Resolution by passing an ordinary resolution to that effect.[19] An Elective Resolution shall cease to have effect if the company is re-registered as a public company.[20]

The detailed provisions of the Elective Regime will be considered at the appropriate point in later chapters.

---

[17] 1985 Act, s.379A(2).

[18] 1985 Act, s.379(A)(2A) (introduced by the Deregulation (Resolutions of Private Companies) Order 1996 (S.I. 1996 No. 1471)).

[19] 1985 Act, s.379(A)(3).

[20] 1985 Act, s.379(A)(4).

CHAPTER 12

MEMBERS' MEETINGS: STATUS AND CONVENTION

1   THE AUTHORITY OF THE GENERAL MEETING

12–01   The general meeting of members represents the source of ultimate authority within the company structure, in that it elects the directors, receives the annual accounts, and passes as special resolutions those matters which most significantly affect the constitution of the company. The general meeting is the repository of any powers of the company that have not been delegated to the directors.[1] This remains an important sanction in spite of the very extensive powers of management which are invariably conferred on the board by the company's articles. For listed companies the Listing Rules require a number of matters to be submitted to shareholders in general meeting for approval. This affords shareholders the opportunity to receive an explanatory circular about the proposal, often accompanied by an up-to-date note of the company's trading position; they will then be able to lobby the board and obtain publicity for their views either in the press or by the circulation of a statement under section 376 of the 1985 Act.[2]

The general meeting, too, retains the right to cure a want of authority on the part of the directors. For example, where a board was alleged to have acted in bad faith in issuing shares to "friendly hands" during a take-over bid and their action had been confirmed in general meeting, an attempt to set aside the allotment failed on the ground that the meeting possessed the power to remedy any lack of proper authority on the part of the board.[3]

In the words of Harman L.J.:

> "It is trite law, I had thought, that if directors do acts, as they do every day, especially in private companies, which . . . they go on doing for years, carrying on the business of the company in the way in which, if properly constituted, they should carry it on, and then they find that everything has been so to speak wrongly done because it was not done by a proper board, such directors can, by making a full and frank disclosure and calling together the general body of shareholders, obtain absolution and forgiveness of their sins . . . Of course, if the majority of the general meeting will not forgive and approve, the directors must pay for it."[4]

---

[1] See paras. 20–01.
[2] See paras. 13–25 to 13–30.
[3] *Bamford v. Bamford* [1970] Ch. 212.
[4] *ibid.* 237. See also *Rolled Steel Products (Holdings) v. British Steel Corp.* [1985] 2 W.L.R. 908 C.A. and *Malaga Investments Ltd (Petitioners)* (1987) 3 B.C.C. 569.

The ratification, however, must be carried out while the opportunity exists: if, for example, the company goes into liquidation, it will not be sufficient to say that if the shareholders had known of the improper act before the liquidation they would have ratified it—by then it will be too late.[5]

2   KINDS OF GENERAL MEETING

Meetings of members of companies are known as general meetings and the   **12–02** decisions they take are spoken of as having been taken by the company in general meeting. The normal requirement of the 1985 Act is that every company must hold an annual general meeting. Other meetings may be called for special purposes, and these are called extraordinary general meetings.

Where the capital of a company is divided into shares of different classes, it may be necessary to convene a class meeting: these are dealt with in Chapter 17, below.

The procedure before and at a general meeting is described in detail in Chapter 19.

(a) Annual general meetings

Basic obligation

Every company must (unless it has passed an appropriate Elective Resolu-   **12–03** tion—see para. 12–05 below) in each year hold a general meeting as its annual general meeting, in addition to other meetings in that year, and not more than 15 months must elapse between the date of one annual general meeting and that of the next. The meeting must be specified as such in the notice calling it. In the case of the first annual general meeting, so long as it is held within 18 months of incorporation, the company need not hold it in the year of its incorporation or in the following year. Default renders the company and every officer of it who is in default liable to fines.[6]

There is a dual responsibility: the holding of the meeting in the calendar year and within the period of 15 months after the preceding general meeting:

A company held a general meeting on March 21, 1916 and, as no general meeting was held in 1917, an information was laid against a director for not holding the meeting in 1917. *Held*, that two offences had been committed: (1) not holding the meeting within the calendar year; and (2) not holding the meeting within 15 months of the preceding one. Each default was liable to be dealt with separately.[7]

The calendar year is the period of time to be calculated from January 1 and   **12–04** ending on December 31 and not the 12 months from the date of registration of the

---

[5] *Re D'Jan of London Limited* [1993] B.C.C. 646.
[6] 1985 Act, s.366(1)–(4).
[7] *Smedley v. Registrar of Companies* [1919] 1 K.B. 97.

company.[8] Month means calendar month[9]; a calendar month is the period expiring on the corresponding day in the following month.

Regard must, however, be paid to the interests of shareholders:

> The articles of a company provided that the ordinary general meeting of shareholders should be held in the month of August. This meeting had never in the past been held prior to the third of fourth Monday in August. Differences occurred between a large shareholder (the plaintiff) and the directors as to the management of the company, and the directors called the meeting for August 3, at which date it would be too early for the plaintiff to exercise voting rights acquired under recent transfers. The court granted an injunction against holding the meeting before August 13, by which time the plaintiff's rights would have accrued.[10]

Failure to convene the annual general meeting may result in the directors ceasing to hold office.[11]

If default is made in holding an annual general meeting of the company, the Department of Trade and Industry may, on the application of any member of the company, call or direct the calling of a general meeting of the company. The Department may give such ancillary or consequential directions as it thinks expedient, including directions modifying or supplementing, in relation to the calling, holding and conduct of the meeting, the operation of the company's articles.[12] The directions may provide that one member of the company present in person or by proxy shall be deemed to constitute a meeting.[13]

A general meeting held in pursuance of the above provisions is, subject to any directions of the Department, deemed to be an annual general meeting of the company. Where, however, a meeting so held is not held in the year in which the default in holding the company's annual general meeting occurred, the meeting is not to be treated as the annual general meeting for the year in which it is held, unless at that meeting the company resolves that it is to be so treated.[14] In effect, this means that provided appropriate notice is given, the meeting may be treated as the annual general meeting for both years. For example, if default is made in holding the annual general meeting for 2002, and in 2003 the Department orders a meeting to be held, the meeting will be treated as the meeting for 2002 (and the annual general meeting for 2003 will have to be held later in that year) or the company may resolve that it shall be treated as the annual general meetings for 2002 and 2003. In the latter case, a copy of the resolution must be forwarded to the Registrar within 15 days.[15]

---

[8] *Gibson v. Barton* (1875) L.R. 10 Q.B. 329.
[9] Interpretation Act 1978, s.5, Sched. 1.
[10] *Cannon v. Trask* (1875) 20 Eq. 669.
[11] *Alexander Ward Co. Ltd v. Samyang Navigation Co. Ltd* [1975] 1 W.L.R. 673.
[12] 1985 Act, s.367(1).
[13] 1985 Act, s.367(2).
[14] 1985 Act, s.367(4).
[15] 1985 Act, s.367(5).

Elective Resolution not to hold AGM

By section 366A of the 1985 Act, a private company may elect, by Elective Resolution,[16] to dispense with the holding of annual general meetings. Such an election has effect for the year in which it is made and subsequent years, but does not affect any liability already incurred by reason of default in holding an annual general meeting. In any year in which an annual general meeting would be required to be held but for the Elective Resolution, and in which no such meeting has been held, any member of the company may, by notice to the company not later than three months before the end of the year, require the holding of an annual general meeting in that year. **12–05**

If the election ceases to have effect, the company is not obliged under section 366 to hold an annual general meeting in that year if, when the election ceases to have effect, less than three months of that year then remains.

Certain changes have been proposed as part of the Company Law Review being carried out by the Department of Trade and Industry. These changes have been designed to make the administration of a small company easier. Under the proposals, not holding an AGM would be the default position, and companies would have to elect to hold one. However, it is not certain when the draft companies act will be placed before Parliament. At the time of writing, the Bill is expected to go before the House before the end of 2005.

Laying of accounts

In practice, annual general meetings are timed to accord with the laying before shareholders of periodic accounts and the declaration of dividends. In respect of each financial year of a company the directors must lay before the company in general meeting copies of the company's annual accounts, the directors' report and the auditors' report on those accounts.[17] The accounts must be laid before the company within ten months after the end of the relevant accounting reference period for a private company, and within seven months for a public company (in the case of a newly-incorporated company which has a first accounting reference period of more than twelve months, the period allowed is (a) 10 months or seven months, as the case may be, from the first anniversary of the company, or (b) three months from the end of the accounting reference period, whichever last expires). These periods can be extended by three months where the company carries on business or has interests outside the United Kingdom, the Channel Islands and the Isle of Man.[18] **12–06**

Under section 252 of the 1985 Act, a private company may, however, pass an Elective Resolution[19] under which it dispenses with the laying of accounts and reports before the company in general meeting. An election has effect in relation to the accounts for the year in which the election is made and subsequent financial

---

[16] See para. 11–14. It may be desirable to make some consequential changes to the articles. See *Administrator*, November 1990, p. 19.

[17] 1985 Act, s.241(1).

[18] 1985 Act, s.244. A listed company must issue an annual report and accounts within six months of the end of the financial period to which they relate although in exceptional circumstances the Stock Exchange can extend this time limit (Listing Rule 12.42(e)).

[19] See para. 11–14.

years (*i.e.* there can be no back-dating of the effect). However, the accounts still have to be sent to members, and this has to be done not less than 28 days before the end of the period allowed for laying and delivering them (*i.e.* 10 months after the end of the relevant period). Each member must be sent a notice informing him of the right to require the laying of the accounts and reports before a general meeting. Before the end of 28 days beginning with the day on which the accounts and reports are sent out, any member or auditor may by notice in writing deposited at the registered office require that a general meeting be held for the purpose of laying the accounts and reports before the company.

By section 233(1) of the 1985 Act, a company's annual accounts must be approved by the board of directors and signed on behalf of the board by a director of the company. The signature shall be on the company's balance sheet. Each copy which is laid before the company in general meeting, or which is otherwise circulated, published or issued, shall state the name of the person who signed the balance sheet on behalf of the board. The copy which is delivered to the Registrar must be signed on behalf of the board by a director of the company.

Change in accounting reference date

12–07   The following is an example of the procedure to be followed where there is a change in accounting reference date; for example, during the year 2003 the date is changed from April 30 to August 31. Even if no accounts are ready, the annual general meeting must still be held on or before December 31, 2003 or, if earlier, within 15 months after the annual general meeting for 2002.[20] The only business to be dealt with will be that required by the articles, for example the re-election of directors retiring by rotation. Since no accounts are being laid before the meeting, there will be no requirement to re-appoint the auditors.[21] When the accounts are ready, early in 2004, they can be laid before the annual general meeting for that year to be held in, say, February 2004, the date of the meeting falling into step with the new timetable for the accounts; at that meeting, too, the auditors would be re-appointed.

(b) Extraordinary general meetings

12–08   There is no definition of an extraordinary general meeting in the Acts, but the term is understood to cover all meetings of a company other than annual general meetings. Article 36 of Table A provides that all general meetings other than annual general meetings shall be called extraordinary general meetings.

Meetings convened by directors

12–09   The directors have the power to convene an extraordinary meeting on their own motion whenever they think it appropriate in the interests of the company.[22]

---

[20] 1985 Act, s.366(3).

[21] 1985 Act, ss.384(1) and 385(2). Similar principles apply if the accounting reference date remains the same, but the accounts have not been prepared in time to lay before an annual general meeting in the earlier year.

[22] See *Currie v. Cowdenbeath Football Club* [1992] BCLC 1029. Art. 37 of Table A confers such a power.

Whenever shareholder consent has to be obtained, it will be necessary to convene an extraordinary general meeting for the purpose (unless, which is often impracticable, the matter can be dealt with as special business at the annual general meeting).

Section 142 of the 1985 Act provides that where the net assets of a public company are half or less of the amount of the company's called-up share capital (not including any treasury shares held by the company), the directors of the company shall, not later than 28 days from the earliest day on which that fact is known to a director of the company, duly convene an extraordinary general meeting of the company for a date not later than 56 days from that day. The purpose of the meeting is to consider which steps, if any, should be taken to deal with the situation. The net assets of a company are the aggregate of its assets less the aggregate of its liabilities.[23]

Meetings on requisition by members

Section 368 of the 1985 Act provides that the directors must, on a member's **12–10** requisition, forthwith proceed duly to convene an extraordinary general meeting of the company. A member's requisition is a requisition of (a) members holding at the date of the deposit of the requisition not less than one-tenth of such of the paid-up capital as at that date carries the right of voting at general meetings; or (b) in the case of a company not having a share capital, members representing not less than one-tenth of the total voting rights of all the members having at that date a right to vote at general meetings. The word "members" includes the singular under section 6 of the Interpretation Act 1978. In the case of joint holders, the requisition should be signed by all the joint holders.[24] Apparently, a holder of a share warrant, if deemed under the articles to be a member, may join in requisitioning the meeting.

The above provisions are overriding, and nothing in the articles can deprive members of their benefits. Conversely, if the articles permit a meeting to be requisitioned by a smaller number of members than that mentioned in section 368, this will be effective.

The reference in the section to one-tenth of such of the paid-up capital of the **12–11** company as "at the date of the deposit" of the requisition carries the right of voting makes it clear that if, for example, preference shares carry votes only when dividends are in arrears, or certain shareholders can vote only in the event of a winding up of the company, there will be no right to join in a requisition unless the stated events have then happened.

The requisition must state the objects of the meeting, and must be signed by the requisitionists and deposited at the registered office of the company. The requisition may consist of several documents in like form each signed by one or more requisitionists.[25]

The court will not be too pedantic in construing requisitions by shareholders:

---

[23] It is believed that this definition, in s.264(2) of the 1985 Act, applies by analogy to s.142. "Called-up share capital" is defined in s.737.
[24] *Patent Wood Keg Syndicate v. Pearse* [1906] W.N. 164.
[25] 1985 Act, s.368(3).

Shareholders of the Isle of Wight Railway Company required the directors to call a general meeting (1) to appoint a committee to enquire into the working expenses of the company and to require the directors to act on its recommendations; and (2) to remove any of the directors and to fill any vacancy in the board. At first instance, the court held that proposal (1) was illegal because directors' powers could not be transferred to a committee, and that proposal (2) was too vague. The Court of Appeal however held that all the objects of proposal (1) could be carried out in a legal way and, in relation to proposal (2), that a general meeting had power to remove directors, that a notice of a proposal to remove "any of the directors" was sufficiently distinct and that the general meeting could fill up vacancies. The requisition was therefore valid.[26]

12–12   If the directors convened a meeting to consider only some of the matters referred to in a requisition, the requisitionists would be within their rights in ignoring it and convening their own meeting.[27]

It would not however be permissible to discuss at a meeting convened by requisitionists any matter not covered by the terms of the requisition.[28]

If the directors do not within 21 days from the date of the deposit of the requisition proceed duly to convene a meeting, the requisitionists, or any of them representing more than one half of the total voting rights of all of them, may themselves convene a meeting. Any meeting so convened by the requisitionists must not be held after the expiration of three months from the date of deposit of the requisition.[29] The directors are deemed not to have duly convened a meeting if they convene it for a date more than 28 days after the date of the notice convening the meeting.[30]

12–13   The power of calling the meeting upon requisition is vested in the directors, and the secretary has no such power.[31]

A meeting convened under section 368 by the requisitionists must be convened in the same manner, as nearly as possible, as that in which meetings are to be convened by the directors. Any reasonable expenses incurred by the requisitionists by reason of the failure of the directors duly to convene a meeting must be repaid to the requisitionists by the company. Any sum so repaid shall be retained by the company out of any sums due or to become due from the company to such of the directors as were in default by way of fees or other remuneration in respect of their services.[32]

Should the requisition be for a meeting to consider passing a special resolution, the directors would have to comply with section 378(2) as to notice.[33]

Further discussion on section 368 procedure is to be found in para. 19–31.

---

[26] *Isle of Wight Railway Co. v. Tahourdin* (1883) 25 Ch.D. 320.
[27] *ibid.*
[28] *Ball v. Metal Industries Ltd*, 1957 S.L.T. 124.
[29] 1985 Act, s.368(4).
[30] 1985 Act, s.368(8).
[31] *Re State of Wyoming Syndicate* [1901] 2 Ch. 431; and see case cited in n. 26 in para. 5–08.
[32] 1985 Act, s.368(5), (6).
[33] 1985 Act, s.368(7); and see para. 15–04.

Meetings convened by members where no provision is made for directors to call meetings

As described above, the articles usually give the directors power to convene a **12–14** general meeting, in which case they can be compelled to do so by requisitionists, acting under section 368 of the 1985 Act. In the rare cases where the articles do not make any such provision, the Act provides that two or more members holding not less than one-tenth of the issued share capital or, if the company does not have a share capital, not less than five per cent in number of the members, may call a meeting.[34]

Meetings convened by the court

Section 371(1) of the 1985 Act provides that if for any reason it is impracticable **12–15** to call a meeting of a company in any manner in which meetings of that company may be called, or to conduct the meeting in the manner prescribed by the articles or the Act, the court may, either of its own motion or on the application of any director or of any member who would be entitled to vote at the meeting, order a meeting of the company to be called, held and conducted in any manner the court thinks fit. Where any such order is made, the court may give such ancillary or consequential directions as it thinks expedient. The court may direct that one member of the company present in person or by proxy shall be deemed to constitute a meeting. Any meeting called, held and conducted in accordance with section 371 is deemed to be a meeting of the company duly called, held and conducted.[35]

The following are examples of the operation of this provision: **12–16**

The applicant held 900 shares in a company; the respondents, who were the only directors, each held 50 shares. No general meeting of the company had ever been held. Under the articles, a quorum at general meetings was two persons present in person or by proxy. The applicant asked the court to convene a meeting under the section; this was opposed by the respondents. It was held that this was a case in which the court ought to exercise its direction; first, because if the court were to refuse to do so it would prevent the applicant from exercising his right as the majority shareholder to remove the directors and, secondly, because the respondents were failing in their duty to call an annual general meeting, which they had a statutory duty to do. A meeting was therefore directed to be held.[36]

In the Scottish case of *Re Edinburgh Workmen's Houses Improvement Co. Ltd*, where a quorum of 13 shareholders personally present was required, the Lord President stated: "I think the expression 'impracticable . . . to *conduct* the meeting of the company in manner prescribed by the articles' is sufficient to cover a case in which it is impracticable, owing to the terms of the articles and the state of the shareholding in the company, to get a quorum present. On the

---

[34] 1985 Act, s.370(3). The same applies where there are no directors available for the purpose of convening a meeting under s. 368: *Re Brick Stone Co.* [1878] W.N. 140.
[35] 1985 Act, s.371(3).
[36] *Re El Sombrero Ltd* [1958] Ch. 900.

facts placed before us it is impracticable in present circumstances to get a meeting with the appropriate quorum. I suggest, therefore, that . . . we order a meeting of the company at which the special resolutions may be proposed and passed, which meeting shall be held and conducted under the provision that the quorum shall be five shareholders personally present." An order was accordingly made to that effect.[37]

The cases make it clear that the fact that the application is opposed by share-holders other than the applicant does not take away the rights of the court, for a minority is not permitted at law to utilise the quorum provisions by failing to attend meetings and thereby preventing any business being done.[38]

The possible reasons why it might be impracticable to call a meeting or to conduct a meeting in the prescribed manner may be varied and numerous. The question of impracticability is one of fact, and the court would have to be satisfied, as it was in the *Edinburgh* case, that all reasonable measures had been taken to surmount the difficulties before granting an order.

The court is prepared to exercise considerable ingenuity in framing a remedy under section 371, as the following case illustrates:

> The British Union for the Abolition of Vivisection (BUAV) was a company limited by guarantee. All votes of BUAV members had to be given personally and no proxies were permitted. A radical faction caused great difficulty at its 1994 AGM. The officers convened an extraordinary general meeting for the purpose of introducing voting by proxy. At the EGM disorder ruled and the police closed the meeting down. The court was asked to convene a meeting under section 371 to vote on a special resolution to alter the articles to introduce voting by proxy. At that meeting personal attendance would be restricted to members of BUAV's executive committee; the other members would have a postal vote. The court decided to make an order in the terms sought: it was clear, from the requirement of BUAV's articles that members should personally attend meetings, that they should not be deterred from doing so by fear of extremism. On the facts, it was clear that it was impracticable to summon a meeting as provided for in the company's constitution.[39]

A meeting may also be convened by the court under section 425 of the 1985 Act, where a compromise or arrangement is proposed between the company and its creditors or members.[40]

---

[37] *Re Edinburgh Workmen's Houses Improvements Co. Ltd*, 1934 S.L.T. 513.

[38] *Re H.R. Paul Son Ltd* (1974) 118 S.J. 166; *Re Opera Photographic Ltd* [1989] 1 W.L.R. 634; *Re Sticky Fingers Restaurant Ltd* [1992] B.C.L.C. 84. The section, however, is not intended for use as a means of overriding the class rights of a minority shareholder to be present in a quorum at a company meeting: *BML Group v. Harman* [1994] 1 W.L.R. 893, C.A. The existence of a petition under s. 459 (see para. 11–11) does not bar the court from making an order under s.371: *Re Whitchurch Insurance Consultants* [1993] B.C.L.C. 1359. Note also *Ross v. Telford* (judgment June 24, 1997).

[39] *Re British Union for the Abolition of Vivisection* [1995] 2 B.C.L.C. 1.

[40] See Chap. 18.

124

Meetings on requisition by auditors

Where the resignation in writing of an auditor, deposited with the company **12–17** pursuant to section 392 of the 1985 Act, is accompanied by a statement of circumstances which he considers should be brought to the attention of members or creditors of the company, the auditor is given the right by section 392A(2) to requisition the directors to convene an extraordinary general meeting of the company to receive and consider such explanation of the circumstances connected with his resignation as he may wish to place before it. He has the right to have a statement in writing circulated to the members.[41] The directors must act on a requisition made by an auditor within 21 days of its deposit and convene the meeting by not more than 28-days notice.[42]

---

[41] 1985 Act, s.392A(3).
[42] 1985 Act, s.392A(5).

CHAPTER 13

CONSTITUTING A MEMBERS' MEETING

1 DEFINITION OF A MEMBER

13–01   The subscribers of the memorandum of a company are deemed to have agreed to become members of the company, and on its registration must be entered as members in the register of members. Every other person who agrees to become a member of a company, and whose name is entered in its register of members, is also a member of the company.[1]

Subject to certain exceptions, a body corporate cannot be a member of its holding company[2] and cannot acquire its own shares unless they are qualifying shares within the meaning of Companies Act 1985, s162(4).[3]

A public company which participates in the CREST system of dematerialised securities (see also para. 14–06) is subject to the Uncertificated Securities Regulations (S.I. 1995 No. 3272). Regulation 34(3) provides that for the purpose of serving notices of meetings, a participating company may determine that persons entitled to receive such notices are those persons entered on the relevant register at the close of business on the day determined by it. Regulation 34(4) provides that the day determined by the company must be not more than 21 days before the day that the notices of the meeting are sent. Suggested practice is that the board meeting which approves the notice of meeting should pass a resolution specifying an appropriate date.[4]

2 NOTICE

In general, the requirements as to notice discussed in Part II, above, will apply to meetings of companies, but additional points which are relevant to shareholders' meetings are summarised below.

(a) To whom notice must be given

(1) In general

13–02   Notice of meetings must be sent to all persons who are entitled, under the company's articles, to receive notice. Article 38 of Table A provides that, subject to

---

[1] 1985 Act, s.22.
[2] 1985 Act, s.23. A company which was a member of another one before it became a susbsidiary of it may retain its shareholding, but has no right to vote in respect of such shares.
[3] 1985 Act, s.143.
[4] See *Chartered Secretary*, June, 1997, p. 7.

the provisions of the articles and to any restrictions imposed on any shares, the notice shall be given to all the members, to all persons entitled to a share in consequence of the death or bankruptcy of a member and to the directors and auditors.

Where the articles make no specific provision, section 370(2) of the 1985 Act provides that a notice of the meeting of a company shall be served on every member of the company in the manner in which notices are required to be served by Table A, and for this purpose "Table A" means that Table A as is for the time being in force.

(2) Deceased or bankrupt members

Table A provides as follows:

13–03

116. A notice may be given by the company to the persons entitled to a share in consequence of the death or bankruptcy of a member by sending or delivering it, in any manner authorised by the articles for the giving of notice to a member, addressed to them by name, or by the title of representatives of the deceased, or trustee of the bankrupt or by any like description at the address, if any, within the United Kingdom supplied for that purpose by the persons claiming to be so entitled. Until such an address has been supplied, a notice may be given in any manner in which it might have been given if the death or bankruptcy had not occurred.

Articles similar to those in Table A will generally govern company practice, but in an older set of articles which did not contain any specific provision for service of notice in the case of a deceased member and notice of meetings had to be served on any "member" either personally or by sending it by prepaid post addressed to "such member" at his registered address, it was held not to be necessary, in the case of a deceased member, either to send a notice addressed to him at his registered address or to serve his legal personal representatives unless they had themselves become members by formal registration.[5]

Another form of article in common use provides that a notice sent to any member shall, notwithstanding that such member be then dead or bankrupt, and whether or not the company has notice of his death or bankruptcy, be deemed to have been duly served unless the member's name shall, at the time of service, have been removed from the register.

The provisions of Table A can be summarised as follows:

13–04

A person becoming entitled to a share in consequence of the death or bankruptcy of a member may, upon such evidence being produced as the directors may properly require, elect either to become the holder of the share or to have some person nominated by him registered as the transferee.[6] A person becoming so

---

[5] *Allen v. Gold Reefs of West Africa Ltd* [1900] 1 Ch. 656.
[6] Table A, art. 30. Under the general law, a personal representative is entitled to be registered as the holder of shares, in the absence of provisions in the articles to the contrary: *Scott v. Scott (London) Ltd* [1940] Ch. 794 and *Safeguard Industrial Investments Ltd v. National Westminster Bank Ltd* [1980] 3 All E.R. 849.

entitled in consequence of the death or bankruptcy of a member shall have the rights to which he would be entitled if he were the holder of the share, except that he shall not, before being registered as the holder of the share, be entitled in respect of it to attend or vote at any meeting of the company, or at any separate meeting of the holders of any class of shares in the company.[7]

A personal representative is thus given the choice either to leave the deceased's name on the register or to become himself registered in place of the deceased. If he takes the former course, the deceased's estate will remain liable for calls if the shares are not fully paid, and will be entitled to dividends, but not to any rights in respect of meetings, *e.g.* the right to vote. If however the personal representative takes the latter course (by means of a "letter of request"), he accedes to full rights of membership so far as, for example, voting at meetings is concerned, but, conversely, he will become personally liable to the company in respect of calls, since the company is not obliged to have regard to his representative capacity. A personal representative of a deceased member may transfer the shares of the deceased member without himself becoming registered.[8]

The position of a trustee in bankruptcy is similar to that of a personal representative but he may, in addition to his other rights, disclaim the bankrupt's shares if they are onerous.[9] Where there is no express provision to the contrary in a company's articles, a bankrupt cannot be debarred from attending the voting at a general meeting so long as he remains a member, but he must vote in accordance with his trustee's direction.[10]

(3) Auditors

13–05   As has been seen, article 38 of Table A confers on an auditor the right to receive notice of meetings, and a similar provision is contained in the articles of most companies.

By section 390 of the 1985 Act, the auditors of a company shall be entitled to attend any general meeting of the company and to receive all notices of, and other communications relating to, any general meeting which a member of the company is entitled to receive, to attend any general meeting and to be heard at any general meeting which they attend on any part of the business of the meeting which concerns them as auditors.

An auditor who has been removed before the expiration of his term of office is entitled to notice either of the general meeting at which his term of office would have expired or of any general meeting at which it is proposed to fill the vacancy created by his removal.[11] If an auditor who has resigned has requisitioned a meeting under section 392A (relating to rights of resigning auditors) he is also entitled to notice of that meeting.[12]

---

[7] Table A, art. 31.
[8] 1985 Act, s.183(3).
[9] 1986 Act, s.315.
[10] *Morgan v. Gray* [1953] Ch. 83.
[11] 1985 Act, s.391(4).
[12] 1985 Act, s.392A(4).

(4) Members situated abroad

In spite of the vastly increased speed of travel and of communications, the law **13–06** remains that if a shareholder is beyond calling distance, he need not be given notice.[13]

Most articles of association reflect this principle; for example Table A, article 112 excepts from the requirement to be given notice a member whose registered address is not within the United Kingdom and who has not supplied to the company an address within the United Kingdom for the giving of notices to him.[14] Under the Listing Rules, quoted companies must send proxy forms to *all* persons entitled to vote.[15] Airmail must be used where available, when sending documents to holders of listed securities residing in countries which are not member states of the European Union.[16]

(5) Joint holders

Table A provides that in the case of joint holders all notices shall be given to the **13–07** joint holder whose name stands first in the register of members in respect of the joint holding and notice so given shall be sufficient notice to all the joint holders.[17]

In view of the way this article is now worded, it would be unwise for a company to act on a request to send the notice to a joint holder other than the first-named.

(6) As between transferor and transferee

Article 38 of Table A provides, in essence, that every member shall receive **13–08** notice. Section 22 of the 1985 Act provides that, to be a member, a person's name must be entered in the register. Therefore, if a person is entered in the register after notices have been despatched, he is not entitled to receive notice of the meeting. However, by article 114 of Table A every person who becomes entitled to a share shall be bound by any notice in respect of that share which, before his name is entered in the register, has been duly given to a person from whom he derives his title.[18]

(7) Persons excluded by the articles

It is quite permissible for articles to exclude particular categories of shareholders **13–09** from the right to receive notice of, to attend, and to vote at general meetings, or from any combination of these rights; this exclusion would normally be associated with a class of share having deferred rights.

---

[13] *Re Union Hill Silver Co.* (1870) 22 L.T. 400.
[14] See *Parkstone Ltd v. Gulf Guarantee Bank plc* [1990] B.C.L.C. 850, in relation to art. 131 of the 1948 Table A.
[15] Listing Rule LR9. See below, para. 14–19.
[16] Listing Rule LR9.
[17] Table A, art. 112.
[18] See para. 14–05, in relation to the rights which such an unregistered member may have. In relation to CREST, see paras. 13–02 and 14–06.

It should be noted, however, that by section 238 of the 1985 Act, copies of the annual accounts of a company and the directors' and auditors' reports and for listed companies a copy of the Operating and Financial Review, must be sent to every member, debenture holder and every person entitled to receive notice of meetings, not less than 21 days before the date of the meeting at which copies of those documents are to be laid. If a notice of a general meeting is printed with the accounts, it should contain a footnote or other mark, to the effect that it is sent only for information to the holders of shares who are not entitled to attend and vote at the meeting.

(8) Accidental omission to give notice

13–10   Care should be taken to ensure that a notice is sent to every member entitled to receive one; otherwise, the proceedings at the meeting may be invalid. A measure of relief is, however available. Table A, article 39, which is repeated in the articles of many companies, provides:

> **39.** The accidental omission to give notice of a meeting to, or the non-receipt of notice of a meeting by, any person entitled to receive notice shall not invalidate the proceedings at that meeting.

For instance, where a company registrar by accident failed to give notice of a meeting to nine shareholders, holding 101 shares out of a total issued capital of 692,718 shares, his omission was excused by the court and the meeting was held to be valid.[19] This type of article would not however apply if, for example, a large block of shareholders who had come on the register following a previous acquisition were inadvertently omitted. Nor does it apply where the decision not to give notice is deliberate, even if based on mistaken assumptions.[20] The onus of proof is on those claiming the omission was accidental.[21]

It is advisable to keep a record of the posting of notices in case service has to be proved in court.

(9) Force Majeure

13–11   In situations where the company is unable to send notices to a member whose registered address is situate in enemy territory, or the right to receive notices is suspended by operation of law, the company can carry on its business without serving notices on such members.[22]

In another case, however, the court granted an injunction restraining the holding of a meeting when the receipt of the notice and agenda by members had been delayed by a postal strike; it was held that in the then current circumstances the alternative methods used by the company in sending out the notices, although sanctioned by the company's articles, would still amount to ineffective service.[23]

[19] *Re West Canadian Collieries Ltd* [1962] Ch. 370.
[20] *Musselwhite v. Musselwhite (C.H.) Sons* [1962] Ch. 964.
[21] *POW Services Ltd v. Claire* [1995] 2 B.C.L.C. 435, at 450.
[22] *Re Anglo-International Bank* [1943] Ch. 233 (C.A.).
[23] *Bradman v. Trinity Estates,* [1989] 5 B.C.C. 33.

(b) Form of notice

Article 111 of Table A provides that any notice given to or by any person pursuant to the articles shall be in writing.[24] It is permissible to give notice electronically, to an email address or via a website (Companies Act 1985 (Electronic Communications) Order 2000). **13–12**

Under section 372(3) of the 1985 Act, in every notice calling a meeting of a company with a share capital there shall appear, with reasonable prominence, a statement that a member entitled to attend and vote is entitled to appoint a proxy or, where that is allowed, one or more proxies to attend and vote instead of him, and that a proxy need not also be a member.

With this exception, and subject to the requirements of the Listing Rules referred to below, there are no prescribed forms for notice of general meetings. They will usually follow a fairly standard pattern, with the type of resolution (for example "ordinary") being stated in the preamble to the text of the resolution; if an extraordinary or special resolution is proposed, the wording of the notice must specify the intention to propose the resolution as such, as required by section 378 of the 1985 Act.

As regards form, it is sufficient that the notice substantially complies with the articles.[25] Of course, it should state the date, place and hour of the meeting.

The notice will state by and on whose authority it is issued, and should be marked with the date on which it is intended to be despatched.

Precedents are contained in Chapter 19.

Stock Exchange requirements

Listing Rule LR9.3.3 provides that whenever holders of listed securities are sent a notice of meeting it should include all of the information needed to help them to exercise their rights. This means that an explanatory circular may have to accompany the notice. **13–13**

Any circular sent by a company to holders of its listed securities must (a) provide a clear and adequate explanation of its subject-matter and (b) if voting or other action is required, contain all information necessary to allow the holders of the securities to make a properly informed decision.

Listing Rule 9.3.6 governs the sending of proxy forms with notices of meetings.[26]

(c) Special business—main principles

In accordance with the principles discussed in Chapter 5, a notice convening a meeting at which any special business is to be transacted must state the nature thereof, otherwise the notice is irregular. The courts have, in the past, been firm in their application of this rule: **13–14**

Certain shareholders and directors entered into an agreement between themselves and the company whereby an action against the directors was dismissed,

---

[24] An exception is made for directors' meetings: see para. 22–04 below.
[25] *Re British Sugar Refining Co.* (1857) 3 K. J. 408.
[26] See para. 14–19.

certain shares were exchanged for debentures, and the capital of the company was reduced. The agreement was approved at a shareholders' meeting, but the notice convening the meeting did not state the effect of the agreement. The articles provided that in the case of special business the notice should state its general nature. Four years later, certain shareholders claimed that the issue of debentures was invalid. The House of Lords agreed, holding that the resolution approving the agreement was ineffective owing to the absence of notice of the contents of the agreement.[27]

The court was influenced by the fact that proxies of shareholders who before the meeting had no opportunity of knowing the contents of the agreement were used in support of the resolution.

Any business transacted outside the scope of the ordinary business, as defined, would be deemed special, and the nature of such special business would have to be set out in the notice convening the meeting:

A notice of a general meeting stated that it would be held for the purpose of receiving the directors' report and electing directors and auditors. The directors' report sent with the notice mentioned certain special business (the ratification of the previous election to the board of a director) not referred to in the notice. The notice and report together were held to be sufficient notice of this special business.[28]

Fullness and frankness are particularly important in situations of possible conflict of interest:

An extraordinary general meeting was convened to pass special resolutions authorising directors of a company to retain remuneration received by them as directors of a subsidiary. Neither the notice nor an accompanying circular stated the amount involved—£51,976 between the years 1907 and 1914—although the circular stated the basis on which the remuneration was calculated. The resolutions were passed, but were later set aside as invalid.[29]

It is not enough merely to refer to "special business" without giving some indication of the matters to be transacted.[30]

In brief, the company should give a clear explanation of important proposals which are placed before shareholders, and in return it is entitled to expect that shareholders will approach matters as practical men of business and that they know the relevant law.

(d) Special business—requirements of the articles

13–15   Articles of association will usually indicate what business transacted at a shareholders' meeting is to be regarded as special. Table A of the Companies Act 1948

---

[27] *Pacific Coast Coal Mines Ltd v. Arbuthnot* [1917] A.C. 607.
[28] *Boschoek Proprietary Co. Ltd v. Fuke* [1906] 1 Ch. 148.
[29] *Baillie v. Oriental Telephone, etc., Co., Ltd* [1915] 1 Ch. 503.
[30] *Wills v. Murray* (1850) 4 Ex. Reps. 843.

(article 52) provides that all business shall be deemed special that is transacted at an extraordinary general meeting, and also all that is transacted at an annual general meeting, with the exception of declaring a dividend, the consideration of the accounts, balance sheets, and the reports of directors and auditors, the election of directors in place of those retiring and the appointment of, and the fixing of the renumeration of, the auditors. Many companies' articles contain an article on these lines.

Table A of the 1985 Act adopted a new approach: article 38 simply states that the notice (of an annual general meeting and an extraordinary general meeting) shall specify the time and place of the meeting and the general nature of the business to be transacted and, in the case of an annual general meeting, shall specify the meeting as such. Many companies have adopted articles which follow this implicit abolition of the distinction between special and ordinary business, relying on the requirement that, whatever the type of business, the notice must indicate the general nature of the business to be transacted. Other companies have retained the list of exceptions contained in the old Table A, but have added extra items of ordinary business, for example the renewal of the authorities of the company in general meeting required in relation to the allotment of shares (under sections 80 and 89 of the 1985 Act).[31]

For special business which it is not thought convenient to add on to the AGM agenda, the directors may convene an extraordinary general meeting to follow on immediately after the close of the annual general meeting, but this will involve extra printing costs and, for a quoted company, the sending of additional proxy forms. If this course is adopted, the notice of the extraordinary general meeting will convene the meeting for, say, September 1, 2004 at 10.45 a.m. "or so soon thereafter as the annual general meeting of the company convened to be held at the same place and on the same date shall have been concluded or adjourned."

(e) Explanatory statement sent with notice

Where a notice and proposed resolution are not self-explanatory, it is customary 13–16 to circulate an explanatory statement with the notice. Indeed, the statement often forms the body of the document sent to members, with the notice of meeting contained in an appendix.

Where the company sends out an explanatory statement (perhaps under the provisions of Listing Rule 9.3.3, see para. 13–13), it must be compiled in good faith and be as complete as is necessary to enable the members to understand the position.

If the company is under some obligation which requires the resolution to be passed, the statement or circular must say so:

An agreement was made by a company with other parties, the fulfilment of which required the company to pass a certain resolution. Arising from litigation, the company was ordered by the court to perform the agreement, and the directors were ordered to recommend the shareholders to vote in favour of the resolution. Instead, they circulated to the shareholders counsel's

---

[31] The remaining business is deemed special, and there is then less risk of an ambush by shareholders because of the need for prior notice. See also para. 5–05.

opinion to the effect that the shareholders could vote as they wished. It was held that the meeting could not proceed since the circulars did not comply with undertakings given by the company to the court.[32]

(f) "Special notice"

13–17   It is proposed here to deal briefly with those situations where, for a resolution to be effective, special notice has to be given *to* the company, usually not less than 28 days before the meeting at which it is to be moved, under the provisions of section 379 of the 1985 Act.

The resolutions of which special notice has to be given to the company are:

(1) To remove a director by ordinary resolution under section 303(1) of the 1985 Act, or to appoint somebody instead of a director so removed at the meeting at which he is removed.[33]

(2) To appoint or approve the appointment of a director over the age of 70. Here, the notice given to the company and by the company to its members must state the age of the person to whom it relates.[34]

(3) In relation to auditors, resolutions:
  (a) filling a casual vacancy in the office of auditor[35]; or
  (b) reappointing as auditor a retiring auditor who was appointed by the directors to fill a casual vacancy[36]; or
  (c) removing an auditor before the expiration of his term of office[37]; or
  (d) appointing as auditor a person other than a retiring auditor.[38]

Procedure under section 379

13–18   Where by any provision of the 1985 Act special notice is required of a resolution, the resolution is not effective unless notice of the intention to move it has been given to the company at least 28 days before the meeting at which it is moved.[39] The company shall give its members notice of any such resolution at the same time and in the same manner as it gives notice of the meeting. If this is not practicable, the company must give its members notice of the resolution, either by advertisement in a newspaper having an appropriate circulation or in any other mode allowed by the articles, at least 21 days before the meeting.[40]

Where, after notice has been given to the company, a meeting is called for a date 28 days or less after it has been given, notice shall be deemed to have been properly given.

---

[32] *Northern Counties Securities v. Jackson Steeple* [1974] 1 W.L.R. 1133. This case was not followed in *Rackham v. Peek Foods Limited* [1990] B.C.L.C. 895 (where the contract was conditional on shareholders' approval).
[33] 1985 Act, s.303(2); see paras. 21–13 to 21–15 as to the procedure to be followed under s.303.
[34] 1985 Act, s.293(5). See paras. 21–06 to 21–08 as to procedure under the age limit provisions.
[35] 1985 Act, s.388(3).
[36] *ibid.*
[37] 1985 Act, s.391A.
[38] *ibid.*
[39] 1985 Act, s.379(1).
[40] 1985 Act, s.379(2).

It must be noted that section 379 merely confers on the members of a company the right to receive notice in the manner provided for by that section of any resolution of which special notice is required and has already been duly given, and which is to form part of the agenda to be dealt with at the relevant meeting. Section 379 does not confer on an individual member the right to compel the inclusion of a resolution in the agenda of a company meeting and the phrase in subsection (2) beginning "The company shall give its members notice" is merely part of the machinery designed to ensure that members generally have at least 21 days' notice of any resolution of which special notice is required:

> An attempt by a member of the Inland Waterways Association to remove the entire Council of the Association under the section (he had given the special notice called for by it) failed because the member, as a single member, did not have sufficient voting weight to be able to take advantage of section 376 and accordingly had no right to compel the inclusion of such an item on the agenda.[41]

On receipt of a notice of an intended resolution to fill a casual vacancy in the office of auditor, or re-appointing as auditor a retiring auditor who was appointed by the directors to fill a casual vacancy, notice has to be sent to the auditor proposed to be appointed or, if the casual vacancy was caused by the resignation of an auditor, to the auditor who resigned.[42] On receipt of notice of an intended resolution to remove an auditor or to appoint as auditor a person other than a retiring auditor, a copy has to be sent to the auditor proposed to be removed, or to the auditor proposed to be appointed and to the retiring auditor.[43] A retiring auditor or auditor proposed to be removed may make to the company, with respect to the intended resolution, written representations of a reasonable length, and request that they be notified to members. The company shall then, unless the representations are received too late for it to do so, in any notice of the resolution state that representations have been made and send a copy to every member to whom notice of the meeting is or has been sent. If the company defaults, or if the resolutions are received too late to be sent out, the auditor may require that they be read out at the meeting. The court may grant relief if satisfied that these rights are being abused to secure needless publicity for defamatory matter.[44]

(g) Manner of service

Notice to members of a company must be given in the manner prescribed by the articles. In theory, this may simply provide for notice by advertisement, but few articles now contain such a provision, which in any event would be inappropriate for a listed company in view of Stock Exchange requirements.   **13–19**

---

[41] *Pedley v. Inland Waterways Association Ltd* [1977] 1 All E.R. 209. See also *Professional Administration*, June 1981. p. 28, and *Fenning v. Fenning Environmental Products Ltd*, (1982) 79 L.S. Gaz. 803. For s.376, see paras. 13–25 to 13–29.
[42] 1985 Act, s.388(3) and (4).
[43] 1985 Act, s.391A(1) and (2).
[44] 1985 Act, s.391A(3)–(6).

In the absence of any provision in the articles, notice has to be served on every member in the manner in which notices are required to be served by the Table A currently in force.[45]

Under Table A of the 1985 Act:

> **112.** A notice may be given by the company to any member either personally or by sending it by post in a pre-paid envelope addressed to the member at his registered address or by leaving it at that address.[46]
>
> **113.** A member present, either in person or by proxy, at any meeting of the company or of the holders of any class or shares in the company, shall be deemed to have received notice of the meeting and, where requisite, of the purposes for which it was called.
>
> **115.** Proof that an envelope containing a notice was properly addressed, prepaid and posted shall be conclusive evidence that the notice was given. A notice shall be deemed to be given at the expiry of 48 hours after the envelope containing it was posted.[47]

"Posted" is taken to mean the placing of the envelope in the post, or delivery to an authorised official of the Post Office. When mail is posted in bulk for franking by the Post office, a certificate of posting should be obtained: reliance should not be placed on the postmark.

Where service has to be made by post, the address for service will be that appearing in the register of members. The register of members is prima facie evidence of any matters which are by the 1985 Act directed or authorised to be inserted in it.[48] A substantially accurate description of the address will suffice even though this may not be literally the address in the register.[49]

Under the provisions of the Companies Act 1985 (Electronic Communications) Order 2000) address can mean an address for the purposes of electronic communications. Delivery of a notice by electronic means such as by email or by posting of the notice on a website is sufficient to cover the obligations of the company.

(h) Length of notice

13–20   Section 369 of the 1985 Act prescribes the following periods of notice for a meeting of members (other than an adjourned meeting):

> (i) in the case of the annual general meeting, 21 days' notice in writing: and
>
> (ii) in the case of a meeting other than an annual general meeting or a meeting for the passing of a special resolution, 14 days' notice in writing (seven days' notice in writing in the case of an unlimited company).

---

[45] 1985 Act, s.370(2).

[46] The remainder of this article deals with joint holders and members outside the U.K. (see paras. 13–07 and 13–06).

[47] In some circumstances, where the senders of a notice know it has not been received, this type of deeming provision cannot be relied on: Re *Thundercrest Limited* [1994] B.C.C. 857; and see *In-House Lawyer*, November 1994, p. 30.

[48] 1985 Act, s.361.

[49] *Liverpool Marine Insurance Co. v. Haughton* (1874) 23 W.R. 93.

The articles may provide for a longer but not a shorter period than the period stated above. To the extent that no other provision is made in the articles, meetings may be called by the periods of notice mentioned in (i) and (ii) above.[50]

The provisions of section 369 are partly reflected in article 38 of Table A, which provides that an annual general meeting and an extraordinary general meeting called for the passing of a special resolution or a resolution appointing a person as a director shall be called by at least 21 clear days' notice. All other extraordinary meetings shall be called by at least 14 clear days' notice. The article goes on to provide for consent to short notice; this is considered below.

"Clear days" is defined by article 1 of Table A as meaning "that period excluding the day when the notice is given or deemed to be given and the day for which it is given or on which it is to take effect"; in this regard note also article 115 (see above, para. 13–18). In the absence of any provisions in the articles calling for clear days, it is established law, at least in England, that the words of the section mean clear days of notice.[51]

If the provisions of a draft companies bill published in March 2005 are adopted, then the notice period will be 14 days for all company meetings. However, it is not expected that these provisions will be in force before 2006.

(i) Consent to short notice

In general, if less than the prescribed period of notice is given, the meeting will be void. There have however for many years been exceptions to the starkness of this rule. For example, the short notice may be cured by the actual presence at the meeting of all the members. As Younger L.J. observed in *Re Express Engineering Works*, "if you have all the shareholders present, then all the requirements in connection with a meeting of the company are observed."[52] This principle has been extended to a situation where all members were present but some abstained:

13–21

> A meeting to pass a winding-up resolution was convened by notice which was one day short of the 14 days which were required under the articles. All five members attended the meeting and two of them voted 500 out of 1,000 votes in favour of the resolution, the other three members abstaining. Shortly afterwards one of the abstainers found out about the short notice, did nothing about it for over three years, and then challenged the validity of the liquidation. It was held that the true quality of the members' acts was to be judged not exclusively by reference to what they did at the meeting but also in the light of what they did and did not do thereafter. The challenge to the winding up therefore failed.[53]

This principle has been confirmed and enlarged by statute. Section 369(3) of the 1985 Act provides that a meeting can be called by a shorter notice than prescribed by section 369(2) or by the company's articles, if so agreed:

---

[50] 1985 Act, s.369(2). See para. 15–04 in relation to special resolutions.
[51] *Re Hector Whaling Ltd* [1936] Ch. 208. See also para. 5–10.
[52] [1920] 1 Ch. 466, 471. See also case cited in n. 49 of para. 5–13.
[53] *Re Bailey Hay Co. Ltd* [1971] 1 W.L.R. 1357.

> (i) in the case of a meeting called as the annual general meeting, by all the members entitled to attend and vote at it; and
>
> (ii) otherwise, by the requisite majority.

13–22   The requisite majority for this purpose is a majority in number of the members having a right to attend and vote at the meeting, being a majority together holding not less than 95 per cent in nominal value of the shares giving a right to attend and vote at the meeting, or, in the case of a company not having a share capital, together representing not less than 95 per cent of the total voting rights at that meeting of all the members.[54] Treasury shares held by the company should not be included in the calculation.

In relation to a company limited by shares, Table A article 38 reflects the above provisions. It should be observed that the requisite majority relates to 95 per cent of the shares giving a right to attend and vote, and not 95 per cent of the votes cast at the meeting.

The provisions relating to shorter notice by consent are widely used. The required consent of shareholders can be given, for example:

> (a) by a resolution passed at the meeting that the relevant provisions of section 369 or of the articles shall apply to the meeting;
>
> (b) by a separate document to the same effect signed by an appropriate number of shareholders; or
>
> (c) by the signature by a sufficient number of shareholders of a form of consent endorsed on the notice of meeting, to the following effect: "Pursuant to section 369 of the Companies Act 1985 (or, to article . . . of the company's articles of association), I, . . . a shareholder in the above company, hereby consent to the convening of the meeting referred to in this notice notwithstanding that it has been called by shorter notice than that prescribed by section 369 of the Act (or, by article . . . of the company's articles of association) . . . "

Consent to short notice can be given orally by a resolution passed on a show of hands, though this is rather less satisfactory.

13–23   It has been held that the consenting members must appreciate that the resolution is being passed without due notice, though such consent may be given later:

> A company sent to its members notice of an extraordinary general meeting to pass a resolution (number one) but omitted to give the full 21 days' notice. It later wished to add resolution number two and the shareholders at the meeting signed a consent to short notice of resolution number two. Subsequently, the company obtained the written consent of every shareholder to both resolutions. The court held that, for a valid short notice under the section, the members had to appreciate that the resolution was being passed on short notice and to agree to its being so passed with that consideration in their minds. In this case, those who signed the consent to resolution number two did not have it in mind that the notice for resolution number one was defective; that consent therefore did not cure the matter. However, in view of

---

[54] 1985 Act, s.369(3) and (4).

the subsequent 100 per cent consent, the court would not hear any of the shareholders to say that the resolution had not been validly passed.[55]

It will be noted that the short notice provisions of section 369 refer only to "members". It is not clear whether the absence of consent from others having the right to attend the meeting, for example auditors, would make any difference. On the face of it, it would appear that the absence of written consent of the auditors to short notice would not invalidate the meeting, but it might be otherwise where the meeting includes business of specific relevance to the auditors.[56] In view of this uncertainty, a company secretary would be well advised to ask the auditors to write a formal letter confirming they have no objection to the short notice.

In all instances, consent to short notice should be recorded in the minutes.

To take advantage of the section 369 procedure notice of some period, however short, must be given: the provisions do not operate in the total absence of notice.

It should finally be noted that a private company may elect by Elective Resolution that the provisions of section 369 shall have effect in relation to the company as if for the references to 95 per cent there were substituted references to such lesser percentage, but not less than 90 per cent, as may be specified in the resolution or subsequently determined by the company in general meeting.

3   POSTPONEMENT OR CANCELLATION; *FORCE MAJEURE*

Once a general meeting has been convened upon due notice, it cannot be **13–24** postponed or cancelled. The correct procedure, where the purpose for which a meeting has been convened has ceased to exist, is to hold the meeting as convened and adjourn it *sine die* without putting the resolution to the members. A purported cancellation will not be valid:

> A notice was issued postponing a general meeting already called. In the belief that the attempted postponement was illegal, an aggrieved director advertised the meeting in the press for the same date as previously arranged. He, with several other shareholders, attended this meeting, and resolutions were approved re-electing himself as a director, refusing to re-appoint another director, and adjourning the meeting to the date of the postponed meeting. The resolutions were held to be valid, for in the absence of express authority in the articles the directors of a company have no power to postpone a general meeting properly convened.[57]

The court may intervene to cancel a meeting if there is evidence of irregularity—for example, a meeting called by directors who had not been properly appointed.[58]

---

[55] *Re Pearce Duff Co. Ltd* [1960] 1 W.L.R. 1014.
[56] See 1985 Act, s.390.
[57] *Smith v. Paringa Mines Ltd* [1906] 2 Ch. 193.
[58] *Harben v. Phillips* (1883) 23 Ch.D. 14.

An example of *force majeure* would be the destruction, by terrorist attack, of the proposed venue. In that situation the company should choose an alternative meeting place and inform members as speedily as possible, in writing and by newspaper advertisement. The meeting must be formally opened at the initial venue, with a quorum of members, and formally adjourned to the new meeting place.

4   CIRCULATION OF MEMBERS' RESOLUTIONS AND STATEMENTS

13–25   Section 376 of the 1985 Act lays down a procedure by which members can, by requisition, bring forward resolutions and have statements circulated. It provides that any number of members representing not less than one-twentieth of the total voting rights of all the members having at the date of the requisition a right to vote at the meeting to which the requisition relates,[59] or not less than 100 members holding shares in the company on which there has been paid up an average sum, per member, of not less than £100,[60] may requisition the company in writing:

(a) to give to members of the company entitled to receive notice of the next annual general meeting notice of any resolution which may properly be moved and is intended to be moved at that meeting[61];

(b) to circulate to members entitled to have notice of any general meeting sent to them any statement of not more than 1,000 words with respect to the matter referred to in any proposed resolution or the business to be dealt with at that meeting.[62]

The effect of the above provisions is that in the case of an annual general meeting the requisitionists may require a resolution to be placed on the agenda and the circulation of a statement, or just the circulation of a statement. In the case of any other meeting, requisitionists are entitled to have a statement circulated relating to any matter pending before that meeting.

13–26   Notice of the requisitioned resolution must be given and the statement circulated by serving a copy on members entitled to receive notice of the meeting in any manner permitted for service of notice. Notice of any such resolution (but no action is here required in respect of statements) must also be given to any other member (*i.e.* one not entitled to receive notice, such as in some companies a preference shareholder), by giving notice of the general effect of the resolution in any manner permitted for service of notice. The copy or notice of the effect of the resolution must be served or given in the same manner and (so far as practicable) at the same time as notice of the meeting, or as soon thereafter as practicable.[63]

Notwithstanding anything in the articles, the business which may be dealt with at an annual general meeting includes any resolution of which notice is given under

---

[59] 1985 Act, s.376(2)(*a*).
[60] 1985 Act, s.376(2)(*b*).
[61] 1985 Act, s.376(1)(*a*).
[62] 1985 Act, s.376(1)(*b*).
[63] 1985 Act, s.376(4) and (5).

the section; and notice is deemed to have been given under the section notwithstanding the accidental omission in giving it, of one or more members.[64]

The company is not bound to give notice of a resolution or circulate a statement unless a copy of the requisition signed by the requisitionists (or two or more copies which between them contain the signatures of all the requisitionists) is deposited at the registered office of the company: (1) in the case of a requisition requiring notice of a resolution, not less than six weeks before the meeting (in this case, the annual general meeting) and (2) otherwise, not less than one week before the meeting.[65] If after a copy of a requisition requiring notice of a resolution has been deposited an annual general meeting is called for a date six weeks or less after deposit, the copy of the requisition is deemed to have been properly deposited.[66] There must be deposited or tendered with the requisition a sum reasonably sufficient to meet the company's expenses in giving effect to it.[67]

The resolution may cover any relevant matter which is *intra vires* the company and can be an ordinary or special resolution. The court can on application by the company or by an aggrieved person order that the company is not bound to circulate a statement if it is satisfied that the section is being abused to secure needless publicity for defamatory matter, and can order the company's costs on such an application to be paid in whole or in part by the requisitionists.[68]

There is a fine for failure by any officer of the company to comply with the provisions of the section.

Practical points

The rights of shareholders under section 376 are often closely linked with their power under section 368[69] to requisition the directors to convene an extraordinary general meeting. The two sections can be compared as follows: **13–27**

(1) The total voting rights required to support a requisition under section 376 are only half those required under section 368, and in addition section 376, unlike section 368, can be invoked by 100 members who have paid up £100 on average on their shares—quite a low requirement in the case of many public companies.

(2) Under section 368, the company pays; under section 376, the requisitionists pay (unless the company otherwise resolves), but since the requisition, if delivered in good time, usually means simply that additional material is added to the notice of the meeting, the cost is unlikely to be great. Members relying on section 376 could require a statement to be circulated between the issue of the notice for an annual general meeting or extraordinary general meeting and its being held, provided the requisition was deposited at the registered office not less than one

---

[64] 1985 Act, s.376(6). See also para. 13–10.
[65] 1985 Act, s.377(1)(*a*).
[66] 1985 Act, s.377(2).
[67] 1985 Act, s.377(1)(*b*). This could cost the requisitionists dearly if, for example the proxy forms for the AGM had already been printed when the requisition was lodged.
[68] 1985 Act, s.377(3).
[69] See above, paras. 12–10 to 12–13, and below, para. 19–31 where an example of a requisitioned meeting is given.

week before the meeting; this would be expensive. A requisitioned resolution can of course contain a sub-clause that the expenses incurred in giving effect to the requisition shall be defrayed by the company.

(3) Under section 376, the company may try and obstruct the requisitionists by alleging defamation. No such specific provision exists under section 368.

(4) In the case of the circulation of statements under section 376 an alternative exists in the event of failure: the dissenting members can obtain a copy of the company's register of members (a right given under section 356)[70] and themselves circulate their statement. No simple alternative to section 368 exists.

Precedents

(1) The requisition

13–28   The following is a precedent for a requisition by a hundred or more shareholders, under section 376, relating to an intended resolution and with a statement in support:

REQUISITION UNDER SECTION 376 OF THE COMPANIES ACT 1985

To the Directors of No Saints plc

We, the undersigned, being [not less than 100] members holding shares in the company on which there has been paid up an average sum, per member, of not less than £100, hereby require you, in accordance with section 376 of the Companies Act 1985, to give to members of the company entitled to receive notice of the next annual general meeting (herein called "the members receiving notice") notice of the following ordinary resolution being a resolution which may properly be moved and is intended to be moved at that meeting, and to circulate to the members receiving notice the annexed statement (which is a statement of not more than 1,000 words) with respect to the matter referred to in the proposed resolution:

ORDINARY RESOLUTION

THAT the Company shall forthwith affiliate to the Work-rate Association.

STATEMENT IN SUPPORT

[Not more than 1,000 words]

Signed: ....[address]

.... ["   ]

(and at least 98 others[71])

Dated .... (at least six weeks before annual general meeting).

---

[70] See para. 19–31.

[71] In this case of joint shareholders, all must sign the requisition: *Patent Wood Keg Syndicate Ltd v. Pearse* [1906] W.N. 164. It would be wise for the requisitionists to count them as one.

(2) The response

If the requisition is received in good time, the company will simply add the **13–29** resolution to the notice of the meeting and proxy form and will, at the same time, circulate the statement in support, probably as a separate document. The notice could be amended by adding an item on the following lines:

> "To consider the following resolution intended to be moved at the meeting, notice of which is given by the company pursuant to section 376 of the Companies Act 1985 on the requisition of certain members."

It will be observed that the company may reply in any way it thinks fit and is not limited to 1,000 words. In addition, the company can take the opportunity to table a resolution of its own, urging shareholders to support it and to reject the requisitioned resolution. If, as sometimes happens, the requisition is received at the registered office within the statutory time limit of six weeks before the annual general meeting but after the report and accounts have gone to the printers, a separate document can be prepared and inserted into the envelope carrying the report and accounts. This may be a three page document: the first page carries a note of explanation from the chairman; the second page will set out the statement by the requisitionists; and the third page will contain a notice of the additional business, as follows:

No saints plc

Notice of resolution

Notice is hereby given, upon the requisition of certain members pursuant **13–30** to the provisions of section 376 of the Companies Act 1985, that No Saints plc has been advised of an intention to move the following resolution, as an ordinary resolution, at the annual general meeting of the members of the company to be held on......, at...... am./pm.:

THAT the Company shall forthwith affiliate to the Work-rate Association.

A member entitled to be present and vote at the above meeting may appoint a proxy [or proxies] to attend and vote instead of him and such proxy need not be a member of the company. A form of proxy is enclosed.

By order of the board, upon requisition pursuant to section 376 of the Companies Act 1985,

....Secretary

No Saints plc
Registered No. .... England.
Registered Office.........
....

Dated......,

5   CHAIRMAN

13–31   The appointment of the chairman is regulated by the articles which also usually provide for the appointment of a deputy, and for the position arising should neither the chairman nor his deputy arrive in time for the meeting.

The articles commonly provide that the chairman of the board of directors shall preside at general meetings of the company. Table A provides as follows:

> **42.** The chairman, if any, of the board of directors or in his absence some other director nominated by the directors shall preside as chairman of the meeting, but if neither the chairman nor such other director (if any) be present within fifteen minutes after the time appointed for holding the meeting and willing to act, the directors present shall elect one of their number to be chairman and, if there is only one director present and willing to act, he shall be chairman.
>
> **43.** If no director is willing to act as chairman, or if no director is present within fifteen minutes after the time appointed for holding the meeting, the members present and entitled to vote shall choose one of their number to be chairman.

In the absence of any provision in the articles, any member elected by the members present at a meeting may be chairman of it.[72]

A difficulty can arise where there are no directors and disputed entitlement to vote:

> B's capital consisted of ordinary and preference shares. The ordinary and preference shareholders disputed each other's right to vote at an EGM. The company had no directors. It had an article similar to article 43 of Table A (see above). The first task of the members at the EGM was therefore to elect a chairman; without one, no business could be done. The solicitor for one of the parties declared that he would act as temporary chairman for the purpose only of supervising the election of a proper chairman. Each faction then put up a nominee; the solicitor ruled that only the preference shareholders were entitled to vote and he declared their nominee elected. The ordinary shareholders withdrew; in their absence resolutions were passed which they subsequently challenged. The court held that the right way to construe B's articles was to hold that the election of a chairman should be entrusted to those members present, in person or by proxy, who were entitled to vote and that (notwithstanding an article similar to article 58 of Table A—see para. 14–06 below) whatever may be the ruling of a self-appointed chairman at the time, that question is open to challenge, in later proceedings, within the limits within which the court will interfere with the internal affairs of companies.[73] In such a case a mere proxy-holder can be chairman.[74]

For an analysis of the duties of the chairman, see Chapter 6.

---

[72] 1985 Act, s.370(5).
[73] *Re Bradford Investments* [1991] B.C.L.C. 224, 229.
[74] *ibid.*

6 QUORUM

A quorum must be present for the valid transaction of business at a general **13–32** meeting. Usually, this will be prescribed by the company's articles, but in the absence of any provision two members personally present are a quorum.[75]

In the case of a single-member company, one person present in person or by proxy shall be a quorum whatever the articles may state.[76]

Table A provides:

> **40.** No business shall be transacted at any meeting unless a quorum is present. Two persons entitled to vote upon the business to be transacted, each being a member or a proxy for a member or a duly authorised representative of a corporation, shall be a quorum.
>
> **41.** If such a quorum is not present within half an hour from the time appointed for the meeting, or if during a meeting such quorum ceases to be present, the meeting shall stand adjourned to the same day in the next week at the same time and place or such time and place as the directors may determine.

The above articles provide for an adjourned meeting (at which the quorum again has to be two), but it is likely that words stating that if at the adjourned meeting a quorum is not present within half an hour from the appointed time the members[77] present shall be a quorum will remain part of the articles of a large number of companies since those words were in previous versions of Table A. The wording of article 41 can produce a rather rigid result: it seems clear that if a quorum is not present, or ceases to be present, at the first meeting then that meeting has to be adjourned to *the same day* in the next week. If no quorum is then present, the meeting fails. The directors thus have no discretion to choose a different day (or even a later time on the same day as the first meeting) for the adjourned meeting; this deprives them of the power either to adjourn the meeting for a longer interval than a week, giving them the chance to issue a fresh notice (even though one might not strictly be required under article 45—see para. 14–29), or, at the other extreme, to adjourn the meeting for a few hours, relying on those members actually present to form a quorum (as they would have done under previous versions of Table A). The point is worth bearing in mind when articles are drafted.

To the extent that the articles do give the directors any discretion over the date, time and place of the adjourned meeting, they have to act reasonably.[78]

Where the articles provide for a quorum to be present "at the time when the meeting proceeds to business," the prescribed number must be present at the start of the meeting but it is not necessary for this situation to be maintained throughout

---

[75] 1985 Act, s.370(4).

[76] 1985 Act, s.370A.

[77] Probably including a single member present in person or by proxy, provided that at least one other person is present by proxy: see *Daimler Co. Ltd v. Continental Tyre and Rubber Co. (Great Britain) Ltd* [1916] 2 A.C. 307, 325 and Palmer's Company Law para. 7.605.

[78] *Byng v. London Life Association Limited* [1989] 1 All E.R. 560, C.A.; and see para. 6–16, above.

the proceedings. This constitutes an exception to the general rule, and was so decided by the court only with reluctance.[79]

13–33   If articles provide for a quorum of persons "present in person or by proxy," persons present by proxy can obviously be included. If however the quorum is to consist of persons present "in person" there must be a physical presence either of the individual shareholder or of a company through its representative appointed under section 375 of the 1985 Act.

Three Scottish cases illustrate the above points:

> One of two persons required to be present in person for a quorum was absent in America and was represented by her attorney. It was held that a quorum was not present (*Harris*).[80]

> A company's articles provided that two or more members present in person or by proxy should form a quorum. One member was personally present and, in addition to his personal ownership, he acted for two trusts of which he was the first-named trustee and also held a proxy for another shareholder. He formally moved the resolution and thereafter, as proxy for another member, seconded the motion. *Held*, there was no quorum (*Prain*).[81]

> On the other hand, in a case where the articles required three members to be personally present as a quorum and two persons attended the meeting, one as an individual member and also as a trustee, it was held that as this person attended in a dual capacity a quorum was present (*McLeod*).[82]

13–34   The above cases are not easy to reconcile; the meeting in *Prain's* case probably failed to attain validity because it was in effect a meeting of one person, whereas in *McLeod's* case two people were physically present. In *Prain's* case, LordMoncrieff thought that "a meeting at which only one member is present to play multiple parts may be thought to be nothing other than a pantomime".

If the provisions in a company's articles as to quorum are abused, for example, by a shareholder deliberately failing to be present so as to frustrate the intended business through want of a quorum, the court may intervene under section 371 of the 1985 Act and fix a quorum which will get round the problem—perhaps that one member present in person or by proxy shall be sufficient.[83]

---

[79] *Re Hartley Baird* [1955] Ch. 143. See para. 6–05 for the general rule.
[80] *Re Harris Ltd, Petitioners*, 1956 S.C. 207.
[81] *Prain Sons Ltd, Petitioners*, 1947 S.C. 325.
[82] *McLeod (Neil) Sons, Petitioners*, 1967 S.C. 16. See also cases referred to in para. 6–03.
[83] *Re H. R. Paul Son Ltd* (1973) 118 S.J. 166 and *Re Opera Photographic* [1989] 5 B.C.C. 601. See para. 12–16.

CHAPTER 14

MEMBERS' MEETINGS: ATTENDANCE AND VOTING

1   CORPORATION REPRESENTATIVES

A corporation may, if it is a member of another corporation being a company **14–01** within the meaning of the 1985 Act, by resolution of its directors or other governing body[1] authorise such person as it thinks fit to act as its representative at any meeting of the company or at any meeting of any class of members of the company.[2] Similarly such a corporation may, if it is a creditor (including a holder of debentures) of another corporation, being a company within the meaning of the Act, by such a resolution appoint a representative at any meeting of any creditors of the company held in pursuance of the Act or of rules made thereunder or in pursuance of the provisions contained in any debenture or trust deed.[3]

It will be noted that the corporation having the power to appoint a representative under either provision need not be a company within the meaning of the Act. Thus a foreign company, for example, could take advantage of the section.

A person so appointed can exercise the same powers on behalf of the corporation which he represents as that corporation could exercise if it were an individual shareholder, creditor or debenture-holder of that other company.[4] This includes the power to speak at the meeting and to vote on a show of hands[5] and on a poll. He is entitled to only one vote on a show of hands even if he acts in the dual capacity of member and corporation representative.[6] He is to be counted in the quorum.

Section 375 does not allow a company to appoint more than one representative for a particular meeting (although an alternative person in the absence of the first-named representative is permitted.)

A specimen form of resolution is appended: **14–02**

UNITED LIMITED
CERTIFIED COPY OF RESOLUTION OF THE BOARD OF DIRECTORS

RESOLVED: THAT Mr......, or, failing him Mr......, be and he is hereby appointed to act as the representative of the company, pursuant to section 375

---

[1] "Other governing body" can include a liquidator: *Hillman v. Crystal Bowl Amusements and Others* [1973] 1 W.L.R. 162, C.A.
[2] 1985 Act, s.375(1)(*a*).
[3] 1985 Act, s.375(1)(*b*). Reference to "the Act" here includes the relevant parts of the 1986 Act—see s.735A of the 1985 Act.
[4] 1985 Act, s.375(2).
[5] *Re Kelantan Coconut Estates Ltd and Reduced* (1920) 64 Sol.J. 700.
[6] See Table A, art. 54.

of the Companies Act 1985, at the annual general meeting of No Saints plc to be held on...... and at any adjournment thereof.

> I hereby certify that the above is a true copy of a resolution of the board of directors of United Limited passed on ....
>
> ....
>
> Secretary
> United Limited

[Address]   [Date]

The certified copy is usually retained by the company of which the corporation is a member as evidence of the representative's right to be present and vote at the meeting.

The resolution sometimes refers to the appointee as the holder of an office such as director, secretary or assistant secretary. In such cases, it is usual for the person attending the proposed meeting to have, in addition to a copy of the resolution, a certificate from the appointing corporation that he is the holder of that particular office; furthermore, where a shareholding company appoints several persons as alternative representatives care should be taken by the company at whose meeting representatives are present to ensure that only one of the alternates attends the meeting or, if by courtesy of the chairman more than one is allowed to be present, only one votes.

In practice, the representative is sometimes not asked to produce the authority under which he acts, and the validity of a resolution passed at such a meeting could not be questioned merely for the reason that the chairman did not ask for the production of the authority.

Conversely, the company may be concerned to ascertain that the representative has been properly authorised; he may not be able to produce evidence that the relevant board resolution of the member corporation to appoint him as its representative had been duly passed. As the effect of the section is that passing the resolution confers the authority, the company may be unwise to debar the representative from attending and voting unless it has, after careful enquiry, formed the view that no resolution had been passed.[7]

One advantage to a shareholder which is a company of appointing a representative under section 375 rather than submitting a proxy in favour of the chairman of the meeting is that the member may, by using section 375, wait until the meeting before deciding which way to vote.[8]

---

[7] In a New Zealand case, the court held that a corporate representative was not required to produce evidence at the meeting that a valid board resolution had been passed: *Maori Development Corporation Limited v. Power Boat International Limited* (1995) 2 N.Z.L.R. 568.

[8] *Administrator*, September 1987, p. 5.

2 VOTING

(a) In general

A company has little or no influence over how its members use their right to **14–03** vote. It is, broadly speaking, not entitled to look behind the bare fact of legal ownership, as recorded in its register, where no notice of any trust, expressed, implied or constructive shall be entered.[9] Even the court has no power to invalidate a vote on the ground that the member did not exercise it in the best interests of the company or because he was tainted by a conflict of interest.[10]

One exception to the above is where a majority attempt, by a vote at a general meeting, to consummate a fraud on the minority—for example, by sanctioning the sale to themselves, at an undervalue, of company property: this will be disallowed.[11]

The court, too, will restrain a shareholder, by injunction, from voting against a resolution where a failure to pass the resolution would bring about the immediate insolvency of the company.[12]

As the following cases illustrate, the freedom of a shareholder to vote in his own interest extends even to a shareholder who is also a director, except where the director is in breach of his fiduciary duty:

> A director was held to be entitled to vote as a shareholder even though his interest in the subject matter was opposed to the interests of the company.[13]

> Where, however, votes were cast in respect of shares issued by the directors themselves or their friends for the purpose or securing the passing of certain resolutions, this was held to be in conflict with the principle that the powers entrusted to the board must be exercised bona fide and in the interest of the company.[14]

> Where three directors of a company obtained a contract in their own names and at a general meeting, by their votes as holders of three-quarters of the issued shares, passed a resolution declaring that the company had no interest in the contract, the resolution was declared invalid as the contract belonged in equity to the company, and the action of the directors amounted to a breach of trust.[15]

While, as between the company and the member, the company has little **14–04** influence (with the exceptions discussed) over the way a member votes, the

[9] 1985 Act, s.360. See also para. 14–05 below.
[10] *East Pant Du United Lead Mining Co. v. Merryweather* (1864) 2 H. M. 254.
[11] *Menier v. Hooper's Telegraph Works* (1874) L.R. 9 Ch. 350. See also para. 7–29.
[12] *Standard Chartered Bank v. Walker* [1992] B.C.L.C. 603.
[13] *North-West Transportation Co. v. Beatty* (1887) 12 App.Cas. 589.
[14] *Punt v. Symonds Co. Ltd* [1903] 2 Ch. 506. See also *Fraser v. Whalley* (1864) 2 H. M. 10.
[15] *Cook v. Deeks* [1916] 1 A.C. 554.

member can freely bind himself by contract to a third party to vote, or not to vote, in a particular way:

> Where shareholders undertook, on a sale of part of the shares held by them, to vote to the office of director of the company a nominee of the purchaser, the agreement was held to be enforceable against both parties.[16]

> In another case, a mandatory injunction was granted compelling the holder of shares to give effect to an agreement to vote in accordance with the wishes of the plaintiff.[17]

> In a case where the owner of fully-paid shares charged them in favour of another person, and gave a blank transfer in respect of the charge, and the owner subsequently became bankrupt, he was held to be entitled to vote so long as his name remained on the register, though, as between himself and the mortgagees, he could only vote as they dictated.[18]

If the contracting party fails to vote in accordance with his agreement, the company must still accept the vote, leaving the aggrieved party to sue the other party to the contract.

(b) Qualification to vote

14–05   The register of members constitutes evidence of the right of a member to vote. The register of members must contain the names and addresses of members, the dates on which they were registered as and ceased to be members, a statement of the shares held by each member with their distinguishing numbers (if any), and details of the class of share and the amount paid or agreed to be considered as paid on each.[19]

The register, however, is only prima facie evidence of matters recorded in it, and section 359 of the 1985 Act permits an application to the court for rectification if the name of any person is entered in or omitted from a company's register of members without sufficient cause.[20]

There is apparently nothing to prevent a person who becomes a member between the dates of an original and adjourned meeting attending and voting at the adjourned meeting. Further, a vendor of shares who remains the holder of them after the contract for sale retains the right to vote in respect of those shares; he should however exercise his vote in accordance with directions given by the purchaser, except where he remains unpaid, in which event his position is analogous to that of a mortgagee and he may disregard the purchaser's instructions to the extent that his right to recover the purchase price is thereby prejudiced.[21]

In private companies, directors sometimes refuse to register transfers; in that case, there is nothing to stop the transferor and transferee entering into a separate

---

[16] *Greenwell v. Porter* [1902] 1 Ch. 530. But see *Wilton Group v. Abrams* [1991] B.C.L.C. 315.
[17] *Puddephatt v. Leith* [1916] 1 Ch. 200.
[18] *Wise v. Lansdell* [1921] 1 Ch. 420. See also *Siemens Bros. v. Burns* [1918] 2 Ch. 324, C.A.
[19] 1985 Act, s.352(2), (3).
[20] See also *POW Services v. Clare* [1995] 2 B.C.L.C. 435, 449.
[21] *Musselwhite v. C.H. Musselwhite Son Ltd* [1962] Ch. 964.

agreement that the transferor, while he remains on the register, will vote in accordance with the directions of the transferee; this can be supplemented by the transferor agreeing to appoint the transferee as his proxy at general meetings, and to forward notice and other documents to the transferee as soon as they are received.

The relevant provisions of Table A are as follows:

54. Subject to any rights or restrictions attached to any shares, on a show of hands every member who (being an individual) is present in person or (being a corporation) is present by a duly authorised representative, not being himself a member entitled to vote, shall have one vote, and on a poll every member shall have one vote for every share of which he is the holder.[22]

A clause in the articles similar to the above would exclude a member present by proxy from voting on a show of hands (but there is no reason in principle why the articles should not permit a proxy-holder to vote on a show of hands).

55. In the case of joint holders the vote of the senior who tenders a vote, whether in person or by proxy, shall be accepted to the exclusion of the votes of the other joint holders; and seniority shall be determined by the order in which the names of the holders stand in the register of members.

The first joint holder thereby has power to give a proxy. Where articles (such as article 55 above) vest in the first joint holder power to vote, the remaining joint holders could attend the meeting, but they would not be allowed to vote.

Joint holders can, however, have their holdings split into two or more joint holdings with their names in different orders.[23]

By article 56, a member in respect of whom an order has been made by any court having jurisdiction in matters concerning mental disorder may vote by his receiver, *curator bonis* or other authorised person.

57. No member shall be entitled to vote at any general meeting or at any separate meeting of the holders of any class of shares in the company, either in person or by proxy, in respect of any share held by him unless all moneys presently payable by him in respect of that share have been paid.

To ensure that difficulties and objections are dealt with promptly, Table A provides that:

58. No objection shall be raised to the qualification of any voter except at the meeting or adjourned meeting at which the vote objected to is tendered, and every vote not disallowed at the meeting shall be valid. Any objection made in due time shall be referred to the chairman whose decision shall be final and conclusive.

---

[22] In the absence of any provision in the articles, under s.370(6) of the 1985 Act, in the case of a company originally having a share capital every member is entitled to one vote in respect of each share or each £10 of stock held by him.

[23] *Burns v. Siemens Brothers Dynamo Works Ltd* [1919] 1 Ch. 225.

(c) Qualification—CREST

14–06   In December 1995 there came into force the Uncertificated Securities Regulations 1995 (S.I. 1995 No. 3272), in order to facilitate the introduction of a new electronic system, CREST, which permits title to certain listed shares to be evidenced and transferred without a written instrument.

Regulation 34(1) provides that for the purposes of determining which persons are entitled to attend or vote at a meeting, and how many votes such persons may cast, the participating issuer (company) may specify in the notice of the meeting a time, not more than 48 hours before the time fixed for the meeting, by which a person must be entered on the relevant register of securities in order to have the right to attend or vote at the meeting. Changes to entries on the relevant register of securities after the time specified by virtue of Regulation 34(1) shall be disregarded in determining the rights of any person to attend or vote at the meeting, notwithstanding any provisions in any enactment, articles of association or other instrument to the contrary.

The purpose of the Regulations is to fix a moment in time at which, on a constantly changing register, voting rights are determined.

Further reference to this topic is made in para. 13–02 and a suggested statement for inclusion in the notice of an AGM is contained in para. 19–09.

(d) Show of hands

14–07   As has been seen, article 54 provides that on a show of hands every member present shall have one vote. This provision is standard form in company articles, and it follows the natural, basic way in which, at common law, the sense of a meeting is obtained.[24] The duty of the chairman, therefore, is to count carefully the hands held up: he can ask for assistance from scrutineers or tellers, or from the secretary.[25] He pays no regard to the number of shares held by each member present and he endeavours to ensure that those present solely as proxy-holders do not vote.[26] Then he declares the result.

14–08   Article 47 provides that unless a poll is duly demanded a declaration by the chairman that a resolution has been carried or carried unanimously, or by a particular majority, or lost, or not carried by a particular majority, and an entry to that effect in the minutes of the meeting shall be conclusive evidence of the fact without proof of the number or proportion of the votes recorded in favour of or against the resolution.

(e) Poll

14–09   The value of a poll lies in the fact that the weighted voting strengths may be more accurately assessed. Section 374 of the 1985 Act provides too that on a poll taken at a meeting of a company or a meeting of any class of members of a

---

[24] See para. 7–19.

[25] The chairman should go through the formality of asking for a show of hands, even if there appears to be no opposition: *The Citizens Theatre Limited* [1946] S.C. 14. See also *Fraserburgh Commercial Company Limited* [1946] S.C. 444.

[26] 1985 Act, s.372(2)(*c*). The particular articles may, exceptionally, allow proxy holders to vote on a show of hands.

company, a member entitled to more than one vote need not, if he votes, use all his votes or cast all the votes he uses in the same way. This facilitates voting by nominee shareholders.

The common law right to demand a poll has been given statutory effect. Section 373 of the 1985 Act provides that the right to demand a poll at a general meeting on any question other than the election of the chairman of the meeting or the adjournment of the meeting cannot be excluded by the company's articles. The section also provides that the articles may not make ineffective a demand for a poll by not less than five members having the right to vote at the meeting, or members representing not less than one-tenth of the total voting rights or one-tenth of the total sum paid up on all the shares conferring the right to vote.

These provisions apply to all general meetings, and to ordinary, special and extraordinary resolutions.

A proxy holder has the right to demand or join in demanding a poll.[27]

The provisions of Table A (which are more liberal than the limits prescribed by section 373) are as follows:

46. A resolution put to the vote of a meeting shall be decided on a show of hands unless before, or on the declaration of the result of, the show of hands a poll is duly demanded. Subject to the provisions of the Act, a poll may be demanded—
  (a) by the chairman, or
  (b) by at least two members having the right to vote at the meeting; or
  (c) by a member or members representing not less than one-tenth of the total voting rights of all the members having the right to vote at the meeting; or
  (d) by a member or members holding shares conferring a right to vote at the meeting being shares on which an aggregate sum has been paid up equal to not less than one-tenth of the total sum paid up on all the shares conferring that right;
and a demand by a person as proxy for a member shall be the same as a demand by the member.

A chairman of a meeting is under no obligation to inform shareholders of their rights, under the articles, to demand a poll.[28]

By article 48, the demand for a poll may, before the poll is taken, be withdrawn **14–10** but only with the consent of the chairman. The article provides that a demand so withdrawn shall not be taken to have invalidated the result of a show of hands declared before the demand was made.[29] (If, on the other hand, a poll is demanded before the declaration of the result of a show of hands and the demand is duly withdrawn, the last sentence of article 51 provides that the meeting shall continue as if the demand had not been made).

---

[27] 1985 Act, s.373(2).
[28] *Re Hockerill Athletic Club Limited* [1990] B.C.L.C. 921.
[29] This reverses what would otherwise be the position: see *R. v. Cooper* (1870) L.R. 5 Q.B. 457, para. 7–20, n. 20.

Subject to the articles, a poll can be validly demanded without going through the formality of a show of hands.[30]

Where the chairman has the right to demand a poll, he must exercise it in the interests of the whole body over whom he presides, including those who have chosen to vote by proxy:

> At a meeting of debenture stockholders, a resolution had to be passed by a three-quarters majority. The state of the proxies was such that if a poll were demanded and the proxies used for the purpose of the vote, the necessary three-quarters majority could not be obtained. The chairman therefore decided not to demand a poll after a show of hands had passed the resolution with the necessary majority. It was held that the chairman should have demanded a poll and then voted the proxies in accordance with the instructions they contained, so as to ascertain the true sense of the meeting.[31]

Another occasion when the chairman should ask for a poll is where new material has been added to the agenda for the meeting after the notices have been sent out; by demanding a poll (to be held at a later date) the chairman may enable members to take the new factors into account by lodging proxies prior to the poll.[32]

14–11 A poll must be conducted in the manner laid down by the articles. Table A provides:

> **49.** A poll shall be taken as the chairman directs and he may appoint scrutineers (who need not be members) and fix a time and place for declaring the result of the poll. The result of the poll shall be deemed to be the resolution of the meeting at which the poll was demanded.
> **51.** A poll demanded on the election of a chairman or on a question of adjournment shall be taken forthwith. A poll demanded on any other question shall be taken either forthwith or at such time and place as the chairmen directs not being more than 30 days after the poll is demanded. The demand for a poll shall not prevent the continuance of a meeting for the transaction of any business other than the questions on which the poll was demanded . . .
> **59.** On a poll votes may be given either personally or by proxy. A member may appoint more than one proxy to attend on the same occasion.

14–12 Many difficulties as to a poll at company meetings relate to the interpretation of the articles. The following are examples:

> The articles of a company provided that if a poll should be demanded, it should be taken "in such manner as the chairman shall direct." A poll having been demanded at a meeting summoned to consider a resolution for a voluntary winding up, the chairman directed the poll to be taken then and

---

[30] *Holmes v. Lord Keyes* [1959] Ch. 199. This is sometimes used as a tactic in difficult meetings (see para. 19–19).

[31] *Second Consolidated Trust Ltd v. Ceylon Amalgamated Tea Rubber Estates Ltd* [1943] 2 All E.R. 567.

[32] For a discussion of the circumstances when this can be done, see paras. 14–22 to 14–24.

there, and it was held that the poll was rightly taken and the resolution was accordingly carried.[33]

In a case, however, where the articles of a company provided that the poll was to be taken at a time and place to be agreed by the directors within seven days of the date of the meeting, and the chairman declared the poll to be taken "then and there," this was held to be invalid as it was not in accordance with the strict interpretation of the articles.[34]

The articles of a company provided that if a poll were demanded it should be taken "in such manner and at such time and place as the chairman of the meeting directs." At a general meeting of the company a resolution was lost upon show of hands and the chairman demanded a poll and directed that it should be taken by means of polling papers signed by the members and delivered at the offices of the company on or before a fixed day and hour. The direction of the chairman was held to be irregular as under the articles the personal attendance of the voter or the person appointed was necessary, and the chairman had no right to enlarge the power of voting by issuing voting papers.[35]

If the articles provide for a poll to be taken "immediately", this means as soon as practicable.[36]

If a group of associated resolutions is to be voted on, and a poll is demanded, it is proper for each resolution to be submitted to a vote separately. In one such case,[37] the resolutions having been passed on a show of hands were submitted to a poll vote en bloc; it was ruled that the resolutions were not properly carried. In a later case, however, where this procedure was adopted and no objection was registered at the time, the earlier precedent was not followed and the resolutions were confirmed as having been carried.[38] It appears, therefore, that in such circumstances a group of resolutions may be taken en bloc for voting on a poll, but only if the meeting so agrees.

On a poll, votes will be counted in accordance with the provisions of the articles. **14–13** A common provision is one vote for each share held[39] but in cases where the share capital of the company is split into different classes of shares the voting powers will be determined according to the rights given under the regulations to particular classes of shareholders.

A member holding a proxy for another member may, on a poll, wish to vote in respect of his own holding in a manner contrary to that of the person whom he represents by proxy. In such a case, he would demand two ballot papers, one for

---

[33] *Re Chillington Iron Co.* (1885) 29 Ch. D. 159.
[34] *Re British Flax Producers Co., Ltd* (1889) 60 L.T. 215.
[35] *McMillan v. Le Roi Mining Co.* [1906] 1 Ch. 331.
[36] *Jackson v. Hamlyn* [1953] Ch. 577.
[37] *Patent Wood Keg Syndicate v. Pearse* [1906] W.N. 164.
[38] *Re R.E. Jones Ltd* (1933) 50 T.L.R. 31. See also 1985 Act, s.292 (see para. 19–27, n. 2).
[39] See Table A, art. 54 (para. 14–05) and 1985 Act, s.370(6).

recording the vote of his own interest and the other for recording the vote of his principal's interest.

Sometimes scrutineers are appointed, but this procedure is not obligatory unless the regulations so provide. If there is no provision in the regulations, the meeting itself can make the appointment. For a large meeting or where the subject is controversial, it is desirable to appoint scrutineers to be responsible for arranging the best way of collecting the voting papers and expediting the checking of the votes against the register.

There is no requirement that polls should be confidential; although if the articles or other rules (for example a debenture trust deed) under which the poll is taken give the chairman the right to control the procedure he may, it appears, introduce an obligation of confidentiality.[40]

The procedure on a poll is explained in detail in paras. 19–32 to 19–36.

(f) Casting vote

14–14 Table A provides:

> **50.** In the case of an equality of votes, whether on a show of hands or on a poll, the chairman shall be entitled to a casting vote in addition to any other vote he may have.

In the absence of such a provision, the chairman has no second or casting vote (see para. 7–26).

(g) Restriction on voting rights

14–15 Under section 445 of the 1985 Act, the Secretary of State for Trade and Industry has power to impose restrictions on shares and debentures, if in connection with an investigation under either section 442 or 444 it appears to him that there is difficulty in finding out the relevant facts about any shares.

Sections 442 and 444 relate to investigations about the ownership of shares in the company. The restrictions which can be imposed include a provision that no voting rights are to be exercisable in respect of those shares.[41] A public company itself has power under section 212 of the 1985 Act to obtain information from its members about the identity of the owner of shares, and under s.216 may, if it fails to get the information, apply to the court for the imposition of the restrictions.

Articles of public companies sometimes provide that a member shall not be entitled to be present or to vote, in person or by proxy, if he or any person appearing to be interested in shares held by him, has been served with a notice under section 212 of the 1985 Act and has failed to supply to the company the required information within a specified period.

---

[40] *Haarhaus Co. GmbH v. Law Debenture Trust Corp.* [1988] B.C.L.C. 640.
[41] 1985 Act, s.454(1)(*b*).

3 PROXIES

(a) The authority

There is no common law right to vote by proxy, and such power must therefore **14–16** be conferred by statute or by the regulations of the body concerned.[42]

Section 372 of the 1985 Act provides that any member of a company entitled to attend and vote at a meeting of it may appoint another person (whether a member or not) as his proxy to attend and vote instead of him; and in the case of a private company a proxy appointed to attend and vote instead of a member has also the same right as the member to speak at the meeting. Unless the articles otherwise provide, (i) these provisions do not apply to a company not having a share capital; (ii) a proxy may vote only on a poll; and (iii) a member of a private company is not entitled to appoint more than one proxy to attend on the same occasion.[43]

It appears that a proxy-holder has no right to propose resolutions and amendments.[44] He can, however, demand or join in demanding a poll.[45]

In every notice calling a meeting of a company having a share capital there must appear with reasonable prominence a statement that a member entitled to attend and vote is entitled to appoint a proxy or, where that is allowed, one or more proxies to attend and vote instead of him, and that a proxy need not also be a member.[46]

The above provisions apply not only to general meetings but also to meetings of any class of members of a company.[47]

It is permissible for a company to use its funds in the expenses of printing and **14–17** posting proxies; it has been held that it is the duty of the directors to inform shareholders about their policy and they are justified in trying to secure votes, and expenses thus bona fide incurred in the interests of the company are payable out of the funds of the company.[48]

Section 372(6) of the 1985 Act however provides that if for the purpose of any meeting of a company invitations to appoint as proxy a person or one of a number of persons specified in the invitations are issued at the company's expense to some only of the members entitled to be sent a notice of the meeting and to vote at it by proxy, the company officer responsible for the issue is subject to a fine. An offence is not however committed by reason only of the issue to a member at his request in writing of a form of appointment naming the proxy, or of a list of persons willing to act as proxy, provided the form or list is available on request in writing to every member entitled to vote at the meeting by proxy.

---

[42] *Harben v. Phillips* (1883) 23 Ch. D. 14.

[43] 1985 Act, s.372(2). In relation to (iii), Table A does otherwise provide; see article 59, which entitles a member to appoint more than one proxy to attend on the same occasion.

[44] See Pennington, *Company Law,* 1990 p. 637; conveners of meetings should bear in mind the difficulties this may cause if a meeting is attended only by proxy-holders. See also *Administrator,* February 1994, p. 25.

[45] 1985 Act, s.373(2).

[46] 1985 Act, s.372(3).

[47] 1985 Act, s.372(7).

[48] *Peel v. London North Western Ry Co.* [1907] 1 Ch. 5. For example a proxy form can be coloured to show the board's preference as to how it should be completed.

The rights of a proxy-holder should be contrasted with those of a representative[49] appointed under section 375; a representative can speak at a meeting of a public company and can vote on a show of hands as if he were an individual shareholder.

(b) Form of proxy

14–18   The proxy must comply with the regulations. Table A, article 60, provides that an instrument appointing a proxy shall be in writing and executed by or on behalf of the appointer; this article, and article 61, provide specimen forms.

It has been held, in connection with the Insolvency Rules, that a proxy form can be sent by fax and that it will be signed if it carries some distinctive or personal marking placed there by, or with the authority of, the creditor. In the same limited context, it was held that a proxy form could be signed by a rubber stamp or by means of a signature applied electronically.[50] In practice some registrars will accept a faxed proxy but the original should be sent immediately after the fax has been transmitted. The company's articles can carry a specific authority to the board to accept a faxed proxy, either generally or in any specific case; but the board should be wary here as it cannot pick and choose which faxed proxies to accept.

Alternate persons may be named to guard against the possibility of any one of the appointees being absent. If the articles provide for attestation an unattested proxy will be invalid:

> The articles of a company provided for proxies to be attested, but at a general meeting of the company certain unattested proxies were admitted by the chairman. An action by shareholders to set aside resolutions passed at the meeting was upheld on the ground that the proxies referred to were improperly admitted.[51]

Neither of the forms prescribed by articles 60 and 61 of Table A require to be witnessed.

The rule that a proxy capable of being used for more than one meeting had to be stamped 50p has been abolished[52] and all proxies are now exempt from stamp duty.

Cases involving defective proxies are:

> The form of proxy in a company's articles provided for the insertion of the number of votes which a proxy was entitled to use. Proxies were sent out which did not contain such information and were held to be invalid.[53]

---

[49] See para. 14–01.
[50] *I.R.C. v. Conbeer* [1996] B.C.C. 189. See also para. 26–02, below.
[51] *Harben v. Phillips* (1883) 23 Ch. D. 14.
[52] s.85 and Sched. 24, Finance Act 1985.
[53] *Davey v. Inyaminga Petroleum* (1954) (3) S.A. 133.

By a printer's error the date of a meeting was left blank and several proxies were returned by shareholders duly executed and stamped but without filling in the blanks. The secretary subsequently filled in the date of the meeting and lodged the proxies with the company, and these were held to be valid.[54]

A proxy which was otherwise in the usual form was not invalidated by a palpable mistake on the face of the proxy, where it referred to a meeting as "the general meeting," when it was in fact an extraordinary general meeting.[55]

If a company rejects a proxy because, for example, it has not been signed, the shareholder should be informed. The operative parts of a proxy, *e.g.* the name of the appointee or the date of the meeting at which the proxy is to be used, may be filled in afterwards by any person authorised to do so.[56]

Stock Exchange requirements

The Listing Rules require as follows: **14–19**

A proxy form must be sent with the notice convening a meeting of holders of listed securities to each person entitled to vote at the meeting (LR9.3.6)

LR9.3.6 A proxy form must:

(a) be sent with the notice convening a meeting of holders of listed securities to each person entitled to vote at the meeting;
(b) provide for two-way voting on all resolutions intended to be proposed (except that it is not necessary to provide proxy forms with two-way voting on procedural resolutions);
(c) state that a shareholder is entitled to appoint a proxy of his own choice and provide a space for insertion of the name of such proxy; and
(d) state that if it is returned without an indication as to how the proxy shall vote on any particular matter, the proxy will exercise his discretion as to whether, and if so how, he votes.

LR9.3.7 A listed company must ensure that, if the resolutions to be proposed include the re-election of retiring directors and the number of retiring directors standing for re-election exceeds five, the proxy form gives shareholders the opportunity to vote for or against the re-election of the retiring directors as a whole but may also allow votes to be cast for or against the re-election of the retiring directors individually.

---

[54] *Ernest v. Loma Gold Mines Ltd* [1897] 1 Ch. 1.
[55] *Oliver v. Dalgleish and Others* [1963] 1 W.L.R. 1274.
[56] *Sadgrove v. Bryden* [1907] 1 Ch. 318.

Specimen

14–20   A specimen of proxy form for use at the annual general meeting of a public company is appended.

THE TRADING COMPANY, plc

Form of proxy

I/we, the undersigned, being a member of the above-named Company, hereby appoint

The Chairman of the Meeting or★

_____

as my/our proxy to attend and [on a poll[57] to] vote for me/us and on my/our behalf at the Annual General Meeting of the Company to be held on . . . . , and at any adjournment thereof.

> ★[Delete if it is desired to appoint any other person and insert his or her name and address in the space provided. A proxy need not be a member of the Company.]

The Proxy is to vote as instructed in respect of the resolutions specified below:

Notes

1 To be valid, this form of proxy, together with any authority (or a notarially certified copy of such authority) under which it is signed, must reach the company's registered office not less than [forty-eight] hours before the time for holding the meeting.

2 Where the appointor is a corporation this form must be executed in due form by or under the hand of an officer or attorney duly authorised.

3 In the case of joint holders, the vote of the senior who tenders a vote whether in person or by proxy, shall be accepted to the exclusion of the vote of the other joint holders. Seniority shall be determined by the order in which the names stand in the register.

4 Instructions as to voting on the specified resolutions should be indicated by an "X" in the appropriate box. If you wish to abstain on a particular resolution, please write "Abstain" across the boxes against that resolution.

5 If you do not tell your proxy how to vote, your proxy can vote or abstain as he or she thinks fit on the resolutions or any other business which may come before the meeting (including any motion to amend a resolution or to adjourn the meeting).

6 This form of proxy confers authority to demand or join in demanding a poll.

7 The return by a member of this form of proxy will not preclude such member from attending in person and voting at the meeting.

---

[57] Most articles do not give a proxy-holder under the right to vote on a show of hands (see para. 14–16, above).

Resolution No. 1

To receive the Report
of the Directors and the
Accounts of the Company
for the year ended
....

For   Against

☐   ☐

Resolution No. 2

To receive the
Remuneration Report for
the year ended.....

☐   ☐

Resolution No. 3

To declare a dividend.

☐   ☐

Resolution No. 4

To re-elect Mr...........
as a director (Chairman of
Remuneration Committee)

☐   ☐

Resolution No. 5

To re-elect Mrs ....
(Group Chief Executive) as
a director.

☐   ☐

Resolution No. 6

To re-appoint........... & Co.
as the auditors of the
Company

☐   ☐

Resolution No. 7
To authorise the board to
fix the remuneration of
the auditors for ....

☐   ☐

Date:
Signed:

Name [IN CAPITAL LETTERS]:

[Shareholder's register number and name
and address to be pre-printed on the form]

[Bar coding, if required]

[To be connected to attendance card if
required—see para. 14–21 below]

161

14–21   The following points relating to the proxy form may be noted:

(1) The form is usually printed so as to be capable of being returned by the member under the business reply service of the Post Office. First class or (more usually) second class prepaid mail may be used for the reply but postal arrangements are left to the company and there is no obligation on the company to pay the return postage.

(2) To the proxy form is often attached an attendance card (or "intention to attend" card) which has been pre-printed with the same details about the member as are given on the proxy form; this can be detached from the proxy form, retained, and handed over at the door, thus saving some time on the day of the meeting.

(3) If the member wishes to abstain on any resolution, he must mark the proxy form clearly to this effect; if he does not do so his shares will, as the notes indicate, be voted at the discretion of the chairman—this will usually be in favour of resolutions put forward by the company and against any put forward by requisitionists (but see para. 14–28, below).

(4) The reference in the proxy form to the responsibilities of the two directors standing for re-election is to meet the requirement contained in paragraph 4.12 of the Greenbury Code (contained in the Report of a Study Group on Directors' Remuneration chaired by Sir Richard Greenbury, published in July 1995).

(c) Deposit of proxies

14–22   Most articles stipulate a time limit within which, and the place where, proxies must be deposited. Where under the regulations the instrument must be deposited a specified number of hours before the meeting, a proxy deposited after the time prescribed cannot be admitted.[58]

Table A states that:

62. The instrument appointing a proxy and any other authority under which it is executed or a copy of such authority certified notarially or in some other way approved by the directors may:

(a) be deposited at the registered office or such other place within the United Kingdom as is specified in the notice convening the meeting or in any instrument of proxy sent out by the company in relation to the meeting not less than 48 hours before the time for holding the meeting or adjourned meeting at which the person named in the instrument proposes to vote; or

(b) in the case of a poll taken more than 48 hours after it is demanded, be deposited as aforesaid after the poll has been demanded and not less than 24 hours before the time appointed for the taking of the poll; or

(c) where the poll is not taken forthwith but is taken not more than 48 hours after it was demanded, be delivered at the meeting at which the

---

[58] *McLaren v. Thomson* [1917] 2 Ch. 261.

poll was demanded to the chairman or to the secretary or to any
    director;

and an instrument of proxy which is not deposited or delivered in a manner
so permitted shall be invalid.

The above article is in conformity with the Act, which provides that a provision **14–23**
contained in a company's articles is void so far as it would have the effect of
requiring the instrument appointing a proxy, or any other document necessary to
show the validity of, or otherwise relating to the appointment of a proxy, to be
received by the company or any other person more than 48 hours before a meeting
or adjourned meeting.[59]

The article also addresses the difficulties relating to proxies which are lodged
after a meeting has been concluded (*i.e.* not adjourned—see para. 14–24 below)
except for the taking of a poll; the article lays down the time-limits within which
such proxies can be admitted.[60]

It is to be noted that to be effective a proxy must be actually received by the
company, and if delayed in the post there is no provision by which its receipt is
deemed to be other than the actual time of receipt. In this respect, it differs from
notice of a meeting.

There is nothing in law to exclude Sunday in the computation of the relevant
periods, and where the 48-hour rule applies a proxy delivered by hand before noon
on Sunday for a meeting to be held at noon on Tuesday would be valid, provided
the receipt of the proxy at the time stated could be identified in some way.
Whether a document put through a letter box at a time when an office is known
to be unattended can be said to have been "received" at that point in time is,
nevertheless, a fine point. Particularly where some controversy surrounds the
meeting, it may be necessary for the company's registrar to attend his office at
unsocial hours in order to be able to establish the time of receipt, and if necessary
(and possible) to make special arrangements with the Post Office.

A company can provide in its articles a period less than 48 hours for the deposit
of proxies, but this may not allow sufficient time for counting and checking.

(d) Proxies at adjourned meetings

Proxies deposited prior to the original meeting may be used at the adjournment, **14–24**
for in the absence of any provisions to the contrary, an adjourned meeting is a
continuation of the original meeting.[61] Conversely, proxies deposited between the
date of the meeting and adjourned meeting can be used at the adjourned meeting.[62] As has been seen, article 62(a) follows the section in this respect.

It will be noted that the suspension of business merely for the purpose of a poll
does not usually constitute an "adjournment":

---

[59] 1985 Act, s.372(5).
[60] For the position where pre-1985 articles apply, see para. 14–24.
[61] *Scadding v. Lorant* (1851) 3 H.L.Cas. 418; see para. 6–17, n. 47.
[62] 1985 Act, s.372(5) (and the corresponding section in earlier Acts) makes this clear in principle; but
    subject to that overriding sub-section, any time limits contained in the articles will apply.

A poll demanded at a company meeting was directed to be taken at a future date, but the meeting itself was not adjourned. *Held*, that the mere postponement of the poll was not adjournment of the meeting within the meaning of an article allowing for the lodgment of proxies before the meeting "or adjourned meeting"; the original meeting continued for the purpose of taking a poll and no fresh proxies could be lodged between the two dates.[63]

A meeting, held on January 20, 1953, ceased to transact business because the hall was no longer available. A resolution to adjourn the meeting for 30 days was the subject of a poll held at once; the resolution was defeated. On January 29, 1953 the directors reconvened the meeting. It was held that this was a continuation of the meeting held on January 20, 1953, that there had been no adjournment (in fact, a resolution to adjourn had been lost) and therefore no proxies deposited after January 18, 1953 would be valid as the articles required proxies to be deposited 48 hours before the holding of a meeting.[64]

The effect of the above is to impose on the chairman of the meeting the duty to be clear as to whether he is adjourning the meeting or closing it subject only to the holding of a poll at a future date.[65]

(e) Revocation and change of instructions

14–25   A proxy can be revoked. The most sure way in which a person member may revoke a proxy is to attend and vote in person:

It was held that there was nothing in the articles of a company to deprive a shareholder who was at a meeting of the right to vote in person, even though he had given a proxy to some other person to vote for him at the same meeting; the fact that the proxy was not revoked in the manner laid down in the articles did not prevent the member recording his vote in person to the exclusion of the proxy holder.[66]

Revocation can also be effected by a determination of the authority by the donor himself prior to the meeting[67] or by deposit of another instrument in substitution for the former instrument (see below).

The death of the appointor will also effect revocation, as will a mental health order or the registration of a transfer. Table A however stresses the importance of notice to the company:

---

[63] *Shaw v. Tati Concessions Ltd* [1913] 1 Ch. 292.
[64] *Jackson v. Hamlyn* [1953] Ch. 577. Table A, article 62(*b*), if applicable, would now deal with this type of situation.
[65] See also paras. 6–14 to 6–17 and 14–29 to 14–30.
[66] *Cousins v. International Brick Co. Ltd* [1931] 2 Ch. 90, C.A.
[67] On the basis of *R. v. Wait* (1823) 11 Price 518, dealing with revocation of a power of attorney, it appears that oral notice, though most unsatisfactory from the company point of view, will suffice except where the articles require (as Table A article 111 now does) that notices shall be in writing.

63. A vote given or a poll demanded by proxy or by the duly authorised representative of a corporation shall be valid notwithstanding the previous determination of the authority of the person voting or demanding a poll unless notice of the determination was received by the company at the registered office or at such other place at which the instrument of proxy was duly deposited before the commencement of the meeting or adjourned meeting at which the vote is given or the poll demanded or (in the case of a poll taken otherwise than on the same day as the meeting or adjourned meeting) the time appointed for taking the poll.

Article 63 and similar articles are obviously useful to prevent the subsequent **14–26** invalidating of proceedings which appeared at the time to be regularly conducted. The particular wording of older forms of article however might present a problem where the appointer wishes to revoke the proxy before the taking of a poll which has been deferred to a later date (though still forming part of the original meeting in accordance with the principles explained above):

A proxy was deposited for a meeting to be held on December 15. A poll was ordered to be taken on December 22, but on December 18 the appointer wrote revoking the proxy. Under the articles, a revocation had to be received before the commencement of "the meeting." *Held*, the vote given by the appointer was valid notwithstanding the purported revocation, since the date of the meeting was December 15.[68]

In a contested bid situation, shareholders may be sent a proxy card which contains a revocation of any earlier proxy lodged by them with the company; they are invited to sign and send it to the company. In that event, subject to anything to the contrary in the company's articles:

(a) a properly completed proxy in the later form which is lodged before the deadline for proxies will be effective to revoke an earlier proxy and to act as a new proxy;

(b) a completed proxy in the later form lodged after the deadline but handed in at the registered office before the start of the meeting will be effective to revoke the earlier proxy but will not itself be operative as a proxy because it is lodged out of time;

(c) where Table A, articles 62 and 63 apply (see above), the later form will be an effective revocation up to the time of the poll (in the case of a poll taken otherwise than on the same day as the meeting or adjourned meeting) and may, depending on circumstances be operative as a proxy if the meeting is adjourned or a poll taken on a later date.

It is clear that, without following any particular formality, a shareholder is entitled to change his instructions to his proxy-holder at any time before the vote is cast. The situation often arises where a company sends out forms by which the chairman is appointed as the member's proxy. Letters are then received at the office which change the instructions given on the previously lodged proxies (again, this

---

[68] *Spiller v. Mayo (Rhodesia) Development Co. (1908) Ltd* [1926] W.N. 78.

may happen in a contested situation). The chairman would ignore such instructions at his peril.

(f) Joint holders; personal representatives; nominees; creditors

14–27   The question may arise whether more than one of registered joint holders can vote by proxy. Most articles contain a clause to the effect that only one of such joint holders may vote at any meeting either personally or by proxy, and the person whose name stands first on the register is usually the person appointed. Table A, article 55, is to this effect.

The position of legal personal representatives is also governed by the articles. Many articles, such as article 31 of Table A, exclude personal representatives from the right to attend or vote until they have become registered as members. If this is what the articles say, a personal representative cannot sign a form of proxy. If the articles are silent, a personal representative does not have the right to vote until registration (see also para. 13–04).

Where shares in a public company are held by nominee companies on behalf, for example, of customers of banks, such companies will, on request, execute separate proxies in favour of parties nominated by the customer in respect of his holding. Even though the shares of the nominee company are shown in one account in the company's register of members, several persons may thus be represented at the meeting.[69]

Creditors in the winding up of a company may vote by proxy.[70]

(g) Duties of a proxy-holder

14–28   The holder of a proxy is the lawfully constituted agent of the member.[71] The duty of an agent is "to carry out, generally in person, the business he has undertaken, or to inform his principal promptly if it is impossible to do so".[72]

Thus, the proxy-holder should vote in accordance with the instructions on a duly completed proxy form, and should vote all the proxies.[73] This particularly applies to those named (usually the directors of the company) on the two-way proxy forms sent out to shareholders in accordance with the Listing Rules[74] and to proxies solicited in connection with a scheme of arrangement under section 425 of the 1985 Act.[75] If the proxy-holder fails to vote in accordance with his instructions he may be liable to his principal for damages caused by his breach of the agency contract. Only in rare circumstances, for example where he genuinely considered that his principal would have changed his instructions, and no special or fiduciary circumstances exist, would the proxy-holder escape such liability.

A question might arise as to how a proxy-holder should vote on any amendment to a resolution which comes before the meeting. It may be that the chairman of the meeting is himself the holder of proxies for members; it might indeed have been

---

[69] See n. 43, above.
[70] See Chap. 26.
[71] *Re English, Scottish Australian Bank* [1893] 3 Ch. 385.
[72] Halsbury, *Laws of England* (4th ed., re-issue) Vol. 1(2), para. 88.
[73] *Second Consolidated Trust Ltd v. Ceylon Amalgamated Tea Rubber Estates* [1943] 2 All E.R. 567.
[74] See para. 14–19.
[75] *Re Dorman, Long Co.* [1934] Ch. 635.

the chairman himself who demanded the poll (see para. 14–09) in order to bring the proxy votes into play. On the assumption that the proxy form is the same as that given in para. 14–20, some guidelines are as follows:

(i) The chairman is the agent of those who have appointed him as their proxy-holder. He should therefore vote in accordance with what he conceives, in his best judgment, to be their wishes. This might mean, if time permits, that he should consult them, especially where a large block of shares is involved.

(ii) The chairman would generally be safe in voting the "yes" and "at discretion" proxies in favour of the amendment, if the amendment imposes a less onerous burden on the company than the resolution as unamended.

(iii) The "no" proxies involve a more difficult decision. It might be impossible to determine the attitude to the amendment of those who have issued the proxies. The wisest course may be to abstain. The chairman will bear in mind that he will have the opportunity (assuming a poll is demanded) to vote the "no" proxies against the substantive resolution, when put, in its amended or unamended form (see para. 19–24).

If a proposal to adjourn the meeting is put forward, the chairman, in the interests of seeing the business through, will normally be able to vote the "yes" and "at discretion" proxies against the proposal.[76]

4   ADJOURNMENT OF COMPANY MEETINGS

In principle, the rules relating to adjournment of a company meeting are the same as for the meeting of any other body, and have been discussed in Part II.[77]   **14–29**

Thus, the chairman has power to adjourn a meeting to facilitate its business, to avoid disorder, or if he is given power to do so by the articles. If however he stops the meeting while business remains to be done, or improperly attempts to adjourn it, the meeting can choose another chairman and carry on with the business.[78]

Since an adjourned meeting is by operation of law a continuation of the original meeting, there is, in principle, no need to give notice of the adjourned meeting, but here the articles may make specific provision.

With the above in mind, the relevant article of Table A can be examined:

45. The chairman may, with the consent of a meeting at which a quorum is present (and shall if so directed by the meeting), adjourn the meeting from time to time and from place to place, but no business shall be transacted at an adjourned meeting other than business which might properly have been transacted at the meeting had the adjournment not taken place. When a meeting is adjourned for 14 days or more, at least seven clear days' notice shall

---

[76] *Re Waxed Papers Limited* [1937] 53 T.L.R. 676.
[77] Chap. 6.
[78] *Catesby v. Burnett* [1916] 2 Ch. 325.

be given specifying the time and place of the adjourned meeting and the general nature of the business to be transacted. Otherwise, it shall not be necessary to give any such notice.

Under an article similar to the above the chairman is bound to adjourn the meeting if a resolution to adjourn is duly passed; the words in brackets make this clear.

> In a case, however, where shareholders resident in England would have been prejudiced had an adjournment been insisted upon by the members present at a meeting in South Africa, and where the words "and shall if so directed by the meeting" were not included in the company's articles, the action of the chairman in refusing to allow adjournment was upheld.[79]

In view of the practical difficulties which arose in the *Byng* case (see para. 6–16) some company articles have been amended to provide that the chairman has the power to adjourn a meeting *without its consent* if he decides that it has become necessary to do so in order to secure the orderly conduct of the meeting or to give all persons present in opportunity to speak and vote or to ensure that the business of the meeting is properly disposed of.

If a poll is demanded on the question of adjournment, it should be taken immediately.[80]

14–30   Article 45 provides for notice of the adjourned meeting if the adjournment is for 14 days or more. There is nothing however to prevent a company giving its members notice even though the adjournment be for a period less than 14 days, as by so doing members absent from the first meeting will be reminded of their right to be present at the adjourned meeting. Further, the board can arrange for newspaper advertisement of the adjourned meeting (and the articles can provide for this).

The directors can, if they have sufficient time, convene an extraordinary general meeting to be held on the same day as the adjourned meeting.

Meetings sometimes stand adjourned automatically, and Table A, article 41, makes such a provision in the event of a quorum not being present.[81]

Section 381 of the 1985 Act provides that where a resolution is passed at an adjourned meeting of:

(a) a company;
(b) the holders of any class of shares in a company;
(c) the directors of a company;

the resolution is for all purposes to be treated as having been passed on the date on which it is in fact passed, and it not to be deemed passed on any earlier date.

---

[79] *Salisbury Gold Mining Co. v. Hathorn* [1897] A.C. 268.
[80] See Table A, art. 51.
[81] See para. 13–31.

CHAPTER 15

MEMBERS' MEETINGS: RESOLUTIONS

1 ORDINARY RESOLUTION

An ordinary resolution is the basic way in which the sense of a company general **15–01** meeting is given specific and formal shape. It requires a simple majority of the members who, being present and entitled to vote on the resolution, do vote.[1] Abstainers will not count; in other words, if an ordinary resolution is put to the vote and six vote in favour, five vote against and twelve abstain, the resolution is carried. In general, the wording of the notice relating to an ordinary resolution does not call for the exacting standards of accuracy which are required for a special resolution, as described below. It will be sufficient if the agenda gives the broad intention of what is proposed; for example, notices of annual general meetings often simply include an item—"to authorise the directors to fix the remuneration of the auditors"—leaving the secretary to prepare the exact words for the chairman to read out at the meeting. With ordinary resolutions as with others, however, the more detail that can be given, the less chance of later misunderstanding.

There are instances in the Acts calling for the sanction of an ordinary resolution. **15–02** For example, section 303 of the 1985 Act provides that a director may be removed from office by ordinary resolution; section 319 requires that directors' service agreements for more than five years must be first approved by "a resolution of the company in general meeting"; and section 320 relates to the validation of substantial property transactions involving directors where the arrangement is approved by such a resolution. These expressions refer to the same need: a resolution passed by a simple majority of the members present and voting.

Where a company's shares are quoted on the Stock Exchange, certain major transactions have to be approved by members in general meeting.

2 EXTRAORDINARY RESOLUTION

An extraordinary resolution is one which has been passed by a majority of not less **15–03** than three-fourths of such members as (being entitled to do so) vote in person or, where proxies are allowed, by proxy, at a general meeting of which notice specifying the intention to propose the resolution as an extraordinary resolution has been duly given.[2]

For example:

---

[1] See *Bushell v. Faith* [1970] A.C. 1099, *per* Lord Upjohn at 1108.
[2] 1985 Act, s.378(1). On a poll, the requisite majority is three-quarters of the votes cast (s.378(5)).

Number of persons present	100
Number of votes cast	80
Number of votes in favour required to pass resolution	60

On the other hand:

Number of persons present	200
Number of votes cast	110
Number of votes in favour required to pass resolution	
($\frac{3}{4} \times 110 = 82.5$)	83

In other words, where a fraction occurs it is necessary to round up.

The intention to propose the resolution as an extraordinary resolution must be set out in the notice. A notice in general terms without specifying the nature of the proposals to be submitted will be insufficient to comply with the Act.[3] The resolution in the form in which it is to be passed should be set out in the notice.

For the purpose of section 378, notice of a meeting is deemed duly given, and the meeting duly held, when the notice is given and the meeting held in the manner provided by the Act or the company's articles.[4]

In practice, this means that if the resolution is to be proposed at an annual general meeting, at least 21 clear days' notice is required, but if it is to be proposed at an extraordinary general meeting at least 14 clear days' notice is all that is necessary.[5]

An extraordinary resolution is required when it is proposed to put a company into voluntary liquidation because it cannot by reason of its liabilities continue in business and it is advisable to wind up, and for sanctioning other steps in a winding up.

The articles do, moreover, sometimes provide that matters not normally requiring an extraordinary resolution must receive the sanction of such a resolution (for example, to alter class rights). Further, an extraordinary resolution is one of the ways in which rights attached to a class of shares otherwise than by the memorandum can be varied where the articles do not contain provisions with respect to variation.[6]

3   SPECIAL RESOLUTION

15–04   By section 378(2) of the 1985 Act, a resolution is a special resolution when it has been passed by such a majority as is required for the passing of an extraordinary resolution and at a general meeting of which not less than 21 days' notice, specifying the intention to propose the resolution as a special resolution, has been duly given. If it is so agreed by a majority in number of the members having the right to attend and vote at such a meeting, being a majority together holding not

---

[3] *MacConnell v. E. Prill Co. Ltd* [1916] 2 Ch. 57.

[4] 1985 Act, s.378(6).

[5] See para. 13–19 above. The circumstances in which shorter notice may be given, with consent, are explained in para. 13–21.

[6] 1985 Act, s.125(2); see paras. 17–03 *et seq.*

less than 95 per cent in nominal value of the shares giving that right (or, in the case of a company not having a share capital, together representing not less than 95 per cent of the total voting rights at that meeting of all the members) a resolution may be proposed and passed as a special resolution at a meeting of which less than 21 days' notice has been given.[7] A private company may, by Elective Resolution, elect that the above provisions shall have effect in relation to the company as if for the references to 95 per cent there were substituted references to such lesser percentage, but not less than 90 per cent, as may be specified in the resolution or subsequently determined by the company in general meeting. The consents under above provisions should be those of persons who appreciated that the resolution was defective in point of time.[8]

The intention to propose a motion as a special resolution should be set out in the notice convening the meeting, and the exact wording of the resolution must be given.

A special resolution is required for many of the most important acts in the life of a company: for example, to alter its memorandum[9] or its articles,[10] to change its name,[11] or to enter into voluntary winding-up.[12]

4 RESOLUTIONS IN WRITING SIGNED BY ALL MEMBERS

General—Table A

The articles of many companies provide that a resolution signed by each **15–05** shareholder of a company shall be valid. An article to this effect is contained in Table A:

> **53.** A resolution in writing executed by or on behalf of each member who would have been entitled to vote upon it if it had been proposed at a general meeting at which he was present shall be as effectual as if it had been passed at a general meeting duly convened and held and may consist of several instruments in the like form each executed by or on behalf of one or more members.

It may be unwise to rely on this type of article in relation to extraordinary or special resolutions, as section 378 (see paras. 15–03 and 15–04 above) refers expressly to the convening of a general meeting.

Private Companies—Written Resolutions

Under the heading of "Deregulation of private companies", the 1989 Act **15–06** introduced into the 1985 Act new sections 381A, 381B, 381C, 382A and Schedule

---

[7] 1985 Act, s.378(3).
[8] *Re Pearce Duff Co. Ltd* [1960] 1 W.L.R. 1014. See para. 13–23.
[9] 1985 Act, s.4.
[10] 1985 Act, s.9(1).
[11] 1985 Act, s.28(1).
[12] 1986 Act, s.84(1)(*b*).

15A. These sections (as subsequently amended, for example by the Deregulation (Resolutions of Private Companies) Order (S.I. 1996 No. 1471), which introduced a new section 381B) provide that anything which in the case of a private company may be done:

(a) by resolution of the company in general meeting; or
(b) by resolution of a meeting of any class of members of the company

may be done, without a meeting and without any previous notice being required, by resolution in writing signed by or on behalf of all the members of the company who at the date of the resolution would be entitled to attend and vote at such a meeting. The signatures need not be on a single document provided each is on a document which accurately states the terms of the resolution. The date of the resolution means when the resolution is signed by or on behalf of the last member to sign (until then it has no effect). The new provisions cover a resolution which would otherwise require to be passed as a special, extraordinary or Elective Resolution (for the latter, see para. 11–12).

There is an important qualification. Under section 381B if a director or secretary or a company knows that it is proposed to seek agreement to a resolution in accordance with section 381A, and knows the terms of the resolution, he shall, if the company has auditors, secure that a copy of the resolution is sent to them, or that they are otherwise notified of its contents, at or before the time the resolution is supplied to a member for signature. There is a fine for default.

The above sections have effect notwithstanding anything in the private company's articles, but do not prejudice any power conferred by any such provision (a company could, therefore, make use of article 53 of Table A, if it applied, without bothering with the more cumbersome section 381A procedure). An appropriate record book of resolutions agreed under the above procedure must be kept. This must include a note of the signatures.[13] Any such record of a resolution, if purporting to be signed by a director of the company or by the company secretary, is evidence of the proceedings in agreeing to the resolution; and where a record is made in accordance with this section (*i.e.* section 382A of the 1985 Act), then, until the contrary is proved, the requirements of the 1985 Act with respect to those proceedings shall be deemed to be complied with.[14]

Part I of Schedule 15A provides that the procedure described above does not apply to:

(a) a resolution under section 303 of the 1985 Act removing a director before the expiration of his period of office; or
(b) a resolution under Section 391 of the 1985 Act removing an auditor before the expiration of his term of office.

Part II of Schedule 15A adapts certain requirements of the 1985 Act to proceedings under section 381A:

section 95—disapplication of pre-emption rights

---

[13] 1985 Act, s.382A(1).
[14] 1985 Act, s.382A(2).

section 155—financial assistance for purchase of company's own shares
sections 164, 165 and 167—authority for off-market purchase of own shares, etc.
section 173—approval for payment out of capital
section 319—approval of director's service contract
section 337—funding of director's expenses

Reference should be made to Schedule 15A for details of the relevant provisions.

5 Record of Decisions of Single Member Companies

Under section 382B, the sole member of a single member company must provide **15–07** the company with a written record of any decision which he takes which has the effect of an agreed decision of the company in general meeting. A suitable record for the purposes of the section would come into being if the written resolution procedure is available and can be used (see paras. 15–05 and 15–06 above), or if the decision is simply recorded in the minute book and signed by or on behalf of the sole member. There is a fine in case of default, but failure to comply with the formalities described above does not affect the validity of the decision reached.

6 Unanimous Consent in Lieu of Meeting

A line of cases makes it clear that where there has been a unanimous consent of **15–08** shareholders, an act may be valid even without a meeting. The principle was expressed as follows by Astbury J.:

" . . . where a transaction is *intra vires* the company and honest, the sanction of all the members of the company, however expressed, is sufficient to validate it, especially if it is a transaction entered into for the benefit of the company itself."[15]

The learned judge said that he saw nothing to prevent all the corporators from arranging to carry out such a transaction, "even if they do not meet together in one room or place, but all of them merely discuss and agree to it one with another separately."[16]

The same principle has been applied to an agreement between all the shareholders of a company which had the effect of removing the chairman's casting vote under the articles, even though there had been no meeting and no special

---

[15] *Parker Cooper Ltd v. Reading* [1926] 1 Ch. 975, at p. 982. (See also *Re Zinotty Properties Ltd* [1984] 3 All E.R. 754, at 766.)

[16] *ibid.* at 984. See also *Re Express Engineering Works* [1920] 1 Ch. 466 and *Re Oxted Motor Co.* [1921] 3 K.B. 32, summarised in para. 5–13.

resolution as would normally be used to amend the articles under section 9 of the 1985 Act.[17]

It was held in another decision that with such unanimous consent an extraordinary resolution can be passed without any meeting being held.[18]

In another case, the purchase of a pension for a retired director was held to be valid against a liquidator who sought subsequently to impeach it, where it had been approved by all shareholders, even though there had been no confirmatory board meeting or general meeting.[19]

The principle underlying these cases may be of assistance if through inadvertence the due formalities are overlooked, or in other exceptional circumstances. It should not be relied on where there is time and capacity to arrange matters properly or where any of the actions of the company, its directors or members are likely to be challenged. Further, it will not apply if the assenting shareholders could not properly have carried through the act in question at a meeting, if one had been held.[20]

In *Cane v. Jones* the learned judge commented:

> "I would also add that one of the most striking features of this case has been the almost total failure of all concerned to observe the simplest requirements of company law."[21]

There is always the possibility that the courts may take the view, as did the report of the Jenkins Committee in 1962,[22] that shareholders should take the trouble to get together and go through the procedure of holding a formal meeting, as part of the legitimate price paid for the benefits of incorporation.

7   AMENDMENTS TO COMPANY RESOLUTIONS

(a) To an ordinary resolution

15–09   An ordinary resolution may, before being put to the meeting, be the subject of amendment, provided that the proposed alteration is not so fundamental as to destroy the intent of the original resolution or to alter its effect to a major degree, qualitatively or quantitatively. For example, if an ordinary resolution is proposed:

> THAT the ordinary capital of the company shall be increased by the creation of 1,000,000 new ordinary shares of £1 each

—it would be improper for the chairman to admit an amendment substituting the figure of "2,000,000" for "1,000,000" or the word "preference" for "ordinary".

---

[17] *Cane v. Jones* [1981] 1 All E.R. 533. The relevant section was then s.10 of the Companies Act 1948.
[18] *Re M. J. Shanley Contracting Ltd (in voluntary liquidation)* (1980) 124 S.J. 239.
[19] *Re Horsley Weight Ltd* [1982] 3 W.L.R. 431, C.A.
[20] *Re New Cedos Engineering Co. Limited* [1994] 1 B.C.L.C. 797.
[21] [1981] 1 All E.R. 543.
[22] Cmnd. 1749 (1962). See also on this topic generally, L.S. Gaz. [1983] p. 3085.

Similarly, an amendment which added onerous conditions to a resolution proposing the approval of a contract would not be admissible.[23]

An amendment, too, must follow the principles laid down in Chapter 7, paras. 7–03 to 7–05. For example, it must fall within the scope of the notice convening the meeting:

> A meeting was convened to consider a company reconstruction, for which a winding up resolution was necessary prior to the registration of a new company. At the meeting, it was simply resolved to wind the company up. It was held that this resolution was invalid, as not being in accordance with the notice.[24]

On the other hand, if under the Acts there is a general power to carry out an action the fact that the notice proposes one particular method will not prevent the meeting from dealing with matters by another method:

> Notice of a meeting to confirm a voluntary winding up proposed that W be appointed liquidator. At the meeting the proposal to appoint W failed and M was appointed. It was held that the appointment was good since anyone at the meeting had the power with or without notice to propose the appointment of a liquidator; shareholders who did not attend were deemed to know of this power and could not complain of its exercise.[25]

Some modern articles provide that an amendment to an ordinary resolution of which the text has been set out in full in the notice convening the meeting may only be voted on if its terms have been sent to the registered office, say, 48 hours before the meeting; and may also provide that if the chairman rules an amendment out of order, the proceedings on the substantive resolution shall not be invalidated by any error in his ruling provided it was made in good faith.

(b) To an extraordinary or special resolution

In general, an extraordinary or special resolution cannot be amended. In *Re* **15–10**
Moorgate Mercantile Holdings[26] a special resolution was proposed to the effect that "the share premium account of the company amounting to £1,356,900.48 be cancelled". That figure included an amount of £321.17 which, it was discovered, could not be regarded as lost. Therefore, at the extraordinary general meeting the chairman proposed that the special resolution should be in the form:

> "That the share premium account of the company amounting to £1,356,900.48 be reduced to £321.17."

On this basis the resolution was passed, but it was not confirmed by the court, which held that it had not been validly passed because it differed not only in form

---

[23] *Wright's Case* (1871) L.R. 12 Eq. 335n.
[24] *Re Teede Bishop* (1901) 70 L.J. 409.
[25] *Re Trench Tubeless Tyre Co.* [1900] 1 Ch. 408.
[26] [1980] 1 All E.R. 40.

but also in substance from the one set out in the notice. The court summarised the relevant principles relating to notices of, and the subsequent amendment of, special resolutions, as follows (the relevant passage is quoted substantially in full):

(1) If a notice of the intention to propose a special resolution is to be a valid notice for the purpose of section 378(2), it must identify the intended resolution by specifying either the text or the entire substance of the resolution which it is intended to propose. In the case of a notice of intention to propose a special resolution, nothing is achieved by the addition of such words as "with such amendments and alterations as shall be determined on at such meeting".

(2) If a special resolution is to be validly passed in accordance with section 378(2), the resolution as passed must be the same resolution as that identified in the preceding notice.

(3) A resolution as passed can properly be regarded as "the resolution" identified in a preceding notice, even though (i) it departs in some respects from the text of a resolution set out in such notice (for example, by correcting those grammatical or clerical errors which can be corrected as a matter of construction, or by reducing the words to more formal language) or (ii) it is reduced into the form of a new text, which was not included in the notice, provided only that in either case there is no departure whatever from the substance.

(4) However, in deciding whether there is complete identity between the substance of a resolution as passed and the substance of an intended resolution as notified, there is no room for the court to apply the *de minimis* principle or a "limit of tolerance". The substance must be identical.

(5) An amendment to the previously circulated text of a special resolution can properly be put to and voted on at a meeting if, but only if, the amendment involves no departure from the substance of the circulated text, in the sense indicated in propositions (3) and (4) above.

(6) References to notices in the above propositions are intended to include references to circulars accompanying notices. In those cases where notices are so accompanied, the notices and circulars can and should ordinarily be treated as one document.

(7) All the above propositions may be subject to modification where all the members, or a class of members, of a company unanimously agree to waive their rights to notice under section 378(3).[27]

In a subsequent case where a resolution for the reduction of a company's capital contained a latent error of an insignificant character, which would not prejudice anyone, the court held that it had either a statutory power under section 137 of the 1985 Act or an inherent power to confirm the reduction of capital in a form or upon terms which would correct the error. The notice had mis-stated the number of existing unissued shares as 2,073,420 instead of 2,073,417 and mis-stated the number of issued shares as 14,926,580 instead of the correct figure of 14,926,583.

---

[27] See para. 15–04. See also 1985 Act, section 380(4)(*c*); *Re Pearce, Duff Co. Ltd* [1960] 1 W.L.R. 1014 (summarised in para. 13–23), *Re Duomatic Ltd* [1969] 2 Ch. 365.

The judge observed that it was manifestly ridiculous to suppose that it could have been intended to leave three issued shares unaffected.[28]

(c) To other types of resolution

The same principles as apply to the amendment of extraordinary and special resolutions apply also to Elective Resolutions.[29] It is arguable that they apply, too, to ordinary resolutions proposed on the requisition of shareholders and to ordinary resolutions requiring special notice.[30]   **15–11**

8 CONCLUSIVENESS OF CHAIRMAN'S DECLARATION

At any meeting at which an extraordinary or special resolution is submitted to be passed, a declaration of the chairman that the resolution is carried is, unless a poll is demanded, conclusive evidence of the fact without proof of the number or proportion of the votes recorded in favour of or against the resolution.[31] When once the declaration has been made by the chairman that an extraordinary or a special resolution has been passed, the court will not interfere unless there is evidence of fraud or manifest error: **15–12**

> At a meeting where there was considerable confusion, it was claimed that a special resolution was not in fact passed, but that an adjournment of the meeting had been carried. A minute was entered in the company's books that the resolution had been carried by the requisite majority and that no poll had been demanded at the meeting. It was held that the declaration by the chairman to that effect would preclude any inquiry into the number of shareholders who voted for or against the resolution and, in the absence of fraud, was absolutely, and not merely prima facie, conclusive.[32]

> The court, on a petition for the compulsory winding up of a company on the ground of an improper declaration on the part of a chairman, refused to entertain the question whether an extraordinary resolution was carried by the requisite majority.[33]

> A company petitioned for confirmation of reduction of capital and for approval of a special resolution. Nine shareholders attended the meeting; on a show of hands, seven voted in favour and two against the resolution. As no poll was demanded the chairman declared the resolution carried. The Court of Session decided that the declaration was legally made, and on being satisfied

---

[28] *Re Willaire Systems* [1987] B.C.L.C. 67. See also *Re European Home Products plc* (1988) 4 B.C.C. 779. A further slight relaxation may be seen in *Re Fenner plc* (unreported, but noted in *Practical Law for Companies* (P.L.C.), June 1994, p. 19).

[29] See para. 11–12, above.

[30] See paras. 13–25 to 13–30 and 13–17, and P.L.C., July 1995, p. 12.

[31] 1985 Act, s.378(4). See also para. 16–02.

[32] *Arnot v. United African Lands Ltd* [1901] 1 Ch. 518.

[33] *Re Hadleigh Castle Gold Mines*, [1900] 2 Ch. 419.

that the conduct of the meeting was regular and that the proceedings were not fraudulent, was bound to accept the chairman's declaration as conclusive without further inquiry. The statute intended by the use of the word "conclusive" that the chairman's declaration should be so regarded unless a poll was demanded. The suggestion that the regulation was not duly carried because two of the members attending the meeting lacked the necessary qualification was not upheld.[34]

15–13   The court however will intervene if it can be proved that the chairman has acted on a mistaken principle:

A chairman put a resolution and declared the result in the following form:
"Those in favour 6
Those against 23
but there are 200 voting by proxy and I declare the resolution carried as required by Act of Parliament."
Buckley J. remarked: "I am asked to affirm a proposition that if a chairman makes a declaration and in it actually gives the numbers of votes for and against the resolution, which he is bound to recognise, and adds that there are proxies (which in law he cannot regard), and then declares that the result is that the required statutory majority has been obtained, although the numbers stated by him show that it has not been obtained, the declaration is conclusive. In my judgement that proposition cannot be supported."[35]

9   FILING OF RESOLUTIONS WITH REGISTRAR

15–14   Under section 380(1) of the 1985 Act, a resolution or agreement to which the section applies shall, within 15 days after it is passed or made, be forwarded to the Registrar and recorded by him. It must be in a form approved by the Registrar.[36] The Registrar will not however accept copies of resolutions passed as extraordinary or special resolutions unless they have been passed at a duly constituted meeting.[37]

Where articles have been registered, a copy of every such resolution or agreement for the time being in force shall be embodied in or annexed to every copy of the articles issued after the passing of the resolution or the making of the agreement.[38] By section 19 of the 1985 Act, each member of a company is entitled to receive from the company, on request, a copy of the memorandum and articles on payment of a sum not exceeding 5p.

The above provisions of section 380 apply to special, extraordinary and Elective Resolutions and to resolutions revoking Elective Resolutions and to certain other resolutions and agreements as set out in section 380(4)(c) to (k).

---

[34] *Graham's Morocco Co. Ltd*, (1932) S.L.T. 210.
[35] *Re Caratal (New) Mines Ltd* [1902] 2 Ch. 498.
[36] 1985 Act, ss.706 and 707.
[37] 53 *The Secretary* 148.
[38] 1985 Act, s.380(2).

10 The Company Law Review

Certain changes are being proposed by the Company Law Review to make the **15–15** administration of small private companies easier. In a draft company law bill published by the Department of Trade and Industry as part of a White Paper in March 2005, it was proposed that a written resolution could be passed by a simple majority of those eligible to vote for an ordinary resolution and by 75% for a special resolution.

However, the draft bill is unlikely to be placed before Parliament before early 2006 and the provisions of the new bill are unlikely to be in force before the end of 2006, possibly even 2007.

CHAPTER 16

MEMBERS' MEETINGS: MINUTES

1 OBLIGATION TO KEEP

16–01 It has always been recognised as the duty of a company to keep minutes of what takes place at its general meetings.[1] This obligation is made explicit in section 382(1) of the 1985 Act which prescribes that every company shall cause minutes of all proceedings of general meetings and board meetings[2] to be entered in books kept for that purpose.[3]

Under the Act, minutes may be kept either by making a bound book or by recording them in any other manner provided adequate precautions are taken against falsification and for facilitating discovery.[4] Penalties are prescribed for failure to take such precautions. What precautions are "adequate" has not yet emerged in the courts, but in principle would seem to require that each page of the minutes should be signed or initialled and that the minute book should be kept in a safe place by a responsible officer of the company. A further useful step would be to number consecutively the pages of the minute book and the minutes themselves.

The power conferred on a company by the above provision includes the power to keep the minutes by recording them otherwise than in a legible form (for example, by the use of a computer), so long as the recording is capable of being reproduced in a legible form.[5]

A fine is prescribed for failure to keep minutes. It is imposed on the company and every officer of it who is in default.[6]

2 MINUTES AS EVIDENCE

16–02 Any minute made under section 382(1), if purporting to be signed by the chairman of the meeting at which the proceedings were had, or by the chairman of the next succeeding meeting, is evidence of the proceedings.[7]

Some company articles go further and provide that a minute shall be "conclusive evidence". For example, article 47 of Table A provides that unless a poll is duly

---

[1] *Re British Provident Life and Fire Insurance Society, Lane's Case* (1863) 1 De G.J. & S. 504, 509.
[2] In relation to directors' meetings, see para. 22–10.
[3] "Purpose" probably means a book or books used exclusively for that purpose: see *POW Services v. Clare* [1995] 2 BCLC 435, 444.
[4] 1985 Act, s.722(1), (2).
[5] 1985 Act, s.723(1).
[6] 1985 Act, s.382(5).
[7] 1985 Act, s.382(2).

demanded a declaration by the chairman about a resolution[8] and an entry to that effect in the minutes of the meeting shall be conclusive evidence of the fact without proof of the number or proportion of the votes recorded in favour of or against such resolution:

A company convened an extraordinary general meeting to sell shares standing in the name of a member over which the company had a lien for an unpaid debt. The plaintiff claimed that he was the highest bidder at the meeting and had thus bought the shares; but this was inconsistent with the minutes of the meeting. The company produced the minute book in evidence and proved that the signature to the minutes was that of the chairman of the meeting at which they were confirmed. This was sufficient to shut out evidence by the plaintiff to the contrary.[9]

The words "conclusive evidence" which appeared in the article of the company above-noted are the words which appear in section 378(4) as to a declaration by the chairman of the passing of an extraordinary resolution or a special resolution.[10] Such an article however does not debar a shareholder from establishing, if he can, that the minutes are not a bona fide record of what took place but have been written up after the event, falsely and fraudulently.

With reference to section 382(2), minutes of a members' meeting are seldom signed by the chairman at the next general meeting as this would complicate the agenda. A common practice is for the minutes to be approved by the meeting of directors, following that of the meeting of members, and for them then to be signed by the person who took the chair at the general meeting, so as to take advantage of the section. Frequently, certified copies of the minutes of the general meeting will be required, and these will usually be signed by the chairman, although section 41 of the 1985 Act makes it clear that a document or proceedings requiring authentication by a company may be signed by a director, secretary or other authorised officer of the company.

Where minutes have been made in accordance with section 382 of the proceedings at any general meeting or directors' meeting of the company then, until the contrary is proved, the meeting is deemed to have been duly held and convened, and all proceedings had at the meeting to have been duly had; and all appointments of directors, managers or liquidators are deemed to be valid.[11]

Conversely, a matter may be established by or against the company even though there is no entry in the minute book.[12] If minutes are not forthcoming, it will be assumed against the company that whatever the directors ought, for example, to have submitted to the shareholders was actually so submitted.[13]

Minutes of general meetings should record the type of voting used (*i.e.* a show of hands or a poll); this may be important in the event of a subsequent challenge to the vote. If the minutes are not specific, it will be assumed that voting has been by means of a show of hands.

---

[8] See paras. 15–12 and 15–13.
[9] *Kerr v. John Mottram Ltd* [1940] Ch. 657.
[10] See paras. 15–12 and 15–13.
[11] 1985 Act, s.382(4).
[12] *Re Pyle Works (No. 2)* [1891] 1 Ch. 173; *Re Fireproof Doors Ltd* [1916] 2 Ch. 142.
[13] *Re British Provident Life and Fire Assurance Society, Lane's Case* (1863) 1 De G.J. & S. 504, 509.

3. Where to be Kept: Rights of Inspection

16–03 The books containing the minutes of proceedings of any general meeting of a company held on or after November 1, 1929, shall be kept at the registered office of the company, and shall be open to the inspection of any member without charge.[14]

Any member shall be entitled, on payment of the prescribed fee, to be furnished within seven days after he has made a request in that behalf to the company with a copy of any such minutes.[15]

In respect of the above, the minimum period during which the minutes should be available for inspection is two hours between 9 a.m. and 5 p.m. each business day. Copying, by means of the taking of notes or transcription of the information, must also be allowed. A member is entitled to a copy of the minutes on payment of a small charge, currently 10p per hundred words or part thereof.[16]

If any inspection so required is refused, of if any copy so required is not sent within the proper time, the company and every officer of the company who is in default is liable to a fine.[17] In any case of refusal or default, the court may by order compel an immediate inspection of the books in respect of all proceedings of general meetings, or direct that the copies required be sent to the persons requiring them.[18]

When a member makes an inspection under section 383(1), he is entitled to be accompanied by an adviser.[19]

If the minutes are kept in non-legible form (*e.g.* on a computer), the company must make a reproduction of the minutes, or the relevant part of them, in a legible form so as to allow inspection to be made and a copy supplied.[20]

---

[14] 1985 Act, s.383(1).
[15] 1985 Act, s.383(3).
[16] Companies (Inspection and Copying of Register, Indices and Documents) Regulations 1991 (S.I. 1991 No. 1998). A business day means any day other than a Saturday or Sunday, Christmas Day, Good Friday or a Bank Holiday.
[17] 1985 Act, s.383(4).
[18] 1985 Act, s.383(5).
[19] *McCasker v. Rae* (1966) S.C. 253.
[20] 1985 Act, s.723(3).

CHAPTER 17

CLASS MEETINGS

The rights attaching to shares in a company can differ. Subdivision of capital into deferred or preference shares is common, and since the Companies Act 1981 the powers of a company to issue redeemable shares have been enhanced. In addition, shares are often divided into 'A' and 'B' shares to suit the character of the company—for example, a joint venture between two principal shareholders. All these are "classes" of share. **17–01**

Ordinary shares, which confer on the holders the residue of rights which do not attach to other classes of shares, constitute the "equity" in the company, and themselves constitute a class of share.

Meetings of separate classes of shareholders will require to be convened whenever the Acts or the articles so provide.

1 VARIATION OF CLASS RIGHTS

Members of a company, acting in accordance with the Acts and the constitution of the company, may, provided they act in good faith for the benefit of the company as a whole, and subject to any necessary consent of the class affected, vary the relative voting rights attached to the various classes of shares.[1] As will be seen, this is an area where the courts have been granted specific powers to protect a dissentient minority.[2] **17–02**

"Variation" will not, however, include a situation where the contractual rights of the class in question are being fulfilled and satisfied in accordance with the articles:

> A company registered in Scotland passed a special resolution at an EGM attended by ordinary shareholders only, reducing its capital by paying off the whole preference capital. Certain preference shareholders objected, on the ground that the failure to hold a class meeting of preference shareholders was in breach of the articles, which required such a meeting wherever the special rights attached to a class of shares were "modified, commuted, affected or dealt with." The House of Lords found against this view: variation presupposed the existence to the right, the variation of the right and the continued existence of the right as varied. It was a different situation where a right was fulfilled and satisfied and thereafter ceased to exist.[3]

[1] *Rights & Issues Investment Trust Ltd v. Stylo Shoes Ltd & Others* [1965] Ch. 250.
[2] 1985 Act, s.127. See J.B.L. (1996) at 554 for a full, radical survey of the modern position.
[3] *House of Fraser plc v. ACGE Investments Ltd* [1987] A.C. 387. It is a different matter if the class rights, as defined in the articles, expressly include any reduction of capital: *Re Northern Engineering Industries plc* [1994] B.C.C. 618, C.A.

Where a variation, properly defined, of class rights is proposed, the class rights can be varied in the manner laid down by the articles, subject to and in accordance with section 125 of the 1985 Act. The section makes it clear that the variation, except where the context otherwise requires, is to include abrogation.

The regime laid down by section 125 (described in more detail below under the heading "Procedure") applies to two categories of cases:

(i) where rights or benefits contained in the company's articles are annexed to particular shares—classic examples of rights of this kind are dividend rights and rights to participate in surplus assets on winding up; and

(ii) where rights or benefits, although not attached to any particular shares, are none the less conferred on the beneficiary in the capacity of member or shareholder.[4]

The distinction between the instances where a right is a class right falling within section 125 and where it is a non–class right but it is capable of being altered by special resolution is an important one: if section 125 applies it may be difficult to obtain the consent of the class concerned, but if a special resolution is required the entire body of shareholders will become the constituency:

The right of petitioning shareholder to be president of a company was not a class right but one personal to her and it could be altered by special resolution.[5]

A company cannot, by contract, deprive its members of their rights to alter the articles by special resolution.[6]

2 PROCEDURE

17–03 The situation differs according to whether the class rights are attached by the memorandum (which has always, in law, been a most difficult document to alter) or otherwise than by the memorandum, for example, in the articles or in a resolution increasing the company's capital by the creation of the new class in question. The categories are as follows:

(a) Where rights are attached otherwise than by the memorandum and the articles do not contain provision for variation: the rights may be varied only if (i) the holders of three-quarters in nominal value of the issued shares of that class consent in writing, or (ii) with the sanction of an extraordinary resolution passed at a separate general meeting of the

---

[4] *Cumbrian Newspapers Group Ltd v. Cumberland and Westmorland Herald Newspapers Printing Co. Ltd* [1986] BCLC 286.

[5] *Re Blue Arrow* [1987] BCLC 585.

[6] *Punt v. Symons & Co. Ltd* [1903] 2 Ch. 506; and see *Cumbrian Newspapers Group Ltd v. Cumberland and Westmorland Herald Newspaper Printing Co. Ltd* [1986] BCLC 286, 305.

holders of that class; this is subject in both cases to complying with any additional requirement which may specifically attach to the rights[7];

(b) where the rights are attached by the memorandum or otherwise and (i) where they are so attached by the memorandum, the articles contain provision with respect to their variation which had been included in the articles on incorporation or (ii) where they are so attached otherwise, the articles contain such provision (whenever first included)—those rights may only be varied in accordance with the provisions in the articles,[8] and

(c) where the rights are attached by the memorandum, and the memorandum and articles do not contain provision for variation: rights may be varied if all the members of the company (not just the members of the class) agree.[9]

Special provisions apply to variations of class rights which are connected with section 80 (authority to directors to allot shares) and section 135 (reduction of share capital).[10]

In relation to any class meetings required under this section, the provisions of the **17–04** Act as to length of notice (section 369), meetings and votes (section 370), the circulation of members' resolution (section 376 and 377) and the provisions of the articles relating to general meetings shall, so far as applicable, apply.[11] This however is subject to the following modifications: (i) the quorum at any meeting other than an adjourned meeting shall be two persons holding or representing by proxy at least one-third in nominal value of the issued shares of the class in question, and, at an adjourned meeting, one person holding shares of the class in question or his proxy; and (ii) any holder of such shares present in person or by proxy may demand a poll.[12]

The persons present at a class meeting or represented by proxy must be members of that particular class but the proxies need not be members either of the company or the class.[13] A class meeting may consist of one person:

> Where a person signified his assent, in a document signed in the minute book, to an increase in the preference share capital of the company of which he was the sole holder, it was held that in the particular circumstances the term "meeting" could not be interpreted in the ordinary sense, and that the expressed assent of the one shareholder was sufficient to treat the resolution as a valid resolution.[14]

A person who is not a member can usually neither be chairman nor present at meetings, and this would also apply to class meetings, but the chairman of the

---

[7] 1985 Act, s.125(2).
[8] 1985 Act, s.125(4).
[9] 1985 Act, s.125(5). An alternative would be to make use of s.425; see Chap. 18.
[10] 1985 Act, s.125(3).
[11] 1985 Act, s.125(6).
[12] 1985 Act, s.125(6)(a), (b).
[13] 1985 Act, s.372(1), (7).
[14] *East v. Bennett Bros. Ltd* [1911] 1 Ch. 163.

board of directors would properly take the chair at a class meeting even though he held no shares of the class concerned. He would however have no vote.

3 REVIEW BY THE COURT

17–05 Section 127 of the 1985 Act is designed to protect dissentient minorities by enabling the court to review the majority decision in spite of what might or might not be contained in the company's articles. It provides that where pursuant to a provision in the memorandum or articles for authorising the variation of class rights, subject to the consent of a specified proportion of the holders of the shares of that class, or with the sanction of a resolution of a separate meeting, or pursuant to section 125(2), class rights are varied, the holders of not less than 15 per cent of the issued shares of the class in question (being persons who did not consent to or vote in favour of the resolution for the variation) may apply to the court to have the variation cancelled. Where any such application is made, the variation shall not have effect unless and until it is confirmed by the court.[15]

An application to the court must be made within 21 days after the date on which the consent was given or the resolution was passed. It may be made on behalf of the dissenting shareholders by such one or more of their number as they may appoint in writing for the purpose. If the court is satisfied, having regard to all the circumstances of the case, that the variation would unfairly prejudice the dissenting shareholders, it may disallow the variation; it not so satisfied, it shall confirm the variation.[16]

4 THE MEETINGS

17–06 As has been seen above, a class meeting may be required to sanction a change in the rights attaching to shares of that class.

In this situation, it will be necessary to call both a class meeting and a meeting of all the shareholders. Separate notices must be sent for each meeting, and the requirements of the articles as to quorum and procedure generally have to be followed at each meeting. Specimen notices might be as follows.

...... PLC

NOTICE CONVENING MEETING OF PREFERENCE SHAREHOLDERS

NOTICE IS HEREBY GIVEN that a separate general meeting of the holders of the 10 per cent cumulative preference shares of £1 each in the capital of the company will be held at ...... on ...... at ...... a.m./p.m. to

---

[15] 1985 Act, s.127(2).
[16] 1985 Act, s.127(3), (4).

consider and, if thought fit, to pass the resolution set out below which will be proposed as an extraordinary resolution:

RESOLUTION

THAT this meeting of the holders of the 10 per cent cumulative preference shares of the company hereby sanctions the passing and carrying into effect of the special resolution set out in the notice convening an extraordinary general meeting of the company to be held on ...... (a print of which notice is comprised in the same document as contains the notice convening this meeting), and all variations of the rights of the said cumulative preference shares involved therein or intended to be effected thereby.

DATED ....

By order of the board,

. . .

Secretary.

A holder of 10 per cent cumulative preference shares entitled to attend and vote at the meeting is entitled to appoint a proxy [or more than one proxy][17] to attend and vote in his stead. A proxy need not be a member of the Company.

...... PLC

NOTICE CONVENING EXTRAORDINARY GENERAL MEETING

NOTICE IS HEREBY GIVEN that an extraordinary general meeting of the Company will be held at ...... on ...... at .... a.m./p.m. (or so soon thereafter as the separate general meeting of the holders of the 10 per cent cumulative preference shares of £1 each in the capital of the company convened for the same date shall have been concluded or adjourned) to consider and, if thought fit, to pass the resolution set out below which will be proposed as a special resolution:

RESOLUTION

Subject to and conditionally upon the passing of the resolution to be put to a separate class meeting of the 10 per cent cumulative preference shares of £1 each in the capital of the company convened for [name date]:
THAT article ...... of the company's articles of association be altered by deleting the words "one vote for every five preference shares" and substituting therefor the words "one vote for every six preference shares."

DATED ......

By order of the board,

......

Secretary.

---

[17] See para. 14–16.

A member entitled to attend and vote at the meeting is entitled to appoint a proxy [or more than one proxy] to attend and vote in his stead. A proxy need not be a member of the company.

17–07   The method of conducting the proceedings of class meetings of shareholders was reviewed in *Carruth v. Imperial Chemical Industries Ltd*:

> In 1935, I.C.I. decided to reorganise its share capital and convened three separate meetings to follow the general meeting for that year; an extraordinary general meeting for a reduction of capital, an ordinary shareholders' meeting and a meeting of deferred shareholders. The annual general meeting was convened for 10.30 a.m. on May 1, 1935; the other meetings were timed for 10.45 a.m., 11.00 a.m. and 11.15 a.m., respectively. On the day, 1600 shareholders were present. After the annual meeting and on the commencement of the extraordinary general meeting, the chairman stated that that meeting would be followed by the ordinary shareholders' and deferred shareholders' meetings, that he proposed to make one speech and to take the vote at each meeting without any further speeches. No attempt was made to clear the room of shareholders who were not entitled to attend any particular meeting; there was some dissent expressed from the floor about the proposal and at all three meetings the proposals were the subject of a poll. The House of Lords held that, since the conduct of the meeting lay in the hands of the chairman, the presence, at a separate meeting of one class of shareholders, of shareholders of a different class did not invalidate the meeting as a separate meeting.[18]

17–08   It is to be noted that the decision was based partly on matters of convenience, and Lord Maugham observed:

> "in my opinion the better and wiser course is to make provision for the holding of truly separate meetings in the ordinary way, even at the risk of inconvenience."[19]

The procedure adopted in the *I.C.I.* case has been followed in other cases where no objection has been raised. The practical question is whether the proposals are likely to be approved as a formality, or whether they have attracted attention and possible controversy. If the first, it will probably be satisfactory for all members present to meet in one room.

5   CLASS MEETINGS—EXAMPLE IN PRACTICE

17–09   In 1996, West Bromwich Albion Football Club decided to seek admission to the Alternative Investment Market. For historical reasons, the club had a complex share

---

[18] *Carruth v. Imperial Chemical Industries Ltd* [1937] A.C. 707.
[19] *ibid.*, at 767.

structure and it was necessary to convene meetings in order to create a new, single class of ordinary shares. The meetings were held in the cavernous surroundings of The Gala Leisure Centre in West Bromwich and the company secretary, Dr. John Evans, describes as follows the procedure followed at this successful event in the club's illustrious history:

"We used separate coloured cards for proxies. We also used separate coloured cards for voting purposes.

So far as checking-in procedures were concerned, we used a system which I have developed over the past few years. It may not be particularly sophisticated, but it tends to work.

A couple of weeks prior to the meeting, we wrote to every shareholder outlining what we believed their shareholding to be and explaining our procedures for the evening. Under separate cover, we sent out the actual formal documentation for the evening including an attendance slip which we asked them to complete and bring with them to the meeting.

As regards the evening itself, the first meeting held was the smallest one, that of bonus warrant holders. This took place in a small room (actually, the bar) where it was easy to sign them in and later record their votes.

We then moved to the major meeting. Experience had taught us to expect around 200 shareholders (out of 1600) but we were prepared for up to 800 and could probably have handled that number.

Shareholders and proxy-holders checked in through one of ten 'turnstiles', arranged alphabetically. There they handed in their attendance slips and also signed a separate entry sheet. They were then given pre-prepared envelopes containing voting slips tailored to their individual voting rights for the main meeting, together with the appropriate coloured slips for the separate class meetings for which they were qualified to attend.

We did not ask for proof of identity, but I have never yet come across anyone attempting to attend our meetings as a voting member on a fraudulent basis.

Once all that was over, we conducted the main meeting, voting being on a poll basis. We then ran the three class meetings in the same room, one after the other. Voting was again on a poll basis with each class being represented by a different coloured voting slip. Since we went through the same explanation three times, it all got very tedious, but we had been warned that that was the correct way in which we should proceed.

As it happens, a number of Premier Shareholders were concerned about what they feared could be an infringement of their rights, so that particular class meeting was quite lively. Since it was also the last meeting people from other classes were able to slope off early."

CHAPTER 18

MEETINGS UNDER SECTION 425
(COMPROMISES AND ARRANGEMENTS)

18–01   The 1985 Act provides a procedure whereby, with the aid of the court, companies can reorganise their capital structure or enter into an arrangement with their creditors, or both.

The procedure may be used where difficulties exist in changing the rights attaching to a class of shares by the variation of class rights procedure.

Section 425 of the Act provides that where a compromise or arrangement is proposed between a company and its creditors or any class of them or between the company and its members or any class of them, the court may, on the application of the company or of any creditor or member of it, or, in the case of a company being wound up or an administration order being in force in relation to a company, of the liquidator or administrator, order a meeting of the creditors or class of creditors, or of the members of the company or class of members (as the case may be) to be summoned in such manner as the court directs.[1] A "three-fourths majority" (see para. 18–07) is required.

1   Scope of the Section

18–02   It will be noted that the words "compromise" and "arrangement" are to have a common sense meaning:

> A scheme was proposed for a company without a share capital (a farmers' association) under which, for administrative savings, it was proposed that the number of ordinary members should be reduced from about 94,000 to seven. Members had paid a small admission fee and the company had considerable assets. Members were not entitled to dividends, but on a winding-up surplus assets would be divided in accordance with the board's determination, or, in default of that, equally. Each member had a right to vote at a general meeting, and, indirectly, to elect members of the board. At the meeting directed by the court, 1,439 votes were cast, seven in person and the remainder by proxy. 1,211 votes were cast in favour of the scheme and 228 against, a majority of almost 85 per cent. The court refused to sanction the scheme. Since the rights of members were being expropriated without any compensating advantage, it could not be said that they were entering into any compromise or arrangement with the company.[2]

Section 425 should not be used to sanction an act which would be *ultra vires*:

---

[1] 1985 Act, s.425(1).
[2] *Re NFU Development Trust Ltd* [1973] 1 All E.R. 135.

It was held in *Re Oceanic Steam Navigation Co. Ltd* that there was nothing in the language of the section under which the company could make and the court could sanction an arrangement which was in excess of the powers defined by the company's memorandum of association. In the case in question, the company petitioned the court to sanction a scheme of arrangement with its creditors under which the company would sell its undertaking for the benefit of the creditors. Simonds J., in refusing the petition, said: "It would be strange if by a side-wind under the section, without observing the particular prescription of the Act with regard to alterations, new powers could be conferred on the company."[3]

In a recent case, however, the Court of Appeal upheld the validity of an option agreement between a company and one of its members which had been sanctioned under section 425, even though it was assumed to amount to an illegal reduction of capital and so outside the powers of the company.[4]

The court will not normally sanction a scheme of arrangement under section **18–03** 425 in the absence of the consent of the company:

A company, Trust Houses Forte Limited, proposed a scheme of arrangement under section 425 in respect of Savoy Hotel Limited under which Trust Houses Forte hoped to gain control of the Savoy. T.H.F. sought the court's permission to convene separate meetings of the A and B shareholders of Savoy Hotel Limited, who between them held all the equity capital. The voting rights attached to these shares were weighted so as to give the B shareholders 49 per cent of the total voting rights, although if a three-quarters majority of the A shareholders voted in favour of the scheme that would be sufficient for the scheme to be approved under section 425. The board of the Savoy company held 65 per cent of the B shares, *i.e.* 32 per cent of the total voting rights. The board opposed the scheme. *Held*, that in the absence of the board's consent or of a provision in the scheme for obtaining the approval of the company by a simple majority in a general meeting, the court had no jurisdiction to sanction the proposed scheme.[5]

The term "arrangement" is wider than "compromise" and can cover a situation where there is no pre-existing dispute or difficulty to be resolved.[6] By section 425(5) "arrangement" includes a re-organisation of the company's share capital by the consolidation of shares of different classes or by the division of shares into shares of different classes, or by both of those methods.

2 PROCEDURE

Where the proposed arrangement is one between the company and its members, **18–04** meetings of creditors are not necessary under section 425.[7] No meeting is required

---

[3] *Re Oceanic Steam Navigation Co. Ltd* (1938) 108 L.J. Ch. 74.
[4] *Barclays Bank plc v. British & Commonwealth Holdings plc* [1996] 1 BCLC 1.
[5] *Re Savoy Hotel* [1981] 3 W.L.R. 441.
[6] *Re Guardian Assurance Co.* [1917] 1 Ch. 431.
[7] *Clydesdale Bank, Petitioners*, 1950 S.L.T. 123.

of any class that is not involved in the proposed scheme. A meeting should be convened, however, of any class that is affected, and great care must be taken in considering what constitutes a class for the purpose of the section. In this context, class rights can arise by reason of difference in interests, and regard must be paid to this in framing the proposed arrangement:

> For the purposes of an arrangement affecting policy holders of an assurance company, the holders of policies which had matured formed a different class from those whose policies had not matured: they had different interests.[8]
> Within a total body of ordinary shareholders, those whose interests lay with certain intended purchasers formed a separate class from the other shareholders.[9]

The important point is that each class should be so defined as to comprise those, and only those, whose rights are not so dissimilar as to make it impossible for them to consult together with a view to their common interest. It is for the company, not the court, to decide on what constitutes a class (although if the company gets it wrong, the court may eventually not approve the scheme). The members of any class can assent individually to the scheme (to save the inconvenience of calling a meeting) but there must be at least one class meeting for the court to have jurisdiction under the section.

Section 426 provides that with the notice must be sent a statement explaining the effect of the compromise or arrangement and in particular stating any material interests of the directors (in whatever capacity). Material changes occurring between the issue of the explanatory statement and the meetings under the scheme should be made known to those entitled to vote at the meetings.[10] If a meeting is convened by advertisement, the advertisement must state where a copy of the explanatory statement may be obtained.[11] The provision of this section should be carefully observed:

> Separate meetings of different classes of shareholders were authorised by the court to consider a scheme of arrangement, and the sending of notices by post and the giving of notice by advertisement were authorised. The advertisement had stated where the scheme could be seen but did not refer to the explanatory statement. *Held*, that the meetings had not been properly convened.[12]
> An explanatory statement sent out to the shareholders stated that the directors had no interests in a proposed scheme whereas they had extensive interests. *Held*, that there had not been a sufficient disclosure.[13]

18–05 An originating summons is the means by which application is made to the court for leave to convene the meeting or separate meetings. Upon the court approving the application, it will direct the company to convene the meeting by giving notice and for the meeting to be advertised.

---

[8] *Sovereign Life Assurance v. Dodd* [1982] 2 Q.B. 573.
[9] *Re Hellenic & General Trust Ltd* [1976] 1 W.L.R. 123.
[10] *Re MB Group plc* [1989] BCLC 672.
[11] 1985 Act, s.426(3).
[12] *City Property Investment Trust Corp., Petitioners*, 1951 S.L.T. 371.
[13] *Coltness Iron Co., Petitioners*, 1951 S.L.T. 344. See also *Re MB Group* [1989] BCLC 672.

The notice must be in a special form used for the purpose, and copies of the scheme of arrangement, statement pursuant to section 426 and proxy form will accompany the notice of the meeting. A special form of two-way proxy is used. In practice it is now customary for the company to send to members or creditors a composite document including a letter from the chairman supported, if applicable, by one from the company's financial advisers recommending acceptance of the scheme.

Directors who, pursuant to the court's order, receive proxies for or against the scheme, must use them.[14] Voting at the meeting will be by poll and not by show of hands because, as is noted below, the value of the votes cast will be relevant in determining the size of the majority. It has been held that the power of voting conferred on the holder of a proxy is wide enough to enable him to vote against a resolution to defer the consideration of the scheme to a future occasion.[15] **18–06**

3 MAJORITY

The majority in favour of the scheme must be a majority in number representing **18–07**
three-fourths in value of the creditors or class of creditors or members or class of members, as the case may be, present and voting either in person or by proxy at the meeting.[16]

It should be noted that the majority is dual, in number *and* in value; a simple majority of those voting is sufficient, whereas the "three-fourths" requirement relates to value.

By way of illustration:

A All 1,000 members of a class holding 10,000 shares vote; of these, one member holds 3,000 shares and he votes against; the remaining 7,000 shares are spread among the other 999 members. Even if all 999 vote in favour, they will not constitute the necessary majority because they cannot muster three-fourths in value.

B The member holding 3,000 shares is persuaded to abstain from voting; when the votes are counted 500 members holding 5,300 shares are found to have voted in favour and 499 members holding 1,700 shares to have voted against. The resolution is carried.

C If, in example B, one more member, holding one share, had been persuaded to vote against the resolution, the result would have been: in favour, 499 members holding 5,299 shares; against, 500 members holding 1,701 shares. The resolution is lost.

D (A more extreme version of C.) The big shareholder decides to cast his vote for the resolution. In the result, 500 members (including the large holder) vote 8,299 shares in favour; there are 500 members, carrying 1,701 shares, against. The resolution is lost.

---

[14] *Re Dorman Long & Co. Ltd* [1934] Ch. 635.
[15] *Re Waxed Papers Ltd* (1937) 53 T.L.R. 676.
[16] 1985 Act, s.425(2).

4   SANCTION BY THE COURT

After the class meetings convened under section 425 have been held, the chairman prepares a report supported by affidavit which is presented to the court. The court will then decide whether or not to sanction the scheme. In doing this, it normally takes into account three factors:

(a) *The meetings must have complied with sections 425 and 426*

18–08   The court will check that the meetings have been duly convened and held and that the resolutions have been passed by the appropriate majorities prescribed by section 425(2) and that all relevant classes have given their consent. The court will also check that the explanatory circular under section 426 has been issued and remains correct at the date of the meetings.

As noted, at this stage the court will check that the company has been correct in its definition of the classes of members or creditors affected by the scheme. If the company has omitted a class, and the court decides that that omission was improper, the scheme will fail even if the court decides that the class concerned is being fairly dealt with or that, anyway, it would have approved the scheme.[17]

(b) *Each class must have been fairly represented at the meetings*

18–09   The court will look behind the majorities achieved for each resolution to ensure that each class is fairly represented. For instance, it will not usually be satisfied if only a very small number of votes are cast in total, either in person or by proxy. If, following the examples above, not only the large shareholder, but many others as well, abstained from voting, so that the result was:

Total shareholding	1,000 members holding 10,000 shares;
In favour	50 members holding 500 shares;
Against	40 members holding 100 shares;

the scheme would be unlikely to be sanctioned. Equally, the court will be vigilant to ensure that no part of any majority is tainted by bias or conflict of interest.[18]

(c) *The proposal must be reasonable in an objective sense*

18–10   The court will take note of the size of the majorities at the meetings, but will refuse to sanction an inequitable scheme or one which does not accord with other principles set out in the Act. In a case where the scheme was in effect an acquisition of one company by another, the court refused its sanction because one shareholder with 13.95 per cent of the shares objected; it was held that if the purchasers had proceeded by way of section 209 of the Companies Act 1948 (relating to the power

---

[17] *Re Neath & Brecon Railway* [1892] 1 Ch. 349; *Re Hellenic & General Trust Ltd* [1976] 1 W.L.R. 123.
[18] *Re Hellenic & General Trust Ltd* [1976] 1 W.L.R. 123.

to acquire dissenting shares in a takeover) that percentage would have been sufficient to block the scheme.[19]

The general rule has been summarised as follows: the court must be satisfied that "the proposal is such as intelligent and honest members of the classes concerned, acting in respect of their own interests, would approve",[20] but provided that the persons with whom the scheme is made have been accurately and adequately informed by the explanatory statement and the requisite majority has approved the scheme, the court will not be concerned with their commercial reasons for approval.

The compromise or arrangement, if sanctioned by the court, is then binding on all creditors or class of creditors, or on the members or class of members, as the case may be, and also on the company, or, in the case of a company in the course of being wound up, on the liquidator and contributories of the company.[21]

An order under section 425(2) will have no effect until an office copy of the order has been delivered to the Registrar, and a copy of every such order must be annexed to every copy of the memorandum of the company issued after the order has been made, or, in the case of a company not having a memorandum, of every copy so issued of the instrument constituting the company or defining its constitution. Default fines are prescribed for non-compliance.[22]

5   MERGERS AND DIVISIONS OF PUBLIC COMPANIES

Section 425 is capable of being used in connection with a merger of two or more   **18–11**
public companies or a division (demerger) of one public company amongst two or
more companies. The companies (Mergers and Divisions) Regulations 1987 (S.I.
1987 No. 1991) added a new section 427A and a new Schedule 15B to the 1985
Act. The requirements imposed by the new provisions are in addition to those laid
down in section 425, and apply in three categories of case:

Case 1:   merger by acquisition, where a public company proposes to transfer all
of its undertaking to another pre-existing public company, with shareholders in the transferor company receiving shares in the transferee
company by way of consideration;

Case 2:   merger by formation, where two or more public companies propose to
transfer their undertakings to a third company, their members receiving
shares in the third company in return;

Case 3:   division, where a public company proposes to divide its undertaking
between two or more other companies, its shareholders receiving shares
in the transferee companies in return.

---

[19] ibid.
[20] Re Dorman Long & Co. Ltd [1934] 1 Ch. 635.
[21] 1985 Act, s.425(2).
[22] 1985 Act, s.425(3).

CHAPTER 19

MEETINGS OF MEMBERS OF COMPANIES: EXAMPLES IN PRACTICE

19–01 In this chapter it is proposed to examine in more detail some of the practical aspects of typical meetings of shareholders. For the purpose, it is assumed that the company is a public company with a Stock Exchange quotation, although much of what is written would apply also to other companies. It should be noted that a private company may elect to dispense with the AGM and other related formalities by following the requirements of s.379A Companies Act 1985.

1 ANNUAL GENERAL MEETING

19–02 Paragraph 6.1 of the Cadbury Committee's Report on the Financial Aspects of Corporate Governance, published in 1992, defines the relationship between the board of a company and its shareholders as follows:

> "The formal relationship . . . is that the shareholders elect the directors, the directors report on their stewardship to the shareholders and the shareholders appoint the auditors to provide the external check on the directors' financial statements. Thus the shareholders as owners of the company elect the directors to run the business on their behalf and hold them accountable for its progress."

The AGM is a significant focal point of this relationship. In spite of this, criticisms in recent years have centred on:

Attempts by pressure groups and single-issue factions to hijack the meeting.

Shareholder apathy, measured by the low number of proxy cards returned (on one survey, about ten per cent by number of members and one-third by number of shares) and the almost complete non-attendance of institutional shareholders.

The time and expense involved in an occasion which is treated as a social event and which produces little or no strategic or executive outcome.

In the mid–1990s, these difficulties led some to call for the abolition of the AGM and its replacement by a system of postal voting on the matters requiring decision.

The response of the Department of Trade and Industry was to set the discussion within the context of an improvement in company-shareholder relationships. The

Department was of the opinion that events had demonstrated the importance which shareholders attached to the opportunity offered by the AGM to express their views. It also wanted to continue to offer support for wider share ownership, which had received a significant boost through the then government's privatisation policy. It accordingly set about finding ways in which shareholder rights could be improved (prompted in part by the report of a House of Commons Select Committee). It established a Committee under the chairmanship of Paul Myners of Gartmore plc which reported that virtually all participants viewed the AGM as an expensive waste of time and money (Myners Report "Developing a Winning Partnership" 1995). In April 1996 the DTI then issued a consultative document, "Shareholder Communications at the Annual General Meeting", which contained proposals for the amendment of the law in two particular areas:

(1) a proposed right of requisitionists to have resolutions considered at the AGM free of charge (see paras. 13–24 to 13–29); and

(2) whether it should be made easier for institutional investors to appoint multiple representatives to speak at an AGM (see para. 14–01).

This was followed by a further consultative document published in November 1996, "Private Shareholders: Corporate Governance Rights" which considered the potential impact on members' rights if, as a result of the moves towards rolling settlement of share bargains and other factors, a substantial number of owners were to move their holdings into nominee arrangements. The document invited views on whether legislation should be introduced to enable investors holding through nominees to have the statutory right to opt to enjoy certain rights (such as to receive companies' reports and accounts and to attend, speak and vote at AGMs) to which they would be entitled if they, and not their nominees, were members of the company.

No proposals for legislation have yet emerged from this consultative exercise. In the meantime, the Institute of Chartered Secretaries and Administrators, picking up its cue from the first consultative paper but widening the scope of the review to cover AGM procedure and best practice generally, in September 1996 published "A Guide to Best Practice for Annual General Meetings".[1] The recommendations of the Guide, which in part reflect practices which are already in use, are increasingly becoming seen as authoritative: they are referred to in the text which follows as "ICSA" with the relevant paragraph number. They are endorsed by the National Association of Pension Funds, the Association of British Insurers and ProShare. It should be noted that this Guide is currently being updated.

The passing of the Directors' Remuneration Report Regulations 2002 requiring quoted companies to prepare a Remuneration Report which must be laid before the members in general meeting and giving members the right to a separate "advisory" vote on this report has led to some lively AGMs.

In 1988/99 the National Association of Pension Funds sponsored an independent inquiry into proxy voting, the Newbold Inquiry. Paul Myners was asked to review the UK proxy voting system on behalf of the Shareholder Voting Working Group in 2004 to take the recommendations of the Newbold Inquiry forward. His report is entitled "Review of the impediments to voting UK shares" and is available

---

[1] Obtainable from ICSA, www.icsa.org.uk

from www.aitc.co.uk. His key recommendations to streamline the voting process are that electronic proxy voting should be encouraged, pension schemes should play a more active role in ensuring that their votes are cast and AGM votes should be put to a poll so all votes are counted, not just hands raised at the meeting. Results of the vote should also be published including abstentions. The Government is currently considering the report.

The question of possible disorder remains a matter of concern to boards and company secretaries. In most instances, however, AGMs pass off peacefully. It is proposed in this chapter to deal first with those AGMs which can be described as normal, and then to deal with situations of potential difficulty. In the notes for an agenda of a normal AGM (see paras. 19–03 to 19–16) a more active style of meeting is described in which there is, by company choice, some extra participation by shareholders and directors. This has been observed to work well, and the more friendly atmosphere will itself help to change the mood of any shareholder who has entered the meeting with aggressive intent. This type of meeting is a good show-piece for the company. It will be referred to as a "longer meeting" in the text which follows. Some companies prefer the traditional style in which proceedings are kept to the minimum required to ensure the necessary resolutions are passed. This minimalist approach is referred to as a "shorter meeting" below.

Then, the text will contain a checklist of items for an AGM where some difficulties are expected.

A.   A Normal AGM

The choice of hall

19–03   The venue chosen for the annual general meeting is a matter of individual preference, but it may be wise to select a place with some historic or architectural merit, both as an aid to company prestige and to bring out the best qualities in the shareholders attending. It is better for too much accommodation to be available than too little.

The organisers will take care to ensure that sufficient car parking space is available and that there are adequate signs to enable members to find their way to the hall. The cloakroom facilities must be readily accessible, and the organisers should check the availability of first aid in an emergency. The venue should be suitable for disabled attendees, including those with poor hearing (ICSA 1.4).

The meeting room should have a dais of sufficient height and size to accommodate the directors[2] and their advisers comfortably, and the secretary will check that sound amplification equipment is available, together with a lectern for the chairman. Questions from the floor should be audible to the meeting and, in particular, to the directors who have the duty to respond.

The lighting in the hall should be adequate for shareholders to be able to read their documents comfortably. A helpful design feature is for the directors' table to be lit more prominently than the rest of the hall and for the board to be seated in

---

[2] ICSA 2.1 and 2.2 recommends that, wherever possible, all directors attend the AGM, and that the directors should be seated with the chairman, facing the shareholders.

front of a large-scale representation of the company's logo. Any audio–visual or presentation equipment should be tested some hours in advance.

There should be adequate security at the entrance to the hall, and a large table for people to check in: shareholders tend to arrive in large numbers shortly before the meeting starts. If refreshments are being offered, they should be in a separate room or screened off until the close of the meeting. The availability of free food and drink will increase the numbers attending.

The company's registrars and press agents will need a telephone, together with access to telephone lines and power for the on-line link.

A room should be available for last-minute preparations by the board or for their use during any adjournment. This should be accessible but at the same time sufficiently far away from the meeting hall to avoid the directors being buttonholed by shareholders prior to the meeting. The same, or another, room might be required in the event of a poll.

The secretary should ensure that a representative of the hall or hotel staff where the meeting is being held should be in attendance to deal with urgently arising points.

Chapter 4 contains a more extensive check-list of items, many of which may be relevant to an AGM.

Preparations before the meeting

The starting signal for the annual meeting is the board meeting, held some two **19–04** months before, at which the directors settle the form of preliminary announcement.

This meeting, at which the company's auditors are often in attendance, crystallises all the preliminary work which has taken place on the accounts, decides on the final dividend to be recommended and approves the arrangements for the meeting. These matters should be covered by a formal board resolution which authorises the signature by the secretary of the notice of the meeting, by a director or the secretary of the directors' report and, by a director, of the annual accounts.[3] The secretary will also be authorised to release the preliminary announcement to the Stock Exchange and to despatch the accounts, containing the notice of the meeting, to shareholders.

It is usual practice to appoint a sub-committee at that board meeting which will meet the night before the intended release of the preliminary announcement to the Stock Exchange to deal with all the final approvals.

The secretary will devote particular attention to the form of the notice of the meeting (see para. 19–09, below) and the proxy form (see para. 14–20, above). He will then send a final copy of the documents to the printers with instructions for them to proceed to prepare a final proof which will then be comprehensively reviewed by senior management, the Board and the auditors. The order to print will then be given, and the secretary will organise the arrangements for despatch of the report and accounts to shareholders. It is customary for the registrars to

---

[3] Under s.233(1) of the 1985 Act a company's annual accounts must be approved by the board and signed by a director; under s.234A and s.234C the directors' report and remuneration report must be approved by the board and signed by a director or the secretary. Every copy of these documents which is laid before the company in general meeting must state the name of the person who signed them on behalf of the board.

deliver addressed labels to the printers; the registrars must make clear which envelopes are to include the proxy form[4] (usually those going to ordinary shareholders) and those which do not require the inclusion of a proxy form (for example copies required to be sent to debenture holders for information, or other complimentary copies in accordance with an additional list provided by the company).

Instead of sending a paper copy of the accounts, a company may now use electronic communication to send the accounts and reports in full to any person who has agreed to accept service in this manner and has provided an "address" for that purpose (s.238(4A) Companies Act). See useful guidance in the ICSA guide "Electronic Communications Order 2000—Guide to Recommended Best Practice" available from www.icsa.org.uk.

Under section 251 of the 1985 Act, a public company whose shares or debentures or any class of whose shares are listed need not, in such cases as are specified in regulations, send to entitled persons (as defined in the section) the full accounts and reports but may instead send them a summary financial statement. This option is becoming increasingly used: the relevant regulations are the Companies (Summary Financial Statement) Regulations (S.I. 1995 No. 2092).

It may also be useful to prepare a likely questions and suggested answers paper to help the Board prepare for the AGM.

19–05   Under the instructions of the secretary, the registrars and the company's bankers will make arrangements for the payment of the dividend to be approved by the annual general meeting. In normal circumstances this will follow the amount recommended by the directors since the articles invariably provide, as does article 102 of Table A, that a final dividend shall not exceed the amount they recommend.

The secretary will, from time to time, check with the registrars as to the progress of the proxy vote. If this is moving slowly, it is open to him to remind one or two of the larger shareholders that, if they wish to support the resolutions to be proposed at the meeting, return of a proxy card would be helpful. At the due date contained in the Company's Articles of Association for closure of the proxy lists (typically 48 hours before the meeting), the registrars will report the final result to the company and this forms one of the documents the chairman and company secretary will need to have available at the meeting.

19–06   Before the meeting, the secretary will attend to the following final details:

(1) Arrange for stewards at the meeting (including people to control the flow of shareholders and others at the checking-in desk and to receive the shareholders' attendance cards).

(2) Arrange for a note, and possibly an audio recording, to be taken of the proceedings.

(3) Ensure that the register of members, the register of directors and secretaries, the register of charges and the register of substantial interests in the company are available at the meeting.

(4) Ensure that the register of directors' interests (which has, under the 1985 Act, Sched. 13, para. 29, to be produced at the commencement of

---

[4] Often, the proxy card will be personalised so as to show the address of each shareholder in a window envelope, and will be bar-coded.

the company's annual general meeting and to remain open and accessible during the continuance of the meeting to any person attending the meeting) and copies of directors' service contracts[5] will also be available.

(5) Arrange for plenty of copies of the report and accounts and a print of the company's memorandum and articles to be available at the meeting.

(6) Prepare attendance sheets for signature by members; these should require details of full name and number of shares, and whether the individual attends in person or as a proxy for a member, or as a corporate representative.[6]

(7) Prepare attendance sheets for signature by persons other than members, *e.g.* press, stockbrokers, employees and others attending by invitation.

(8) Ensure that all proxy cards are taken to the meeting.

(9) Ensure that poll cards and voting lists are available in case a poll is demanded.[7]

(10) Prepare a detailed chairman's script (see paras. 19–10 to 19–16),

(11) Agree whether the chairman will make a current trading statement and, if so, make arrangements for this to be announced to the Stock Exchange simultaneously with its transmission at the AGM (see para. 19–07 below).

Press arrangements

It is convenient at this point to consider the arrangements which are typically **19–07** made for press coverage, often with the help of specialists in financial public relations. The period starting with the preliminary announcement and leading up to the annual general meeting is a time when companies often adopt a high profile. First, after the preliminary announcement has been released to the Stock Exchange, the company or its press/financial PR agents will send copies direct to the press and selected brokers, analysts and major shareholders with the name of a person (usually the chairman or chief executive) who may be contacted for further information. Sometimes, the company will insert a paid advertisement relating to the results in the main financially-orientated newspapers, so that all conspires to give maximum coverage to the world at large.

When the annual report is posted to shareholders, the company or its agents will send copies to the press, often accompanied by a copy or synopsis of the chairman's statement.

By the time the annual general meeting has been reached, attention has switched to the current trading position, and, if the chairman makes a statement about it at the meeting, it is immediately released to the press. Simultaneous release to the Stock Exchange is obligatory; otherwise the members who have come to the meeting will be in possession of information, probably price-sensitive, which is not available to other members.[8]

---

[5] See para. 19–05.
[6] See para. 14–01.
[7] See paras. 19–32 to 19–36.
[8] See Disclosure Rules available from www.fsa.gov.uk.

If the press attend a meeting of shareholders they do so at the invitation of the company. They have no right to be present. If, therefore, a member objects to their presence the meeting's agreement should be sought; on public relations grounds it might be unwise to ask the press to leave unless there is good reason.

The directors' report

19–08   The directors' report must set out, in respect of the financial year in question, a fair review of the development of the business of the company and its subsidiary undertakings during that year and of their position at the end of it. The 1985 Act also provides for the report to give particulars of any proposed dividend and details of the directors and the principal activities of the company and its subsidiary undertakings together with the information listed in Schedule 7.[9]

In addition to these statutory requirements, any company having a Stock Exchange listing is obliged under Listing Rule 9.8.4 to include a number of items in the annual report and accounts; in practice, many of these are put within the directors' report. Where business other than ordinary business is to be considered at an AGM, Listing Rule 14.17 requires an explanatory circular or, more conveniently, an explanation in the directors' report.[10] (ICSA 1.7 suggests that the company should give a brief description of the directors standing for re-election)

Precedent of notice and agenda

19–09   It may now be helpful to provide a precedent for a notice of an annual general meeting and notes from which a detailed chairman's script can be prepared by the secretary. The resolutions are the same as those shown in the example of a proxy form above, at paragraph 14.20.

NOTICE OF ANNUAL GENERAL MEETING

The .... th Annual General Meeting of the Company will be held at .... on .... at .... a.m./p.m. to transact the following business:

1 To receive [and consider[11]] the accounts and the reports of the directors and auditors thereon for the year ended .....
2 To receive the Remuneration Report for the year ended .....
3 To declare a final dividend of ...p per ordinary share, payable on .... to shareholders on the register on ...
4 To re-elect Mr .... as a director.
5 To re-elect Mrs .... as a director.
6 To re-appoint .... as auditors.
7 To authorise the directors to fix the remuneration of the auditors for ....

---

[9] 1985 Act, s.234.

[10] See para. 13–15, above. ICSA 1.6 emphasises the need for plain English to be used in these explanatory documents.

[11] ICSA 2.5 refers to the "consideration" of the report and accounts, which implies that there could be discussion on them.

A member entitled to attend and vote is entitled to appoint a proxy [or proxies][12] to attend and [on a poll][13] to vote instead of him. A proxy need not be a member of the company.

By order of the board,

....

Secretary.

[Address]   [Date]

A form of proxy is enclosed for the use of shareholders. To be effective it must be completed, signed and returned so as to reach the [Company's Registrars] at least 48 hours[14] before the time of the meeting. By signing and returning the form of proxy a shareholder will not be precluded from attending and voting in person should he subsequently decide to do so.

The Company specifies, pursuant to regulation 34 of the Uncertificated Securities Regulations 1995, that for members to be entitled to attend and vote at the meeting (and for the purpose of the determination by the Company of the number of votes they may cast) they must be entered on the Company's register of members at [date and time not more than 48 hours before the time fixed for the meeting] ("the specified time"). Changes to entries on the register after the specified time will be disregarded in determining the rights of any person to attend or vote at the meeting.[15]

Notes for an AGM Agenda

The following text contains notes rather than a suggested script. The secretary can, **19–10** from it, prepare either a summarised version for the board, or, if the chairman prefers it, a complete verbatim text for use by the chairman.

Opening of meeting

At the appointed time, and assuming a quorum is present, the chairman declares **19–11** the meeting open. If there is congestion at the back of the hall, he may be able to point out some vacant seats further forward. He checks that his words are fully audible.

Notice convening the meeting

The chairman checks that everybody has a copy of the notice and may refer to **19–12** the page in the annual report where it is printed. He asks whether it may be taken

---

[12] See para. 14–16.

[13] Delete the words in square brackets if the articles permit a proxy-holder to vote on a show of hands.

[14] Or as the articles may require—but not more than 48 hours before the meeting (see 1985 Act, s.372(5)).

[15] This is the statement required by CREST. See paras. 13–02 and 14–06.

as read. In the unlikely event of this not being agreed, the secretary would read out the notice.

Auditors' report

19–13   Section 235 of the 1985 Act does not require this to be read out. The chairman may therefore ask for it to be taken as read. At the longer type of meeting (see para. 19–02), the chairman may ask a representative of the auditors to give a summary of the report: the auditors can then also refer to the extent to which the company has complied with the corporate governance matters referred to in the Combined Code on Corporate Governance, about which a separate report by the auditors will be set out in the annual report.

Current trading

19–14   It is often the practice (one which is encouraged by ICSA 2.18) that before the chairman puts the formal resolutions to the meeting, he makes a statement about the company's current trading (which is simultaneously released to the Stock Exchange—see para. 19–07). In the longer meeting, this can be accompanied by short presentations by other executive members of the board covering their areas of responsibility (see ICSA 2.19).

In the shorter meeting (see para. 19–02) it may be preferable to leave this item until the end of the meeting.

Resolutions

19–15   The chairman reads out each resolution in turn, and briefly summarises their effect and purpose (ICSA 2.7). He then puts them to a vote by a show of hands in accordance with the following procedure. Following each vote on a show of hands, the chairman should indicate the level of proxies lodged on each resolution, and the balance for and against the resolution and the number of abstentions (Combined Code provision D.2.1)

(1) That the accounts and the reports of the directors and auditors thereon for the year ended .... as printed and distributed to shareholders, be and they are hereby received.
The chairman seeks a proposer and seconder.
Questions are then invited. These are dealt with by the chairman or the appropriate board member (see ICSA 2.6 and 2.8 and para. 19–23 below).
The chairman then puts the resolution to the vote. If the result is not obvious, the secretary will count the hands. The chairman then declares the result.

(2) That the Remuneration Report for the year ended .... as printed and distributed to shareholders, be and it is hereby received. As above a proposer and seconder are sought. The resolution is put to the vote in the same way. That a final dividend of ... per ordinary share payable on .... to the shareholders on the register on ... be and the same is hereby approved.

The chairman seeks a proposer and seconder. He then puts the resolution to the vote and declares the result.

(3) That Mr .... be and he is hereby re-elected a director of the company.

The chairman invites the director to stand up. The chairman may choose to briefly describe the director's role in the company, and seeks a proposer and seconder for the resolution. He then puts the resolution to the vote and declares the result. If elected, the director concerned expresses his thanks.

(4) That Mrs .... be and she is hereby re-elected a director of the company.

The chairman follows the same procedure as in (3). In any resolution where the chairman's own re-election is proposed, he or she should hand the chair to to the deputy chairman or to another director to put the proposal to the meeting (see ICSA 2.4).

(5) That the auditors ...., be and they are hereby re-appointed to act as the auditors of the company until the conclusion of the next general meeting at which accounts are laid before the company.[16]

The chairman seeks a proposer and seconder. He then puts the resolution to the vote and declares the result.

(6) That the directors be and they are hereby authorised to fix the remuneration of the auditors for .....[17] The chairman follows the same procedure as in (5).

In the shorter meeting, it is enough for the chairman to propose each resolution, put it to the vote and declare the result. He does not need to seek a seconder.

At the longer meeting, the chairman will ask for a proposer and seconder for each resolution. It helps to create a good atmosphere if the proposers and seconders are drawn from shareholders in the body of the hall. This may involve some planning, and those who offer to take on the role of proposer or seconder like to have a slip on which is written their script: "I have pleasure, Mr. Chairman, in proposing/seconding the motion".

Close of meeting

As mentioned, in the shorter meeting the statement as to current trading may be **19–16** made after all the resolutions have been voted on.

In the longer meeting it is customary for the directors to receive a vote of thanks from the members present: a company official may perhaps have been instrumental in arranging this.

The chairman will then indicate where the shareholders and visitors should proceed in order to receive any refreshments provided by the company. He then thanks everyone for their attendance and declares the meeting closed.

---

[16] 1985 Act, s.385(2).

[17] *ibid.*, s.390A(1). Resolutions (5) and (6) should not be run together as one resolution (see ICSA 2.5).

B.   A POTENTIALLY DIFFICULT AGM

19–17   Set out below is a check-list of points which might be taken into account by companies when they face the prospect of a difficult AGM.

Generally

19–18   The better the relationship with shareholders and with other interest groups, the less likelihood of trouble at the annual meeting. The following advice is given in the Administrator[18]:

> Throughout the year you must be tireless in putting your message across to your important target audiences. These target audiences might include employees, customers, institutional and small shareholders, the Stock Exchange and UK Listing Authority for quoted companies, trade associations and institutions, government, and the broadcast and print media (local, trade, vertical trade, national publications).[19]
>
> Depending on what you have to say, there are numerous methods that can be used to ensure that all your target audiences are kept informed of your actions, comments and feelings on events which impact on your business. These methods include for example: newsletters, media relations, conferences, workshops, corporate entertaining, personalised letters from the chairman/managing director, reports, positioning papers, crisis management plans, issues management programmes, monitoring of competitors and pressure groups.

In general, consultations with major shareholders over controversial items should continue down to and including the day of the AGM, bearing in mind at all times the need to be aware of the potential for disclosing inside information.

Check the articles

19–19   There are several ways in which a company's articles can be amended, if an opportunity permits (without itself arousing controversy), so as to introduce some potential improvements in the conduct of an AGM:

> The company's articles can make it clear that the chairman may take such action as he considers necessary to ensure the proper and orderly conduct of the meeting, and that his ruling on any matters of procedure or incidental to the business being conducted, (including whether or not to allow any amendment to a resolution) shall be final and binding (Extra Article A).
>
> The articles may provide that the chairman may, *without the consent of the meeting*, interrupt, suspend or adjourn it if he decides it is necessary to do so in order to secure the proper and orderly conduct of the meeting, or to give

---

[18] February 1996, p. 24; article by Sue Ashe, account director at Charles Barker.
[19] Disclosure Rules available at www.fsa.gov.uk.

all those present a proper opportunity to speak and vote, or to ensure that the business of the meeting is properly disposed of (Extra Article B).

Arising out of the *Byng v. London Life Association* case,[20] articles now frequently provide that a meeting is duly constituted if the chairman is satisfied that adequate additional premises are available to ensure that a member who cannot be accommodated in the main meeting is able (by means of such audio-visual or other equipment as may be necessary) to participate in the business for which the meeting has been convened and to hear and see and to be heard and seen by all other persons present (Extra Article C).

If the company is seriously concerned that there may be an attempt by some shareholders to smuggle in weapons or other offensive objects, the articles should afford the company a right of search. In the absence of this, the company may have no right to exclude a shareholder who refuses to submit to a search (Extra Article D).

In regard to the incidental rights attaching to a share, it is good practice for the articles to make clear the basis on which the individual classes of shares in the company afford the right to receive notice, to attend the meeting, to speak at the meeting and to vote (Extra Article E).

The presence in the articles of provisions on the lines of Articles 76 and 77 of Table A should be checked. Article 76, for example, states that no person other than a director retiring by rotation may be appointed or reappointed a director at a general meeting without either (i) the recommendation of the board or (ii) a period of prior notice having been given.[21] It may be useful, too, to insert a provision that the election of directors to replace those retiring is ordinary business while the appointment of additional directors is special business[22] (Extra Article F).

An attempt to amend, at a general meeting, a resolution which has been placed before it by proper notice can place the chairman in considerable difficulty,[23] because of the need to make an immediate decision in what might be disadvantageous circumstances and because of possible unfairness to shareholders who do not attend the meeting in person. In general, extraordinary and special resolutions are very difficult to amend[24]; some protection against late amendment of an ordinary resolution can be given by an article which provides that no amendment to an ordinary resolution shall be considered or put to the vote (other than an amendment to correct a patent error) unless (i) written notice of the intention to move the amendment is lodged at the registered office no later than (say) 72 hours prior to the time appointed for the holding of the meeting (or adjourned meeting), or (ii) the chairman in his absolute discretion agrees that the amendment may be considered and voted upon (Extra Article G). Alternatively, or in addition, the articles can provide that if an amendment to a resolution is ruled out of order by the chairman the proceedings on the substantive resolution are not invalidated by an error in his ruling (see para. 7–03).

---

[20] See para. 6–16.
[21] See para. 21–12.
[22] See para. 13–14.
[23] See para. 14–28.
[24] See para. 15–10.

It is helpful, too, for the articles to provide that, with the consent of the chairman, an amendment may be withdrawn by its proposer[25] (Extra Article H).

A number of larger companies have introduced a provision that votes on all resolutions shall be by means of a poll: this allows the chairman to omit the possibly contentious stage of a show of hands (Extra Article I).

Venue

19–20   The Company will wish to choose the venue for its annual general meeting well in advance. The best time is immediately after the previous AGM. Points relevant to the choice are as follows:

> **Size.** Choose a place which will, on any reasonable reckoning, be of more than ample size. An overflow room can be hired if it is in the same building, convenient of access, and will permit members to be "electronically in each other's presence so as to hear and be heard and to see and be seen".[26] Even then it might be wise to book an alternative, even bigger, venue which could be used if exceptionally large numbers turn up (see para. 19–22 below).
>
> **Overflow room.** If this is needed, careful preparation will be necessary to overcome a number of inherent disadvantages. The audio/visual equipment must be of a sophisticated nature, allowing each room to have a clear view of the other, and of the main points of activity. The overflow room will require to be separately chaired, and each chairman must be in easy communication with the other. The chairman in the main hall should be able to see the voting on a show of hands in the overflow room. The principal chairman should be able, and in fair rotation, to take questions from members in the overflow room.
>
> **Seating.** If extra chairs have to be hired, choose a reliable firm and make a pre-meeting check that the order is in hand.
>
> **Layout.** The dais should be high up, in a well-lit position, and with a fair distance between it and the first row. Wide and long aisles are an advantage.
>
> **Entrance.** The way in which arriving members and visitors will be controlled requires careful planning in conjunction with the company's registrars. One method is for shareholders to pass through a security check and registration formalities into a large foyer where members may congregate and which has a social function (the main hall will lie beyond). In the foyer can be situated the registrar's desk and an information point for shareholders.
>
> **Conditions of hire (hall).** The company should ensure that there are no conditions imposed by the owners of the hall which are relevant to the meeting, and with which the company might have difficulty in complying —items relating, for example to security (Extra Article D will help).
>
> **Equipment.** Plenty of microphones should be available. It is for consideration whether to use roving microphones, or to have a number of standing

---

[25] Otherwise, strictly, the consent of the meeting to the withdrawal of the amendment is necessary: see para. 7–03.

[26] *Byng v. London Life Association* [1989] 2 W.L.R. 738, C.A. See para. 6–16.

microphones at strategic places in the hall. All this will need to be controlled, on the day, by the chairman. He should have the ability to switch off the microphones in the body of the hall.

If any audio-visual or sound-reproducing equipment is required, this should be ordered, installed and tested in advance. It ruins the atmosphere of a meeting if the engineers are still testing equipment as people start to arrive.

Other items. Those items which are relevant to all AGMs will, of course, have to be taken into account.[27]

Before the meeting

Important points to watch are: 19–21

The company should field its strongest **team** to plan the meeting.[28]

Precise wording to cover the proposals before the meeting should be included in the **notice**. For example, it is less easy to amend or add to a motion which reads:

"To re-elect Mr. X as a director of the company"

than one which reads:

"To elect directors"[29]

A close watch should be kept on the **proxies**, as they arrive. Any points of difficulty (for example, whether a proxy is validly given under a power of attorney) should be promptly cleared up.

If the company has published a **summary financial statement**, copies of the full statement should be available immediately on request: supplies must not run out.

It may be helpful to shareholders, and to the company, to prepare a special form of **agenda**, or programme, for the meeting: this can be handed out to shareholders on their arrival. A folded A4 document could contain: a page of welcome and explanation in large type, a page setting out the resolutions or a summary of them, and remaining pages containing the meeting procedure (voting and questions), information about the layout of the venue and the stage, the location and timing of refreshments and arrangements for security.

Security arrangements should be firm but discreet. Shareholders dislike being frisked. The stewards should be given a careful briefing, in good time. If the decision is taken to exclude or eject anyone from the meeting, this should be taken by the chairman of the meeting. In the case of ejection, only reasonable force may be used.[30]

---

[27] See paras. 19–03 to 19–07.
[28] For example, The "Shell" Transport and Trading Company plc assembles a five-strong team several months in advance (*Financial Times*, May 8, 1996).
[29] See para. 5–05.
[30] See para. 3–02.

19–22   **Attendance cards**[31] are a useful way of regulating the flow of arriving members. They can be accepted in lieu of a signature on attendance sheets (but of course two people—for example a shareholder and a visitor, such as the member's spouse, may arrive with only one card: then the person without a card should sign in). Alternatively visitors, too, should be issued with an attendance card, possibly of a different colour from that of members.

The stewards and those who are manning the entrance areas should be in touch with the company secretary with news of the arrival of persons for whom a **special watch** is being kept. It will be helpful for the chairman to know where any dissident faction is seated.

The attendance of the **press**, at an AGM is, in general, acceptable.[32] Television is, however, a different matter: programme makers are usually more interested in the sensational aspects of a meeting than in serious reporting, and should be dealt with outside the meeting if possible.

Punctuality is important. Delay causes irritation, and detracts from the punctilious observance of legal form on which the chairman may need to rely later in the meeting. Even if people are still queuing for admittance at the hour appointed for the meeting, the chairman should open the meeting on time. If the late arrivals are causing a considerable distraction, the chairman can informally ask the indulgence of the members present for a few minutes, and then proceed with the formal business when the noise has subsided. It might be helpful for the agenda to begin with an innocuous item, such as a more extended introduction to the persons at the top table or a short presentation: this will help to set a constructive tone to the proceedings, and can be begun even if there is still a certain amount of movement at the back of the hall.

If, in spite of everyone's best forecasts, the meeting attracts a much **greater attendance** than anticipated, the secretary has to work through the alternative arrangements in the following order:

1. Ask the stewards to see whether there are additional unoccupied seats here and there in the body of the hall which can be filled by those crowded at the back. It may be possible to remove some "reserved" labels. Perhaps some extra chairs can be brought in.
2. Bring into use the overflow rooms, in accordance with the principles set out in the *Byng* case and, if applicable, Extra Article C.
3. Adjourn the meeting (and to that extent it is a "meeting" capable of adjournment) to the stand-by accommodation which has been reserved for such an emergency (see above). The adjournment should be of minimum length, *i.e.* to allow people time to get to the new venue. Adequate directions would need to be given.
4. Adjourn the meeting to another day, time and place. The exercise of this power (which is a common law one, arising where the views of the majority cannot validly be ascertained[33]) is subject to the company's articles (which may, it is hoped, include Extra Article A). This power must be exercised reasonably with a view to facilitating the discussion of

---

[31] See para. 14–21.
[32] See para. 19–07.
[33] *Byng*; see para. 6–16.

the business before the meeting. The length of the adjournment will depend on the urgency of the business.[34]

In cases 3 and 4, the meeting should be opened at the first venue and then formally adjourned to the alternative venue.

At the meeting: questions

Questions to the directors have always been part of an annual general meeting, **19–23** although no right is conferred by statute. Questions are encouraged by the ICSA Code of Practice, which puts forward the following principles:

1. Companies should provide adequate time for shareholder questions. The chairman should permit shareholders to raise questions on any item concerning the company's past performance, its results and its intended future performance. Questions which are irrelevant to the company or its business or which might lead to the release of commercially sensitive information, should not be permitted.[35]
2. Repetitive questions can be brought to an end by the chairman who has the right to limit the amount of debate permitted on each resolution.[36]
3. The Code encourages companies to allow questions to be submitted in advance of the meeting.[37]

The above principles, of course, permit a good deal of latitude to the individual member. They probably go no further than the law allows: shareholders have the right to debate matters which are the business of the meeting. The chairman can, however, bring about some order in the discussion by trying to ensure that only one topic at a time is debated, that each person speaks once only, and by terminating debate.[38] However, he must be impartial and must allow all points of view a full hearing. He may need to be very patient.[39] The best plan, if possible, is to allow the discussion to run its course; in the end, a proposal to move to the next item on the agenda will command the approval of many in the hall. Strictly, such a proposal is a closure motion and can be debated.

Questions are normally taken under the item relating to the approval of the accounts. It is possible, however, for the agenda to provide that only questions relevant to the accounts will be taken at that stage, with more general questions and comments being taken at the end. In the hurly-burly of a contentious meeting, however, the distinction may be hard to enforce.

The chairman will, in practice, ask for questions at only one point in the meeting, but if they are raised by members in relation to any proposal before shareholders they must be answered.

---

[34] For adjournment of company meetings, see Chap. 14.
[35] ICSA 2.6.
[36] ICSA 2.8.
[37] ICSA 2.9.
[38] See "Rules of Debate" in Chap. 7.
[39] The AGM of Sony in Tokyo in 1984 lasted 13212 hours.

Anyone who asks a question should give his or her name and that of any organisation represented.

At a large meeting, members who wish to ask questions may be directed to a central question point with its own light and microphone. The latter items will be under the control of the chairman; it is courteous to allow these to remain switched on while the chairman replies to a member's question.

Proxy-holders do not have the right to ask questions at any AGM of a public limited company unless the articles so allow.[40] In practice, the chairman may allow a proxy-holder to speak to avoid creating the impression that debate is being stifled; but to permit one will be to permit all.[41]

At the meeting: amendments to proposed resolutions

19–24 This topic has been dealt with elsewhere: see in particular paras. 7–03 to 7–05 and 14–28.

In summary, the chairman should reject amendments which are:

(1) Negative (negate the substantive motion)
(2) Onerous (impose more of a burden than the main resolution)
(3) Outside the scope of the notice
(4) Redundant (re-open previously settled business)

Poll on an amendment

19–25 The questions to be put to members will require careful thought. In accordance with the principles described earlier,[42] the questions will be:

(1) Does the meeting approve the amendment?
(2) Does the meeting approve the resolution as amended?
(3) Does the meeting approve the original resolution as unamended?

Depending on the result of question (1), either questions (2) or (3) will be irrelevant.

At the meeting: other points

19–26 (1) **Motion to adjourn:** if a shareholder proposes the adjournment of the meeting, the chairman should resist the proposal as it is irrelevant to the meeting and the AGM is required to be held under the 1985 Act.

(2) **Directions to the board:** a member may attempt to introduce a resolution which requires the board to act in a certain manner. Since matters of management have been delegated to the board, such a proposal would almost certainly require a special resolution.[43] This in

---

[40] See para. 14–16.
[41] ICSA 2.31 encourages chairmen to seek the consent of the meeting to proxy-holders speaking and participating in the debate. One possibility is for the chairman to take questions from proxy-holders after those from members attending in person.
[42] See Chap. 7.
[43] See paras. 20–01 and 20–02.

turn would require prior notice. The company's articles may also cover the point.

(3) Vote of no confidence: if such a vote is proposed, the chairman should state that it would, in practice, amount to no more than a call upon the board to do better—and the board's efforts are (it will have been said) already being redoubled. If the point is pressed, the chairman could indicate that an alternative would be to vote against the adoption of the accounts.

(4) Points of order: the chairman should be quick to reject any bogus points of order (*i.e.* those which deal with substantive and not procedural matters).[44] On genuine points he should give an immediate ruling and indicate that it is final. He may be able to point to an article on the lines of Extra Article A.

(5) Disturbances: the atmosphere and tone of the proceedings may do much to discourage unruly elements.[45] If, in spite of the evident good humour and reasonableness of the chairman and the care which has been taken over the choice of venue and layout of the hall, bad behaviour breaks out, the chairman will have to take one or more of the following steps:

Rule the shareholder out of order and ask him to desist so that the meeting can proceed; the request should, if necessary, be repeated. Only if that fails should the chairman ask the shareholder to leave the meeting. If the shareholder does not leave, the chairman should direct the stewards and/or security staff to remove the person from the meeting; only reasonable force may be used.

In cases of more serious disturbance, for example where protesters storm the directors' table, they can be ejected summarily and without warning.[46]

(6) Adjourn the meeting: this is a more drastic step and may be appropriate where there is a body of demonstrators and attempts to encourage them to put their points of view through a spokesperson have failed and disorder persists. The adjournment can be for a short period while, for example, the chairman has discussions with the demonstrators to see whether a basis for progress can be made—perhaps by offering them separate discussions outside the meeting. In desperate cases, the meeting could be adjourned for a longer period—perhaps a week or so.[47] At the adjourned meeting it will be possible to exclude those who have been identified as disruptive troublemakers; although, with good fortune, the second event is likely to be conducted in a calmer atmosphere.

(7) Defamation: if the chairman thinks a member is making defamatory remarks, he should call him to order at once.[48]

---

[44] For a discussion of other procedural points, see Chap. 7.
[45] An established procedure is good practice: ICSA 2.24.
[46] ICSA 2.24; and see para. 3–02.
[47] See para. 3–04.
[48] See Chap. 30. Equally, the chairman should be careful in attributing base motives to a questioner.

Appointing an additional or substitute director

19–27   If the company thinks that an attempt will be made to appoint a director in addition to or in substitution for those named in the notice it will be necessary to take early legal advice. The member who wishes to appoint such a director (the "proposing member") may give prior notice to the company, thus meeting the requirements of articles such as Extra Article F, in particular the Table A, article 76 type of provision. He may, alternatively, have acted under section 303.[49] It will then be for the company to take such steps as are appropriate, depending on the nature and contents of the notice received, the company's articles, Stock Exchange requirements and the time available before the meeting.[50]

If the proposing member waits until the meeting, whether he will succeed in his proposal depends on:

(1) **The articles:** if they contain provision on the lines of article 76 of Table A, the proposal will fail. It will also fail if the proposing member moves the appointment of an additional director, and the number of board members is already at the maximum permitted.

(2) **The form of notice:** as mentioned,[51] the most restrictive form of notice will be: "To re-elect Mr. X as a director". Then the chairman would be in order in accepting an extra resolution to elect a director in substitution for Mr. Y, if the proposal to re-elect Mr. X fails to be carried. He will need to put the exact form of resolutions to the meeting, to explain their effect and to make sure he knows how to vote the proxies.[52] In the circumstances, the company may be advised to adjourn the meeting, so that all shareholders will have an opportunity of considering and voting on the additional resolution.

Voting Points

19–28   (1) **Inspection of proxies:** when a keenly contested vote is expected, one or more shareholders may ask to inspect the proxies already lodged. There is no right for a member to do this, but in the interests of transparency the company may allow it. The inspection should be carried out, in the presence of a company representative, by a single individual only.

(2) **Forestalling demands for a poll:** it is a frequent practice for chairmen to attempt to deflect a demand for a poll by announcing the number of valid proxy votes he has for/against a resolution, together with the number in respect of which he may exercise his discretion. ICSA 2.14 points out that some proxy voters might, however, have attended the meeting, either in person or by company representative. They may have decided to cast their votes differently from the instructions given to their proxy. It is suggested that good practice calls for:

---

[49] See paras. 21–13 to 21–15.
[50] While tempting to try, it is not possible to deal with all eventualities in this book.
[51] See paras. 5–05 and 19–21.
[52] See para. 14–28. The 1985 Act, s.292, prevents the appointment of two or more persons as directors by a single resolution unless the meeting agrees without dissent.

    (a) the provisional figures not to be revealed before any discussion on a resolution—this may look like an attempt to stifle debate;

    (b) such a statement to be made only when it is clear that the majority want to move on to the next item without a poll being taken; and

    (c) any statement to indicate that the number of proxy votes held relates to the number lodged before the meeting, and that those who have lodged proxies may be present at the meeting and have decided to vote differently.

  (3) **Polls—timing:** it may be an advantage for the chairman (especially where polls are validly demanded by members present) to take them at the end of the meeting, thus minimising disruption. ICSA 2.12, however, stresses the need for polls to be taken promptly; it is recommended that if companies conduct polls at the end of a meeting, shareholders and proxy-holders should be given poll cards as they enter so that those who depart early may deposit their cards with the registrars as they leave (see generally as to polls procedure, paras. 19–32 to 19–36 below).

After the meeting

(1) **Questions to be answered:** where concerns are raised by shareholders and where the chairman undertakes at the AGM to consider these, the shareholder should later receive a full report of the action taken.[53]   **19–29**

(2) **Minutes:** after a meeting in which there has been controversy, it is good practice to prepare minutes as quickly as possible, and have them signed by the chairman, so that they can be inspected by any member, and copies can be sent to any member within the prescribed seven days after request.[54]

(3) **Authorise payment of dividend and file resolutions as appropriate with Companies House and the UK Listing Authority.**

2   Extraordinary General Meeting

(a) Convened by directors

    The circumstances in which a company may need to arrange for the holding of an extraordinary general meeting are, as has already been seen, many and various; it is less easy therefore to offer detailed practical suggestions but it will be obvious that many of the matters which apply to the annual meeting—for example, the choice of hall—will apply also to an extraordinary meeting.   **19–30**

    A precedent for a notice of an extraordinary general meeting is as follows:

---

[53] ICSA 2.10.
[54] 1985 Act, s.383. See also ICSA 3.1 and para. 16–03.

NOTICE OF EXTRAORDINARY GENERAL MEETING

NOTICE is hereby given that an extraordinary general meeting of ...... plc will be held at .... at ...... a.m./p.m. for the purpose of considering and (if thought fit) passing the following resolution, which will be proposed as an ordinary resolution:

> THAT the share capital of the company be increased to £10,000,000 by the creation of 3,000,000 additional ordinary shares of £1 each.

A member entitled to attend and vote is entitled to appoint a proxy [or proxies] to attend and [on a poll] to vote instead of him. A proxy need not be a member of the company.

Dated ......

By order of the board,

....

Secretary

Registered Office ....

(b) Requisitioned by members (see para. 12–10)

19–31   The difficulties facing members of a company who seek to requisition a meeting under section 368 of the 1985 Act are formidable. The following is an outline of the steps that will have to be taken, and of some of the snags.

> (1) It will usually be necessary to co-ordinate the activities of the requisitionists, so that a proper section 368 notice can be served. This can be done by a newspaper advertisement addressed to all the shareholders of the company describing the matter in issue and asking them to sign and return a tear-off form on the following lines (a simple wording has been used as being more suitable for an advertisement):

I hereby call on the directors of Stone Walls plc to convene an extraordinary general meeting of shareholders to consider the following resolution:

[Text]

Signed .... Date ....
Name ....
Address ....
Number of shares held ....

The tear-off form should usually be sent back to the sponsors of the advertisement so that the strength of the response can be gauged and the number of shares counted; if they amount to the necessary one-tenth of the paid-up capital they will be lodged with the company.

(2) Alternatively, an informal meeting can be held, following press publicity, at which forms of requisition can be signed.

(3) As a preliminary step to the above, the sponsors would be well advised to order from the company a copy of its register of members, under section 356 of the 1985 Act. Delivery of the copy must be made within a period of 10 days beginning with the day next after the request is received.[55] It would be advisable, too, for a member to order a copy of the company's memorandum and articles pursuant to section 19 of the 1985 Act. These requests can be made by recorded delivery letter addressed to the registered office.

(4) Assuming sufficient people turn up at the informal meeting, the requisition can be served. In our imaginary example, it can take the following form:

Requisition for Extraordinary General Meeting
To: The Directors,
Stone Walls plc,
Crab End,
Nottingham.
Pursuant to section 368 of the Companies Act 1985 ("the Act"), we, the undersigned, being the holders of not less than one-tenth of the paid-up share capital of Stone Walls plc ("the company") which at the date hereof carries the right of voting at general meetings of the company hereby require you pursuant to section 368 of the Act forthwith to convene an extraordinary general meeting of the company for the purpose of considering and if thought fit passing the following resolution which will be proposed as an ordinary resolution:

Ordinary Resolution

"THAT this meeting of shareholders of Stone Walls plc considers that the proposed sale of the company's subsidiary Midfield Limited would be contrary to the long-term interests of the company, and it accordingly recommends the directors of the company not to permit such transaction to proceed."

Dated ....

[Signatures] [Addresses] [Number of shares held]

(5) The requisition must be deposited at the registered office and the company then has 21 days from the date of deposit to convene a meeting and the meeting must be convened for a date not more than 28 days after the date of the notice convening the meeting.[56]

---

[55] If a member cannot obtain a list of other members with their true addresses (for example, if the register of members is seriously defective) then it is not possible to hold a proper company meeting: *POW Services Ltd v. Clare* [1995] 2 B.C.L.C. 435, 450.

[56] See para. 12–12.

(6) Provided they convene the meeting, the directors can respond to the requisition in whatever way they like. They can accompany the notice to shareholders with their own circular recommending rejection. If the company is subject to the Listing Rules, the notice must be accompanied by a two-way proxy form.

(7) If the directors fail to requisition a meeting, the requisitionists, or any of them representing more than one-half of their total voting rights, may themselves convene a meeting; but the directors are unlikely to be so foolish as to allow the initiative to pass in this way to the requisitionists.

(8) The requisitionists can send out their own form of proxy (with the names of their own nominees as proxies) to shareholders with an appropriate circular. Provision can be made for these forms of proxy to be sent to an address nominated by the requisitionists, so that they can be checked and listed; they can then be taken in bulk to the place named in the articles for the deposit of proxies, care being taken to get them in by the hour prescribed.

(9) Shareholders who are companies and who are favourable to the requisitionists should be encouraged to send a representative to the meeting, properly authorised under section 375 of the 1985 Act.

(10) The arrangements for the meeting are under the control of the company, and this is one of the biggest disadvantages the requisitionists face. Little can be done about the choice of date and venue, but as company boards do not like being associated with disorderly meetings the requisitionists have some bargaining strength in asking that certain ground rules for the meeting should be established, by agreement, in advance. These could cover items such as—who is to take the chair (if the chairman of the board is for any reason an interested party he should not take the chair at the meeting), the order of debate and the length of time allowed for speeches, the admission of legal advisers and the press (solicitors and reporters can be appointed as proxies as a last resort) and the way in which a poll will be taken and who will be appointed scrutineers.

(11) At the meeting, any ruling by the chairman with which the requisitionists do not agree should be challenged on the spot.

(12) If the requisitionists wish to challenge the qualification of any voter, this should be done at the meeting—articles such as article 58 of Table A will make it too late to do so afterwards.

3   PROCEDURE FOR CONDUCTING A POLL

(a) *Before the meeting*

19–32   Ensure that the final proxy statement is available, with an up-to-date list of members accurately reflecting actual register balances (in practice, the company's registrars may be connected to this data by an on-line link). Ascertain, by reference to the articles, the number of votes to which each member is entitled (this may be one vote for every share held or be based, for example, on a sliding scale to a maximum number). Establish who is to be responsible for conducting the poll and for explaining the procedure to the meeting.

Ensure an adequate supply of poll cards (Specimen A).

Establish who are to be scrutineers[57] and go through the procedure with them.

Ensure that everyone who arrives at the meeting signs the appropriate attendance sheet or has handed in his attendance card.

Check that those who sign in as members are shown on the list of members.

Check that those attending as representatives of companies are properly authorised in writing.

Those who attend as proxies must have been properly appointed by the shareholders concerned, and will therefore have been marked off on the register in preparing the final proxy statement; if possible, hand each proxy a poll card marked as shown in Specimen B—this helps identification when the poll starts and saves time.

Prepare a briefing note for the chairman.

(b) *When a poll is demanded*

Check the demand is valid by reference to the articles.[58] If invalid, it can be **19–33** ignored. If the demand is in order, consider whether to ask for it to be withdrawn.[59] If not withdrawn, ask those concerned to sign a form of demand for a poll (Specimen F).

Inform the meeting when the poll will be taken.

(c) *Before the commencement of the poll*

Make a statement to the meeting on the following lines: **19–34**

> Poll cards will now be distributed. Only shareholders or their proxies or corporate representatives are entitled to vote. If a voter is both shareholder and proxy, please use separate poll cards, one as a shareholder and one as a proxy. A member wishing to vote part of his holding "for" and part "against" can have two cards. Those shareholders who have already voted by proxy and do not wish to change the way in which they voted need not complete a poll card as their proxy vote will stand. Poll cards should be completed by inserting the full name of the shareholder, including, if applicable, the names of all joint holders; insert an X to indicate a vote for or against the resolution. It is not necessary for members to insert the number of shares held, provided the vote is being cast in respect of the entire holding. (A list of members is available for reference.) The poll card must be signed.

---

[57] ICSA 2.13 suggests the company's registrars or auditors. In cases where the vote may be close, or a particular demonstration of independence is required, the Electoral Reform Society can be used: see www.electoral-reform.org.uk.

[58] See para. 14–09.

[59] See para. 14–10.

Inform the meeting when the poll will be closed and when, where and how the result will be announced.

Advise the meeting of the names of the scrutineers.

(d) *During the poll*

19–35   Distribute poll cards.

After a short interval, collect them (or arrange for their deposit in boxes provided for the purpose).

Arrange for the chairman (or other person named in the proxy form) to sign two poll cards—one in respect of those shareholders who have appointed him as proxy to vote "For" the resolution or "At Discretion"[60] (Specimen C) and the other in respect of those who have appointed him to vote "Against" (Specimen D).

Check poll cards against the register. Eliminate double counting, *e.g.* where a member who has signed a proxy votes in person. Total the result.

(e) *At the conclusion of the poll*

19–36   The results should be calculated by the scrutineers (they will have to make all necessary decisions in a close situation—no re-vote or "recount" is permitted after they have reported). They should sign the certificate (Specimen E) and make their report to the chairman. Pass original certificate to the chairman to enable him to announce the result of the poll. He should give the total number of votes cast in favour of, and against, the resolution.[61]

NOTE: *The above procedure is based on the assumption that a poll is likely. Some of the preliminary steps would not be taken if the meeting is uncontroversial, but the secretary should have all the appropriate documents ready in case a poll is unexpectedly demanded.*

POLL CARD   *Specimen A*

Name(s) of Holders(s) (Block Letters)	Holding	Resolution No.	VOTE	
			FOR	AGAINST
		1	....	....
		2	....	....
		3	....	....
		4	....	....
Signature of Holder, Proxy or Corporate Representative	Has a Proxy Form already been submitted? YES/NO	Please insert 'X' in the appropriate column above		

---

[60] Assuming that the chairman casts his discretionary votes in favour of the resolution.
[61] ICSA 2.13.

SPECIMEN—FOR USE BY PROXY (OTHER THAN CHAIRMAN)

POLL CARD

Specimen B

Name(s) of Holders(s) (*Block Letters*)	Holding	Resolution No.	VOTE	
			FOR	AGAINST
.... Acting as proxy for .... by whom he/she has been duly appointed		1 2 3 4	....	....
Signature of Holder, Proxy or Corporate Representative	Has a Proxy Form already been submitted? YES/NO		Please insert 'X' in the appropriate column above	

SPECIMEN—FOR USE BY CHAIRMAN OF MEETING RE "FOR" AND "DISCRETION" PROXY VOTING

POLL CARD

Specimen C

Name(s) of Holders(s) (*Block Letters*)	Holding	Resolution No.	VOTE	
			FOR	AGAINST
The chairman of the meeting of .... plc acting for shareholders by whom he has been appointed to act as proxy	(See separate list)	1 2 3 4	..X.. ..X.. ..X.. ..X..	....
Signature				

SPECIMEN—FOR USE BY CHAIRMAN OF MEETING RE "AGAINST" PROXY VOTING

POLL CARD   *Specimen D*

Name(s) of Holders(s) (*Block Letters*)	Holding	Resolution No.	VOTE	
			FOR	AGAINST
The chairman of the meeting of .... plc acting for shareholders by whom he has been appointed to act as proxy	(See separate list)	1 2 3 4	....	..X.. ..X.. ..X.. ..X..
Signature				

SCRUTINEERS' CERTIFICATE

(Addressed to the chairman)

Specimen E

Dear Sir,

As Scrutineers appointed for the purpose of the Poll taken at the Annual/Extra-ordinary General Meeting of the Members of the Company held on .... we HEREBY CERTIFY that the result of the Poll is correctly set out as follows.

	Present and Voting		For		Against	
	No.	Representing Shares	No.	Representing Shares	No.	Representing Shares
In person	21	5,927,000	20	4,910,000	1	1,017,000
By Proxy	891	5,975,700	692	4,992,700	199	1,983,000
TOTALS	912	11,902,700	712	9,902,700	200	3,000,000

Yours faithfully,

(Scrutineers)

[COMPANY NAME]

DEMAND FOR A POLL

(Addressed to the Chairman)   *Specimen F*

AGM/EGM

We, the undersigned, being ordinary shareholders in the Company, hereby demand that a poll be held on the resolution set out below:

Date:	*Resolution No.*	
Name	*Number of ordinary shares*	*Signature(s)*

Date....

CHAPTER 20

POWERS AND DUTIES OF DIRECTORS

1 RELATIONSHIP WITH SHAREHOLDERS

20–01 Under common law, a company's powers must be exercised by its members in a general meeting unless its memorandum or articles of association provide otherwise (*Mayor, Constables and Company of Merchants of the Staple of England v. Governor and Company of the Bank of England* (1887) 21 WBD 160). In other words, the directors will have no power to act on behalf of the company at all unless the memorandum or articles say so. In United Kingdom company law, however, the management of a company is vested in its directors who are, in effect, agents for the company in relation to the transactions into which they enter on behalf of the company, and trustees for the company so far as concerns the company's funds and property.[1]

In practice the articles of most companies delegate wide powers of management to the directors, reversing the common law rule that the company's powers must be exercised by the members in general meeting. The relationship between directors and shareholders finds expression in Table A of the Companies Act 1985 and this clause is commonly known as the "general management clause":

> **70.** Subject to the provisions of the Act, the memorandum and the articles and to any directions given by a special resolution, the business of the company shall be managed by the directors who may exercise all the powers of the company. No alteration of the memorandum or articles and no such direction shall invalidate any prior act of the directors which would have been valid if that alteration had not been made or that direction had not been given . . . .

This type of article, which vests the management of the company in the directors, means that the shareholders cannot in general meeting exercise a power given by the articles to the directors or overrule the directors when exercising such a power:

20–02 Articles of a company contained a clause similar to the predecessor of article 70. A resolution of the company in general meeting for payment of preference dividends in advance by instalments was held to be invalid as being inconsistent with the delegation clause in the articles.[2]

Articles of another company contained a similar clause, except that shareholders could by extraordinary resolution regulate the powers of the directors. At a general

---

[1] *Great Eastern Railway v. Turner* (1872) 8 Ch.App. 149, 152.
[2] *Scott v. Scott* [1943] 1 All E.R. 582; and see *Quin Axtens Ltd v. Salmon* [1909] A.C. 442.

meeting a resolution was passed by simple majority for the sale of the company's assets, and the directors were directed to carry the sale into effect. They declined to do so, being of the opinion that the sale was not for the benefit of the company. *Held*, that the articles had vested the power of management in the directors and, except as provided in the articles, they could not be deprived of this power: there had been no extraordinary resolution as prescribed and therefore the directors could not be compelled to carry though the sale.[3]

The shareholders are, however, not without remedies in the event of a conflict with directors:

(i) directors can be removed from office by an ordinary resolution of which special notice is given[4];

(ii) the shareholders can pass a special resolution changing the articles so as to give the general meeting powers which were vested in the directors—and can then exercise such powers;

(iii) the shareholders can apply for relief under the unfair prejudice provisions of the 1985 Act.[5]

Directors are in a fiduciary position. They must exercise their powers for the company's benefit and, if abuse of these powers is threatened, the court will intervene. There have been cases, for example, of directors having been restrained by the court from abusing powers in the articles relating to the registration of transfers and the issue of shares under their control.[6] Directors should act fairly as between different shareholder groups.[7]

Alternatively, the court may order a general meeting:

Under a scheme designed to avoid a take-over bid, the board altered the voting rights attaching to shares so that the board and its associates could rely on the support of a majority of votes. The court held that this conduct was invalid unless ratified by the company in general meeting. Proceedings were stayed to enable such a meeting to be held.[8]

It is also worth mentioning that where the board of directors is unable or unwilling to conduct the company's business, the members in general meeting may be entitled in default to exercise powers given to the directors.[9]

---

[3] *Automatic Self-Cleansing Filter Syndicate Co. v. Cunninghame* [1906] 2 Ch. 34. Article 70 vests authority in the board as a whole and not in individual directors: *Mitchell Hobbs (U.K.) Ltd v. Mill* [1996] 2 BCLC 102.

[4] 1985 Act, s.303.

[5] See ss.459–461.

[6] *Piercy v. S. Mills Co. Ltd* [1920] 1 Ch. 77; and see *Marshall's Valve Gear v. Manning Wardle Co.* [1909] 1 Ch. 267, *Clemens v. Clemens Bros Ltd* [1976] 2 All E.R. 268; and *Popely v. Planarrive Limited, The Times,* April 24, 1996. See para. 14–05.

[7] *Re BSB Holdings (No. 2)* [1996] 1 BCLC 155.

[8] *Hogg v. Cramphorn Ltd* [1967] Ch. 254.

[9] *Barron v. Potter* [1914] 1 Ch. 895 and *Foster v. Foster* [1916] 1 Ch. 532.

2 VALIDITY OF ACTS

(a) *Where appointment defective*

20–03   By section 285 of the 1985 Act, the acts of a director or manager are valid notwithstanding any defect that may afterwards be discovered in his appointment or qualification[10]; and under Table A:

> **92.** All acts done by a meeting of directors, or of a committee of directors, or by a person acting as a director shall, notwithstanding that it be afterwards discovered that there was a defect in the appointment of any director or that any of them were disqualified from holding office, or had vacated office, or were not entitled to vote, be as valid as if every such person had been duly appointed and was qualified and had continued to be a director, and had been entitled to vote.

It will be noted that article 92 extends section 285 to acts done by a meeting of directors. Examples are:

> The articles of a company contained a clause similar to the above. B was appointed secretary of the company, and under the articles he thereby vacated office as director. He continued to act as director, and at a meeting of directors B and the only other director of the company passed a resolution electing X a director under a power in the articles to fill casual vacancies. The three directors continued to act as directors and throughout acted in good faith. *Held*, that the irregularities were validated by the articles and the Act (section 67 of the 1862 Act, now section 285 of the 1985 Act), and the appointment was confirmed.[11]

> A call was purported to be made by persons who were acting as directors of the company, and the call was resisted by certain shareholders on the ground that the directors were not directors *de jure*, as one of them had vacated office as a result of his having been for six days without a share qualification. The Court of Appeal held that such irregularities as there might have been were cured by the relevant article, but only on the footing that the call was made by directors in ignorance of any possibility of disqualification.[12]

The section will protect transactions by a director who was appointed at a meeting of which insufficient notice had been given.[13]

It is clear that section 285 and article 92 are designed only as machinery to prevent questions from being raised as to the validity of transactions where there has been a slip in the appointment of a director. The section does not apply when

---

[10] Including a resolution to appoint which is void under section 292(2)—see para. 19–27, n. 2.
[11] *British Asbestos Co. v. Boyd* [1903] 2 Ch. 439.
[12] *Dawson v. African Consolidated Land and Trading Co. Ltd* [1898] 1 Ch. 6.
[13] *Briton Medical and General Life Assurance v. Jones* (1889) 61 L.T. 384.

bad faith is present or when there has been no appointment at all, and cannot be relied upon for the purpose of ignoring or overriding the substantive provisions relating to appointments of directors. Neither the section nor the article can assist a party if that party has knowledge of the facts giving rise to the invalidity; nor do they operate if that party is put on enquiry and does not enquire.[14]

(b) *Where powers and duty are delegated*

Committees. In principle, directors have no power under the Acts to delegate their authority.   **20–04**

> In an old case, where a power of allotment was vested in the directors, three of whom constituted a quorum, and an allotment was made by a committee of two directors, the allotment was held to be invalid as the directors had no right to delegate such power without express authority.[15]

Table A, however, provides as follows:

> **72.** The directors may delegate any of their powers to any committee consisting of one or more directors . . . . Any such delegation may be made subject to any conditions the directors may impose, and either collaterally with or to the exclusion of their own powers, and may be revoked or altered. Subject to any such conditions, the proceedings of a committee with two or more members shall be governed by the articles regulating the proceedings of directors so far as they are capable of applying.

The last words of the above article apply to such matters as notice, quorum, chairman, majority and casting vote. Thus, in the absence of conditions imposed by the full board, notices are covered by article 88, quorum by articles 89 and 95, chairman by article 91, and majority and chairman's casting vote by article 88. Declarations of interest in relation to committee members are covered specifically in articles 94–98. A committee may make resolutions in writing (article 93).

It is usual for the board to specify the quorum in the committee's terms of reference. In the absence of any such specification, and on the assumption that the present Table A does not apply and the articles make no specific provision for what is to be the quorum of a committee, all the members of the committee must be present to enable the business to be transacted.[16]   **20–05**

There is nothing to prevent a committee of one being appointed.[17] Article 72 in terms covers such a possibility.

In a case under a previous Table A:

> A company had only two directors, one of whom was resident in Germany, and these two directors met and decided that the director resident in London should conduct the business of the company, and that he alone should

---

[14] *Morris v. Kanssen* [1946] A.C. 459.
[15] *Howard's Case* (1866) 1 Ch. 561.
[16] *Liverpool Household Stores Association v. Smith* (1887) 37 Ch.D. 170.
[17] *Re Taurine Co.* (1884) 37 Ch.D. 118.

constitute a quorum. The latter subsequently agreed to an issue of debentures and authorised the sealing of the documents, the secretary and himself signing them on behalf of the company. The validity of the debentures was challenged. It was held that under the articles there was power to appoint a committee of one, and the allotment was valid.[18]

Delegation to a committee may at any time be revoked by the board. This retains responsibility for the actions of the committee.[19]

Committees cannot sub-delegate their powers unless authorised to do so by the board.[20]

For a general review of the committee system see Chapter 9.

Restrictions on power to delegate

A particular instance of the rule that a committee must not exceed the powers delegated to it arose in *Guinness plc v. Saunders*[21]:

> A committee of the board of the plaintiff company agreed to pay W, a non-executive director, £5.2m. for his services in connection with a take-over bid. The company subsequently claimed recovery of the money. It was held that, under the plaintiff's articles, special remuneration could be awarded to a director serving on a committee only by the board, not by the committee itself.

Following the decision in the Guinness case, some listed companies have adopted articles along the following lines to clarify that the general power to delegate is not intended to be limited by anything in the articles that requires powers to be exercised by the board:

> "Where a provision of the articles refers to the exercise of a power, authority or discretion by the board and that power, authority or discretion has been delegated by the board to a committee, the provision shall be construed as permitting the exercise of the power, authority or discretion by the committee".

20–06   **Executive directors.** Article 72 of Table A provides that the directors may delegate any of their powers to any managing director or any director holding any other executive office, subject to any conditions the directors may impose, and either collaterally with or to the exclusion of their own powers. The delegation may be revoked or altered. Limits on individual directors' authorities may be reinforced by the adoption of a schedule of matters reserved to the board. Formal service agreements for salaried executive directors would be expected which would include the title of the job to be performed and a general provision stating that the

---

[18] *Re Fireproof Doors* [1916] 2 Ch. 142.
[19] Article 72 of Table A; *Huth v. Clarke*.
[20] *Cook v. Ward* 1877 2 CPD 255.
[21] [1990] 2 A.C. 663.

director shall have such powers and duties as the board may determine from time to time.

This article is supplemented by article 84 which makes it clear that any such appointment to an executive office shall terminate if the appointee ceases to be a director, but without prejudice to any claim under a service contract.[22] Under this article, a managing director and a director holding another executive office shall not be subject to retirement by rotation except at the first annual general meetings following their appointment.[23] However, under the Combined Code, provision A.7.1,which applies to listed companies, it is recommended that all directors should retire and offer themselves for re-election at least once every three years.

Alternate directors. It is not permissible under the Companies Acts, unless authorised by the articles, for a director to appoint another person to act on his behalf at board meetings, *i.e.* attend and vote. A director is, in this respect, in the position of a trustee acting on behalf of the shareholders, and he has no power to delegate his authority. Articles do however frequently provide for the appointment of an alternate or substitute director to act in the absence of another. The terms of the appointment, share qualification, scope of duties and remuneration are matters that must be clearly defined in the articles, for the alternate can only act within the powers therein conferred. In Table A alternate directors are dealt with in articles 65–69.

20–07

In some sets of articles the power to appoint an alternate is exercisable by the board, in others by the director in whose place the alternate is to act, in which case it may be subject to the approval of the board. Where the company is a wholly-owned subsidiary the articles may place the power in the hands of "the person or persons holding the majority of the shares," *i.e.* the parent company.

The question of appointing an alternate under the articles should not be confused with the question of assignment of office under section 308 of the 1985 Act, which provides that where any provision is made in the articles or by any agreement between any person and the company, for empowering a director or manager to assign his office to another person, any such assignment shall be of no effect unless and until it is approved by a special resolution of the company.

Local boards. Authority for the appointment of local boards is normally given in the articles of association and such boards remain under the control of the parent body. An arrangement of this nature would apply to a company with a head office and branches or factories located throughout the country or in different parts of the world.

20–08

Members of these bodies are not generally directors for the purpose of the Acts. Their rights and duties and the rules of procedure at their meetings are entirely within the control of the appointing board.[24]

---

[22] See *Southern Foundries (1926) Ltd v. Shirlaw* [1940] A.C. 701 and *Shindler v. Northern Raincoat Co. Ltd* [1960] 1 W.L.R. 1038.

[23] See paras. 21–09 and 21–10. In relation to an executive director other than a managing director, this article differs from the previous Table A.

[24] If they are called "directors" they may have ostensible authority to bind the company in its relations with third parties.

Similarly, a company may divide its operations into divisions, each run by a "board" whose members may carry the designation of director. Again, these units are outside the formal procedures of the Acts.

(c) *Where number less than prescribed minimum*

20–09 The question as to the validity of the acts of directors, in cases where the number of directors falls below the minimum number of directors prescribed by the articles, will depend upon whether provision is made in the articles for continuing directors to act. Where no such provision is made, the acts of directors, when their number is less than the minimum prescribed, would be invalid:

The articles provided that the business of the company should be conducted by not less than five directors. The number of directors in the course of time dropped to four and these four made a call. There was no power in the articles for continuing directors to act, and it was held that the call was invalid.[25]

Where however the articles make provision for continuing directors to act, the position would be different:

The articles provided that the number of directors should not be less than four, nor more than seven; two directors were to form a quorum, and the continuing directors might act notwithstanding any vacancy in the board. Four directors were in the first place appointed but two of them subsequently resigned. At a directors' meeting the remaining two proceeded to allot shares. The allottee sought to have his name removed from the register. *Held*, the allotment by the two directors was valid in view of the provisions of the articles empowering continuing directors to act despite vacancies.[26]

20–10 The above case was decided in circumstances where the number of directors fixed by the articles had at some time existed. The position would be different if the minimum number had never existed:

A company's articles provided for not less than four nor more than eight directors, and a quorum of three directors. At a meeting of three directors an allotment of shares was made although the minimum number of directors prescribed, *i.e.* four, had not yet been appointed. Another article gave the directors power to act notwithstanding vacancies in their body, but it was held that such an article applied only where the actual number of directors was reduced below the minimum because of proper and reasonable cause; the allotment was therefore invalid.[27]

Where the number of directors falls below the minimum prescribed by the articles, the procedure laid down by the articles for filling up any vacancies must be

---

[25] *Re Alma Spinning Co., Bottomley's Case* (1880) 16 Ch.D. 681.
[26] *Re Scottish Petroleum Co.* (1883) 23 Ch.D. 413.
[27] *Re Sly, Spink and Co.* [1911] 2 Ch. 430.

followed. If the articles do not prescribe any procedure, the vacancies will have to be filled by the company in general meeting.

It is not clear on the authorities whether, when there are fewer remaining directors than the minimum prescribed, those directors can appoint new directors in reliance solely on a clause in the articles empowering the board to fill up any casual vacancy. The better view appears to be the positive one taken by the Court of Appeal in *Channel Collieries, Trust Ltd v. Dover, etc., Railway Company*:

> The minimum number of directors was three; a quorum was two. Their number had fallen to one. Section 89 of the Companies Clauses Consolidation Act 1845 applied to the company: this provided that the directors had power to fill occasional vacancies in the office of director. *Held*, that the remaining director had the power to elect new directors.[28]

Table A provides as follows:

20–11

> **90.** The continuing directors or a sole continuing director may act notwithstanding any vacancies in their number, but, if the number of directors is less than the number fixed as the quorum, the continuing directors or director may act only for the purpose of filling vacancies or of calling a general meeting.

The above article makes the loss of the *quorum* the point at which the directors' powers become limited to making up their number or calling a general meeting. Even after that point has been reached, their acts may be valid in favour of a person dealing with the company in good faith.[29] Thus, whether the number of directors is less than the minimum prescribed by the articles or there are not sufficient directors to form a quorum, the directors may bind the company in a transaction with an innocent third party. By doing so, however, the directors will have acted in breach of duty and may therefore be liable to compensate the company.

If there are no directors at all, for example because no annual general meetings have been held and the directors will thus be deemed to have retired by rotation, no other officers of the company, for example, the secretary, can act.[30]

(d) Upon subsequent ratification

The actions of a board of directors which were irregular when carried out can be cured by:

(i) a subsequent properly convened board meeting[31]; or
(ii) an extraordinary general meeting of shareholders.[32]

---

[28] *Channel Collieries Trust, Ltd v. Dover, St. Margaret's and Martin Mill Light Railway Co.* [1914] 2 Ch. 506, C.A.; but see *Faure Electric Accumulator Co. Ltd v. Phillipart* (1888) 58 L.T. 525.
[29] 1985 Act, s.35A (see para. 11–08 above).
[30] *Re Zinotty Properties Ltd* [1984] 3 All E.R. 754.
[31] *Southern Counties Deposit Bank v. Rider Kirkwood* (1895) 73 L.T. 374.
[32] See para. 12–01, above.

CHAPTER 21

APPOINTMENT TO AND DEPARTURE FROM OFFICE

1 APPOINTMENT

21–01 Section 282 of the 1985 Act provides that every company registered on or after November 1, 1929 (other than a private company) shall have at least two directors; and every company registered before that date, and every private company, shall have at least one director. Subject to this minimum, the Ωnumber of directors will be prescribed by the articles. In practice, Table A does not cater for a sole director, so articles 64, 89 and 90 will require modification where it is wished that only one director shall be appointed.

First

21–02 The articles will usually name the first directors, or will provide for their appointment.

The subscribers to the memorandum may execute a document nominating the first directors; if this method is used, all subscribers should sign.[1] The document could read as follows:

... LIMITED

We, the undersigned, being the subscribers of the memorandum of association of the above company hereby in pursuance of article ...... of the company's articles of association appoint ...... of ......, ... of ...... and ...... of ...... to be the first directors of the company.

Dated ...... 19...... [Signature]

Subsequent

21–03 Directors other than first directors will be appointed at general meetings except when appointed by the board to fill a casual vacancy.[2]

In a public company, appointments of directors at a general meeting must be voted on individually, unless the meeting has previously resolved without any

---

[1] *Re Great Northern Salt and Chemical Works* (1890) 44 Ch.D. 472.
[2] See para. 21–05.

dissenting vote that they be taken together.[3] Many articles, including Table A article 75, provide that a retiring director, if willing to act, is automatically re-elected unless the meeting elects any other person to the vacancy or resolves not to fill it, or a resolution for the re-appointment of the director is lost.[4]

A director cannot become a director of a company merely by willing himself into that position.[5] However, a person may be a de facto director by virtue of behaving and acting like a director.[5a]

Nominated

In some companies, the articles provide that directors may be appointed or removed from office by a notice in writing signed by the holders of a majority of the shares. This is useful for wholly-owned subsidiaries and avoids the necessity for a meeting. Equally, power may be reserved to shareholders of a particular category to appoint directors; for example, in a jointly-owned company the "A" shareholders and the "B" shareholders may each have the right to appoint directors. In a case where "governing directors" had the power to appoint additional directors, this power had to be exercised by all the governing directors and not just a majority of them.[6]   **21–04**

Casual vacancies: additional directors

Under Table A: **21–05**

79. The directors may appoint a person who is willing to act as a director, either to fill a vacancy or as an additional director, provided that the appointment does not cause the number of directors to exceed any number fixed by or in accordance with the articles as the maximum number of directors. A director so appointed shall hold office only until the next following annual general meeting and shall not be taken into account in determining the directors who are to retire by rotation at the meeting. If not re-appointed at such annual general meeting, he shall vacate office at the conclusion thereof.

Article 79 and articles based on its predecessor are in very common use and represent a convenient way in which the board can add to its number, subject, in effect, to ratification at the next annual general meeting. Any such appointment must be made at a valid meeting of the board.[7] In principle, where this power of addition is vested in the directors, the company cannot usurp it,[8] except where the articles contain a provision similar to article 78 of Table A, which provides that the company may by ordinary resolution appoint a person who is willing to act to be

---

[3] 1985 Act, s.292.
[4] See paras. 21–10 and 21–11.
[5] *National Rivers Authority v. Stockinger, The Times,* March 27, 1996.
[5a] *Secretary of State for Trade and Industry v. Tjolle* [1998] 1 B.C.L.C. 333.
[6] *Perrott and Perrott Ltd v. Stephenson* [1934] 1 Ch. 171.
[7] *POW Services Ltd v. Clare* [1995] 2 B.C.L.C. 435
[8] *Blair Open Hearth Furnace v. Reigart* (1913) 108 L.T. 665, but see *Worcester Corsetry Ltd v. Witting* [1936] Ch.640.

a director either to fill a vacancy or as an additional director. The company can act in general meeting, too, when the directors are unable or unwilling to act.[9]

Casual vacancies are those which occur through death, resignation, disqualification, or reasons other than those arising by rotation. Where articles provide that vacancies in the board can be filled up by the company in general meeting, and that casual vacancies may be filled up by the directors, the power of the directors to fill such a vacancy continues even though a general meeting has intervened and the vacancy was not then filled up.[10]

2 QUALIFICATION: AGE LIMIT

21–06 With one exception, it is not proposed to deal in detail in this work with the various disqualifications which attend the office of director. For example, some articles provide that directors shall hold a minimum number of shares in the company and in general a person who fails to obtain this qualification will vacate office[11]; similarly, disqualification orders may be made under the Company Directors Disqualification Act 1986, and the articles may themselves contain a disqualification provision (see, for example, article 81 of Table A).

The exception, which will be discussed, relates to the age limit for directors prescribed by section 293 of the 1985 Act. A company is subject to section 293 if it is a public company, or, being a private company, it is a subsidiary of a public company.[12]

In the case of a company first registered after the beginning of the year 1947, the section has effect subject to the company's articles. In the case of a company first registered before the beginning of 1947, section 293 will apply subject to any alteration in the articles made after the beginning of the year 1947, and if at that date the articles contained provisions relating to an age limit those provisions shall apply to the exclusion of the section.[13] In relation to a company to which the section applies, the general rule is that no person shall be capable of being appointed a director if at the time of his appointment he has attained the age of 70; furthermore, upon reaching that age a director must vacate office at the conclusion of the annual general meeting next after reaching the age of 70, but any acts done by such a director are valid notwithstanding that it is afterwards discovered that his appointment had so terminated.[14] Where a person retires under these provisions, no provision for the automatic re-appointment of retiring directors in default of another appointment applies; and if at the meeting at which he retires the vacancy is not filled it may be filled as a casual vacancy.[15]

---

[9] *Barron v. Potter* [1914] 1 Ch. 895.
[10] *Munster v. Cammell Co.* (1882) 21 Ch. 183.
[11] 1985 Act, s.291.
[12] 1985 Act, s.293(1).
[13] 1985 Act, s.293(7). An amendment to a company's articles to disapply section 293 in its entirety might not find favour with some institutional shareholders; the revised article should at least require the company to refer in the notice convening the meeting to the age of any director who has passed the age of, say, 70 and who is proposed for appointment or reappointment.
[14] 1985 Act, s.293(2),(3).
[15] 1985 Act, s.293(4).

The Company Law Review, in a draft company law bill published in March 2005, proposed that the age limit be removed altogether. However this provision is unlikely to be in effect before late 2006. The proposals also include making 16 the minimum age limit for a director. (See *www.dti.gov.uk/cld/whitepaper.pdf*.)

Nothing in the above provisions prevents the appointment of a director at any age, or requires a director to retire at any time, if his appointment is or was made or approved by the company in general meeting; but special notice to the company shall be required of any resolution appointing or approving the appointment of a director for it to have effect for this purpose. The notice given to the company and by the company to its members must state or must have stated the age of the person to whom it relates.[16] The following are suitable precedents: **21–07**

SPECIAL NOTICE TO COMPANY WHERE SECTION 293 APPLIES

To: The Directors,

...... Limited [Date]

Pursuant to sections 293 and 379 of the Companies Act 1985 I HEREBY GIVE YOU NOTICE of my intention to move the following resolution as an ordinary resolution at the next annual general meeting of the company:

RESOLUTION

THAT Mr......, who has attained the age of 70 years, be and he is hereby re-elected a director of the company.

[Signature★][Address]

★ The notice will often be given by another member of the board in his capacity as a shareholder.

ITEM FOR INCLUSION IN NOTICE BY COMPANY TO MEMBERS

To re-elect Mr...... a director, special notice having been given to the company pursuant to sections 293 and 379 of the Companies Act 1985 of the intention to propose the following resolution as an ordinary resolution:

[Text as above]

A person who retires by virtue of the age limit provisions and who is reappointed and a person who is appointed in the place of a director so retiring, are each to be treated, for the purpose of determining the time at which he or any other director is to retire, as if he had become a director on the day on which the retiring director was last appointed before his retirement; but otherwise the retirement out of turn is to be disregarded in determining when any other directors   **21–08**

---

[16] 1985 Act, s.293(5). See *Administrator*, September 1982, p. 26.

are to retire.[17] For example, if a company has six directors and two retire each year by rotation under provisions similar to those of Table A:

> 2001—E and F retire and are re-elected.
> 2002—A and B retire and are re-elected.
> 2003—C and D retire and are re-elected.
> 2004—E and F retire and are re-elected.
> 2005—A and B retire and are re-elected.

If E becomes 70 on January 1, 2003 the consequence will be:

> 2001—E and F retire and are re-elected.
> 2002—A and B retire and are re-elected.
> 2003—C, D and E★ retire and are re-elected.
> 2004—E★ and F retire and are re-elected.
> 2005—A and B retire and are re-elected.

★Special notice would be necessary in relation to each re-appointment of E. If a new director, X, is appointed in 2003 in place of E, the directors to retire in 2004 would be X and F.

A person who is appointed or to his knowledge proposed to be appointed as a director who is affected by age limit provisions under section 293 or under the company's articles must give notice of his age to the company. This will not apply where he is being reappointed.[18]

3   ROTATION

21–09   The following are the relevant articles in Table A as to the rotation of directors.[19]

> **73.** At the first annual general meeting all the directors shall retire from office, and at every subsequent annual general meeting one-third of the directors who are subject to retirement by rotation, or, if their number is not three or a multiple of three, the number nearest one-third shall retire from office; but, if there is only one director who is subject to retirement by rotation, he shall retire.

The object of an article in the above form is to give the shareholders an annual opportunity to review the composition of the board. If this opportunity is lost, through failure, for example, to hold an annual general meeting, the consequences can be serious:

---

[17] 1985 Act, s.293(6). (The sub-section has been paraphrased rather more than usual). For the rotation provisions, see paras. 21–09 and 21–10.

[18] 1985 Act, s.294(1), (3).

[19] The provisions are often modified or omitted, particularly in relation to private companies.

The articles of a company provided that all the directors should retire at an ordinary meeting in a certain year, but no ordinary meeting was held in that year or the next. The directors continued to act, and in the liquidation claimed remuneration on the footing that they had not ceased to be directors because there had been no ordinary meeting in the particular year in which they should have retired. The liquidator contended that the directors vacated office on the last day of the year. This contention was upheld by the court.[20]

The effect of this decision is that a director who is bound to retire at a meeting to be held in a certain year in effect holds office until the end of that year, or until the earlier date on which the meeting for that year may be held.

If a director who should retire at an annual general meeting fails to do so, it appears that his office will be vacated at the conclusion of that meeting, where Table A applies to the company.[21]

It is, however, common to disapply this provision of Table A for small private companies for ease of administration.

Even without the final words of article 73, it is clear that if the number of **21–10** directors is reduced to one, that director shall retire by rotation; to hold otherwise would give the single director permanent tenure of office.[22]

Table A continues:

74. Subject to the provisions of the Act, the directors to retire by rotation shall be those who have been longest in office since their last appointment or re-appointment, but as between persons who became or were last re-appointed directors on the same day those to retire shall (unless they otherwise agree among themselves) be determined by lot.

Where article 79 of Table A applies and directors are appointed to fill a casual vacancy, it is clear from the terms of article 79 that those directors are not to be taken into account in determining the directors who are to retire by rotation. Thus, if a company to which articles 73, 74, 79 and 84 of Table A apply has the following directors (of whom only B is an executive director):

A—chairman (re-appointed at 1994 annual general meeting)
B—managing director (appointed 1991)
C—re-appointed at 1993 annual general meeting
D—re-appointed at 1993 annual general meeting
E—appointed on January 1, 1995 to fill a casual vacancy
F—appointed on January 1, 1995 to fill a casual vacancy.

Only three directors, A, C, and D, are subject to retirement by rotation at the 1995 annual general meeting, and one must therefore retire. (As managing director, B is not subject to retirement by rotation—see article 84). C and D have been the

---

[20] *Re Consolidated Nickel Mines Ltd* [1914] 1 Ch. 883; *Alexander Ward Co. Ltd v. Samyang Navigation Co. Ltd* [1975] 1 W.L.R. 673.
[21] (1964) 4 *The Chartered Secretary* 347.
[22] *Re New Cedos Engineering Co. Ltd* [1994] 1 BCLC 797.

longest in office, and must agree among themselves who is to retire by rotation, or decide the issue by lot. This director (under article 73) and E and F (under article 79) will retire from office at the annual general meeting.

The following provisions of Table A apply to the re-appointment of directors retiring by rotation:

> **75.** If the company, at the meeting at which a director retires by rotation, does not fill the vacancy the retiring director shall, if willing to act, be deemed to have been re-appointed unless at the meeting it is resolved not to fill the vacancy or unless a resolution for the reappointment of the director is put to the meeting and lost.

21–11   It is a well-established principle that articles are binding on the members until altered and that a procedure in conflict with the articles cannot be carried out by ordinary resolution. In *Grundt v. Great Boulder Gold Mines*:

> An article provided that "If at any general meeting at which an election of directors ought to take place, the place of any director retiring by rotation is not filled up, he shall, if willing, continue in office until the ordinary meeting in the next year, and so on from year to year until his place is filled up, unless it shall be determined at any such meeting on due notice to reduce the number of directors in office." At the annual general meeting held in 1947, G retired by rotation from the board and offered himself for re-election, but the resolution for re-election was defeated. There was no resolution passed to reduce the number of directors in office, nor was any election made of another director to fill the office vacated. G claimed that notwithstanding that the express resolution to re-elect him had been defeated, the effect of the article was that, in the circumstances, he continued in office. This contention was upheld by the Court of Appeal.[23]

An article on the lines of article 75 of Table A will prevent this particular situation being repeated.

ICSA 1.8 (see para. 19–02) recommends that all directors of public companies should be subject to retirement by rotation. The same view is taken by the National Association of Pension Funds.

4   Appointment of a Director at a General Meeting

21–12   The 1985 Table A introduced newly-worded provisions (article 95 of the 1948 table A being much more onerous on the company) which are particularly relevant when a group of shareholders wishes to introduce its own nominees to a company board. In view of their complexity, there is no alternative but to quote the relevant articles in full:

---

[23] [1948] Ch. 145.

76. No person other than a director retiring by rotation shall be appointed or re-appointed a director at any general meeting unless:
   (a) he is recommended by the directors; or
   (b) not less than 14 nor more than 35 clear days before the date appointed for the meeting, notice executed by a member qualified to vote at the meeting has been given to the company of the intention to propose that person for appointment or re-appointment stating the particulars which would, if he were so appointed or re-appointed, be required to be included on the company's register of directors together with notice executed by that person of his willingness to be appointed or re-appointed.

77. Not less than 7 nor more than 28 clear days before the date appointed for holding a general meeting notice shall be given to all who are entitled to receive notice of the meeting of any person (other than a director retiring by rotation at the meeting) who is recommended by the directors for appointment or re-appointment as a director at the meeting or in respect of whom notice has been duly given to the company of the intention to propose him at the meeting for appointment or re-appointment as a director. The notice shall give the particulars of that person which would, if he were so appointed or re-appointed, be required to be included in the company's register of directors.

Further detailed mention of this topic is made in paras. 19–19 and 19–27.

5   REMOVAL FROM OFFICE UNDER SECTION 303

Section 303 of the 1985 Act provides that a company may by ordinary resolution   **21–13** remove a director before the expiration of his period of office, notwithstanding anything in its articles or in any agreement between it and him. An ordinary resolution is expressly provided for in section 303, something that is rare in company law.

The section is generally regarded as conferring ultimate supremacy on the shareholders over the directors and is the foundation of the control which a parent company has over a subsidiary. It should be noted however that the section does not deprive a person removed under it of compensation or damages payable to him in respect of the termination of his appointment as a director, or of any appointment terminating with that of director.[24] This proviso has the effect, for example, of preserving the director's right to damages for termination of a service agreement if this is brought to an end on his ceasing to be a director.

It is clear that the operation of the section can be avoided by articles of association which provide, in relation to the ordinary resolution required under the section, for additional or weighted votes:

A company had a share capital of £300 divided equally among the plaintiff, the defendant and the plaintiff's sister, as to 100 shares each. Under article 9

---

[24] 1985 Act, s.303(5).

of the company's articles, in respect of any resolution for the removal of a director from office, any shares held by that director would carry three votes per share. At a members' meeting, a resolution for the removal of the defendant from the board was voted in favour by the plaintiff and her sister, and against by the defendant. It was held that the article was valid and that the resolution had been defeated by 300 votes to 200.[25]

Procedure

21–14 An example of procedure under section 303 is set out below. It will be necessary to follow closely the requirements of the articles (for example, articles 76 and 77 of Table A[26]) but for ease of illustration only the statutory framework is described.

1. Special Notice, under section 379 of the 1985 Act, is required of any resolution to remove a director under section 303 or to appoint somebody instead of a director so removed at the meeting at which he is removed.

The precedent of a notice is as follows:

SPECIAL NOTICE TO REMOVE A DIRECTOR

To: The Directors,

...... Limited [Date]

Pursuant to section 303 and 379 of the Companies Act 1985 I HEREBY GIVE YOU NOTICE that I intend to move the following resolution as an ordinary resolution at the next [annual] general meeting of the company:

Resolution

That Mr. X be and he is hereby removed from office as a director of the company.

[Signature] [Address]

Under section 379, notice of the intention to move the resolution has to be given to the company at least 28 days before the meeting. If, after notice of the intention to move such a resolution has been given to the company, a meeting is called for a date 28 days or less after the notice has been given, the notice is deemed properly given, though not given within the time required.[27]

2. On receipt of notice of an intended resolution to remove a director the company shall forthwith send a copy to the director concerned, and the director (whether or not he is a member of the company) is entitled to be heard on the resolution at the meeting.[28]

---

[25] *Bushell v. Faith* [1970] A.C. 1099; and see [1980] J.B.L. 17.
[26] See para. 21–12.
[27] See para. 13–17. See *Administrator*, May 1990, p. 33, for a suggested method by which the procedure can be accelerated.
[28] 1985 Act, s.304(1).

The following would be a suitable form of letter to be sent to the director concerned:

To: Mr. X. [Date]

Dear Sir,

The company has received notice from Mr...that he intends to move a resolution at the next [annual] general meeting of the company that you be removed from office as a director. A copy of the notice is attached.

I would draw your attention to the provisions of the Companies Act 1985 which are referred to in the notice, and to section 304 of that Act which gives you a right to be heard on the proposed resolution and to make representations with respect to it.

Yours, etc.,

[Secretary] [address]

3. The company must, under section 379, give notice of the resolution to its members at the same time and in the same manner as it gives notice of the meeting or, if that is not practicable, by advertisement in a newspaper having an appropriate circulation or in any other mode allowed by the articles at least 21 days before the meeting.

If there is time to include the item in the notice of the meeting, an extra item on the following lines will be added:

> To consider the following resolution which will be proposed as an ordinary resolution, special notice having been given pursuant to sections 303 and 379 of the Companies Act 1985:

[text as above]

If an advertisement has to be inserted the wording could be as follows: **21–15**

X LIMITED

Notice is hereby given that the company has been notified that at the [annual] general meeting of the company to be held at ...... on ......, notice of which has already been sent to members, it is intended that a resolution to move Mr. X from the office of director will be moved.

[Date] ...... [Secretary] [Address]

4. The director may make representations in writing to the company (not exceeding a reasonable length) and request their notification to members. Unless they are received too late for it do so, the company must, in any notice of the

resolution given to members, state that representations have been made and send a copy of the representations to every member to whom notice of the meeting is sent (whether before or after receipt of representations by the company). If this is not done, because the representations are received too late or because of the company's default, the director may require that, without prejudice to his right to be heard orally, the representations shall be read out at the meeting.[29] The above would not apply if the court is satisfied that the rights conferred by the section are being abused to secure needless publicity for defamatory matter.[30]

5. A vacancy created by the removal of a director under section 303, if not filled at the meeting at which he is removed, may be filled as a casual vacancy.[31]

6. Procedure under section 303 often has to be combined with initiatives under other sections of the Act. For example, the persons wishing to remove the director may have to take steps to ensure that the resolution is placed before members, since, as has been noted, section 379 does not give the right to compel the inclusion of any item on an agenda where the standing of the member does not justify it.[32] Indeed, it may be necessary for the members who wish to remove a director to join forces in requisitioning a meeting under section 368. The following is an example where members convene an extraordinary general meeting under section 368,[33] to remove two directors and to appoint two in their place:

REQUISITION UNDER COMPANIES ACT 1985, s.368

To: the Directors,
    Shepherds' Turf Limited,
    [Address]

Pursuant to sections 303 and 368 of the Companies Act 1985 ("The Act") we, the undersigned, being the holders of not less than one-tenth of the paid-up capital of Shepherds' Turf Limited ("the Company") which at the date hereof carries the right of voting at general meetings of the Company hereby require you pursuant to section 368 of the Act forthwith to convene an extraordinary general meeting of the Company ("the Requisitioned Meeting") for the purpose of considering and, if thought fit, passing the following resolutions each of which will be proposed as an ordinary resolution:

(1) That ...... be and he is hereby removed from office as a director of the company.

(2) That ...... be and he is hereby removed from office as a director of the Company.

(3) That any person appointed by the directors as an additional director pursuant to article ...... of the Company's articles between the date of this requisition and the conclusion of the Requisitioned Meeting be and is hereby removed from office as a director of the Company.

---

[29] 1985 Act, s.304(3).
[30] 1985 Act, s.304(4).
[31] 1985 Act, s.303(3).
[32] *Pedley v. Inland Waterways Association Ltd* [1977] 1 All E.R. 209, dicussed at para. 13–17.
[33] See paras., 12–10 to 12–13.

(4) That ...... be and he is hereby appointed a director of the Company in place of either one of the directors removed pursuant to resolutions (1) or (2) hereof.

(5) That ...... be and he is hereby appointed a director of the Company in place of either one of the directors removed pursuant to resolutions (1) or (2) hereof.

Dated ......

[Signatures] [Addresses] [Number of shares held]

NOTE: *Resolution (3) is to deter the board from making new appointments under the article relating to additional directors, for example article 79 of Table A.*

Section 303 is not to be taken as derogating from any power to remove a director which may exist apart from it.[34] One possibility is that a director may, under the articles, be removed by extraordinary resolution; then, there will be no need for special notice under section 379 and the director will have no right to make written representations and have them circulated.[35]

The section 303 procedure is not suitable where there is doubt as to whether the object of it is in fact a director.[36]

6   VACATION OF OFFICE

Table A article 81 provides (*inter alia*) that the office of a director shall be vacated   **21–16** if he resigns his office by notice to the company or if he shall for more than six consecutive months have been absent without permission of the directors from the meetings of directors held during that period and the directors resolve that his office be vacated.[37]

Under the previous Table A which did not provide for such a directors' resolution in the event of prolonged absence, it was held that a director vacated office automatically, and the board had no power to waive the event or condone the offence.[38]

Involuntary absence caused, for example, by cogent medical reasons, might not be enough to disqualify a director under this type of provision; further, it is not clear whether the words "without permission" imply a board resolution or whether informal consent would suffice.[39]

Resignation

The proper course for a director who wishes to resign is to serve notice on the   **21–17** company. Under articles 81(d) and 111, the notice should be in writing. Section

---

[34] 1985 Act, s.303(5).
[35] *Professional Administration*, May 1979, February 1981.
[36] See *Currie v. Cowdenbeath Football Club* [1992] BCLC 1029.
[37] See *POW Services Ltd v. Clare* [1995] 2 BCLC 435, 453.
[38] *Re Bodega Co. Ltd* [1904] 1 Ch. 276, *Glossop v. Glossop* [1907] 2 Ch. 370.
[39] *Mack's Claim* [1900] W.N. 114, *Willsmore v. Willsmore Tibbenham Ltd* (1965) 109 S.J. 699.

725 of the Act provides that a document may be served on a company by leaving it at or sending it by post to the registered office. It has however been held that an oral resignation is effective if given and accepted at a general meeting, even though the articles provide that a director shall vacate office if he resigns by notice in writing.[40] In another case, an oral resignation was accepted at a board meeting when the facts were such as to show that the resigning director had clearly intended to resign.[41] The important point in these two cases is that the resignation was accepted. In instances where the articles do not specifically provide for the resignation of a director, a director may resign by notice to the company.[42]

Once a notice in writing of resignation has been given it cannot be withdrawn without the consent of the company:

> A director gave notice of resignation in conformity with the articles, but before the board had met he withdrew his resignation. The board subsequently met and a resolution was passed to the effect that the director had vacated his office. *Held*, that the director could not under the articles withdraw his resignation without the consent of the company, that by letter he had vacated the office, and that the resolution of the board was effective.[43]

Removal

21–18   Some articles provide that a director can be removed from office by the other board members. There exists an institutional shareholders' recommendation that such a power should only be exercised by a written resolution of at least 75 per cent of the director's co-directors, for failure to attend a specified number of board meetings or board meetings held during a specified period.[44]

Suspension

21–19   A board member guilty of obstruction or disorderly conduct during the continuance of any meeting may be suspended for at least the remainder of the meeting.[45]

---

[40] *Latchford Premier Cinema v. Ermion* [1931] 2 Ch. 409.
[41] *Sawyer v. Mann (Financiers) Ltd* (1937) 184 L.T.J. 42.
[42] *Transport Ltd v. Schonberg* (1905) 21 T.L.R. 305.
[43] *Glossop v. Glossop* [1907] 2 Ch. 370.
[44] Institutional Shareholders' Committee: The Role and Duties of Directors (August 1993).
[45] *Barton v. Taylor* [1886] 11 App. Cas. 197 at 204.

CHAPTER 22

CONSTITUTION AND CONDUCT OF DIRECTORS' MEETINGS

1 DIRECTORS MUST ACT AS A BODY

Since the board of directors is entrusted with the management and administration of the company, its affairs must be conducted with reasonable formality. Decisions of the board will govern internal matters such as capital expenditure and personnel policy, and board resolutions constitute the authority for dealings with third parties. In relation to how the board shall conduct its business, Table A states:

22–01

> **88.** Subject to the provisions of the articles, the directors may regulate their proceedings, as they think fit . . .

In the words of Fry, L.J.: "As they think fit. Must they not meet in order to think?" The learned judge made his remark in a case in which the facts were as follows:

An application was made for shares in a company and on the same day there was a meeting of two out of four directors, the other two not having been given sufficient notice. The meeting resolved that two should form a quorum, and allotted shares. They adjourned the meeting until the next day. On that day the allottee withdraw his application and the meeting was again adjourned to the following day. On this third occasion three directors were present; one of those who had previously been absent approved the resolution relating to the quorum and the meeting confirmed the allotment. The fourth director on the same day wrote approving the quorum and his letter was received on the next day. The Court of Appeal held that as there had been no notice of the original meeting none of the subsequent meetings was valid and the allotment was therefore bad.[1]

The case is authority for the rule that, in general, the only way in which directors can exercise their constitutional powers is at or under the authority of a meeting of which proper notice has been given to all the directors entitled to attend.

A board meeting can be held in informal circumstances:

22–02

> There was a vacancy on the board. A board meeting had been properly summoned for the purpose of filling it. S intimated to B (they were both directors) that he would see B in his (S's) office at 2.30 p.m. B went there and saw S outside the office door, in a passage. B explained the purpose of the

---

[1] *Re Portuguese Consolidated Mines Ltd* (1889) 42 Ch.D. 160.

meeting and a vote was taken; B exercised his casting vote and the records were written up. *Held*, it was a valid board meeting.[2]

However, the casual meeting of two directors even at the office of the company cannot be treated as a board meeting at the option of one against the will and intention of the other:

> A company consisted of two directors, Canon Barron and Mr. W. J. Potter, and not being able to agree as to the conduct of the business they refused to meet each other in board meeting. Canon Barron requisitioned a general meeting for the purpose of approving resolutions removing Mr. Potter from the board and for appointing an additional director. The day before the general meeting, Mr. Potter met Canon Barron coming off his train at Paddington Station and proposed that certain persons be elected directors of the company. The Canon replied that he had nothing to say and continued towards his taxi, but Mr. Potter as chairman of the company gave his casting vote and declared the resolution carried. Realising that this might not have been good enough, Mr. Potter went up to the Canon in the office before the general meeting and proposed certain additional directors. Canon Barron made a non-committal answer, but Mr. Potter again exercised his casting vote and declared them elected. *Held*, these were not board meetings.[3]

The importance of the act to the company will have some bearing on whether or not the meeting will be vitiated by a technical irregularity. For example, a matter such as a winding up would require a greater observance of strict formality than minor matters of administration.[4]

However, it is not necessary for the directors to state that a meeting is a board meeting for it to be one. In the case of *Hunter v. Senate Support Services Limited*[5] the directors, who were all present, did not decide to treat their meeting as a formal board meeting, but the judge stated that it would be unrealistic not to treat it as such.

It is not essential to the validity of an act of the board that the directors shall, at the time of reaching a binding decision, have been all assembled together in one place under one roof.[6] In today's conditions, for example, directors situated in several different places can be connected for a conference by telephone or television; provided it had been duly convened as such, this would constitute a valid board meeting.

An example of a modern form of article[7] providing for a meeting to be held by telephone conference is as follows:

> Any or all of the directors, or members of a committee of directors, can take part in a meeting of the directors or of a committee of directors:

---

[2] *Smith v. Paringa Mines* [1906] 2 Ch. 193.

[3] *Barron v. Potter* [1914] 1 Ch. 895.

[4] *Re Haycroft Gold Reduction and Mining Co.* [1900] 2 Ch. 230.

[5] *Hunter v. Senate Support Services Limited* [2004] WL 10744336.

[6] See for example, *Re Bonelli's Telegraph Co.* (1871) L.R. 12 Eq. 246. For further discussion of some of the above cases, see 83 S.J. 577.

[7] It is taken from the Plain English articles adopted by National Westminster Bank plc in May 1996.

- by way of a conference telephone, or similar equipment, designed to allow everybody to take part in the meeting; or
- by a series of telephone calls from the chairman of the meeting.

Taking part in this way will be counted as being present at the meeting. A meeting which takes place by a series of calls from the chairman will be treated as taking place where the chairman is calling from. Otherwise meetings will be treated as taking place where most of the participants are.

It should be noted that proper notice of the meeting still has to be given. In the article quoted, the first bullet point is declaratory of the existing position; the second bullet point breaks new ground in that without it such a series of calls would not constitute a meeting. In view of the unusual nature of the provision, it is preferable to use it only where the matters to be discussed are formal and uncontroversial or in cases of urgency. Otherwise, the chairman would be wise to set up a more conventional meeting or arrange for a resolution to be circulated for signature.[8]

In the light of the importance of the principle that directors must act as a body, the courts will intervene where a director is improperly excluded from board meetings by his fellow directors, by granting an injunction restraining the exclusion.[9] The injunction will however be refused if a general meeting of shareholders resolves that it does not wish the excluded director to act as a member of the board.[10]

2 MEETINGS OF A SOLE DIRECTOR

It is clear that there can be a directors' meeting when there is only one director of a company. The meeting is all the more important where there are no other directors to control the sole director's actions, and it could be held in the presence of the company secretary. If the director, however, holds the meeting by himself he must deliberate carefully (a "statutory pause for thought") and pay special regard to the wording of the minutes.[11]   **22–03**

3 NOTICE OF BOARD MEETINGS

In general, notice of a board meeting should be given to each member. Table A continues: **22–04**

> **88.** . . . A director may, and the secretary at the request of a director shall, call a meeting of the directors. It shall not be necessary to give notice of a meeting to a director who is absent from the United Kingdom . . .

---

[8] See para. 22–09. For a general review of recent practice, see *PLC*, May 1997, at 31.
[9] *Pulbrook v. Richmond Consolidated Mining Co.* (1878) 9 Ch.D. 610, and see *Hayes v. Bristol Plant Hire Ltd* [1957] 1 W.L.R. 499.
[10] *Bainbridge v. Smith* (1889) 41 Ch.D. 462.
[11] *Neptune (Vehicle Washing Equipment) Ltd v. Fitzgerald* [1995] 1 BCLC 352; see also para. 22–07 below.

It will be observed that article 88 is silent as to the length of notice. Reasonable notice is all that is required, and if a directors' meeting is being convened in an emergency (for example, if a take-over bid for the company has been announced) notice could be extremely short. It need not be given in writing. The contents and style of the notice are generally left to the discretion of the board, which will make its own rules of conduct.

Each director should receive notice of a board meeting, because otherwise it would be possible for some members of the board to meet and transact business which may not receive the concurrence of other members:

> A board consisted of five directors. Two directors called a meeting for two o'clock in the afternoon of the same day, knowing that the third director could not attend until three o'clock, and not knowing whether the fourth director could attend or not; no notice was sent to the fifth director who was abroad. No intimation of any special business was set out in the notice. The two directors (who constituted a quorum) then met at the time appointed, but their acts were declared irregular as "what was done on that occasion was not the act of the board, and did not bind the company."[12]

Where a director is absent from the United Kingdom, the articles usually excuse the sending to him of a notice of meeting.[13] Even without this provision, notice need not be given to a director who is abroad unless he is within easy reach[14]—a situation which has become progressively more likely to arise with the development of modern communication systems. In practice, if the matter for which the meeting is being convened is important and urgent, an attempt will usually be made to contact all the directors (even those who are abroad) so that those who are necessarily absent can at least have their views reported to the meeting. It might be sensible to amend articles based on Table A to provide that notice of a board meeting shall be sent to a director who is outside the United Kingdom at the relevant time, and that it shall be the responsibility of the director concerned to notify the company of an overseas address where he can be contacted.

If the board has decided to meet on fixed dates at the same place, the distribution of a formal notice can be waived. Otherwise, notice must be sent to a director even if he has stated that he will not be able to attend.[15]

In principle, unless the articles otherwise provide the notice does not have to specify the nature of the business to be transacted.[16]

4 CHAIRMAN

22–05 Under Table A:

> **91.** The directors may appoint one of their number to be the chairman of the board of directors and may at any time remove him from that office. Unless

[12] *Re Homer District Consolidated Gold Mines* (1888) 39 Ch.D. 546.
[13] See Table A, art. 88.
[14] *Halifax Sugar Refining Co. v. Francklyn* (1890) 62 L.T. 563.
[15] *Re Portuguese Consolidated Mines Ltd* (1894) 42 Ch.D. 160. See para. 22–01 (n. 1).
[16] *Compagnie de Mayville v. Whitley* [1896] 1 Ch. 788.

he is unwilling to do so the director so appointed shall preside at every meeting of directors at which he is present. But if there is no director holding that office, or if the director holding it is unwilling to preside or is not present within five minutes after the time appointed for the meeting, the directors present may appoint one of their number to be the chairman of the meeting.

Even in the absence of a specific provision, the appointment of a chairman does not entitle him to fill the office for as long as he retains his directorship, and the directors have power at any time to substitute another chairman in his place.[17]

The chairman should make himself familiar with the regulations of the company, although in practice the secretary is usually the person who brings to his notice such matters as absence of quorum, qualification of directors, disclosure of interests in contracts and other matters that must be observed in order to make the proceedings valid.

Beyond these practical details, the chairman is responsible for seeing that the business of the directors is conducted efficiently. Some practical aspects are discussed below, in Chapter 23.

The chairman of the board normally takes the chair at general meetings.[18]

5   QUORUM

If a quorum is not present, the meeting cannot transact business. In practice, no **22–06** business can be done, even if all the directors are present, if their number is less than the prescribed quorum,[19] unless the articles provide that they may act notwithstanding any vacancies.[20]

The articles usually fix whatever quorum is deemed necessary. Exceptionally, the number required for a quorum can be established by usual practice.[21] It is possible for there to be a quorum of one director.[22] In practice, however, articles of association are unlikely to provide for a quorum of one. (Under section 282 of the 1985 Act, a private company may have only one director.) Table A provides that:

> **89.** The quorum for the transaction of the business of the directors may be fixed by the directors and unless so fixed at any other number shall be two. A person who holds office only as an alternate director shall, if his appointor is not present, be counted in the quorum.

If no quorum is established by the articles, the board must act by a majority of directors,[23] or a majority of the directors may fix a quorum. A director prohibited

---

[17] *Foster v. Foster* [1916] 1 Ch. 352.
[18] See para. 13–31.
[19] *Faure Electric, etc. Co. v. Phillipart* [1888] 58 L.T. 525.
[20] *Re Bank of Syria* [1900] 2 Ch. 272.
[21] *Lyster's Case* (1867) L.R. 4 Eq. 233.
[22] *Re Fireproof Doors Ltd* [1916] 2 Ch. 142.
[23] *York Tramways Co. v. Willows* (1882) 8 Q.B.D. 685. See also para. 6.04, n. 17.

from voting, for example by reason of his interest in a contract, cannot be taken into account for the purpose of ascertaining whether a quorum of directors is present.[24] Where two or more directors are interested in a contract, any arrangement by which the resolution is split to enable a director to abstain from voting on the part in which he is interested would not be permissible:

> The articles of a company provided that a director should not be disqualified from contracting with the company, but that he could not vote in respect of such contract; the quorum fixed by the directors was three. At a board meeting at which four directors were present, including X and Y, a debenture was issued to X pursuant to a resolution on which X did not vote, and another to Y pursuant to another resolution on which Y did not vote. The issue of the two debentures was held to be invalid because the two debentures formed part of the same transaction and the two resolutions were invalid for want of a disinterested quorum. At a subsequent meeting a resolution was passed reducing the quorum to two to enable a resolution for another debenture to be passed. *Held*, that the resolution relating to the debenture was invalid for want of a disinterested quorum, and the resolution relating to the reduction of the quorum was not passed in the interest of the company but only for the purpose of enabling X and Y to obtain an interest in the company's property.[25]

Similarly, article 95 of Table A provides that a director shall not be counted in the quorum present at a meeting in relation to a resolution on which he is not entitled to vote. (The conflict of interest obligations of a director are discussed in para. 22–07 below).

Where there is difficulty in obtaining a disinterested quorum, or where a director refuses to attend board meetings and his absence makes it impossible to secure a quorum, there must be recourse either to the shareholders in general meeting, for example by the use of the procedure laid down by section 368 of the 1985 Act,[26] or to the court:

> The whole of the issued share capital of the company was held by two persons who were also its directors. The quorum for the board meeting was two. One director refused to attend a board meeting to consider the registration of share transfers executed by the other director. It was held that the right of a shareholder to dispose of his shares can only be restricted subject to an express provision in the articles, and the court ordered the transfers to be registered.[27]

---

[24] *Re Greymouth Point Elizabeth Ry.* [1904] 1 Ch. 32. See para. 22–07 for a fuller discussion of the matter of conflict of interest.

[25] *Re North Eastern Insurance Co.* [1919] 1 Ch. 198.

[26] See paras. 12–10 to 12–13.

[27] *Re Copal Varnish Co.* [1917] 2 Ch. 349. See also *Re Opera Photographic* (1989) 5 B.C.C. 601. Note, however, *Hood Sailmakers Ltd v. Axford* [1997] 4 All E.R. 830, where it was held that a resolution passed by a single director, where the quorum for board meetings was fixed at two, was invalid notwithstanding the fact that the absent director was not entitled to receive notice of the board meeting in question because he was out of the jurisdiction.

It will be recalled, that section 371 of the 1985 Act provides that if for any reason it is impracticable to call a meeting of the company, the court may requisition one, either of its own motion or on the application of any director of the company or of any member of the company who would be entitled to vote at the meeting.[28]

6   Conflict of Interest

Under section 317 of the 1985 Act, it is the duty of a director of a company who is in any way, whether directly or indirectly, interested in a contract or proposed contract with the company to declare the nature of his interest at a meeting of the directors. In the case of a proposed contract, the declaration shall be made at the meeting at which the question of entering into the contract is first taken into consideration, or, if the director was not at the date of that meeting interested in the proposed contract, at the next meeting of the directors held after he became so interested. In a case where a director becomes interested in a contract after it is made, the declaration shall be made at the first meeting of the directors held after the director becomes so interested.[29]   **22–07**

For the purpose of section 317, the director may give a general notice to the directors that:

(a) he is a member of a specified company or firm and is to be regarded as interested in any contract which may, after the date of the notice, be made with that company or firm; or

(b) he is to be regarded as interested in any contract which may after the date of the notice be made with a specified person who is connected with him (within the meaning of section 346 of the 1985 Act);

but such a notice shall be of no effect unless either it is given at a meeting of the directors or the director takes reasonable steps to secure that it is brought up and read at the next meeting of the directors after it is given.[30]

A reference in section 317 to a contract includes any transaction or arrangement (whether or not constituting a contract) made or entered into on or after December 22, 1980.[31]

Where a director has a conflict of interest (for example he is also a director of a company in a competing field of activity), that should be declared. An interest should be declared even if it is patently obvious. The declaration should be full and frank, and cover the precise nature of the interest held.

Disclosure had to be made to a meeting of the full board of directors, not to a committee of directors; it makes no difference that all the board members knew of the interest in question, if there was no disclosure to a duly convened meeting of the board.[32] In certain circumstances, however, if the failure to disclose is a mere

---

[28] See para. 12–15.
[29] 1985 Act, s.317(1), (2).
[30] 1985 Act, s.317(3), (4).
[31] 1985 Act, s.317(5).
[32] *Guinness plc v. Saunders* [1988] 2 All E.R. 940; see also [1990] 2 A.C. 663 (H.L.).

technicality the company, in an action by the director, may not be able to rely on it.[33] A sole director has to show that he made the necessary declaration to himself at a director's meeting.[34] The disclosure should be recorded in the board minutes.

Amplification of the statutory obligations is to be found in articles 85, 86 and 94. The underlying rule is that a director should not allow a position to arise where his interest and that of the company may conflict; in such a situation the contract may be voidable and the director will not be allowed to retain the profit arising.[35] Article 94 (which reflects the provisions to be found in many sets of articles) provides that, with certain exceptions, a director shall not vote at a meeting of directors or of a committee of directors on any resolution concerning a matter in which he has, directly or indirectly, an interest or duty which is material and which conflicts or may conflict with the interests of the company. Paragraph 20 of Appendix 1 to Chapter 13 of the Listing Rules provides that the articles of a listed company must prohibit a director from voting on any contract or arrangement or any other proposal in which he has an interest which (together with any interest of any person connected with him) is to his knowledge a material interest otherwise than by virtue of his interests in shares or debentures or other securities of, or otherwise in or through, the listed company (certain exceptions are permitted). Article 95 provides that a director shall not be counted in the quorum present at a meeting in relation to a resolution on which he is not entitled to vote.

Article 96 provides (in essence) that the company may, by ordinary resolution, suspend or relax any provision in the articles prohibiting a director from voting (but the director must still declare his interest under section 317). In other words, if too many directors are disqualified from voting in relation to a particular matter, a general meeting of shareholders will be necessary either to operate article 96 (if applicable), or to appoint additional disinterested directors, or to change the articles.

Certain changes to the regulation of conflicts of interest are being proposed by the company law review. See 22–13.

7   VOTING

22–08   An attempt is usually made at directors' meetings to obtain a consensus rather than to press matters to a vote. There may be instances, however, when votes are taken or at any rate the possibility of voting is contemplated, for example when the composition of the board reflects the differing ownership of blocks of the company's share capital. This might arise where the company is formed to carry on the business of a consortium or a joint venture. Irreconcilable differences of opinion can of course develop in any company, and then a vote will be necessary when a board decision has to be taken.

Under article 88 of Table A, questions arising at any meeting are decided by a majority of votes, and in the case of an equality of votes the chairman has a second

---

[33] *Runciman v. Walter Runciman plc* [1992] BCLC 1085.
[34] *Neptune (Vehicle Washing Equipment) Ltd v. Fitzgerald* [1995] 1 BCLC 352.
[35] *Parker v. McKenna* (1874) 10 Ch.App. 96.

or casting vote. Articles not infrequently provide, however, that the chairman has no second or casting vote. He has no such vote at common law.[36] As a general rule, voting is by show of hands. Every director has one vote at a board meeting unless the articles otherwise provide. Should there not be unanimity in voting, a director is entitled to have the fact that he voted against the motion recorded in the minutes.

There is no provision in Table A for voting at a directors' meeting by poll. A director not entitled to vote at a board meeting, for example, because of an interest in a contract cannot, however, be excluded from the meeting.[37]

Under article 88 of Table A, a director who is also an alternate director shall be entitled in the absence of his appointer to a separate vote on behalf of his appointer in addition to his own vote.

8 RESOLUTIONS IN WRITING SIGNED BY ALL DIRECTORS

It is common for articles to include a provision similar to article 93 of Table A: **22–09**

> **93.** A resolution in writing signed by all the directors entitled to receive notice of a meeting of directors or of a committee of directors shall be as valid and effectual as if it had been passed at a meeting of directors or (as the case may be) a committee of directors duly convened and held and may consist of several documents in the like form, each signed by one or more directors, but a resolution signed by an alternate director need not also be signed by his appointer and, if it is signed by a director who has appointed an alternate director, it need not be signed by the alternate director in that capacity.

Under the provisions of such an article, the practice has developed of circulating among directors a prepared resolution for their signature. The arrangement is convenient where the business is purely formal and it would be difficult or inconvenient for the directors to meet. In such circumstances the resolution should be signed by each director, and the date for inclusion in the minutes would be the date when the last director signed. The document can be faxed but the signed original should be retained.

The article cannot be used where the business would not be capable of being transacted by a meeting of the directors—for example, through the absence of a disinterested quorum. There appears, however, to be no reason why a director who is interested (in the technical sense) in a matter covered by the resolution should not sign it, with a note to the effect that he has signed for the purposes of article 93 and not as a vote on the resolution.[38]

---

[36] *Nell v. Longbottom* [1894] 1 Q.B. 767.
[37] *Grimwade v. B.P.S. Syndicate Ltd* (1915) 31 T.L.R. 531.
[38] [1978] *Prof. Admin.* (March) and Corporate Administrator p. xvi in *Administrator* magazine, November 1989. See also *Davidson and Begg Antiques Ltd v. Davidson* [1997] B.C.C. 77.

9 MINUTES

22–10   It is proposed here to deal with the statutory provisions relating to minutes of directors' meetings and relevant case law. General comments on minutes of meetings are contained above, in Chapter 8, and Chapter 23, below, contains some precedents and comments on the drafting of board minutes.

Duty to keep minutes

22–11   Section 382(1) of the 1985 Act requires minutes to be made and kept of all proceedings of general meetings of a company and of meetings of its directors or managers, and provides for penalties in case of default. The subsection is amplified by article 100 of Table A, which states:

> **100.** The directors shall cause minutes to be made in books kept for the purpose:
> (a) of all appointments of officers made by directors; and
> (b) of all proceedings at meetings of the company, of the holders of any class of shares in the company, and of the directors, and of committees of directors, including the names of directors present at each such meeting.

The general duty of directors has been summarised as follows:

> "Directors ought to place on record, either in formal minutes or otherwise, the purport and effect of their deliberations and conclusions; and if they do this insufficiently or inaccurately they cannot reasonably complain of inferences different from those which they allege to be right."[39]

The records of the meetings of directors need not necessarily be in the form of resolutions, so long as the minutes show the substance of the decision arrived at.[40]

In cases where directors arrive after the start of the proceedings or leave before their conclusion, it is the usual practice to record in the minutes that a director joined or left a meeting during the proceedings.

The provisions of section 722 of the 1985 Act in relation to the form in which minutes are to be kept, apply equally to board minutes as to minutes of general meetings and are referred to in para. 16–01.

Minutes as evidence

22–12   Section 382(2) of the 1985 Act states that a minute, if purporting to be signed by the chairman of the meeting at which the proceedings were had, or by the chairman of the next succeeding meeting, is evidence of the proceedings. This

---

[39] *Re Liverpool Household Stores Assoc.* (1890) 59 L.J. Ch. 616, 619.
[40] *Re Land Credit Co. of Ireland* (1869) 4 Ch.App. 460, 473.

gives statutory embodiment to the rule, long accepted in common law, that minutes will be prima facie evidence of the matters to which they relate:

> The articles of a company provided that a minute, if signed by a person purporting to be chairman of the company, was to be receivable as evidence with further proof. The minute of a meeting signed by the chairman represented him as having subscribed for 100 shares, and he was held liable for this amount.[41]

Entries in the minute book must be made within a reasonable time, otherwise there may be difficulty in enforcing a contract agreed to at a meeting:

> The remuneration of a director for services as manager of the company was increased, and the minute recording such increase was not written up until 12 months after the meeting, although the articles provided that in disclosure of interest situations such disclosure should be entered in the minutes. *Held*, the plaintiff could not recover the excess since the entry covering the arrangement was not made within a reasonable time.[42]

In an action for the enforcement of a service agreement submitted in draft and approved at a meeting of directors, it was held that although the signature of the chairman was entered in the minute book for the purpose of verifying the accuracy of the entry, it nevertheless operated as an admission of the contract contained in the draft and submitted to the meeting.[43] While this was so in the particular circumstances of that case, the conclusion must not be drawn that a resolution of a board or other executive body itself creates a contractual relationship between the body and a third party. Thus, the resolution of a board of managers to appoint an applicant to be headmaster of a school, which resolution had not been communicated to him and was subsequently rescinded, provided no ground for action.[44]

Minutes of directors' meetings are prima facie evidence only and "other evidence is admissible, though the existence of a minute is a circumstance to be considered in judging of its weight".[45]

The presence of a director at a meeting at which the minutes of the previous meeting were confirmed is not sufficient to make him liable for an *ultra vires* investment when he knew nothing of the irregularity agreed upon at the former meeting. Where, however, a fellow director had taken an active part in and had assented to the investment, he could not escape personal liability in the repayment of the illegal investment.[46] A director, by voting at a subsequent meeting for the confirmation of the minutes, does not make himself responsible for acts done at a board meeting at which he was not present.[47]

---

[41] *Stock's Case* (1864) 4 De G.J. S. 426.
[42] *Toms v. Cinema Trust Ltd* [1915] W.N. 29.
[43] *Jones v. Victoria Graving Dock Co.* (1877) 2 Q.B.D. 314. See also *Orion Insurance Co. v. Sphere Drake Insurance* [1992] 1 Lloyd's Rep. 239, C.A.
[44] *Powell v. Lee* (1908) 99 L.T. 284.
[45] *Re Pyle Works* (No. 2) [1891] 1 Ch. 173, 184.
[46] *Re Lands Allotment Co.* [1894] 1 Ch. 616.
[47] *Burton v. Bevan* [1908] 2 Ch. 240.

22–13   A director has the right at common law to inspect the minutes of meetings of the board: he may be accompanied by his professional adviser.[48]

10   COMPANY LAW REVIEW

22–14   The Company Law Review has been ongoing for a number of years now, and a draft companies bill was published in March 2005. This draft bill was part of a White Paper published by the Department of Trade and Industry and has been supplemented since that date by more draft clauses. In respect of directors it will introduce a new statutory statement of duties. This statement of duties will put the duties of a director on a statutory footing, instead of the current situation where much of a directors duties have been established by common law and precedent.

The law on the regulation of conflicts of interest is thought to be too complex and in need of simplification. The draft companies bill addresses this. Types of transaction requiring shareholder approval will be grouped together. It will become possible to make loans to directors without shareholder approval.

Since the draft bill is not yet before Parliament, it is unlikely that any of these changes will take effect before the middle or end of 2006.

---

[48] *McCusker v. McRae*, 1966 S.C. 253.

CHAPTER 23

BOARD MEETINGS:
EXAMPLES IN PRACTICE

In this chapter, examples of the procedure followed at board meetings will be described in more detail. An example of an agenda and minutes of the first meeting of a company after incorporation is provided: these are in fairly standard form. The next section relates to the procedure which might be followed at board meeting of a public company. This section attempts to paint a realistic picture, but cannot be taken as definitive: it would be impossible to encompass all the situations which can arise in practice. More information on good boardroom practice is contained within the ICSA's Code on Good Boardroom Practice for Directors and Company Secretaries, available from the ICSA's website at *www.icsa.org.uk*

23–01

1   First Board Meeting

At the first meeting of the directors of a newly formed company, a number of special matters call for attention, as is indicated in the following specimen agenda and minutes of Springer Limited, a private company.

23–02

Springer Limited

A board meeting of the company will be held at The Whitethorns, High Point, West Midlands on December 1, 2005 at 11.30 a.m.

Agenda

(1) To table the certificate of incorporation of the company and a print of the memorandum and articles of the company, as registered.[1]

(2) To table a copy of the statement delivered to the Registrar (Companies Form No. 10) and naming Mr .... and Mrs .... as the first

23–03

---

[1] If an "off-the-shelf" company is used, appropriate stock transfer forms should also be tabled, together with resignations of the first directors and secretary, notices of appointment of new directors and secretary, and a resolution relating to change of registered office. Minutes 2 and 7 will not be required.

directors and Mr .... as the secretary of the company, and giving the intended situation of the registered office.[2]

(3) To produce the statutory books of the company.[3]

(4) To elect a chairman of the board.

(5) To appoint Messrs .... Co. as auditors of the company.

(6) To appoint ...... Bank as the company's bankers, in accordance with the Bank's standard form of mandate, a copy of which is annexed hereto.

(7) To confirm the situation of the company's registered office.

(8) To adopt the common seal of the company.

(9) To produce and read to the meeting notices given by the directors pursuant to s.317(3) of the Companies Act 1985.[4]

(10) To issue and allot shares in the company.

(11) To fix an accounting reference date.

(12) To arrange the dates of future board meetings.

(13) Any other business.

MINUTES

23–04 Minutes of a board meeting of Springer Limited held at the Whitethorns, High Point, West Midlands on December 1, 2005.

Present:

Mr ....

Mrs ....

In attendance: Mr .... (secretary)

1. There was tabled the certificate of incorporation of the company (No ....) dated ...... 1997 and a print of the memorandum and articles of association as registered.

2. It was confirmed that, in accordance with the statement delivered to the Companies Registrar with the memorandum and articles of the company, Mr ...... and Mrs ...... were the first directors of the company, and that Mr ...... was the secretary of the company.

3. The statutory books of the company were produced to the meeting.

4. It was resolved that Mr ...... be and he is hereby appointed chairman of the board.

5. It was resolved that Messrs ...... and Co. be and they are hereby appointed auditors of the company to hold office until the conclusion of the first general meeting at which accounts are laid before the company. Authority was given to the chairman to negotiate with the auditors in order to fix their fee.

---

[2] 1985 Act, s.10.

[3] Initially these will usually comprise a register of members (1985 Act, s.352), a register of directors and secretary (1985 Act, s.288) and a register of directors' interests (1985 Act, s.325).

[4] Directors' interests in shares and contracts.

6. It was resolved that a bank account for the company be opened with ...... Bank and that the Bank be authorised:

(a) to honour and comply with all cheques, drafts, bills, promissory notes, acceptances, negotiable instruments and orders expressed to be drawn accepted, made or given on behalf of the company at any time or times whether the banking account of the company is overdrawn or in credit or otherwise; and

(b) to honour and comply with all instructions to deliver or receive or dispose of any securities or documents or property held by the Bank or to be held by the Bank on behalf of the company:

provided that any such cheques, drafts, bills, promissory notes, acceptances, negotiable instruments, orders or instructions are signed on behalf of the company by: [detailed signing instructions].

7. It was resolved that the registered office of the company be situated at The Whitethorns, High Point, West Midlands, which address had already been given in the statement on registration as the intended location of the registered office.[5]

8. It was resolved that the seal, an impression of which is affixed to these minutes, be adopted as the common seal of the company.

9. There were produced and read to the meeting notices given by [names of directors] pursuant to s317(3) of the Companies Act 1985.

10. (a) There were produced to the meeting forms of application for shares as follows, together with cheques in payment in full:

Date	Applicant	Number of shares
	[details]	

(b) It was accordingly resolved that shares of £ each in the capital of the company be and they are hereby allotted as follows:

Allottee	Number of shares	Distinctive
	[details]	numbers

(c) It was resolved that share certificates prepared in respect of the subscribers' shares and the allotment made pursuant to (b) above be approved and that the common seal of the company be thereto affixed.

11. It was resolved that the accounting reference date for the company should be ......

12. It was agreed that the next meeting of the directors would be held on January 10, 2006 at 11.30 a.m. at the registered office.

2   Board Meeting: Public Company

This section gives an outline of practice at the board meeting of a public company. It is assumed that a typical board structure applies: that the chairman is non-executive, that there is a chief executive, a finance director and some other   **23–05**

---

[5] 1985 Act, s.10(6).

executive directors and that, in addition to the chairman, there are other non-executive directors. Such a board will normally meet at regular intervals, say monthly, and it is these meetings which are described below.

Notice and agenda

23–06   It is standard practice for the secretary to prepare a set of papers which are circulated a week or so in advance. They consist of a combined notice and agenda.

The secretary must impose a tight deadline by which papers in support of each agenda item have to be delivered to his office. The assembly of the total agenda is a large task and it is not satisfactory to send out supporting papers after the main agenda has been despatched or table them at the meeting as directors will not have sufficient time to digest the information and make informed decisions at the meeting.

It is good practice for the secretary to mark each board paper with the agenda item number for ease of reference.

ENGINEERS PUBLIC LIMITED COMPANY

A board meeting will be held at [address] on September 30, 2005 at 10.30 a.m.

AGENDA

	Supporting Paper No.
1. Minutes	
1.1 To approve the minutes of the board meeting held on 21 August 2005	1.1
1.2 To note the minutes of the remuneration committee held on 22 August 2005	1.2
2. Chief Executive's Report:	
2.1 to consider the Chief Executive's report for the month of August 2005.	2.1
2.2 to consider the divisional directors' reports for the month of August 1997.	2.2
3. Finance Director's Report	2.2
3.1 to consider the management accounts for the month of August 2005	
4. Capital Expenditure	
To consider the capital expenditure requests for the month of September 2005.	3

5. Acquisition

To consider a paper by the Chief Executive dated September 22, 2005 recommending the acquisition of Shirley Widgets Limited. (Mr ... will be in attendance for this item).

4

6. Secretary's Report

a. Shareholder analysis, share price, share trading volumes
b. Update on legislative and corporate governance developments
c. Sealing register
d. Directors' share dealings

....

Secretary

Date ....

Notes:

1. Minutes. A draft of the minutes of the previous meeting will be circulated with the board papers. These will have been compiled by the secretary from his notes taken at that meeting. A preliminary draft should have been approved by the chairman before being included with the board papers. If the minutes are not approved by the board meeting, any minor correction to the typed minutes can be made by the secretary and initialled by the chairman; a major alteration should be the subject of a new minute approved at the next meeting.

2. Chief Executive's report. There will be wide variation in practice over this item. The Chief Executive is likely to circulate his own report with the board papers; Questions are likely to come mainly from the chairman and non-executive directors: in answering them the Chief Executive will be assisted by other executive directors with special responsibilities. Those directors themselves may present regular reports to the board.

3. Capital expenditure. Again, the relevant requests, with details, will be included in the circulated papers.

4. Acquisition. The purchase of Shirley Widgets Limited will probably be the subject of a separate paper in which the arguments for and against the purchase are examined in detail, culminating in the Chief Executive's recommendation. (A board paper should always make clear what it is that the author is asking of the board: for example, that the proposal should be approved, or that the situation be noted; exceptionally, the paper might conclude simply with a request that the matter be discussed. Each supporting paper should be dated and indicate who has taken the responsibility for its preparation.) Here it is assumed that as well as the paper there will be an oral presentation by the Chief Executive and the divisional manager, who is to attend the board meeting for this item on the agenda.

The chairman's role

23–07   The chairman will have conferred with the secretary and the Chief Executive in the framing of the above agenda, making sure that all relevant issues are included. He will also need to make himself aware of the most significant aspects of each item; it is customary for a non-executive chairman to talk frequently with the Chief Executive about the company's operations. He will need to ensure that the board's business is conducted in a logical and timely sequence.

Where disagreement exists among board members, the chairman's duty is to take time and trouble in seeking a consensus, since good relationships in the boardroom are important for the health of the company. He will work behind the scene to reconcile differences, but if the disagreement surfaces at the board table he will ensure that the views of each director are fairly heard. This patient work is usually successful: a vote by show of hands is an infrequent event in the life of a public company board. If one does take place, a dissentient director can ask to have his name and comments recorded in the minutes.

23–07a   Corporate governance

Corporate governance is concerned with ensuring that decisions are taken in an appropriate manner by appropriate people after due consideration of the relevant facts. Good boardroom practice can play a significant part in ensuring sound decision making. For listed public companies, boardroom practice and effectiveness are regulated, in large measure, by the current version of the Combined Code on Corporate Governance published in July 2003. Companies must include a statement in their Annual Report and Accounts as to how the provisions of the Code have been applied throughout the financial year; where companies have not complied with any provision, an explanation is required. This code consolidated (with some modifications) the recommendations made in other codes of practice such as the Cadbury Committee's Code of Best Practice and the Greenbury Code on directors' remuneration policy and practice. The Combined Code covers the responsibilities of the board, best practice in the workings of the board, eg the requirement to have regular meetings, the role of the chairman and non-executive directors, the system of reporting and controls and the membership of committees.[6] The Code states at provision A.5.3 that the company secretary is responsible to the board for ensuring that board procedures are complied with.

Minutes

23–08   Observations on the drafting of minutes are contained in Chapter 8. Those apply also to board minutes, and the purpose of this note is merely to offer some further advice on style:

(1) Each minute should refer briefly to how the matter comes before the board, for example, that a paper was submitted by the Chief Executive, that the chairman raised the matter at the meeting or that it was carried forward from a previous meeting.

[6] Copies can be obtained from the Financial Reporting Council at *www.frc.org.uk*

(2) The minute should summarise the essential facts on which the board had to make a decision.

(3) The minute should summarise the conclusion and give sufficient detail for the minute to be self-standing—so that, for example, it could be produced to the company's auditors without the need for oral explanation or reference to another document. If reference to another document is however made (for example, where a long list of items of capital expenditure is approved) that other document should be cross-referenced to the paper or attached to or kept in safe custody with the signed minutes.

(4) There is usually no need to record individual expressions of opinion by board members. If there has been disagreement, the minute can include a note of the main arguments for and against the matter before the board, without attribution.

(5) Expressions such as "the chairman," "the Chief Executive," "the secretary" are preferable to the use of names, both to make the minute easier for third parties to read (if that is appropriate) and to set the remarks made by the people concerned in the context of their authority.

(6) In items such as the Chief Executive's report, the minutes need only record that (on the basis of the agenda described above) the reports were discussed. Note can however be made of salient items if they are significant or if the item is likely to recur—for example, where a division is operating at a loss and the Chief Executive describes the action being taken.

Duties of secretary

The above outline is typical of current practice. The note details some additional **23–09** practical matters which may fall to be handled by the secretary.

(1) *Before the board meeting*

(a) The secretary should send the board papers (notice, agenda and supporting papers) to each director. It is good practice to mark the envelope "confidential", to use registered post, recorded delivery or courier, and to affix an "if undelivered please return to. . . ." sticker. A robust envelope is desirable.

(b) Arrangements for the meeting room, with any necessary overhead projector and other conference-type equipment, should be made in good time before sending out the board papers.

(c) If anyone has to be in attendance at the board meeting, he or she should be given full instructions well in advance of the meeting.

(d) In making sure nothing has been omitted from the agenda, it is useful to refer to the following:
 (i) minutes of the previous two or three meetings;
 (ii) any "bring-up" system in use;
 (iii) the minutes of the corresponding meeting in the previous year
 (iv) any rolling agenda programme in use, eg grant of share options may be scheduled to take place twice a year

    (e) Where possible, if a formal resolution is required, a draft should be prepared and circulated in advance.

    (f) The secretary will prepare a check-list of administrative details which should not be overlooked, for example, arrangements for transport to the meeting, for any refreshments before or at the end of the meeting, for a supply of stationery in the board room, visual aids, and the availability of basic documents of reference, (*e.g.* minute book and memorandum and articles.

    (g) The minutes of the previous meeting should be ready for approval and signature by the chairman.

(2) *During the board meeting*

23–10

    (a) First, the directors should sign the attendance book, if there is one (it is no longer required by Table A).

    (b) The secretary should check that a quorum is present before the meeting proceeds to business (Table A Reg 88 specifies that the quorum for meetings of directors shall be two).

    (c) The secretary should take handwritten notes of the proceedings, from which the minutes will be compiled. These notes should be retained.

    (d) It will be the secretary's responsibility to ensure that the business conducted by the meeting follows the provisions of the company's articles and any relevant statute or procedural requirement, including any declaration of an interest by a director. If the proceedings risk becoming irregular, this should be pointed out immediately to the chairman. It should be noted, however, that the secretary has no inherent power to ensure compliance; he does not even have a right to attend board meetings.

    (e) At the end of the meeting, the room should be cleared of any confidential papers which may have been accidentally left behind. Some companies insist that board papers are retained by the company after the meeting.

(3) *After the board meeting*

23–11

    (a) If the company is listed, and there has been a decision about a dividend, or figures in respect of any financial period have been approved, there must be immediate communication to the Stock Exchange under the Listing Rules.[7]

    (b) The secretary will follow through items of implementation (for example, the execution of documents) which have been delegated to him, and will communicate the board's decisions to those persons in the company and outside it who are affected by them.

    (c) The minutes must be prepared in a timely fashion; comment on this task has been made above, at paragraph 23–08.

---

[7] Listing Rules 9.7.2(2) and 9.7.1.

CHAPTER 24

MEETINGS IN INSOLVENCY SITUATIONS, SHORT OF WINDING UP

The Insolvency Act 1986 ("the 1986 Act") and the Insolvency Rules 1986,[1] gave **24–01** effect to many of the reforms recommended by the Review Committee on Insolvency Law and Practice.[2] The Enterprise Act 2002 made major changes to the 1986 Act and changed the emphasis of law generally to favour the recovery of businesses and individuals.

The Act substantially reformed the law, and there are now five main ways in which the affairs of a company which is insolvent (or close to it) may be regulated:

(1) A voluntary arrangement (Part I of the 1986 Act).
(2) An administration order (Part II).
(3) Administrative receivership (Part III).
(4) Winding up by the Court (Part IV).
(5) Voluntary winding up (also Part IV).

This chapter and the next will provide a brief description of the main features of each method,[3] an outline of the relevant meeting procedure and a brief summary of the points which creditors should particularly note.

The provisions are complex and reference should be made to the full text of the Act and Rules. Chapter 26 will deal with proxies and company representation in an insolvency. A members' voluntary winding up generally relates to solvent rather than insolvent companies and will be dealt with in Chapter 27.

1 VOLUNTARY ARRANGEMENT

The 1986 Act introduced a new method by which a company can make a binding **24–02** arrangement with its creditors. The provisions are simpler than those contained in section 425 of the 1985 Act,[4] and, in general, do not involve the active participation of the court. Trading can continue.

---

[1] S.I. 1986 No. 1925. See also the Insolvency (Amendment) Rules 1987 (S.I. 1987 No. 1919), the Insolvency (Amendment) Rules 1989 (S.I. 1989 No. 397), the Insolvency (Amendment) Rules 1991 (S.I. 1991 No. 495), the Insolvency (Amendment) Rules 1993 (S.I. 1993 No. 602) and the Insolvency (Amendment) Rules 1995 (S.I. 1995 No. 586). In this and the following chapter these rules will be referred to as "the Rules".
[2] Cmnd. 8558 (1982) (the Cork Report).
[3] The text relates to the law in force in England and Wales.
[4] See Chap. 18.

The proposal

24–03   The procedure calls for the making of a proposal to the company and its creditors for a composition in satisfaction of its debts or a scheme of arrangement of its affairs.[5] The proposal must provide for some person (the "nominee") to act in relation to the voluntary arrangement either as trustee or otherwise for the purpose of supervising its implementation.[6] The nominee must be a "qualified insolvency practitioner".[7] The directors may make the proposal, (following a duly convened board meeting) but only where no administration order is in force and the company is not being wound up.[8] Unlike the situation in the case of an administration order, the directors are not deprived of the power to continue to manage the company while the voluntary arrangement is being implemented.

The nominee, who will normally have been advising the company, will receive written notice of the proposed arrangement and a statement of the company's affairs.[9]

The first duty of the nominee is within 28 days after he is given notice of the proposal for the voluntary arrangement (or such longer period as the court may allow) to submit to the court a report stating:

(a) whether, in his opinion, meetings of the company and of its creditors should be summoned to consider the proposal, and

(b) if in his opinion such meetings should be summoned, the date on which and the time and place at which, the meetings should be held.[10]

The nominee will normally act quickly. If his recommendation is positive, he must convene the meetings unless the court otherwise directs.[11] If the company is in administration or being wound up, and the nominee is the liquidator or administrator, he must summon meetings of the company and of its creditors to consider the proposed arrangement for such a time, date and place as he thinks fit.[12]

The meetings

24–04   The meetings must be held not less than 14, nor more than 28 days, from the date the nominee's report is filed in court.[13] Notices calling the meetings must be sent by the nominee at least 14 days before the day fixed for them to be held—

---

[5] 1986 Act, s.1(1).

[6] *ibid.*, s.1(2).

[7] See ss.388–398 of the 1986 Act. The same qualification is required for administrators, administrative receivers and liquidators.

[8] 1986 Act, s.1(1). In the excepted cases, the proposal may be made by the administrator or liquidator, respectively (s.1(3)). In that situation the administrator or liquidator can himself become the nominee or another insolvency practitioner can be appointed as nominee.

[9] 1986 Act, s.2(3). See also rr. 1.2 to 1.6. In practice, the nominee may be identified by the directors before the proposal is put together; he is then asked for his help in preparing the report and accompanying statement of affairs.

[10] 1986 Act, s.2(2); r. 1.7. See also *Re a Debtor (No. 222 of 1990)* [1992] BCLC 137. No nominee's report to the court is necessary if the nominee is the liquidator or administrator.

[11] *ibid.*, s.3(1).

[12] *ibid.*, s.3(2).

[13] r. 1.9(1); r. 1.11 relates to the position where the administrator or liquidator is himself the nominee.

(a) in the case of the creditors' meeting, to all the creditors specified in the statement of affairs, and any other creditors of the company of whom he is otherwise aware; and

(b) in the case of a meeting of members of the company, to all persons who are, to the best of the nominee's belief, members of it.[14]

The purpose of the meetings is to decide whether to approve the proposed voluntary arrangement, with or without modifications.[15] The nominee has to have regard primarily to the convenience of creditors in fixing the venues.[16] The meetings must be held on the same day and in the same place, but the creditors' meeting must come first; they must be held between 10.00 a.m. and 4.00 p.m. on a business day.[17] In practice, the two meetings are often held together.

The convener must give at least 14 days' notice to attend the meetings to all directors of the company, and to any persons in whose case the convener thinks that their presence is required as being officers of the company, or as having been directors or officers (including auditors) of it at any time in the two years immediately preceding the date of the notice.[18]

However, even if they have been sent notice, such persons can, at the chairman's discretion, be excluded from attendance at a meeting or any part of it.[19]

Normally, the nominee, as the convener of the meetings, takes the chair but there are provisions for an alternative in his absence.[20]

Quorum

The quorum for the members' meeting will be determined by the articles. The quorum for the creditors' meeting is one creditor present in person or by proxy and entitled to vote.[21]   **24–04a**

Voting and resolutions

Creditors and members can vote by proxy, and forms of proxy must be sent together with the notices of the meetings.[22] Since, in relation to creditors' meetings, the Rules make no provision for proxies to be delivered by any particular time, they can be delivered by a creditor at any time up to the time a vote is taken.   **24–05**

In relation to the voting rights of creditors, the general rule is that every creditor who was given notice of the meeting is entitled to vote at the meeting or any adjournment, but he should give written notice of his claim to the chairman prior to or at the time of the meeting. Votes are calculated according to the creditor's debt at the date of the meeting, or, where the company is being wound up or is

---

[14] r. 1.9(2). The notice must contain the information set out in r. 1.9(3).
[15] 1986 Act, s.4(1).
[16] r. 1.13(1).
[17] r. 1.13(2), (3).
[18] r. 1.16(1).
[19] r. 1.16(2).
[20] r. 1.14.
[21] r. 12.4A.
[22] r. 1.13(4).

subject to an administration order, the date of its going into liquidation or of the administration order. A creditor shall not vote in respect of a debt for an unliquidated amount, or a debt whose value is not ascertained, except where the chairman agrees to put an estimated minimum value on the debt.[23] A creditor who should have been given notice of a meeting and was not given such notice but who learned about the meeting independently can validly vote at the meeting.[24] The chairman may admit or reject a claim, in whole or in part. The chairman's decision is subject to appeal (within a prescribed time limit) to the court. If the chairman is in doubt about a vote, he must mark it as objected to and allow the creditor to vote, subject to his vote being declared invalid if the objection is sustained. If, on appeal, the chairman's decision is reversed or varied or a creditor's vote is declared invalid, and the court considers there has been unfair prejudice or material irregularity, the court may order another meeting to be summoned or may make such other order as it thinks just.[25]

The prescribed majority at the creditors' meeting for any resolution approving any proposal or modification is a majority in excess of three-quarters in value of the creditors present in person or by proxy and voting on the resolution. Any other resolution at a creditors' meeting requires a majority of one-half of the creditors so present and voting.[26] The Rules contain provisions for a creditor's vote in certain cases to be left out of account in whole or in part, and to prevent misuse of a proxy by the chairman. The resolution will fail at the creditors' meeting if those voting against it include more than half in value of the creditors, counting only those (a) to whom notice of the meeting has been sent, (b) whose votes are not to be left out of account under the provisions described above and (c) who are not, to the best of the chairman's belief, persons connected with the company.[27]

In relation to the members' meeting, as a general rule the articles determine the voting rights.[28] Where no voting rights attach to a member's shares, he is nevertheless entitled to vote either for or against the proposal or any modification of it.[29] The requisite majority is one-half in value of the members present in person or by proxy and voting on the resolution; the value of members is determined by

---

[23] r. 1.17(1)–(3). On the powers and duties of a chairman in this regard, see *Re Cranley Mansions Ltd, Saigol v. Goldstein* [1994] B.C.C. 576 and *Re a Debtor (No. 162 of 1993) Doorbar v. Alltime Securities* [1994] B.C.C. 994; the latter case was affirmed on appeal ([1995] B.C.C. 1149) and is to be preferred. It establishes that an "agreement" exists if the chairman of the meeting agrees that the creditor's claim shall have a value attributed to it for voting purposes; the chairman determines the value (but he must act bona fide in deciding the figure). This stops the creditor refusing to agree a figure: then he would not be bound by the voluntary arrangement and could scupper it by presenting a winding-up petition. In relation to a creditor with an unliquidated claim who does not turn up at the meeting, see *Beverley Group plc v. McClue* [1995] B.C.C. 751; and for a more general review of the meaning of "creditor", see *Re Cancol Ltd* [1995] B.C.C. 1133. See also *Re Kenneth George Hoare (No. 47 of 1996), The Times*, March 20, 1997: H.M. Customs is entitled to vote at the meeting in respect of all sums which would be owed to it if a VAT return were drawn up as at the date of the meeting; it is bound in respect of that sum; it cannot later claim that it was owed some other debt which was not included in an earlier estimate.
[24] *Re Debtors (Nos. 400 and 401 of 1996), The Times*, February 27, 1997.
[25] r. 1.17(4)–(8).
[26] r. 1.19(1)–(2).
[27] r. 1.19(3), (4) and (6). The chairman has the power to decide if a vote is to be left out of account, or if a person is connected with the company. The purpose of the provision is to prevent connected persons from forcing a proposal on to a majority of unconnected creditors.
[28] r. 1.18(1).
[29] r. 1.18(2).

reference to the number of votes conferred on each member by the articles (excluding those who have no votes under the articles).[30]

The rules contain provisions for the chairman to consolidate the creditors' and members' meetings in order to facilitate the obtaining of agreement to the proposal and for the adjournment of the meetings for not more than 14 days.[31]

Approval of the proposal

The meetings must decide whether to reject the proposed voluntary arrange- **24–06** ment or to approve it with or without modifications. At the conclusion of either meeting, the chairman must report the result to the court within four days, and give notice of the result to all who were sent notice of the meeting.[32]

Once a voluntary arrangement has been approved by each of the meetings, it takes effect as if made by the company at the creditors' meeting and binds every person who, in accordance with the rules, had notice[33] of, and was entitled to vote at the creditors' meeting (whether or not he was present or represented at the meeting) as if he were a party to the voluntary arrangement.[34] However, there is a right of appeal to the court where either the arrangement unfairly prejudices the interests of a creditor, member or contributory, or there has been some material irregularity at or in relation to either of the meetings.

The possibility of the directors being reported for disqualification, under the terms of section 7 of the Company Directors Disqualification Act 1986, does not extend to a voluntary arrangement (it does apply to winding up, administration and administrative receivership).

The supervision of the proposal then rests mainly in the hands of the person identified for this purpose by the terms of the arrangement (the "supervisor"). Normally, the nominee becomes the supervisor. If any of the company's creditors or any other person is dissatisfied by any act, omission or decision of the supervisor, he may apply to the court.

Creditors—points to note

From the point of view of a creditor, the meeting convened by the nominee **24–07** under the 1986 Act, s.3, will be of vital importance (see para. 24–03, above). He should attend the meeting, or appoint a carefully-instructed proxy-holder (see Chapter 26), because, at the meeting, proposals will be put forward which will become binding on him if they are accepted by a sufficient majority. Further, the proposals adopted at the meeting might differ substantially (by reason of amendments accepted at the meeting) from what had been circulated in advance.

The creditor will have to weigh up the relative advantages of a company voluntary arrangement, which may allow the debtor to trade out of its difficulties, and putting the company into liquidation. He should bear in mind that there are no laws to prevent the debtor from giving way to claims (for example recovery of

---

[30] r. 1.20(1), (2).
[31] r. 1.21.
[32] *ibid.*, r. 1.24.
[33] See para. 24–05.
[34] See also *Johnson v. Davies* [1997] 1 BCLC 580.

goods under reservation of title clauses) while the voluntary arrangement is being formulated.

The future role of the supervisor will need to be carefully checked: to what extent is he planning to intervene in the management of the company?

[Paragraph 24–08 has been deleted]

2 ADMINISTRATION ORDER

24–09 The administration order procedure was introduced by the Insolvency Act 1985 and consolidated as Part II of the 1986 Act. Part II was replaced in its entirety by s.248 of the Enterprise Act 2002, which inserted a new Schedule B1 to the 1986 Act.

The essence of the scheme remains the same and it provides a means whereby a company in financial difficulties can obtain a moratorium against creditors while its affairs are in the hands of a qualified insolvency practitioner[35] and a rescue plan is formulated.

There are two main conditions which must be satisfied for the court to make an administration order:

(a) it must be satisfied that the company is or is likely to become unable to pay its debts (within section 123 of the 1986 Act[36]); and

(b) the administration order is reasonably likely to achieve the purpose of the administration: para 11 Sch B1 of the 1986 Act.

An administrator may not be appointed if the company is subject to a voluntary winding up resolution or a winding up order (subject to exceptions in paras 38 & 39, Sch B1, Insolvency Act 1986).

Appointment of Administrator

24–10 Following the introduction of the Enterprise Act 2002 an administrator may be appointed by:

- the court
- the holder of a floating charge
- the company or its directors.

The changes introduced by the Enterprise Act make it easier to appoint a receiver but place the onus on the administrator to make all possible efforts to guide the company to recovery rather than acting merely to gain the best possible payout for creditors.

The appointment of the administrator dismisses any petition for winding up of the company and removes any administrative or other receiver and commences the moratorium which lasts so long as the company is in administration.

[35] See para. 25–02.
[36] See para. 25–02.

The administrator has to send notice of his appointment to the company and to creditors, so far as he is aware of their addresses.

After the making of the order, the powers of the directors are suspended; they remain in office, but the administrator has power to remove any director and to appoint new directors. He may also call a meeting of the members or creditors of the company and must call a creditors' meeting if requested so to do by one-tenth in value of the company's creditors, or if he is directed to do so by the court. He has the power to do all things necessary for the management of the company, together with the additional powers given by Schedule 1 of the 1986 Act. He has to begin by obtaining a statement of the company's affairs from the officers and appropriate employees of the company and certain others associated with it.

Administrator's proposals

The administrator must send a notice of appointment to the company and **24–11** publicise his appointment as soon as reasonably practical after appointment. A copy must be sent to the Registrar of Companies within seven days. Copies must also be sent to all the creditors that the administrator can gain details of.

The administrator will then require some person (usually a director) to provide a statement of affairs of the company. This must be provided within 11 days and verified as a statement of truth..

Within eight weeks from the day the company enters administration the administrator must formulate his proposals for achieving the purposes specified in the order. He must send a copy of his proposals to, among others, all creditors of whose addresses he is aware, and must lay a copy before the initial meeting of creditors. This meeting must take place within ten weeks from the day administration commenced.

There must be annexed to the administrator's proposals a statement by him giving certain information, including details as to his appointment, the purposes for which an administration order was applied for and made and any subsequent variation by the court of those purposes; it should also include an account of the circumstances giving rise to the application for an order, a statement of affairs or details of the financial position of the company, and a description of the way in which the affairs of the company have been managed and financed since his appointment and will be managed and financed if his proposals are approved.[37] This meeting has to be convened in accordance with the Rules. Salient points (which apply in practice to all creditors' meetings summoned by the administrator) are:

- (i) in fixing the venue, the administrator must have regard to the convenience of creditors;
- (ii) normally, the meeting must begin between 10.00 a.m. and 4.00 p.m. on a business day;
- (iii) notice has to be given to all creditors who are known to the administrator and had claims against the company at the date of the administration order;

---

[37] r. 2.16.

    (iv) the notice has to specify the purpose of the meeting and give details of the entitlement to vote;

    (v) forms of proxy have to be sent out with the notice; and

    (vi) there are provisions for adjournment for a period of not more than 14 days.[38]

The administrator or a representative appointed by him acts as chairman.[39]

  The resolution to approve the proposals requires a simple majority in value of those present or represented; a resolution is, however, invalid if those voting against it include more than half in value of the creditors to whom notice of the meeting was sent and who are not, to the best of the chairman's belief, persons connected with the company.[40] Such value is taken as at the making of the order.[41] Details in writing of all debts claimed to be due from the company must be given to the administrator not later than twelve noon on the business day before the day of the meeting.[42] The administrator may allow a creditor to vote, notwithstanding that he has failed to give notice of his claim, if he is satisfied that the failure was due to circumstances beyond the creditor's control; the administrator may call for extra evidence to substantiate the creditor's claim.[43] However, an administrator should be wary of excluding any creditor who has submitted a proxy even if that proxy is incomplete.[44]

  Secured creditors and reservation of title creditors are only allowed to vote at the meeting in respect of any unsecured balance of their debt.[45] A creditor shall not vote in respect of a debt for an unliquidated amount, or any debt whose value is not ascertained, except where the chairman agrees to put upon the debt an estimated minimum value for the purpose of entitlement to vote and admits the claims for that purpose.[46] Similar regulations relating to the admission or rejection of a claim apply as in the case of a company voluntary arrangement (see para. 24–05).[47]

  Proxies must be lodged by not later than the start of the meeting.[48]

  The proposal may be approved with modifications, provided the administrator assents to each modification. After the meeting, the administrator must report any decision made at the meeting to the court and the Registrar of Companies. The administrator may revise his proposals; if the change is substantial he must advise creditors and summon a creditors' meeting by not less than 14 days' notice. An administrator must call a meeting of the creditors if so requested by one or more creditors holding at least ten per cent of the debt or by the court.

---

[38] r. 2.19.
[39] r. 2.20.
[40] r. 2.28(1), (1A).
[41] r. 2.22(4). Amounts paid in after that date are deducted.
[42] r. 2.22(1).
[43] r. 2.22(2), (3).
[44] *Roberts v. Pinnacle Entertainment Ltd* [2003] EWHC 2394.
[45] r. 2.24 and 2.26.
[46] r. 2.22(5).
[47] r. 2.23 (there are minor differences which make the position of a creditor at an administration meeting slightly more favourable).
[48] r. 2.22(1).

Creditor's committee

The 1986 Act makes provision for the creditors' meeting to appoint a committee **24–12** to assist the administrator in discharging his functions. The committee must consist of at least three and not more than five creditors. It does not come into being until the administrator has issued a certificate of its due constitution. Meetings are held when and where determined by the administrator. The first meeting must be held within three months and thereafter the administrator must in general follow the committee's wishes as to meetings. Unless waived, seven days' notice of meetings must be given. The administrator or a person nominated by him acts as the chairman. The quorum is two members of the committee. Each member has one vote and a simple majority is required for resolutions. There is provision for the administrator to seek agreement to a resolution by post.[49]

Members' meeting

As mentioned, the administrator has the power under the 1986 Act to convene **24–13** a meeting of members. This right may be useful if, for example, he wishes to vary class rights, to raise fresh capital or to capitalise debt. The meeting must be convened and conducted in the same manner as if it were a general meeting summoned under the provisions of the 1985 Act and the company's articles, but, under Rule 2.31, the administrator must fix a venue for the meeting which has regard to the convenience of members. The administrator or a person nominated by him takes the chair.

Culmination

If the administration succeeds, the company will be returned to its directors and **24–14** shareholders. If it fails, because the administrator has no power to pay off creditors the exit routes are likely to be a compulsory winding-up, a company voluntary arrangement proposed by the administrator, or a scheme under section 425 of the 1985 Act.

Creditors—points to note

The important meeting from a creditor's point of view will be the initial **24–15** creditors meeting summoned by the administrator to consider his proposals. By this time, the administrator will have been in place for some weeks and a considerable amount of the company's money and time will have been used in bringing the application to the court and in preparing proposals to lay before creditors. However, the creditor should, as always, take care in filling in his proxy form (see Chapter 26). He should also lodge details of his debt by twelve noon on the day prior to the meeting. The meeting itself represents probably the only opportunity creditors will have to question the administrator in any depth, and to satisfy themselves that the company's affairs are being improved and not worsened by the administration process and that the administrator's stewardship down to the date of

---

[49] r. 2.32–2.46A.

the meeting has been satisfactory. It would be a good plan to discuss the administrator's proposals with other creditors prior to the meeting. The proposals can be modified at the meeting.

It is important to form a creditors' committee and to give that committee power to sanction further action by the administrator (*i.e.* without having to convene another creditors' meeting, except for major items).

[Paragraph 24–16 has been deleted]

3 ADMINISTRATIVE RECEIVERSHIP

24–17 The changes under the Enterprise Act 2002 greatly restricted the process of administrative receivership. Previously creditors able to appoint an administrative receiver under the provisions in a debenture enjoyed a considerable advantage over other creditors. An administrative receiver owes a rather limited duty of care to those other creditors; his first duty is to the person who appointed him.[50]

The Enterprise Act inserted new ss. 72A to 72H and a new Sch. 2A into the 1986 Act. The new s.72A placed a prohibition on the appointment of administrative receivers by the holders of floating charges. Six exceptions are contained in ss. 72B to 72G, these are where the charge relates to:

- a capital market arrangement expected to be greater than £50 million
- a public-private partnership project with step-in rights
- a project company involved in a utility project which includes step-in rights
- a project company involved in a financed project which includes step-in rights with an expected debt of at least £50 million
- the financial market and is deemed to be a market charge,[51] system-charge[52] or collateral security charge[53]
- a registered social landlord.

The intention of the change is to make receivers rare exceptions rather than the common occurrence they had become. Administrative receivers pursue only the interests of the charge holder that appoints them and this is felt to encourage them to act against the interests of the company and other creditors. The amended legislation favours the appointment of administrators who are bound to act in the wider interest (see para 24–10). Therefore administrative receivership is not as important a subject as it formally was.

The dominant position taken by an administrative receiver means that the influence of other creditors is somewhat limited, but the 1986 Act does require him to prepare and send to secured creditors a report on the events leading up to

---

[50] See *Re B. Johnson Co. (Builders) Limited* [1955] 1 Ch. 634 and *Downsview Nominees Limited v. First City Corporation Limited* [1994] 1 BCLC 49, P.C.

[51] Within the meaning of section 173 of the Companies Act 1989 (c. 40).

[52] Within the meaning of the Financial Markets and Insolvency Regulations 1996 (S.I. 1996 No. 1469).

[53] Within the meaning of the Financial Markets and Insolvency (Settlement Finality) Regulations 1999 (S.I. 1999 No. 2979).

his appointment, the disposal of company property and the carrying on of its business, the amounts due to the debenture holders by whom he was appointed and to preferential creditors and the amount likely to be available for other creditors. This report has normally to be made within three months of his appointment. The receiver has to send a copy to unsecured creditors or publish the address from which copies can be obtained.[54] Unless the court otherwise directs, a copy of the report has to be laid before a meeting of unsecured creditors summoned for the purpose by not less than 14 days' notice.[55] In fixing the venue, the receiver must have regard to the creditors' convenience; the meeting must normally begin between 10.00 a.m. and 4.00 p.m. on a business day; at least 14 days' notice must be given; forms of proxy must be sent with the notice; the notice has to include a statement that secured creditors are not entitled to attend or be represented at the meeting; and the notice must explain the relevant voting rights.[56] The receiver or a person nominated by him takes the chair at the meeting.[57] The provisions of the Rules relating to lodgement of proxies, voting rights (with the exception that in a receivership votes are calculated in accordance with the creditor's debt as at the date of appointment of the receiver), secured creditors, unliquidated or unascertained debts and admission and rejection of claims are similar to those which appertain to creditors' meetings when an administration order is in force; but in a receivership a creditors' meeting shall not be adjourned, even if no quorum is present, unless the chairman decides that it is desirable, and in a receivership a creditors' resolution is passed when a majority (in value) of those present and voting in person or by proxy have voted in favour of it.[58]

The meeting may appoint a creditors' committee to assist the receiver in discharging his functions; that committee may, on giving not less than seven days' notice, require the receiver to attend before it at any reasonable time and furnish it with information.[59] The regulations governing the constitution and proceedings of the committee are similar to those which relate to a creditors' committee established to assist an administrator.[60]

Creditors—Points to Note

The receiver must (unless liquidation supervenes) summon the meeting called **24–18** for by the 1986 Act, s.48, to consider his report. At that meeting, creditors may wish to appoint a creditors' committee. Both the meeting and the subsequent work of the committee will, however, only be concerned with receiving information. There are no decisions of substance to be made: these are for the administrative receiver.

---

[54] *ibid.*, s.48.
[55] *ibid.*, s.48(2), (3).
[56] r. 3.9.
[57] r. 3.10.
[58] See para. 24–11, rr. 3.11–3.15.
[59] 1986 Act, s.49.
[60] See para. 24–12, rr. 3.16 to 3.30A.

CHAPTER 25

MEETINGS IN INSOLVENCY
SITUATIONS—WINDING UP

25–01 A winding up of a company is the way in which its corporate life is brought to an end; its assets are realised and its debts paid, any balance being returned to its shareholders. A winding up may be either:

(a) by the court; or
(b) voluntary.

The latter may be a creditors' voluntary winding up or a members' voluntary winding up.

1   WINDING UP BY THE COURT

Reasons for winding up

25–02 The principal reasons for which a company may be wound up by the court are:

(i) the company has by special resolution resolved that the company be wound up by the court;
(ii) the company does not commence its business within a year from its incorporation or suspends business for a whole year;
(iii) the number of members is reduced below two (except in the case of a private company limited by shares or by guarantee);
(iv) the company is unable to apply its debts; or
(v) the court is of the opinion that it is just and equitable that the company should be wound up.[1]

In relation to (iv) above, a company is deemed to be unable to pay its debts when a creditor to whom the company is indebted in a sum exceeding £750 serves on the company a written demand for payment and the company neglects for three weeks to pay the sum or to secure or compound for it to the reasonable satisfaction of the creditor.[2] The same applies if execution on a judgment is returned unsatisfied[3] or if it is proved to the court that the company is unable to pay its debts as

---

[1] 1986 Act, s.122.
[2] *ibid.*, s.123(1)(a). The demand must be in the prescribed form: see Rules 4.4–4.6 and Form 4.1.
[3] *ibid.*, s.123(1)(b).

they fall due.[4] The latter includes cases where the value of the company's assets is less than the amount of its liabilities, taking into account its contingent and prospective liabilities.[5]

Cases where it has been held to be "just and equitable" that the company should be would up include those where—

    (a) the substratum of the company had gone (*i.e.* the main object had become impracticable)[6];

    (b) the company was formed for fraudulent purposes[7];

    (c) there was complete deadlock[8];

    (d) a member holding a majority of the shares refused to produce accounts or to pay dividends[9];

    (e) the petitioner was excluded from all participation in the business.[10]

The petition and order

Winding up is effected by a petition presented to the court by the company, the directors, any creditor[11] or any contributory, or, in certain cases, other bodies.[12]   **25–03**

The court may then make a winding-up order.[13] By section 127 of the 1986 Act the effect of this is normally to make void all dispositions of the company's property and all transfers of shares or alterations in the status of the company's members made after the commencement of the winding up (which dates back to the presentation of the petition).[14] The company's employment contracts terminate. Control of the company passes immediately out of the hands of the directors. The court may, under section 126 of the 1986 Act, stay or restrain any legal proceedings against the company. The winding up petition may be suspended if the company is in administration, in which case the administrator can do whatever he feels is necessary and s127 of the 1986 Act does not apply.

First meetings of creditors and contributories

When a winding up order is made the official receiver, by virtue of his office, becomes the provisional liquidator and will continue in office until another person becomes liquidator in accordance with the prescribed procedures.[15]   **25–04**

---

[4] *ibid.*, s.123(1)(e).

[5] *ibid.*, s.123(2).

[6] *Re Bleriot Aircraft Co.* (1916) 21 T.L.R. 253.

[7] *Re T. E. Brinsmead Sons* [1897] 1 Ch. 45; on appeal, [1897] 1 Ch. 406.

[8] *Re Yenidje Tobacco Co.* [1916] 2 Ch. 426.

[9] *Loch v. John Blackwood Ltd* [1924] A.C. 783.

[10] *Ebrahimi v. Westbourne Galleries* [1973] A.C. 360, H.L.

[11] Including a contingent or prospective creditor. Even if the company is being wound up voluntarily, a creditor or other interested party may still petition for a compulsory winding up: *Securities and Investments Board v. Lancashire and Yorkshire Portfolio Management Limited* [1992] B.C.L.C. 281; *Re Magnus Consultants Limited* [1995] 1 B.C.L.C. 203; *Re Pinstripe Farming Co. Limited* [1996] B.C.C. 913.

[12] 1986 Act, s.124, and s.124A.

[13] *ibid.*, s.125.

[14] *ibid.*, s.129(2). If the winding up began as a voluntary winding up, it dates back to the passing of the resolution for voluntary winding up.

[15] *ibid.*, s.136(2).

At the request of the official receiver, certain persons connected with the company must send to him a statement as to the affairs of the company, which will detail the assets of the company, list its creditors and give other prescribed information.[16]

Separate meetings (called the "first meetings") of the creditors and contributories may be summoned by the official receiver to enable them to appoint a liquidator of their own choosing, in place of the official receiver.[17]

The official receiver normally has to make his decision within 12 weeks of the winding-up order; if he decides against holding meetings, creditors and contributories must be notified.[18] The meetings can be compelled by one-quarter in value of the company's creditors.[19] The official receiver normally calls a meeting of creditors if he can see there is possibility of passing the case on to a "private sector" insolvency practioner—i.e. if there are any realisable assets.

If they are convened, notice of the meetings must be given by public advertisement and not less than 21 days' notice must be given by post to those persons known to be creditors or contributories.[20] The notice to creditors must state a time, not more than four days before the date fixed for the meeting, within which they must lodge their proofs and (if applicable) proxies in order to entitle them to vote at the meeting; the same applies in respect of contributories and their proxies.[21] No creditor may vote in respect of any unliquidated or contingent debt or any debt whose value is not ascertained.[22] The meetings must confine themselves to the appointment of a liquidator or liquidators and a liquidation committee (formerly known as a committee of inspection) and matters incidental thereto, except that the meeting may consider a resolution to adjourn for not more than three weeks and any other resolution which the chairman thinks it right to allow for special reasons.[23] Where the official receiver has convened the meeting, he or a person nominated by him acts as chairman.[24] Where the convener of the meeting is other than the official receiver, the chairman shall be he or a person nominated in writing by him.[25]

In the case of a resolution for the appointment of a liquidator:

(i) if on any vote there are two nominees for appointment, the person who obtains the most support (meaning a majority in value of those present in person or by proxy at the meeting and entitled to vote) is appointed;

(ii) if there are three or more nominees, and one of them has a clear majority over both or all the others together, that one is appointed; and

(iii) in any other case, the chairman of the meeting shall continue to take votes (disregarding at each vote any nominee who has withdrawn and, if

[16] ibid., s.131.
[17] ibid., s.136(4).
[18] ibid., s.136(5).
[19] ibid., s.136(5)(c).
[20] r. 4.50(2), (3), (5).
[21] r. 4.50(4).
[22] Re Ruffle ex p. Dummelow (1873) 8 Ch. App. 997, C.A.
[23] r. 4.52.
[24] r. 4.55(2).
[25] r. 4.55(3).

no nominee has withdrawn, the nominee who obtained the least support last time), until a clear majority is obtained for any one nominee.[26]

At any time the chairman may put to the meeting a resolution for the joint appointment of any two or more nominees.[27]

If the meetings of creditors and contributories choose different liquidators, priority is given to the person who is the creditors' nominee.[28] However, there is provision for any creditor or contributory, where different persons are nominated, to appeal to the court within seven days of the date of the creditors' nomination; in that case the court may make an order either—

(a) appointing the person nominated as liquidator by the contributories to be a liquidator instead of, or jointly with, the person nominated by the creditors; or
(b) appointing some other person to be liquidator instead of the person nominated by the creditors.[29]

Other matters relevant to the first meetings are set out at paras. 25–18 to 25–29 below, which contains a note of those of the Rules which appertain to all meetings in a winding up ("Generally Applicable Rules"); the scheme of this chapter will be to set out in relation to each individual type of meeting only those of the Rules which are specific to that meeting.

Liquidation committee

Under section 141 of the 1986 Act, the first meetings may establish a liquidation **25–05** committee. The liquidator (not being the official receiver) may, if he thinks fit, summon separate meetings of creditors and contributories to determine whether a liquidation committee should be established; one-tenth in value of the company's creditors may compel the liquidator (not being the official receiver) to summon such a meeting. In general, if either of the first meetings decides that there should be a liquidation committee, this overrides a non-committal or negative decision of the other meeting. When the official receiver is acting as liquidator, or where no committee has been appointed, its functions are vested in the Department of Trade and Industry.

The role of the liquidation committee is to assist the liquidator and to obtain information from him.[30] With the sanction of the liquidation committee, the liquidator can:

(i) bring or defend legal proceedings;
(ii) carry on the company's business so far as necessary for a beneficial winding up;
(iii) pay any class of creditors in full;
(iv) make any compromise or arrangement with creditors;

---

[26] r. 4.63(2), (2A).
[27] r. 4.63(3).
[28] 1986 Act, s.139(3).
[29] *ibid.*, s.139(4.)
[30] r. 4.155(1).

(v) compromise claims by the company against third parties and all questions in any way relative to the assets or the winding up of the company.[31]

The liquidation committee is to consist of at least three and not more than five creditors elected at the creditors' meeting.[32] There are two additional persons who have the right to be members of the committee if they wish. These are:—

(i) a representative of the Financial Services Authority. This right is given to them by the Financial Services and Markets Act 2000 (s.371)

(ii) a representative of the Financial Services Compensation Scheme manager. This right is given to them by the Financial Services and Markets Act 2000 (s.215)

The liquidation committee does not come into being until the liquidator issues a certificate of its constitution.[33] Meetings are held when and where determined by the liquidator; he must call a first meeting within three months of his appointment or of the committee's establishment (whichever is the later) and thereafter must call a meeting if so requested by a creditor member (to be held within 21 days of the request being received), and for a specified date if the committee has previously so resolved. Unless waived, seven days' notice is required.[34] The liquidator or a person nominated by him takes the chair at meetings.[35] A quorum is two creditor members.[36] Members may appoint representatives.[37] Each member has one vote; to pass a resolution, a simple majority of creditor members present or represented must vote in favour of it.[38] The liquidator may seek to obtain agreement to a resolution by post, but if he does, any creditor member of the committee may, within seven business days from its being sent out, require the liquidator to summon a meeting of the committee to consider it.[39] Periodic reports must be made by the liquidator to the committee.[40]

Meetings subsequent to first meetings

25–06   By section 195 of the 1986 Act, the court may, as to all matters relating to a winding up, have regard to the wishes of the creditors and contributories, and, to ascertain those wishes, may direct meetings of creditors and contributories to be called, held and conducted as the court directs. Under section 168 and Rule 4.54, the liquidator may himself summon meetings of contributories and creditors to ascertain their wishes; he has to give 21 days' notice and to specify the purpose of the meeting. Further, under section 168 it is the duty of the liquidator to convene such a meeting when requested to do so by a resolution of the creditors or

---

[31] 1989 Act, s.167, Sched. 4.
[32] r. 4.152(1)(a).
[33] r. 4.153(1).
[34] r. 4.156.
[35] r. 4.157.
[36] r. 4.158.
[37] r. 4.159. The representative must hold a letter of authority entitling him to act and signed by or on behalf of the committee member (a proxy form or company representation document under s.375 of the 1985 Act—see para. 14–01—will suffice).
[38] r. 4.165(1).
[39] r. 4.167(1), (3).
[40] r. 4.168.

contributories or by one-tenth in value of the creditors or contributories, as the case may be. Any such request must be accompanied by a list of those concurring with the request and the amount of their claims, with written confirmation of their concurrence, and a statement of the purpose of the proposed meeting; if he considers the request to be properly made, the liquidator must fix a venue for the meeting not more than 35 days from the date of receipt of the request and give 21 days' notice of it to creditors.[41] The only exception to this is where the Court makes a winding up order under the Financial Services Act 1986 (s.72), the Banking Act 1987 (s.92) or the Financial Services and Markets Act 2000 (s.367). In these cases the court can determine the winding up preceedings.

Again, the "Generally Applicable Rules" (see paras. 25–18 to 25–29) will apply to the above meetings.

In a compulsory liquidation there are no requirements for annual meetings.

Final meeting

If it appears to the liquidator (not the official receiver) that the winding up is for practical purposes complete, the liquidator shall summon a final meeting of the company's creditors to receive the liqudiator's report and to determine whether the liquidator should have his release under section 174 of the 1986 Act.[42] The procedure is governed by Rule 4.125: the liquidator has to give at least 28 days' notice which must be sent to all creditors who have proved their debts. If there is no quorum present, the liquidator reports its absence to the court and the final meeting is then deemed to have been duly held and the liquidator's release given.[43]

    25–07

Dissolution of the company then follows under the provisions of section 205 of the 1986 Act.

Creditors—points to note

The important points for the creditor at a meeting convened by the official receiver under the 1986 Act, s. 136 are: to get a satisfactory liquidator and a liquidation committee. These points are similar to those which concern creditors in a creditors' voluntary winding-up and are dealt with in more detail in para. 25–13 below.

    25–08

In a compulsory winding up, creditors must submit their claims on a statutory form known as a proof of debt. These forms will be issued by the official receiver or liquidator. Obviously, care should be taken over their completion and return.

2   VOLUNTARY WINDING UP

The ways in which a company may be wound up voluntarily are:

    25–09

    (i) where the company was incorporated for a fixed duration which has expired or where an event occurs upon which the articles provide for

---

[41] r. 4.57.
[42] 1986 Act, s.146(1).
[43] r. 4.125(5).

dissolution, and the company passes an ordinary resolution to be wound up voluntarily;

(ii) if the company resolves by special resolution that it be wound up voluntarily; or

(iii) if the company resolves by extraordinary resolution to the effect that it cannot by reason of its liabilities continue its business and that it is advisable to wind up.[44]

A voluntary winding up can be of two kinds; a members' or a creditors' winding up. A winding up will be a members' voluntary winding up where a declaration of solvency is filed, the essence of such a declaration being an honest statement by the directors that the company can meet its debts.[45]

Where the directors cannot make such a declaration of solvency, the liquidation must be a creditors' voluntary winding up, and on the appointment of a liquidator all the powers of the directors cease, except so far as the liquidation committee, or, if there is no such committee, the creditors sanction the continuance thereof.[46]

From the commencement of the winding up the company must cease to carry on its business except as may be required for its beneficial winding up: but the corporate state and the corporate powers of the company, notwithstanding anything to the contrary in the articles, continue until it is dissolved.[47]

Any transfer of shares, unless made to or sanctioned by the liquidator and any alteration in the status of the members made after the commencement of the winding up is void.[48]

The initiating resolution

25–10   As has been noted, two of the instances where a company may be wound up voluntarily are if it resolves by special resolution that it be wound up voluntarily, or if it resolves by extraordinary resolution to the effect that it cannot by reason of its liabilities continue in business and that it is advisable to wind up.[49] An extraordinary resolution is the usual method adopted by the members, and this is followed by a creditors' meeting, as explained below.

Members' meeting

25–11   The directors, acting at a board meeting, would arrange for the convening of an extraordinary general meeting in the usual way.[50] The business at the meeting would be to consider the financial position of the company, to pass the necessary extraordinary resolution as to liquidation, and to nominate a liquidator. (The nomination by the creditors of a liquidator will, if different, normally prevail.)[51]

---

[44] 1986 Act, s.84(1).
[45] See Chap. 27.
[46] 1986 Act, s.103.
[47] *ibid.*, s.87.
[48] *ibid.*, s.88.
[49] See para. 25–09.
[50] See para. 12–09.
[51] See para. 25–14.

The meeting would normally be timed to take place just before the creditors' meeting.

Under section 86 of the 1986 Act, the liquidation commences from the date of the passing of the resolution by the members.

Creditors: first meeting

The company must cause a meeting of creditors (a section 98 meeting) to be **25–12** summoned for a day not later than the 14th day after the date of the members' meeting.[52] Notices must be sent to creditors not less than seven days before the meeting date and the meeting must be advertised in the *London Gazette* and in at least two local papers.[53] The notice must state the name and registered number of the company. It should also state the name and address of a qualified insolvency practitioner who will furnish creditors free of charge with such information about the company's affairs as they may reasonably require, or state a place in the relevant locality where, on the two business days falling next before the day of the meeting, a list of the company's creditors will be available for inspection free of charge.[54] Where there has been more than one principal places of business in the previous six months, requirements as to advertisement and inspection of lists must be met in relation to each of those places.[55] There is a default fine.[56]

The directors must prepare a statement of affairs of the company in the prescribed form; they must cause the statement to be laid before the creditors' meeting and appoint one of their number to preside at the meeting (and it is the duty of the person so appointed to attend and preside).[57] Where a liquidator is nominated by the company at a general meeting held on a day prior to the creditors' meeting, the directors shall forthwith after such nomination or the making of the statement of affairs, whichever is the later, deliver to him a copy of the statement of affairs.[58]

In relation to the formalities of the creditors' meeting, the following points apply:

   (i) the notice must specify a venue for the meeting and the time (not earlier than 12 noon on the business day before the day fixed for the meeting) by which and the place at which, proxies must be lodged[59];

  (ii) only the appointment of a liquidator or liquidators and a liquidation committee and matters incidental thereto may be discussed except that the meeting may consider a resolution to adjourn for not more than three weeks and any resolution which the chairman thinks it right to allow for special reasons[60];

---

[52] *ibid.*, s.98(1)(a).
[53] *ibid.*, s.98(1)(b), (c).
[54] *ibid.*, s.98(2).
[55] *ibid.*, s.98(3).
[56] *ibid.*, s.98(6).
[57] *ibid.*, s.99(1) and r. 4.34. In the absence of the nominated director, it may be possible for the meeting to proceed under the chairmanship of, for example, the solicitor acting for the company: *Re Salcombe Hotel Development Co.* (1989) 5 B.C.C. 807.
[58] r. 4.34A.
[59] r. 4.51.
[60] r. 4.52 and 4.53.

(iii) any resolution passed at a creditors' meeting held before an adjourned members' meeting passes a resolution to wind up takes effect only from the passing of the winding-up resolution[61];

(iv) the directors are required to up-date the statement of affairs if necessary[62];

(v) one of the directors of the company, appointed by the board prior to the meeting, takes the chair (but the prospective liquidator will be in attendance).[63]

Section 166(5) of the 1986 Act provides that if default is made by the company or the directors in meeting their respective obligations in relation to the creditors' meeting or the statement of affairs, the liquidator must apply to the court for directions; it is a criminal offence if he fails to do so.

Creditors—points to note

25–13   The meeting of creditors convened by the company pursuant to section 98 of the 1986 Act will be crucial to the future course of the liquidation.

Before the meeting, a creditor should take steps to obtain further information about the company and its recent trading history. If the claim is large, it may be a good idea for the creditor to make contact with other substantial claimants; the purpose would be to consider whether to nominate a liquidator in place of the person who might be proposed by the members of the company, and to discuss tactics to be followed at the meeting. There may be areas where further enquiry can be made: for example, whether any charges created prior to the liquidation can be set aside and whether the directors may have been guilty of fraudulent or wrongful trading under the provisions of sections 213 and 214 of the 1986 Act. The creditor should, in good time, follow up the invitation contained in the section 98 notice to inspect the list of creditors or to obtain further information. In all these aspects, the creditor can seek advice from an insolvency practioner, who may well be prepared to attend the meeting, free of charge, on the creditors' behalf.

The creditor should prepare his proof. It can be lodged at the meeting but there is merit in getting it in in good time. Proxies must be lodged by the time stated in the notice (not earlier, under Rule 4. 51(2), than noon on the business day before the day fixed for the meeting). The creditor should give careful thought to his choice of proxy-holder: if he inserts the phrase "chairman of the meeting" he may be surrendering authority to one of the very persons (the director appointed by the board to chair the meeting) who has been responsible for the company's difficulties. The choice of liquidator and the names of the people represented on the liquidation committee are crucial decisions for the meeting to take.

Company creditors should arrange for a section 375 representative to attend and vote: a certified copy of the resolution must be presented to the chairman of the meeting (see para. 14–01).

---

[61] r. 4.53A.

[62] r. 4.53B.

[63] 1986 Act, s.99(1). See Statement of Insolvency Practice 8 (Summoning and Holding Meetings of Creditors Convened Pursuant to section 98 of the Insolvency Act 1986) published by the Society of Practitioners of Insolvency.

If the voting is close (and the proxies can be inspected in advance—see para. 26–04) the creditor should call for a ballot. This request may surprise the meeting's conveners, but it should not be difficult for them to prepare ballot papers which show the names of all the nominees for appointment and contain spaces in which can be put the names of the proxy-holder and of the creditor and the amount of the claim. In announcing the result, the chairman should give details of the total value of votes cast in favour of each of the nominees, and of any rejected votes (with reasons therefor).

Appointment of liquidator

The creditors and the company at their respective meetings may nominate a **25–14** person to be liquidator for the purpose of winding up the company's affairs and distributing its assets.[64]

Voting in relation to the appointment of a liquidator is as follows:

(i) if on any vote there are two nominees for appointment, the person who obtains a majority in value of those present and voting in person or by proxy is appointed;

(ii) if there are three or more nominees and one of them has a clear majority over both or all the others together, that one is appointed; and

(iii) in any other case, the chairman of the meeting shall continue to take votes (disregarding at each vote any nominee who has withdrawn and, if no nominee has withdrawn, the nominee who obtained the least support last time), until a clear majority is obtained for any one nominee.[65]

The chairman may at any time put to the meeting a resolution for the joint appointment of any two or more nominees.[66]

The liquidator shall be the person appointed by the creditors, or, where no person has been so nominated, the person (if any) nominated by the company; in the case of different persons being nominated, any director, member or creditor may, within seven days after the date on which the nomination was made by the creditors, apply to the court for an order directing that the company's nominee shall be liquidator instead of or jointly with the creditors' nominee or appointing some other person than the person nominated by the creditors.[67]

One possibility of abusive conduct by the directors prior to the appointment of a liquidator is removed by section 114 of the 1986 Act which provides that where no liquidator has been appointed or nominated by the company the powers of the directors shall not be exercised except with the sanction of the court or so far as may be necessary to comply with their obligations to call a creditors' meeting and prepare a statement of affairs. The only exceptions to this rule relate to the disposal of perishable goods or goods of diminishing value and the taking of such steps as are necessary for the protection of the company's assets. A further abuse (this time one which involved the connivance of a liquidator appointed by the company) has

[64] 1986 Act, s.100(1).
[65] r. 4.63(2).
[66] r. 4.63(3).
[67] 1986 Act, s.100.

been stopped by section 166 of the 1986 Act, which provides that the powers which the liquidator ordinarily enjoys under section 165 (see below) are to be incapable of being exercised, except with the sanction of the court, during the period prior to the holding of the creditors' meeting (with similar exceptions relating to perishable assets, etc.)

Powers of a liquidator; vacancies

25–15   The powers and duties of a liquidator in a voluntary winding up are set out in section 165 and the Fourth Schedule of the 1986 Act. The matters set out in Part I of the Schedule (payment of debts, compromise of claims, etc.) may in a creditors' winding up only be exercised with the sanction of the court or the liquidation committee (or, if there is no such committee, a meeting of the company's creditors). The powers in Parts II (institution and defence of proceedings, carrying on the business of the company) and III (general powers) of the Schedule may be exercised without such sanction. The liquidator may convene general meetings of the company to obtain a special or extraordinary resolution or for any other purpose.[68]

If a vacancy occurs by death, resignation, or otherwise, in the office of a liquidator (other than a liquidator appointed by, or by the direction of, the court) the creditors may fill the vacancy.[69] Any continuing liquidators or any creditor may convene a meeting of creditors for this purpose.[70]

Liquidation committee

25–16   The creditors at their meeting held in pursuance of section 98 of the 1986 Act,[71] or at any subsequent meeting, may, if they think fit, appoint a liquidation committee consisting of not more than five persons, and if such a committee is appointed the company may, either at the meeting at which the resolution for voluntary winding up is passed, or at any time subsequently in general meeting, appoint such number of persons (not exceeding five) as they think fit to act as members of the committee. However, the creditors may, if they think fit, resolve that all or any of the persons so appointed by the company ought not to be members of the liquidation committee, and (if the creditors so resolve) the persons mentioned in the resolution shall not, unless the court otherwise directs, be qualified to act as members of the committee, and on any application to the court under this provision the court may, if it thinks fit, appoint other persons to act as such members in place of the persons mentioned in the resolution.[72]

The powers of the liquidation committee are as follows:

(i) to fix the remuneration of the liquidator[73];

---

[68] *ibid.*, s.165(4)(c).
[69] *ibid.*, s.104.
[70] r. 4.101A.
[71] See para. 25–12.
[72] 1986 Act, s.101(1)–(3).
[73] r. 4.127 (or if liquidator is not official receiver and remuneration is not set under r4.127, then the fee will be fixed in accordance with r4.127A).

(ii) to sanction continuance of the powers of directors[74]:
(iii) to sanction the powers given to the liquidator under Schedule 4, Part I:
(iv) to sanction reconstruction under the provisions of sections 110 and 111 of the 1986 Act;
(v) to receive periodic progress reports from the liquidator[75]; and
(vi) to require the liquidator to submit his financial records for inspection.[76]

The constitution and conduct of meetings of the liquidation committee is similar to that in a winding-up by the court.[77]

Subsequent meetings of creditors

In any creditors' voluntary winding up the liquidator may from time to time summon and conduct meetings of creditors for the purpose of ascertaining their wishes in all matters relating to the liquidation.   **25–17**

Notice has to be given to every known creditor; it must be given at least 21 days before the date fixed for the meeting and must specify the purpose of the meeting. The notice must specify a time and date, not more than four days before the date fixed for the meeting, by which, and the place at which, creditors (if not individuals attending in person) must lodge proxies in order to be entitled to vote at the meeting.[78]

Any request by creditors to the liquidator for a meeting of creditors must be accompanied by a list of those concurring with the request and the amount of their claims, with written confirmation of their concurrence and a statement of the purpose of the proposed meeting; if he considers the request to be properly made, the liquidator must fix a venue for the meeting not more than 35 days from the date of receipt of the request and give 21 days' notice of it to creditors.[79]

The court, too, can convene a meeting to ascertain the wishes of creditors or contributories.[80]

In the event of the winding up continuing for more than one year, the liquidator must summon a general meeting of the company and of the creditors at the end of the first year from the commencement of the winding up, and of each succeeding year, or at the first convenient date within three months from the end of the year or such longer period as the Secretary of State may allow. The liquidator must lay before the meetings an account of his acts and dealings and of the conduct of the winding up during the preceding year.[81]

---

[74] 1986 Act, s.103.
[75] r. 4.155 and 4.168.
[76] Insolvency Regulations 1994, reg. 10(4).
[77] See para. 25–05, but note that in relation to quorum, majority and a request for a committee meeting following the liquidator sending out a proposed resolution by post, the expression "creditor member" should read "member", as in these cases the provisions also operate to cover a liquidation committee which has members who are not creditors.
[78] r. 4.54(5). See also 1986 Act, s.165 (4)(c).
[79] r. 4.57.
[80] 1986 Act, s.195.
[81] 1986 Act, s.105.

As soon as the affairs of the company are fully wound up the liquidator must make up an account of the winding up, showing how the winding up has been conducted and the property of the company has been disposed of. He must also call a general meeting of the company and a meeting of the creditors for the purpose of laying the account before the meetings and giving an explanation of it.[82] The meetings are called by advertisement in the *London Gazette*, specifying the time, place and object and published one month at least before the meeting.[83]

Within one week after the date of the meetings (or, if the meetings are not held on the same date, after the date of the later one), the liquidator must send to the Registrar a copy of the account, and must make a return to him of the holding of the meetings and of their dates. Should there be no quorum present at either of these meetings, the liquidator must make a return to the effect that the meeting was duly summoned and that no quorum was present.[84] On the expiration of three months from the registration of the account and return the company is dissolved.[85]

3 GENERALLY APPLICABLE RULES

The Rules set out a number of items which apply to both a winding up by the court and a creditors' voluntary winding up. It is proposed in this section to set out some of the salient points, although in the space available only a brief summary can be attempted and the reader is referred to the detailed text of the Rules.

Attendance at meetings of company's personnel

25–18   Whenever a meeting of creditors or contributories is summoned, the convener must give 21 days' notice to such of the company's personnel as he thinks should be told of or present at the meeting. In the case of any meeting, the company's personnel may be admitted at the chairman's discretion, but they must have given reasonable notice of their wish to be present. Only such questions may be put to one of the company's personnel as the chairman may allow. (Rule 4.58)

For this purpose, "company's personnel" means:

(a) those who are or have at any time been officers[86] of the company;
(b) those who have taken part in the formation of the company at any time within one year before the effective date (*i.e.* usually, the date on which the company went into liquidation);
(c) those who are in the employment of the company, or have been in its employment (including employment under a contract for services) within that year, and are in the liquidator's opinion capable of giving information which he requires;

---

[82] *ibid.*, s.106(1).
[83] *ibid.*, s.106(2).
[84] *ibid.*, s.106(3), (5).
[85] *ibid.*, s.201.
[86] This may include auditors; see *Re Thomas Gerrard Son Ltd* [1968] Ch. 455, 473.

(d) those who are, or have within that year been, officers of, or in the employment (including employment under a contract of services) of, another company which is, or within that year was, an officer of the company in question; and

(e) in the case of a company being wound up by the court, any person who has acted as administrator, administrative receiver or liquidator of the company.[87]

Notice of meetings by advertisement only

The court may order that notice of a meeting of creditors or contributories be given by public advertisement, and not by individual notice to the persons concerned. In considering whether to make such an order, the court shall have regard to the cost of public advertisement, to the amount of the assets available, and to the extent of the interest of creditors or of contributories, or any particular class of either of them (Rule 4.59).

25–19

Venue

In fixing the venue, the convener shall have regard to the convenience of the persons who are invited to attend. Meetings shall be summoned for commencement between 10.00 a.m. and 4.00 p.m. on a business day, unless the court otherwise directs. A form of proxy has to be sent with the notice (Rule 4.60).

25–20

Resolutions

At a meeting of creditors or contributories, a resolution is passed when a majority (in value) of those present and voting, in person or by proxy, have voted in favour of the resolution (Rule 4.63): Exceptions relate to resolutions for the appointment of a liquidator (see paras. 25–04 and 25–14, above).

25–21

Chairman as proxy-holder

If the chairman holds a proxy which requires him to vote for a particular resolution and no other person proposes it, he must himself propose it unless he considers there is a good reason for not doing so. If he does not propose it, he must inform his principal why not (Rule 4.64).

25–22

Suspension and adjournment

Once only in the course of any meeting, the chairman may, in his discretion, and without an adjournment, suspend the meeting for up to an hour. The chairman may, and shall if the meeting so resolves, adjourn the meeting to such time and place as seems appropriate to him (different provisions apply if the liquidator or his nominee is chairman and a resolution has been proposed for the liquidator's removal).[88] If within 30 minutes of the start, a quorum is not present, the chairman

25–23

---

[87] See 1986 Act, s.235(3) and (4); r. 4.58(2).
[88] rr. 4.113 (3) and 4.114 (3).

may adjourn the meeting to such time and place as he may appoint. An adjournment shall be for a period of not more than 21 days. At an adjourned meeting, proofs and proxies may be lodged up to noon on the immediately preceding business day (Rule 4.65), but, by Rule 8.3.(1), proxies given for the original meeting will be valid for the adjourned meeting.

Quorum

25–24   A quorum at a creditors' meeting is at least one creditor entitled to vote. A quorum at a contributories' meeting is at least two contributories so entitled, or all the contributories if their number does not exceed two. The reference is to persons present or represented by proxy or, in general, by a form of representation under section 375 of the 1985 Act. Where the above requirements are satisfied by the attendance of the chairman alone, or just the chairman and one other, and the chairman is aware that other persons, if attending, would be entitled to vote, the meeting shall not commence until at least the expiry of 15 minutes from the time appointed for its commencement (Rule 12.4A).

Entitlement to vote (creditors)

25–25   A creditor is, in general, entitled to vote only if he has duly lodged a proof of debt and it has been admitted for the purpose of voting, together with any proxy requisite for that entitlement. A creditor shall not vote in respect of a debt for an unliquidated amount, or any debt whose value is not ascertained, except where the chairman agrees to put an estimated minimum value on the debt for the purpose.[89] A secured creditor is entitled to vote only in respect of the balance (if any) of his debt after deducting the value of his security as estimated by him (Rule 4.67(4)). In a compulsory winding up the proof should be in Form 4.25; in a voluntary winding up the proof may take any form permitted by the liquidator and a letter will usually suffice; by way of guidance, claims should, at least, give clear details about the creditor's name and address, set out how the claim is calculated, and be clearly intended to be a formal claim in the liquidation. In either case an affidavit in Form 4.26 may be required.

Delivery of proof

25–26   The creditors' proof may, in a voluntary liquidation, be delivered at any time up to the taking of the vote (Rule 4.67(1)). In a compulsory winding up, the proof must be lodged by the time and date stated in the notice.

Admission and rejection of proof

25–27   At a creditors' meeting, the chairman has power to admit or reject a proof, in whole or in part. This is subject to appeal to the court. If the chairman is in doubt whether a proof should be admitted or rejected, he must mark it as objected to and allow the creditor to vote, subject to his vote being subsequently declared invalid

---

[89] See para. 24–05, for a discussion of the procedural difficulties associated with this type of provision.

if the objection to the proof is sustained. If on appeal the chairman's decision is revised or varied, or a creditor's vote is declared invalid, the court may order that another meeting be summoned, or make such other order as it thinks just (Rule 4.70).

Proofs, claims

Detailed further regulations covering the position of debts in a liquidation are **25–28** contained in Rules 4.73 to 4.94, which cover the procedure for proving, the quantification of claims and the position of secured creditors.

Minutes

The chairman must keep minutes, sign them and retain them. He must also keep **25–29** a list of creditors and contributories who attend the meeting. The minutes must include a record of any resolution passed (Rule 4.71).

A minute of proceedings at a meeting (held under the 1986 Act or the Rules) of creditors, members or contributories, signed by the chairman, is admissible in insolvency proceedings without further proof. The minute is prima facie evidence that the meeting was duly convened and held, that all resolutions were duly passed, and that all proceedings at the meeting duly took place (Rule 12.5).

CHAPTER 26

PROXIES AND COMPANY REPRESENTATION IN AN INSOLVENCY

1 Definition of Proxy

26–01 For the purposes of the Rules, a proxy is an authority given to a person ("the principal") to another person ("the proxy-holder") to attend a meeting and speak and vote as his representative. Proxies are for use at creditors', company or contributories' meetings summoned or called under the 1986 Act or the Rules.[1]

Only one proxy may be given by a person for any one meeting at which he desires to be represented; and it may only be given to one person, being an individual aged 18 or over. The principal may, however, specify one or more other such individuals to be proxy-holder in the alternative, in the order in which they are named in the proxy.[2]

A proxy for a particular meeting may be given to whoever is to be the chairman of the meeting; and for a meeting held as part of the proceedings in a winding up by the court it may be given to the official receiver.[3] Such a person cannot decline to be the proxy-holder in relation to that proxy.[4]

A proxy requires the holder to give the principal's vote on matters arising for determination at the meeting, or to abstain, or to propose, in the principal's name, a resolution to be voted on by the meeting, either as directed or in accordance with the holder's own discretion.[5]

2 Forms of Proxy

26–02 The following forms of proxy are specified for use by creditors in the various proceedings covered by the 1986 Act and which have been discussed in earlier chapters. These must be used with such variations, if any, as the circumstances may require[6]:

> Form 8.1: Proxy—Voluntary Arrangements
> Form 8.2: Proxy—Administration

---

[1] r. 8.1(1), (2).
[2] r. 8.1(3).
[3] r. 8.1(4).
[4] r. 8.1(5).
[5] r. 8.1(6).
[6] r. 12.7(2).

Form 8.3: Proxy—Administrative Receivership
Form 8.4: Proxy—Winding up by the Court
Form 8.5: Proxy—Members' or Creditors' Voluntary Winding up.

(At meetings of shareholders in an insolvency situation, the forms of proxy will generally follow the requirements of the articles and the 1985 Act—see Chapter 14).

When notice is given of a meeting to be held in insolvency proceedings, and forms of proxy are sent out with the notice, no form so sent out shall have inserted in it the name or description of any person.[7]

No form of proxy shall be used at any meeting except that which is sent out with the notice summoning the meeting, or a substantially similar form.[8]

A form of proxy must be signed by the principal, or by some person authorised by him (either generally or with reference to a particular meeting). If the form is signed by a person other than the principal, the nature of the person's authority shall be stated.[9]

Forms of proxy can be faxed:

> HM Revenue and Customs (formerly the Inland Revenue) sent a form of proxy directing the chairman of a creditors' meeting to vote against the debtor's proposals. It did not arrive. On the morning of the meeting the Revenue faxed the form to the chairman who decided not to act on the form as it was not the original document. The Revenue sought reversal of that decision and revocation of the approval of the debtor's arrangement. The district judge dismissed the application holding that the faxed proxy was not "signed" as required. The Revenue appealed. *Held*, allowing the appeal, that a proxy form was signed if it bore some distinctive or personal mark placed there by the creditor. A form that had been faxed to the chairman of a creditor's meeting was a valid proxy form.[10]

As an alternative to arranging for the signature of a proxy, a company can complete an authority under section 375 of the 1985 Act.[11] If this is done, the person named in the authority must produce to the chairman of the meeting a copy of the resolution from which he derives his authority; the copy resolution must be under the seal of the company or certified by the secretary or a director of the company to be a true copy.[12]

3   USE OF PROXIES AT MEETINGS

A proxy given for a particular meeting may be used at any adjournment of that meeting.[13]   **26–03**

---

[7] r. 8.2(1).
[8] r. 8.2(2).
[9] r. 8.2(3).
[10] *I.R.C. v. Conbeer* [1996] B.C.C. 189.
[11] See para 14–01.
[12] r. 8.7(1),(2).
[13] r. 8.3(1).

Where the responsible insolvency practitioner holds proxies to be used by him as chairman of a meeting, and some other person acts as chairman, the other person may use the proxies.[14]

Where a proxy directs a proxy-holder to vote for or against a resolution for the nomination or appointment of a person as the responsible insolvency practitioner, the proxy-holder may, unless the proxy states otherwise, vote for or against (as he thinks fit) any resolution for the nomination or appointment of that person jointly with another or others.[15]

A proxy-holder may propose any resolution which, if proposed by another, would be a resolution in favour of which by virtue of the proxy he would be entitled to vote.[16]

Where a proxy gives specific directions as to voting, this does not, unless the proxy states otherwise, preclude the proxy-holder from voting at his discretion on resolutions put to the meeting which are not dealt with in the proxy.[17]

A proxy-holder should not vote in favour of any resolution which would place him or any associate of his in a position to receive any remuneration out of the insolvent estate, unless the proxy specifically directs him to vote in that way.[18]

4   RIGHT OF INSPECTION

26–04   The responsible insolvency practitioner must, so long as proxies lodged with him are in his hands, allow them to be inspected, at all reasonable times on any business day, by:

  (a) the creditors, in the case of proxies used at a meeting of creditors, and
  (b) a company's members or contributories, in the case of proxies used at a meeting of the company or of its contributories.[19]

In this regard, "creditors" refers to those who, in a liquidation, have proved their debts or, in any other case, have submitted a written claim to be creditors of the company concerned; but the expression does not include a person whose proof or claim has been rejected.[20] Directors also have a right of inspection.[21]

Any person attending a meeting in insolvency proceedings is entitled, immediately before or in the course of the meeting, to inspect proxies and associated documents (including proofs) sent or given, in accordance with directions contained in any notice convening the meeting, to the chairman of that meeting or to any other person by a creditor, member or contributory for the purpose of that meeting.[22]

Copies of proxies may be taken, on payment of a fee.[23]

[14] r. 8.3(3).
[15] r. 8.3(4).
[16] r. 8.3(5).
[17] r. 8.3(6).
[18] r. 8.6.
[19] r. 8.5(1).
[20] r. 8.5(2).
[21] r. 8.5(3)(a).
[22] r. 8.5(4).
[23] rr. 12.15 and 12.15A.

5 Exception

Customs and Excise officers do not need to lodge a proxy; they simply produce their commission at creditors' meetings. **26–05**

6 Proxies at First Meeting of Creditors—Points to Note

The following points relating to the completion by a creditor of Form 8.5 (Proxy- **26–06**
Members' or Creditors' Voluntary Winding Up) may be useful:

(1) Check that the name of the insolvent company is correctly stated at the top of the form.

(2) Insert the creditor's name and address where shown. Ensure the full legal title of the creditor is given (leave out references to credit managers etc.).

(3) Give the full name of the proxy holder against line (1) and of any alternatives in lines (2) and (3). Proxy-holders must have attained the age of 18.

(4) In the printed words which follow, delete the words not required so that the first sentence reads: "I appoint the above person to be the creditor's proxy-holder at the meeting of creditors to be held on . . . , or at any adjournment of that meeting". If the creditor is an individual, the words should read: "I appoint the above person to be my proxy-holder at the meeting of creditors . . . (etc.)". Check that the date is correctly shown. Initial all alterations.

(5) With regard to the second sentence below the printed lines, the best course is to delete and initial the words in square brackets. This will stop the proxy-holder using his own discretion on matters which are not covered by specific instructions from the creditor. Of course, the creditor may trust the proxy-holder's judgment, in which case the square brackets should be deleted (leaving the words within them), and the alterations initialled.

(6) The creditor should give precise instructions as to how the proxy-holder should vote on each of the various matters set out in the notice convening the meeting. The first item covered by the form is the appointment of a liquidator. The creditor's choice (or choices, if he wants joint liquidators) should be inserted after the words "For the appointment of . . . ". Consider whether to delete (and initial) the words in brackets: the decision depends on whether or not the creditor wants the proxy-holder to vote on any other proposed appointment as the proxy-holder thinks fit. If the proxy-holder is given instructions to vote for a particular person as liquidator, this is deemed to include the authority to vote for the appointment of that person jointly with another liquidator, if the proxy-holder thinks fit.

(7) Specific instructions should be given on any other matters expected to come before the meeting.

(8) Make sure the proxy form is correctly signed. It must be an original signature. Write or type, in capital letters, the name of the person signing, below the signature.

(9) The person signing the proxy form must be authorised to sign by the company: this authority can, for example, take the form of a board resolution covering the signatory's capacity to sign either in relation to a single meeting or in relation to creditors' meetings generally. If the signatory is a director or secretary of the company, this should be stated; if the company authorises any other person to sign then his position in the company should be specified and the words "Authorised to sign on behalf of . . . Limited" should be added.

(10) Date the form.

(11) Follow exactly the instructions in the notice convening the meeting as to when, and to where, the proxies should be returned.

(12) Avoid faxing the proxy if at all possible. If this cannot be avoided, follow up immediately by sending the hard copy with its original signature.

CHAPTER 27

MEMBERS' VOLUNTARY WINDING UP

This topic has been left until the end, for convenience, as it is not strictly an **27–01** insolvency matter—unless a crisis occurs while it runs its course.

Declaration of solvency

As mentioned at the commencement of the previous chapter, a voluntary **27–02** winding up can be a members' voluntary winding up where a declaration of solvency under section 89 of the 1986 Act can be filed. The obvious advantage of this procedure is that the involvement with the company's creditors is to a large extent eliminated.

The section provides that where it is proposed to wind up a company voluntarily, the directors of the company (or, in the case of a company having more than two directors, the majority of them) may, at a directors' meeting, make a statutory declaration to the effect that they have made a full inquiry into the company's affairs and that, having done so, they have formed the opinion that the company will be able to pay its debts in full, together with interest at the official rate (as defined in section 251 of the 1986 Act), within such period not exceeding 12 months from the commencement of the winding up as may be specified in the declaration.

The declaration of solvency will be of no effect unless:

(a) it is made within five weeks immediately preceding the date of the passing of the resolution for winding up, or on that date but before the passing of that resolution; and

(b) it embodies a statement of the company's assets and liabilities as at the latest practicable date before the making of the declaration.[1]

The declaration must be delivered to the Registrar before the expiry of 15 days immediately following the date on which the resolution for winding up the company is passed.[2] Where the statutory declaration is not delivered within the 15-day period, the liquidation will remain a members' voluntary liquidation but the company and any officer in default will be liable to a fine.[3]

A director making a declaration of solvency without having reasonable grounds for the opinion that the company will be able to pay its debts in full, together with interest at the official rate, within the period specified is liable to imprisonment or fine, or both. If the company is wound up in pursuance of a resolution passed within the period of five weeks after the making of the declaration and its debts

---

[1] 1986 Act. s.89(2).
[2] *ibid.*, s.89(3).
[3] *ibid.*, s.89(6).

(together with interest at the official rate) are not paid or provided for in full within the period specified, it is to be presumed (unless the contrary is shown) that the director did not have reasonable grounds for his opinion.[4]

In a members' voluntary winding up the resolution will normally be a special resolution under section 84 of the 1986 Act. In the unusual circumstance of the company having been formed to operate for a limited period or until the happening of a particular event, and that period having expired or the event having happened, an ordinary resolution will suffice.

Effect of liquidation

27–03   In a members' voluntary winding up, all the powers of the directors cease, except so far as the company in general meeting or the liquidator sanctions their continuance.[5] The company must cease to carry on business except as required for its beneficial winding up, but its corporate state and powers continue until dissolution.[6]

Any transfer of shares, unless made to or sanctioned by the liquidator, and any alteration in the status of the members made after the commencement of the winding up, is void.[7]

Appointment of liquidator

27–04   The company in general meeting must appoint one or more liquidators for the purpose of winding up the affairs and distributing the assets of the company.[8]

The powers of the liquidator are the same as those of a liquidator in a creditors' voluntary winding up,[9] except that for the matters referred to in Part I of Schedule 4 (payment of debts, compromise of claims, etc.) he needs the sanction of an extraordinary resolution of the company.[10] The restraints imposed by section 166 do not apply in a members' voluntary winding up.

If a vacancy occurs by death, resignation or otherwise in the office of liquidator appointed by the company, the company in general meeting may, subject to any arrangement with its creditors, fill the vacancy. A meeting for this purpose may be called by any contributory or, if there were more liquidators than one, by the continuing liquidators. The meeting is held in manner provided by the Act or by the articles, or in such manner as may, on application by any contributory or by the continuing liquidators, be determined by the court.[11]

Periodic meetings

27–05   In the event of the winding up continuing for more than one year, the liquidator must summon a general meeting of the company at the end of the first year from

---

[4] *ibid.*, s.89(4),(5).
[5] *ibid.*, s.91(2).
[6] *ibid.*, s.87.
[7] *ibid.*, s.88.
[8] *ibid.*, s.91.
[9] See para. 25–15, above.
[10] 1986 Act, s.165(2)(a).
[11] *ibid.*, s.92.

the commencement of the winding up, and of each succeeding year, or at the first convenient date within three months from the end of the year or such longer period as the Department of Trade and Industry may allow. The liquidator must lay before the meeting an account of his acts and dealings, and of the conduct of the winding up during the preceding year.[12]

Position in case of insolvency

If the liquidator is at any time of opinion that the company will be unable to pay **27–06** its debts in full (together with interest at the official rate) within the period stated in the declaration of solvency, he must summon a meeting of creditors for a day not later than the 28th day after the day on which he formed that opinion. He must send notices of the creditors' meeting to the creditors by post not less than seven days before the day on which that meeting is to be held, and advertise the meeting; he must also make information available free of charge to creditors. He has to prepare and lay before the creditors' meeting a statement of affairs in the prescribed form and attend and preside at that meeting.[13] As from the day on which the creditors' meeting is held, the 1986 Act has effect as if there had been no declaration of solvency and as if the creditors' meeting and company meeting at which the resolution to wind up was made were the creditors' and members' meetings appropriate to a creditors' voluntary winding-up.[14]

Final meeting

As soon as the company's affairs are fully wound up, the liquidator must prepare **27–07** an account showing how the members' voluntary winding up has been conducted and the property of the company disposed of, and must also call a meeting of the members for the purpose of presenting the account and giving an explanation of it. This meeting must be called by advertisement in the *London Gazette*, specifying the time, place and object thereof, and published at least one month before the meeting.[15] As with a creditors' voluntary winding-up, a return is made to the Registrar and dissolution follows.[16]

---

[12] *ibid.*, s.93.
[13] *ibid.*, s.95(1),(2),(3).
[14] *ibid.*, s.96.
[15] *ibid.*, s.94(1),(2).
[16] *ibid.*, s.94(3).

CHAPTER 28

MEETINGS OF LOCAL AUTHORITIES

1 THE STRUCTURE OF LOCAL GOVERNMENT

28–01 Local government in England and Wales is administered by authorities elected by universal suffrage. The Local Government Act 1972[1] rearranged local government into a structure based upon (a) counties and (b) districts, each county being divided into a number of districts. The counties were originally divided into metropolitan and non-metropolitan (or "shire") counties but the metropolitan county councils (West Midlands, Greater Manchester, Merseyside, West Yorkshire, South Yorkshire and Tyne Wear) were abolished by the Local Government Act 1985 as from April 1, 1986.

Further changes were introduced by the Local Government Act 1992, Part II, which provides that orders can be made by the Secretary of State for the Environment for the replacement, in any non-metropolitan area in England, of the two principal tiers (*i.e.* the county council and the district council) with a single tier (*i.e.* either a county council or a district council). Orders creating a number of such unitary councils came into force between 1996 and 1998. In Wales, the structure of local government was again reorganised, as from April 1, 1996, by the Local Government (Wales) Act 1994 which replaced the two principal tiers (counties and districts) with a single tier of counties and county boroughs throughout the principality. The councils administering the "principal areas" (*i.e.* in England county councils, district councils and London boroughs, and, in Wales, county and county borough councils) are known as "principal councils".[2] Parish councils and community councils are not designated as principal councils.

In England, districts are divided into metropolitan and non-metropolitan districts. Certain districts are further subdivided into parishes (in Wales, some principal areas are further sub-divided into communities).

The parish or community is an area smaller than a principal area, and includes rural parishes in country areas (which were largely unaffected by the 1972 Act reforms) and parishes created after 1972 from former urban districts or boroughs—the "small free-standing market towns of England".

The 1972 Act made little change in the structure of local government in operation in London; this had been regulated by the London Government Act 1963. Again, there was previously a two-tier structure, the first tier consisting of

---

[1] In Pt. IV, the expression "the 1972 Act" refers to the Local Government Act 1972, and (unless otherwise stated) references to a section or schedule relate to a section or schedule of the 1972 Act.

[2] s.270.

the Greater London Council and the other of the London boroughs. The Greater London Council was abolished by the Local Government Act 1985. The Great London Authority Act 1999 provided for the establishment of an elected Mayor and Assembly for Greater London.

In general, principal areas are governed by principal councils consisting of a chairman and councillors.[3] However, where a council is operating an executive arrangement[4] involving a mayor and a cabinet executive or a mayor and a council manager executive, the council consists of an elected mayor, a chairman and councillors.[5] A member of the executive may not be elected as chairman.[6]

For each parish in England within the category defined above, there must be a parish meeting and for Welsh communities there may be a community meeting, which all local government electors in the area may attend and which has the right to discuss parish affairs.[7] In addition certain parishes will be administered by a council, for example, every parish which is a former borough included in a rural district[8] or established to succeed a former borough or urban district.[9] In England a district council must establish a separate parish council if the population of the parish includes 200 or more local government electors or if, where the population exceeds 150 but is less than 200, the parish meeting so resolves.[10] The district council may establish a parish council in a parish with not more than 150 electors if the parish meeting so resolves.[11] In Wales, the community meeting may apply to the principal council for an order establishing a community council for the community.[12]

Under Part II of the Local Government Act 1992 and sections 53 *et seq.* of the 1972 Act, the Local Government Commission for England and the Local Government Boundary Commission for Wales are responsible for conducting reviews of local government areas in England and Wales respectively and may make proposals for implementation by means of orders made under each Act. Part II of the Local Government and Rating Act 1997 contained further provisions for the establishment and review of parishes and parish councils.

The authority exercised by local authorities is divided between the county and the district. The functions of metropolitan district councils are wider than those of non-metropolitan districts.

---

[3] ss.2, 21, Sched. 2.

[4] The requirement to implement management structures, otherwise known as "executive arrangements," was imposed on local authorities with effect from October 26 2000, by Part II Local Government Act 2000.

[5] Local Government Act 1972 s 2(2A) (inserted by the Local Government Act 2000 s 46, Sch 3 para 1).

[6] Local Government Act 1972 s.3(1A) (inserted by the Local Government Act 2000 s 46, Sch 3 para 2(1), (2))

[7] ss.9(1), 27(1).

[8] s.9(4)(*a*).

[9] s.9(4)(*e*).

[10] s.9(2), repealed by Local Government and Rating Act 1997. The duty is now contained in s.16(2) of the latter Act.

[11] s.9(3), repealed by Local Government and Rating Act 1997. The power is now contained in s.16(4) of the latter Act.

[12] s.28(1).

Although the parish or community exists as a smaller unit, the powers exercised by the council or meeting are small,[13] and, especially in the case of the "meeting", are to be the channel through which local views can be assessed and passed to the district or county council.[14] Parish councils frequently provide facilities such as street lighting, allotments, playing fields and halls and meeting places. Under Part III of the Local Government and Rating Act 1997, they have power to introduce community transport schemes and crime prevention measures. Parish councils can claim to be consulted over planning applications.[15] Parish and community councils are within the definition of "local authority", but parish and community meetings are excluded from the definition.[16]

Elections

28–02   By section 6 of the 1972 Act the members of principal councils are to be elected in accordance with the 1972 Act and with Part I of the Representation of the People Act 1983. By section 7, it is provided that county councils are to be elected as a whole once every four years: metropolitan district councils are to be elected by thirds, *i.e.* by one third of the members going out of office each year and the vacancies filled by election, but without any such retirement and election in the year of the county council election. The term of office of each councillor is thus four years. Non-metropolitan districts may request the Secretary of State to provide for a system of whole council elections or of election by thirds. The term of office for London borough councillors and for parish and community councillors is four years. Where the principal council is headed by an elected mayor, that mayor is to be elected in accordance with regulations made by the Secretary of State under s.44(1).[17]

The ordinary day of election for all local government areas in England and Wales is the first Thursday in May in every year or such other day as may be fixed by the Secretary of State.[18]

---

[13] See ss.189, 210, 214 and 215. But by s.101(1) a power of delegation is given by which county or district councils can arrange for the discharge of functions by parish councils; note that under the Local Government Act 2000, in particular Part II, instituting executive arrangements, the discharge of functions are in certain circumstances prohibited where that function is the responsibility of the executive: see also the Local Authorities (Executive Arrangements)(Modification of Enactments and Further Provisions)(England) Order 2001 (S.I. 2001 No. 1517).

[14] ss.9(1), 27(1).

[15] Town and Country Planning Act 1990, Sched. 1, para. 8, as amended by Planning and Compensation Act 1991, Sched. 7, paras 8, 53(1) and (5). See also Local Government and Rating Act 1997, s.21.

[16] See paras 28–30 ff below.

[17] Namely the Local Authorities (Mayoral Elections) (England and Wales) Regulations 2002, SI 2002/185, as amended by S.I. 2001 No. 225.

[18] Representation of the People Act 1983, s.37.

2 PROVISIONS RELATING TO THE ADMINISTRATION OF LOCAL AUTHORITIES[19]

Requisites of a valid meeting

The following are the essential features of a local authority meeting: **28–03**

    (a) The meeting must be properly convened, *i.e.* there must be public notice of the meeting and a summons sent to every person entitled to attend.[20]

    (b) There must be more than one person present. A meeting of one person, which can in some circumstances apply in company law, has no place in local authority practice.[21]

    (c) There must be a chairman, and the proper person must be in the chair.[22]

    (d) A quorum must be present.[23]

Standing orders

A local authority may make standing orders for the regulation of its proceedings **28–04**
and business and may revoke or vary any such orders.[24]

Standing orders often contain provision for their suspension, subject to the favourable vote of a specified majority. There is nothing to prevent the suspension of standing orders even though no such provision is made in the standing orders themselves, although notice of such intention should be given, and a resolution will be necessary since standing orders cannot be suspended by implication.[25] A ratepayer may apply to the court for an order of mandamus to require a local authority to follow its standing orders.[26]

Standing orders will cover a wide variety of matters, including, for the sake of clarity and completeness, many matters which are the subject of regulation in the 1972 Act. The rules of debate, for example, will usually be set out in detail, and may include a provision that no speech shall exceed, say, seven minutes for a proposer of a motion or amendment and four minutes in any other instance. It is here that details of the composition of committees will be found. Attached to the procedural standing orders will usually be a full list of the powers and duties of each committee, including those which it can exercise under "executive powers", *i.e.* without referring the matter to the full council for a decision. Also annexed will be a list of the powers delegated to the principal officers of the council to be

---

[19] Defined by s.270 as a county council, a district council, a London borough council or a parish council but, in relation to Wales, as meaning a county council, county borough council or community council.

[20] See below, paras 28–17 and 28–24.

[21] *R. v. Secretary of State for the Environment ex p. Hillingdon L.B.C.* [1986] 1 W.L.R. 192 (Woolf J.); [1986] 1 W.L.R. 807 (Court of Appeal); see below, para. 28–05.

[22] paras. 28–18 and 28–25.

[23] paras. 28–20 and 28–27.

[24] Sched. 12, para. 42.

[25] *R. v. Hereford Corporation, ex p. Harrower* [1970] 3 All E.R. 460.

[26] *ibid.*

exercised either in consultation with the chairman and vice-chairman of the relevant committee or, in matters of less importance, on his or her own initiative.

Standing orders will usually contain a provision as to how they may be varied, and that the chairman's decision on their construction shall be final.

Local authorities' standing orders have the force of law: an authority may be required to comply with its own standing orders and decisions taken in breach of them may be declared invalid.

By section 20 of the Local Government and Housing Act 1989 (which will be referred to in this Part as "LGHA 1989") the Secretary of State is empowered to introduce regulations requiring certain authorities as defined in LGHA 1989, including parish and community councils, to incorporate such provision as may be prescribed. This may include:

(i) arrangements for council and committee members to requisition meetings;

(ii) requiring a committee or sub-committee decision to be reviewed by the full council or a committee; and

(iii) requiring that a vote of a council or of any committee or sub-committee is to be taken in a particular manner.

The Local Authorities (Standing Orders) Regulations 1993 (S.I. 1993 No. 202) and the Local Authorities (Standing Orders) (England) Regulations 2001 (S.I. 2001 No. 3384) have been made pursuant to these provisions.[27]

A number of parish and community councils have adopted the model form of standing orders for local councils published by the National Association of Local Councils.[28]

Delegation to committees and others

28–05   Subject to any express provision contained in the 1972 Act or any Act passed after the 1972 Act, a local authority may arrange for the discharge of any of its functions—

(a) by a committee, or sub-committee or an officer of the authority; or

(b) by any other local authority.[29]

Where any functions may be so discharged by a committee of the authority, then, unless the authority otherwise directs, the committee may arrange for the discharge of any of those functions by a sub-committee or an officer of the authority and where by virtue of these provisions any functions may be discharged by a sub-committee, then, unless the authority or the committee otherwise directs,

---

[27] The 1993 regulations relate mainly to the appointment of chief officers. The 2001 Regulations relate mainly to administrative arrangements regarding staff, consequent upon the implementation of executive arrangements under Part II of the Local Government Act 2000.

[28] A copy of the booklet "Standing Orders and Chairmanship" may be obtained from the Council at 109 Great Russell Street, London WC1B 3LD, the most recent edition being April 2002.

[29] s.101(1).

the sub-committee may arrange for the discharge of any of those functions by an officer of the authority.[30]

The 1972 Act permits delegation to a committee, sub-committee or officer. A decision purportedly made by an officer in the absence of a formal delegation to him is in principle *ultra vires*.[31] It has also been made clear that the Act does not allow any function of an authority to be discharged by one of its members acting individually:

> Hillingdon Council had granted planning permission to a local gravel extrac-
> tion company for the erection of two large maintenance buildings at its works
> site. A condition was that by July 31, 1977 activity should be discontinued,
> the buildings and works demolished and the land reinstated. By 1980 this had
> not been done and so on the sole authorisation of the chairman of the
> council's planning committee (who acted in accordance with standing orders)
> two enforcement notices were served. *Held*, the actions of the committee
> chairman were *ultra vires*, as were the standing orders, and the enforcement
> notices were therefore of no legal effect.[32]

At first, it was thought that the *Hillingdon* case would cause inconvenience in matters of urgency. In practice, however, the council can, where it expects that an urgent decision may be required (either in a particular instance or as a general precaution—for example the institution of or response to legal proceedings), delegate the matter to one of the chief officers of the council in consultation with the chairman and vice-chairman of the relevant committee. The decision would then be ratified at the next committee meeting. This solution is not ideal, because it takes away some of the transparency of the decision-making process. The more cumbersome, but more open, procedure is the convening of a special meeting of the committee.

A local authority has the right to set up a working party to consider a particular proposal and on the assumption that no powers are delegated to the working party, which has a purely advisory role, it will not rank as a "committee" for the purposes of the 1972 Act (which may affect, for example, the rights of the public and other members of the council to attend its meetings under standing orders).[33]

The constitution of any committee is determined by the appointing authority and except for a finance committee may include persons who are not councillors.[34] Such co-opted members of committees, joint committees and sub-committees are

---

[30] s.101(2), and see s.102.

[31] *R v. St Edmunsbury Borough Council, ex p Walton* The Times, May 5 1999. In *R (Carlton-Conway) v. Harrow LBC* [2002] JPL 1216 the Court of Appeal examined closely the terms of the scheme of delegation, and emphasised that public policy required that officers (in this case a planning officer) are circumspect in exercising the powers delegated to them where those powers are not clearly defined.

[32] *R. v. Secretary of State for the Environment ex p. Hillingdon L.B.C.* (see n. 21 above). See also: *R. v. Liverpool City Council, ex p. Professional Association of Teachers* (1984) 82 L.G.R. 648i; (1985) 83 L.G.R. 79.

[33] *R. v. Eden District Council, ex p. Moffat, The Independent*, November 8, 1988.

[34] s.102(3). There are, however, certain statutory provisions which govern co-option. Under s.499 of the Education Act 1996, for instance, the Secretary of State may give directions for the appointment as committee members of persons who appoint foundation governors for voluntary schools in the area. They can be appointed as voting members.

non-voting members of those committees.[35] Certain exceptions to this provision are listed in subsections (4) and (5). Where a person will be treated by virtue of section 13 as a non-voting member of any committee, joint committee or sub-committee, he shall not be entitled to vote at any meeting of the committee, joint committee or sub-committee on any question which falls to be decided at that meeting; references to voting include making use of a casting vote.[36]

Every member of a committee who at the time of his appointment was a member of the local authority by whom he was appointed, ceases to be a member of the committee upon ceasing to be a member of the local authority.[37]

A local authority may make standing orders with respect to the quorum, proceedings and place of meeting of a committee, including any sub-committee but, subject to any such standing orders, the quorum, proceedings and place of meeting are such as the committee or sub-committee may determine.[38]

A committee can have no greater powers or authority than those which are conferred on it by its parent body. It must abide by its terms of reference and cannot dissolve itself. In local authority practice the function of a committee is, in part, to administer services which are delegated to it, and, in part, to contribute to the formulation of policy by making recommendations to its parent body. A council has the right to remove members of a committee who vote against policy proposals, because where councils are organised on party lines a political party is entitled to take steps to impose group discipline on elected council members to ensure its cohesion, provided such steps do not amount to punishment of a councillor and are not vindictive or malicious.[39]

The work of a committee is reported upwards by means either of a report prepared on behalf of the committee or by the submission of the committee's minutes. In the case of certain statutory committees, a local authority may not exercise any functions within the scope of the committee until it has considered a report from the committee. For example, every local education authority is required to set up such education committees as it thinks expedient for the efficient discharge of its functions with regard to education, although it may dispense with such a report if, in its opinion, the matter is urgent:

> A local education authority's decision to close a school was held to be *ultra vires* because, among other things, it had not first considered a report from its education committee (which was then required by the Education Act 1944),

---

[35] S.13 LGA 1989.
[36] LGA 1989, s.13(7),(9).
[37] s.102(5).
[38] s.106. A council is not entitled to delegate any of its powers to determine the size and composition of committees and sub-committees and the appointment, replacement and removal of chairmen, vice-chairmen and members: *R. v. Brent London Borough Council, ex p. Gladbaum and Anor.* (1990) L.S.Gaz. at 47. See also *Administrator*, May 1990, p. 22. Note, however, that this decision pre-dates the introduction of ss.15–17 LGA 1989. By s.16, a context-specific duty is imposed on authorities or committees to give effect to party political wishes. *Gladbaum* would therefore not apply to appointment, replacement or removal where such was in line with the duty to comply with the group's political wishes; it would seem to remain good law where no wish has been expressed or the authority is not divided along political lines.
[39] *R. v. Greenwich London Borough Council ex p. Lovelace* [1991] 1 W.L.R. 506, C.A.

or, as an alternative, dispensed by resolution with the need for such a report.[40]

However, the adequacy of an education committee's report to the council must be considered in relation to the education function on which the report would have a bearing:

> Cornwall County Council resolved to close Penwerris Infants' School. In so doing, it had before it its education committee's "report", which comprised the minutes of a prior meeting of the schools sub-committee, together with a report prepared by the Secretary of State summarising parents' objections (which clearly set out the case for and against) and a copy of a consultation document. Parents opposed to closure argued that this did not amount to a report as required by the Education Act 1944. It was held that the documentation was adequate: what was required by way of a report must depend on circumstances, and the authority must be able to deduce from the material before it both the committee's recommendation and the reasons for it.[41]

Committees in local authority practice are sometimes called "Boards" where they have a quasi-commercial function: their legal position is the same.

Committees—political balance

Provisions as to the political balance on committees were introduced by sections 15 to 17 and Schedule 1 to LGHA 1989. Principal councils and certain other authorities (but not parish or community councils) have the duty to review the representation of different political groups on the committees of that authority and its like sub-committees (together with certain other committees and sub-committees which are listed in Schedule 1). The authority (or committee as regards its sub-committee) has the duty under section 15(3) to determine the allocation to the different political groups into which the members of the authority are divided of all the seats which fall to be filled by appointments made from time to time by that authority or committee. Certain principles have to be followed; these are: **28–06**

- (a) that not all the seats on any body (*i.e.* committee or sub-committee) are allocated to the same political group;
- (b) that a majority of the seats is allocated to a particular political group if the number of persons belonging to that group is a majority of the authority's membership;
- (c) subject to (a) and (b), that the number of seats on the ordinary committees[42] of the authority which are allocated to each political group bears the same proportion to the total of all the seats on the ordinary committees of that authority as is borne by the number of members of that group to the membership of the authority; and

---

[40] *R. v. Brent London Borough Council, ex p. Gunning* (1986) 84 L.G.R. 168.

[41] *R. v. Cornwall County Council and Another ex p. Nicholls, The Independent*, March 30, 1989. See also *R. v. Kirklees M.B.C. ex p. Molloy* (1988) L.G.R. 115, *O'Keefe v. Isle of Wight C.C.* (1989) E.G.C.S. 25, and *Local Government Chronicle* September 1, 1989, p. 10.

[42] As defined in Sched. 1.

(d) subject to (a) to (c), that the number of seats on the body which are allocated to each group bears the same proportion to the number of all the seats on that body as is borne by the number of members of that group to the membership of the authority.

In general, non-voting members of committees and sub-committees are to be disregarded.

The Secretary of State has made regulations[43] to facilitate the working of the political balance provisions.

The regulations provide that a political group shall be treated as constituted when there is delivered to the proper officer (as defined in the 1972 Act, s.270(3)) a notice signed by two or more council members who wish to be treated as a political group, which states that those members wish to be treated as a political group, and which gives the name of the group and specifies one of those members as its leader (reg. 8(1)–(3)). A political group shall cease to be constituted if the number of persons who are to be treated as members of that group is less than two (reg. 8(2)).

A councillor is to be treated as a member of a political group if he has either signed a notice under regulation 8 or he has delivered to the proper officer a notice signed by him and the leader or deputy leader of the group or by a majority of the members of the group, stating that he wishes to join the group (reg. 9).

A person ceases to be a member of a group when he ceases to be a councillor, or he notifies the proper officer in writing that he no longer wishes to be treated as a member of the group, or he takes part in the formation of a new group under regulation 8 or he joins another group, or the majority of the members of his group deliver to the proper officer a notice signed by the majority of the group that they no longer wish him to be treated as a member of it (reg. 10).

No person may be a member of more than one political group at any given time (reg. 11).

Ordinarily, the persons to be appointed to committees covered by the political balance provisions will be nominated by the relevant group (regs. 13–15).

Decisions on questions

28–07 With rare exceptions, all questions coming before a local authority are taken by simple majority of those members of the authority present and voting thereon at a meeting of the authority.[44] The chairman or other person presiding has a second or casting vote exercisable in the case of an equality.[45] This applies also to meetings of committees and sub-committees.

There is no provision for voting by proxy.

---

[43] These are: The Local Government (Committees and Political Groups) Regulations 1990 (S.1.1990 No. 1553); The Local Government (Committees and Political Groups) (Amendment) Regulations 1991 (S.I. 1991 No. 1398) and The Local Government (Committees) (Amendment) Regulations 1993 (S.I. 1993 No. 1339); The Local Government (Committees and Political Groups) (Amendment) Regulations 1998 (S.I. 1998 No. 1918); and The Local Government (Committees and Political Groups) (Amendment) Regulations 1999 (S.I. 1999 No. 500).

[44] Sched. 12, para. 39(1).

[45] Sched. 12, para. 39(2).

In the case of parish and community councils, on the requisition of any member of the council the voting on any question is to be recorded so as to show whether each member present and voting gave his vote for or against that question.[46]

By virtue of Part III of the Local Authorities (Standing Orders) Regulations 1993, which have been referred to above (para. 28–04), the local authorities defined in the Regulations (which do not include parish and community councils) are obliged to include in their standing orders a provision that where immediately after a vote is taken at a meeting of a relevant body any member of that body so requires, there shall be recorded in the minutes of the proceedings of that meeting whether that person cast his vote for the question or against the question or whether he abstained from voting. Here "relevant body" means the authority, a committee or sub-committee of the authority or a relevant joint committee or sub-committee of such a committee.

Records of members attending and minutes

The names of the members present at a meeting of a local authority and of its committees and sub-committees must be recorded.[47] **28–08**

Minutes of the proceedings of a meeting of a local authority, or of a committee or sub-committee thereof, must be drawn up and entered in a book kept for that purpose, and must be signed at the same or next suitable meeting of the local authority, committee or sub-committee by the person presiding thereat, and any minute purporting to be so signed shall be received in evidence without further proof.[48]

Until the contrary is proved, a meeting of a local authority, a minute of whose proceedings has been so made and signed is deemed to have been duly convened and held, and all the members present at the meeting are deemed to have been duly qualified[49]; and where the proceedings are proceedings of a committee or sub-committee, the same presumptions apply with the addition that it is deemed to have had power to deal with the matters referred to in the minutes.[50]

Minutes may be kept in a loose-leaf system.[51]

The minutes of a principal council are open to inspection by any member of the public.[52] The minutes of a parish or community council are open to inspection by any local government elector for the area of the council.[53] The same applies to the minutes of a parish meeting.[54]

Vacancy or defect in election or qualification

The proceedings of a local authority, committee or sub-committee are not invalidated by any vacancy among their number or by any defect in the election or **28–09**

---

[46] Sched. 12, paras 13(2), 29(2).
[47] Sched. 12, paras 40,44.
[48] Sched. 12, paras 41,44.
[49] Sched. 12, para. 41(3).
[50] Sched. 12, para. 44(2).
[51] Sched. 12, para. 41(2).
[52] s.100C (see para. 29–05 below).
[53] s.228(1).
[54] s.228(8).

qualifications of any of its members.[55] This provision would not, however, save a meeting at which a quorum was not present.

Conduct of Members

28–10   Drawing on Lord Nolan's report on Standards of Conduct in Local Government in England, Scotland and Wales (Cm 3702–1), the Local Government Act 2000 significantly tightened the rules governing the conduct of members of local authorities. Section 51 of the Local Government Act 2000 (which will be referred to in this Part as "LGA 2000") required all relevant authorities to adopt a code of conduct for their members.[56] The code of conduct must follow the mandatory conditions set down in the relevant model code issued by the Secretary of State and approved by Parliament (for England) or the National Assembly for Wales (for Wales).[57] Authorities had six months after the issue of the relevant model code of conduct in which to adopt their own code of conduct based upon the model; in default the mandatory conditions of the relevant model code applied automatically.[58]

As at the moment when the authority adopted a code of conduct or the national code was imposed upon it by default, the preceding regime governing members' conduct was disapplied as regards that authority.[59]

The Model Code of Conduct for English local authorities ("the Model Code of Conduct") places a range of general obligations on members covering such matters (1) non-discrimination[60]; (2) respect for others[61]; (3) impartiality[62]; (4) access to and confidentiality of information[63]; (5) integrity[64]; (6) stewardship of resources[65]; (7) accountability[66] and (8) confidential reporting.[67]

---

[55] Sched. 12, para. 43.

[56] "Relevant authorities", as defined in s.49(6) included the organs of local government described in paragraph 28–01 above.

[57] For English local authorities, the Model Code of Conduct is contained in the Local Authorities (Model Code of Conduct)(England) Order 2001 (S.I. 2001 No. 3575). There are, in fact, two Model Codes forming Schedules 1 and 2 to this Order, one for authorities operating executive arrangements, and one for those not operating such arrangements. They are to all intents and purposes identical; the discussion in the body of the text and the references uses the paragraph numbers in the Model Code for authorities operating executive arrangements. For Wales, the relevant Order is the Conduct of Members (Model Code of Conduct) (Wales) Order 2001 (S.I. 2001 No. 2289). Parish Councils, National Parks and Broads Authorities and Police Authorities also have their own model Codes, contained in S.I.s 2001 No. 3576, 2001 No. 3577 and 2001 No. 3578 respectively. Lack of space prevents full discussion of each of these.

[58] s.51(5) LGA 2000. Time expired for Welsh local authorities on 28 January 2002 and for English local authorities on 5 May 2002.

[59] Contained in s.94–8 and 105 of the 1972 Act, and on the basis of regulations made under s.19 LGHA 1989. For discussion of the earlier regime, see the ninth edition of this work at paragraphs 28–10 ff.

[60] Paragraph 2(a).

[61] Paragraph 2(b).

[62] Paragraph 2(c).

[63] Paragraph 3.

[64] Paragraphs 4 and 5.

[65] Paragraph 6(1)(a).

[66] Paragraph 6(1)(b).

[67] Paragraph 7.

Members must provide a written undertaking that in performing their functions they will observe the authority's code of conduct for the time being. Without such an undertaking, they may not act.[68]

A complex regime exists for the investigation of and adjudication upon alleged infringements of the rules governing the conduct of members. This is dealt with further at paragraph 28–13 below.

Personal and prejudicial interests

The Model Code of Conduct contains detailed provisions relating to interests.[69] **28–11** These are divided into personal and prejudicial.

By Paragraph 8 of the Model Code of Conduct, a member[70] must regard himself as having a personal interest in any matter if the matter relates to an interest required to be included on the register of members interests (on which see further below), or if a decision upon it might reasonably be regarded as affecting to a greater extent than other council tax payers, rate payers or inhabitants of the authority's area, the well-being or financial position of himself, a relative[71] or a friend or—

(a) any employment or business carried on by such persons;
(b) any person who employs or has appointed such persons, any firm in which they are a partner, or any company of which they are directors;
(c) any corporate body in which such persons have a beneficial interest in a class of securities exceeding the nominal value of £5,000; or
(d) any specified body in which such person holds a position of general control or management.[72]

A prejudicial interest is defined in paragraph 10(1) of the Model Code of Conduct as a personal interest which a member of the public with knowledge of the relevant facts would reasonably regard as so significant that it is likely to prejudice the member's judgement of the public interest. By paragraph 10(2), a member may regard himself as not having a prejudicial interest in a matter if that matter relates to:

(a) another relevant authority of which he is a member;
(b) another public authority in which he holds a position of general control or management;

---

[68] s.52(4) LGA 2000.
[69] In Part 2.
[70] Which includes a co-opted member: Paragraph 1(4).
[71] Defined in Paragraph 8(2).
[72] The bodies are specified in paragraph 15 of the Code of Conduct. They are (1) bodies to which the member has been appointed or nominated by the authority as its representative; (2) a public authority or a body exercising functions of a public nature; (3) a company, industrial and provident society, or body directed to charitable purposes; (4) a body whose principal purposes include the influence of public opinion and policy; and (5) a trade union or professional association.

(c) a body to which he has been appointed or nominated by the authority as its representative;

(d) the housing functions of the authority where the member holds a tenancy or lease with a relevant authority, provided that he does not have arrears of rent with that relevant authority of more than two months, and provided that those functions do not relate particularly to the member's tenancy or lease;

(e) the functions of the authority in respect of school meals, transport and travelling expenses, where the member is a guardian or parent of a child in full time education, unless it relates particularly to the school which the child attends;

(f) the functions of the authority in respect of statutory sick pay under Part XI of the Social Security Contributions and Benefits Act 1992, where the member is in receipt of, or is entitled to the receipt of such pay from a relevant authority; and

(g) the functions of the authority in respect of an allowance or payment made under ss.173 to 176 of the 1972 Act or s.18 LGHA 1989.

A member must also regard himself as having a personal and a prejudicial interest if he is involved in the consideration of a matter at a meeting of an overview and scrutiny committee of the authority or a sub-committee of such a committee and that consideration relates to a decision made or an action taken by another of the authority's committees, sub-committees, joint committees, or joint sub-committees of which he may be a member.[73]

Whether a member has a personal or a prejudicial interest is a question to be determined objectively, and the test for compliance with the Code of Conduct where he has such an interest is equally objective.[74]

Where a member has a personal interest in a matter to be discussed at a meeting, he must disclose to that meeting the existence and nature of that interest at the start of the consideration of that matter, or when the interest becomes apparent.[75]

Where a member has a prejudicial interest in any matter, he must:

(a) withdraw from the room or chamber where a meeting is being held whenever it becomes apparent that the matter is being considered at that

---

[73] Paragraph 11(1). However, by paragraph 11(2), this restriction does not apply if the member attends the meeting of the overview and scrutiny (sub)committee for the purpose of answering questions or otherwise giving evidence relating to the decision or action under scrutiny.

[74] *Scrivens v. Ethical Standards Officer* [2005] EWHC 529 (Admin); [2005] All ER (D) 78 (Apr), [2005] NPC 51, clarifying *R(Richardson and Others) v. North Yorkshire County Council* [2004] 1 WLR 1920. In other words, a member will fail to comply with the Code if he reasonably but mistakenly concludes that he does not have a personal interest or prejudicial interest, as the case may be, in a matter considered by his authority, and as a result does not take the required action. The Council in *Scrivens* was a parish council, but the principle will hold good for other authorities.

[75] Paragraph 9(1). By Paragraph 9(2), where a member has made an executive decision in relation to a matter in which he has a personal interest (in an authority operating executive arrangements), he must ensure that any written statement of that decision records the existence and nature of that interest.

meeting, unless he has obtained a dispensation from that authority's standards committee[76];

(b) (where relevant) not exercise executive functions in relation to that matter; and

(c) not seek improperly to influence a decision about that matter.[77]

However, a member with a prejudicial interest may participate in a meeting of the authority's overview and scrutiny committee or joint or area committee to the extent that such committees are not exercising functions of the authority or its executive, so long as the prejudicial interest is not financial or is of the nature described in Paragraph 11 of the Model Code.[78]

The register of interests

Local authorities are required to establish and maintain a register of the interests of the members and co-opted members of the authority.[79] The register must be available for inspection by members of the public at an office of the authority at all

28–12

---

[76] The Relevant Authorities (Standards Committees) (Dispensations) Regulations 2002 (S.I. 2002 No. 339), made under s.81(5) LGA 2002 set out the circumstances under which dispensations may be granted by the relevant standards committee. The circumstances (as set out at Regulation 3(1)) are that (a) the transaction of business of the authority would, on each occasion on which the dispensation would apply, otherwise be impeded by, or as a result of, the mandatory provisions because—(i) the number of members of the authority that are prohibited from participating in the business of the authority exceeds 50% of those members that are entitled or required to so participate; or (ii) the authority is not able to comply with any duty which applies to it under section 15(4) of LGHA 1989 (the duty to allocate seats in accordance with political groupings); or (b) the member has submitted to the standards committee a written request for a dispensation explaining why it is desirable; and (c) the standards committee concludes that having regard to the matters mentioned in paragraph (a) above, the content of the application made pursuant to paragraph (b) above, and to all the other circumstances of the case, it is appropriate to grant the dispensation. However, by Regulation 3(2), no dispensation can be granted (a) in respect of participation in business of the authority conducted more than four years after the date on which the dispensation is granted; or (b) where the effect of the mandatory provisions from which a dispensation is sought is that—(i) a member is prohibited from participating in the consideration of a matter at a meeting of an overview and scrutiny committee of the authority, or sub-committee of that committee, where that considera-tion relates to any decision made or action taken by any other of the authority's committees, sub-committees, joint committees, or joint sub-committees of which he may also be a member; or (ii) a member of the authority's executive is prohibited from exercising functions which are the responsibility of the executive of the authority and which would otherwise be discharged by him solely. For Wales, the equivalent regulations are the Standards Committees (Grant of Dispensations) (Wales) Regulations 2001 (S.I. 2001 No. 2279).

[77] Paragraph 12(1). In R(Richardson and Others) v. North Yorkshire County Council [2004] 1 WLR 1920, the Court of Appeal held that Paragraph 12(1) referred to members of the council generally, not only to members of the relevant committee (at 1942D per Simon Brown LJ) Further, a member of the council attending a council meeting who would otherwise be barred by reason of a prejudicial interest could not simply by declaring that he was attending in his private capacity thereby divest himself of his official capacity as a councillor (at 1949A-J, per Simon Brown LJ). He was still to be regarded as conducting the business of his office, and it was only by resigning that he could shed the role. In the circumstances, the Court of Appeal therefore concluded that the member in question had properly been excluded from the meeting.

[78] Paragraph 12(2).

[79] s.81(1) LGA 2000. The register must be established and maintained by the monitoring officer for the authority.

reasonable hours.[80] Within 28 days of his election or appointment to office the member must register his financial and other interests in the register by providing written notification to the authority's monitoring officer of the matters set down in Paragraphs 14 and 15 of the Model Code.[81] The member must also provide written notification within 28 days of any change to the interests specified under Paragraphs 14 and 15,[82] and, finally, must notify the monitoring officer in writing of receipt of any gift or hospitality over the value of £25.[83]

Standards Committees

28–13   Each relevant authority must establish a standards committees with the functions conferred upon it by or under Part III LGA 2000.[84] Regulations have been made by the Secretary of State and the National Assembly for Wales amplifying the detail of such standards committees.[85] Statutory guidance has also been issued by the Standards Body for England as to the size and composition of standards committees of relevant authorities in England and police authorities in Wales.[86]

---

[80] s.81(6).

[81] The matters set down in paragraph 14 in respect of a member are: (a) any employment or business carried on by him; (b) the name of the person who employs or has appointed him, the name of any firm in which he is a partner, and the name of any company for which he is a remunerated director; (c) the name of any person, other than a relevant authority, who has made a payment to him in respect of his election or any expenses incurred by him in carrying out his duties; (d) the name of any corporate body which has a place of business or land in the authority's area, and in which the member has a beneficial interest in a class of securities of that body that exceeds the nominal value of £25,000 or one hundredth of the total issued share capital of that body; (e) a description of any contract for goods, services or works made between the authority and himself or a firm in which he is a partner, a company of which he is a remunerated director, or a body of the description specified in sub-paragraph (d) above; (f) the address or other description (sufficient to identify the location) of any land in which he has a beneficial interest and which is in the area of the authority; (g) the address or other description (sufficient to identify the location) of any land where the landlord is the authority and the tenant is a firm in which he is a partner, a company of which he is a remunerated director, or a body of the description specified in sub-paragraph (d) above; and (h) the address or other description (sufficient to identify the location) of any land in the authority's area in which he has a licence (alone or jointly with others) to occupy for 28 days or longer. The matters set down in paragraph 15 are membership of or a position of general control or management in any (a) body to which he has been appointed or nominated by the authority as its representative; (b) public authority or body exercising functions of a public nature; (c) company, industrial and provident society, charity, or body directed to charitable purposes; (d) body whose principal purposes include the influence of public opinion or policy; and (e) trade union or professional association.

[82] Paragraph 16.

[83] Paragraph 17.

[84] s.53(1) LGA 2000. Note that parish and community councils are excluded from the requirements of s.53(1) by virtue of s.53(2). By s.55(1)-(2), parish councils are supervised by the standards committee of the relevant district council or (where relevant) unitary council. The district or unitary council may appoint a sub-committee to discharge its functions in respect of parish councils.55(3) LGA 2000. Similarly, community councils in Wales are supervised by the standards committee of the relevant county council: s.56(1) LGA 2000; similar provisions in respect of the operation of sub-committees are to be found at s.56(3).

[85] Relevant Authorities (Standards Committees) Regulations 2001 (2001 S.I. No 2812), as amended by 2003 S.I. No. 1483 and 2004 S.I. No. 2617, applicable to relevant authorities in England other than parish councils and to Welsh police authorities, and the Standards Committees (Wales) Regulations 2001 (2001 S.I. No. 2283).

[86] Pursuant to s.53(7)(b) LGA 2000.

A standards committee's functions are to (a) advise the authority on the adoption or revision of a code of conduct[87]; (b) monitor the operation of that code of conduct[88]; and (c) advise, train or arrange to train members (including co-opted members) on matters relating to the code of conduct.[89] Regulations have been made by the Secretary of State in respect of the exercise of the functions of relevant authorities in England and police authorities in Wales[90]; the National Assembly for Wales has yet to do the same in respect of the standards committees of relevant authorities in Wales other than police authorities.

A standards committee can appoint one or more sub-committees to discharge any of its functions, whether or not to the exclusion of the committee.[91]

Upholding of the Code of Conduct: Investigation

Investigations into the conduct of members of relevant authorities in England **28–14** and police authorities in Wales are carried out by the Standards Board for England ("the Standards Board").[92] Investigations into the conduct of members of relevant authorities in Wales are at present entrusted to a local commissioner, in other words a member of the Commission for Local Administration in Wales.[93]

A complaint can be brought by way of written allegation to the Standards Board that a member or former member (to include co-opted members) of a relevant authority has failed or may have failed to comply with the authority's code of conduct.[94]

Investigations are carried out by ethical standards officers.[95] Four findings are possible following an investigation:

(a) there is no evidence of any failure to comply with the relevant code of conduct[96];

---

[87] s.54(2)(a) LGA 2000.

[88] *ibid.*, s.54(2)(b).

[89] *ibid.*, s.54(2)(c).

[90] Local Authorities (Code of Conduct) (Local Determination) Regulations 2003 (2003 S.I. No. 1483).

[91] s.54A(1) LGA 2000 (added by s.113(1) Local Government Act 2003). This section does not apply to functions in relation to parish or community councils: s.54A(2).

[92] s.57(1) LGA 2000; Schedule 4 to the Act sets out details of the constitution and operation of the Board.

[93] ss.68(5) and 83(1) LGA 2000. From a date to be appointed, the local commissioner is to be replaced by a Public Services Ombudsman for Wales: Public Services Ombudsman (Wales) Act s.35, Sch.4, paras. 1, 13(a). Considerations of space mean that the discussion in this Chapter are limited to the Standards Board of England.

[94] s.58(1) LGA 2000. Where the Board considers that an allegation is not to be investigated, it must take reasonable steps to give written notification of that decision (and reasons) to the complainant: s.58(3).

[95] s.59(1) LGA 2000. Provisions as to qualifications required to be an ethical standards officer are contained in Sch.4 para. 3(3). Provisions as to the carrying out of investigations are contained at ss.60–1 LGA 2000. Ethical standards officers have the power to compel the production of information by virtue of s.62(1); failure to comply with a request for information is a criminal offence: s.62(10). However, officers may then only disclose information obtained in the limited set of circumstances set down in s.63(1).

[96] *ibid.*, s.59(4)(a).

(b) that no action needs to be taken in respect of the matters which are the subject of the investigation[97];

(c) that the matters which are the subject of the investigation should be referred to the monitoring officer of the authority concerned[98]; or

(d) that that matters which are the subject of the investigation should be referred to the president of the Adjudication Panel for England for adjudication by a tribunal.[99]

An ethical standards officer may produce a report where he reaches conclusions (a) or (b); he must produce a report in the case of reaching conclusions (c) or (d).[1] A report must be sent to the monitoring officer in the case of reaching conclusion (c).[2] He may also produce an interim report during the course of an investigation where he believes it necessary in the public interest.[3]

Provision is also made by s.67 LGA 2000 for coordination of inquiries under Part III with matters falling to be investigated by the Local Commissioner under Part III Local Government Act 1974, i.e. complaints as to maladministration: see further below 28–15.

Where a report is received by a monitoring officer pursuant to s.71(2) LGA 2000, he must arrange for the Standards Committee of the relevant authority to convene to consider it.[4] Regulations have been made covering the procedure to be adopted by the Standards Committee when considering the report and also in respect of appeals that can be made against any subsequent decision of the Committee.[5]

Upholding of the Code of Conduct: Adjudication

28–15   There is now an Adjudication Panel for England and one for Wales.[6] Adjudications are carried out by case tribunals or interim case tribunals, in each case consisting of not less than three members of the Panel.[7] Regulations have been made dictating the procedure to be followed by adjudicating tribunals in Wales only.[8]

---

[97] *ibid.*, s.59(4)(b).

[98] *ibid.*, s.59(4)(c). Where a monitoring officer considers that he ought not to perform particular functions, he can delegate those functions to a nominated individual, who must carry out those functions personally: s.82A LGA 2000 (added by s.113(2) Local Government Act 2003).

[99] *ibid.*, s.59(4)(d).

[1] *ibid.*, s.64(1)–(3).

[2] *ibid.*, s.64(2).

[3] *ibid.*, s.65(1).

[4] Regulation 5 of the Local Authorities (Code of Conduct) (Local Determination) Regulations 2003 (2003 S.I. No. 1483),

[5] *ibid.*, regulations 6–13. Appeals against findings of Standards Committees are to the Adjudication Panel.

[6] Established under ss.75(1) and (2) LGA 2000 respectively. The constitution of the Panels is set down in the balance of s.75. At time of writing, the Adjudication Panel for England has a website at: *http://www.adjudicationtest.com*, which includes determinations.

[7] ss.76(1),(2) and 83(1) LGA 2000.

[8] The Adjudications by Case Tribunals and Interim Case Tribunals (Wales) Regulations 2001 (2001 S.I. No. 2288), made under ss.77(4) and (6) LGA 2000. The Adjudication Panel has set its own rules of procedure pending direction from the Secretary of State under s.77 LGA 2000.

As with investigations by ethical standards officers, case tribunals are restricted in the findings that they can reach. They must decide first whether the person in question has failed to comply with the relevant code of conduct.[9] If they conclude that he has not, they must give notice to that effect to the Standards Committee of the relevant authority.[10] If they conclude that he has failed, they must decide whether the nature of the failure is such that the person should be: (1) suspended or partially suspended from being a member or co-opted member or the relevant authority; or (2) disqualified from being, or becoming, whether by election or otherwise, a member of that or any other relevant authority.[11] It is also open to the case tribunal to decide that the person had failed to comply with the code of conduct, but that they should not be suspended or disqualified.[12] Notices of any findings reached by the tribunal must be disseminated, including to a relevant regional newspaper.[13] The tribunal must give adequate reasons for its decision,[14] and in reaching it must take into account the effect of such decision not only the individual in front of it but also the need to discourage similar actions by others.[15]

An appeal against a decision of a case tribunal lies to the High Court.[16] A case tribunal may also make recommendations to a relevant authority arising out of its adjudication.[17]

Order at meetings

It is the duty of the chairman at local authority meetings to control the proceedings properly and to maintain order.[18]   **28–16**

If the disorderly conduct is being carried on by a councillor, the chairman will usually first call upon the offender to desist. If this fails, standing orders may provide for another council member to put the motion "That the member named be not further heard." If the disorderly member continues his misconduct, another member may put a further motion "That the member named do leave the meeting", or the chairman may adjourn the meeting. The latter may be the wiser course, both in practical terms to allow tempers to cool, and because on legal grounds the chairman may have no power to use force to expel a member from a meeting where he has a statutory right to be present.[19]

Where the disorder arises from the conduct of persons other than members, the chairman will, again, begin by attempting to assert his own authority; if the

---

[9] s.79(1) LGA 2000.
[10] ibid., s.79(2).
[11] ibid., ss.79(4)(a) and (b) respectively.
[12] ibid., s.79(7).
[13] ibid., s.79(12).
[14] Adami v. Ethical Standards Board for England [2005] All ER(D) 321 (Jun).
[15] Sloam v. Standards Board for England [2005] EWHC 124 (Admin).
[16] s.79(15) LGA 2000. Note that this is not simply restricted to an appeal on a point of law as might have been expected.
[17] ibid., s.80(1). A relevant authority must consider any recommendations made within three months of receipt and prepare a report detailing actions that have been taken or that will be taken as a result: s.80(3) LGA 2000.
[18] R. v. D'Oyly (1840) 12 Ad. El. 139, 159. R. v. St. Mary's Lambeth (1832) 8 Ad. El. 356. See also para. 6–10.
[19] See, however, Marshall v. Tinnelly (1937) 81 S.J. 903.

conduct persists, the offender will be asked to leave the chamber. On his refusal, reasonable force may be used to eject him.[20] In this context, standing orders usually confer on the chairman an explicit right to order the offender's removal from the chamber.

A local authority can, where it fears that persons are intent on disrupting a meeting, exclude them in advance.[21] If a large, but legitimate, demonstration is expected, the arrangements (such as the numbers to be allowed into the meeting, whether or not councillors are to meet representatives of the demonstrators in advance, method of access to the meeting, security arrangements and the role of the police) should be discussed in advance by council officers and the organisers of the demonstration.

Defects in administration: ombudsman

28–17   Because local authorities are organs of government whose decisions can affect the rights and duties of members of the public, a distinction must be drawn between the attitude of the law to the conduct of their meetings and those of companies or associations. The courts are, as has been shown, ready to take a commonsense line in allowing a margin of informality in company meetings. No such margin can be admitted in respect of local authority meetings: there is no "rule in *Foss v. Harbottle*". Likewise, in relation at least to principal councils, there is no residual power in a meeting of electors to cure defects in the procedure followed by councils.

Complaints about maladministration may, in practice, be made to:

(a) the local authority itself, under its "How to Complain" procedure; or
(b) the district auditor, where financial impropriety is alleged; or
(c) the court, on the grounds, for example, that the authority has acted outside its statutory powers or illegally, or there has been procedural impropriety; or
(d) the "Ombudsman", *i.e.* the Commission for Local Administration in England or the Commission for Local Administration in Wales.[22]

Complaints to the ombudsman should be made in writing to the local commissioner specifying the action alleged to constitute maladministration. Alternatively, a complaint may be made to a member of the local authority, who can refer the matter to the ombudsman with the consent of the complainant. The requirement for referral through the authority may be dispensed with where a request for a complaint to be referred has not been complied with.[23] In respect of matters within his jurisdiction, the local commissioner may investigate the complaint and report

---

[20] For a discussion of this topic, and relevant cases, see paras. 3–02.
[21] *R. v. Brent Health Authority, ex p. Francis and Another* [1985] Q.B. 869.
[22] Local Government Act 1974, s.26. From a date to be appointed, the Commission for Local Administration in Wales is to be abolished and replaced by the Public Service Ombudsman for Wales: Public Service Ombudsman (Wales) Act 2005. The discussion in the text is limited to that of the English ombudsman.
[23] Local Government Act 1974, s.26(1)–(4). A leaflet, "How to Complain to the Local Government Ombudsman", is obtainable on the Local Government Ombudsman's website which was, at time of writing, to be found at *www.lgo.org.uk.*

or give his reasons for not conducting an investigation; copies of the report have to be made available for public inspection.[24] Where the ombudsman reports that injustice has been caused to a person aggrieved in consequence of maladministration, the report has to be laid before the local authority concerned. The authority must consider the report and within three months, or such longer period as the commissioner may allow, notify the ombudsman of the action it has taken or proposes to take. Default by the authority in taking action to the satisfaction of the ombudsman gives him the right to make a further report with his own recommendations; default in implementing them can lead to the publication of a statement in the local press of details of the actions recommended by the ombudsman which the authority has not taken.[25]

Adverse reports and the action to be taken consequently upon them have, in general, to be considered by the full council and authority members who are named and criticised in the report have no right to vote on any question with respect to it.[26]

A local authority may incur expenditure in making a payment or in providing a benefit to a person who has suffered an injustice in consequence of the maladministration.[27]

In essence, the local ombudsman examines complaints that injustice has been caused by a fault in the way that something has been done, or because an authority has not done something which it ought to have done. Examples of such maladministration include:

(a) unjustified delay;
(b) failure to follow agreed policies, rules or procedures, or failure to have proper procedures; and
(c) malice, bias or unfair discrimination.

The local ombudsmen are established to investigate cases of maladministration rather than breach of the law, and as has been stated by Commissioner Cook, "acceptable administrative action lies within the frame of a wider (and less precise) concept than action taken within the law".[28] The ombudsman must, however, concern himself only with the manner in which the authority reached its decision, and not with the nature, quality or reasonableness of the decision itself.[29] Failure to give an elector a fair chance to have his views expressed to the council or the appropriate committee would probably be regarded as maladministration.[30]

The Commission for Local Administration will not investigate matters which are more appropriate to court proceedings, nor complaints which affect most of the residents of the area (for example, that the council tax has been set at too high a figure), nor complaints which relate to personnel matters or to contractual and commercial transactions. Nor will the Commission have jurisdiction where a

---

[24] *ibid.*, s.30.
[25] *ibid.*, s.31.
[26] *ibid.*, s.31A.
[27] *ibid.*, s.31(3).
[28] *Croydon L.B.C. v. Commissioner for Local Administration* [1989] 1 All E.R. 1033.
[29] See Local Government Act 1974, s.34(3) and *R. v. Commissioner for Local Administration, ex p. Eastleigh BC* [1988] Q.B. 855 at 863.
[30] Some examples are given in [1987] J.P.L. 612.

challenge to a local authority has been properly brought by way of judicial review.[31] The jurisdiction of the Commission covers local authorities (except parish and community councils) and a range of named bodies with public functions.[32]

Complaint must be made within 12 months from the day on which the person aggrieved first had notice of the matters alleged in the complaint, but the local commissioner may waive this requirement.[33]

The report of an ombudsman is subject to judicial review.[34]

The ultra vires rules

28–18   Local authorities are statutory corporations and are subject to the *ultra vires* rule. By Part III of the 1972 Act (which was intended to confirm the position as it had previously been understood) a local authority has the power, subject to the provisions of the Act, to do any thing (whether or not involving the expenditure, borrowing or lending of money or the acquisition or disposal of any property or rights) which is calculated to facilitate, or is conducive or incidental to, the discharge of any of its functions. The Local Government Act 2000 introduced a so-called "well-being provision" for local authorities to do anything which they consider is likely to achieve the promotion of the economic, social or environmental well-being of their area.[35]

Where a local authority has made a resolution in excess of its powers, that part which is not *ultra vires* may be severable and valid.[36]

3   PRINCIPAL COUNCILS

Holding of meetings

28–19   A principal council must in every year hold an annual meeting, and may hold such other meetings as it may determine.[37]

In a year when there has been an ordinary election of councillors, the annual meeting must be held on the eighth day after the retirement of councillors or such other day within the 21 days immediately following the date of retirement as the council may fix.[38]

In any other year the annual meeting must be held on such day in the months of March, April or May as the council may fix.[39]

---

[31] s.26(6)(c) as interpreted in *R (Scholarstica Umo) v. Commissioner for Local Administration in England* [2004] ELR 265.

[32] Local Government Act 1974, ss.25 and 34(1). Complaints about maladministration by parish and community councils are covered by the National Association of Local Council's Code of Practice in Handling Complaints—which recommends a standard procedure.

[33] Local Government Act 1974, s.26(4).

[34] *R. v. Commissioner for Local Administration, ex p. Eastleigh Borough Council* [1988] Q.B. 855.

[35] s.2(1).

[36] *Thames Water Authority v. Elmbridge BC* [1983] 2 W.L.R. 743, C.A. For a full review of the cases on Part III of 1972 Act, see *Hazell v. Hammersmith and Fulham LBC* [1991] 2 W.L.R. 372, H.L. (relating to a speculative interest rate swap transaction).

[37] Sched. 12, paras. 1(1), 2(1). For definition of "principal council", see para. 28–01.

[38] Sched. 12, para. 1(2)(*a*). As to the years of election, see para. 28–02.

[39] Sched. 12, para. 1(2)(*b*).

The annual meeting is to be held at such hour as the council may fix, and if no hour is so fixed, at twelve noon.[40]

Meetings other than an annual meeting must be held at such hour and on such other days as the council decide.[41]

Meetings of a principal council shall be held at such place, either within or without its area, as the council may direct.[42]

Convening of meetings

Three clear days[43] at least before a meeting of a principal council (and of its **28–20** committees and sub-committees) notice of the time and place of the meeting must be published at the offices of the council.[44] Within the same period, a summons to attend the meeting, specifying the business proposed to be transacted and signed by the proper officer of the council, must be left at or sent by post to the usual place of residence of every member of the council.[45] Service by post is deemed to be effective by properly addressing, prepaying and posting a letter containing the document and, unless the contrary is proved, is deemed to have been effected at the time at which the letter would be delivered in the ordinary course of post.[46]

Want of service of the summons on any member of the council will not affect the validity of the meeting.[47] Service, in this connection, means the delivery of the notice if, for example, it is sent by post; the provision does not authorise any laxity on the part of the officials in sending it. It should be noted that no provision is contained in the 1972 Act excusing an accidental failure to give notice *to the public*. Notice of an adjourned meeting is not, strictly speaking, required although standing orders may provide, for example, that where a meeting is adjourned to another day, other than the following day, notice of the adjourned meeting shall be sent.[48]

The chairman of a principal council may call an extraordinary meeting of the council at any time.[49] If the chairman refuses to call a meeting of the council after a requisition for that purpose, signed by five members of the council, has been presented to him, or if, without so refusing, the chairman does not call a meeting within seven days after such requisition has been presented to him, then any five members of the council, on that refusal or on the expiry of those seven days, as the case may be, may forthwith call an extraordinary meeting of the council.[50] The calling of the meeting need not be by the same members as requisitioned it.

Where the meeting is called by members of the council the notice must be signed by them and must specify the business proposed to be transacted.[51]

---

[40] Sched. 12, para. 1(4).
[41] Sched. 12, para. 2(2).
[42] Sched. 12, para. 4(1).
[43] See para. 5–10.
[44] Sched. 12, para. 4(2)(*a*).
[45] Sched. 12, para. 4(2)(b). A member may nominate an alternative address: Sched. 12, para. 4(3).
[46] Interpretation Act 1978, ss.7, 22(1), Sched. 2, para. 3. So far as notification to the public is concerned see, further, para. 29–02.
[47] Sched. 12, para. 4(4).
[48] *Scadding v. Lorant* (1851) 3 H.L. Cas. 418. See para. 6–17.
[49] Sched. 12, para. 3(1).
[50] Sched. 12, para. 3(2).
[51] Sched. 12, para. 4(2)(a).

Except in the case of business required by the 1972 Act or any other Act to be transacted at the annual meeting of the council and other business permitted as urgent business under standing orders, no business can be transacted at a meeting other than that specified in the summons relating thereto.[52]

Further, an item of business may not be considered unless a copy of the agenda including the item has been open to public inspection in the manner prescribed by s.100(B)(4) of the 1972 Act.[53]

Chairman

28–21   The chairman of a principal council is elected annually by the council from among the councillors.[54] However, where a council operates executive arrangements, a member of the executive cannot be so elected.[55] The election of the chairman must be the first business transacted at the annual meeting of a principal council.[56] If he is present, the outgoing chairman must preside for the election except where he is a candidate for re-election, in which case he should arrange for a substitute to take the chair temporarily.[57] Any business transacted prior to the election of the chairman would be invalid.[58] The chairman, unless he resigns or becomes disqualified, continues in office until his successor becomes entitled to act as chairman.[59]

During his term of office the chairman continues to be a member of the council notwithstanding the provisions of the 1972 Act relating to the retirement of councillors.[60] This provision ensures continuity by enabling the chairman to continue in office until the annual meeting, when his successor will be appointed, even if he has ceased to be a councillor under the election procedure. In this situation, however, he must not vote in the election of his successor other than by a casting vote in the event of equality of votes.[61] If a casual vacancy occurs in the office of chairman an election must be held at the next ordinary meeting of the council, or if that meeting is within 14 days after the date on which the vacancy occurs, not later than the next but one meeting.[62]

At each meeting of a principal council the chairman, if present, shall preside.[63] Should he be absent the vice-chairman, if present, will preside[64]; in the event of both being absent such councillor as the members of the council present shall choose shall preside.[65]

---

[52] Sched. 12, para. 4(5).
[53] See para. 29–04.
[54] s.3(1).
[55] s.3(1A), inserted by Local Government Act 2000, Sched. 3, para. 2.
[56] s.4(1).
[57] *R. v. Owens* (1859) 28 L.J.Q.B. 316, *R. v. White* (1867) L.R. 2 Q.B. 557.
[58] *R. v. McGowan* (1840) 11 A. E. 869, *R. v. Parkyns* (1820) 3 B. Ad. 668.
[59] s.3(2).
[60] s.3(3).
[61] s.4(2),(3).
[62] s.88(1).
[63] Sched. 12, para. 5(1).
[64] Sched. 12, para. 5(2)(a). In the case of a London borough council, the deputy mayor, if at that time he remains a councillor and is chosen for that purpose by the members of the council then present, shall preside (Sched. 12, para. 5.2(c)).
[65] Sched. 12, para. 5(3).

Vice-chairman

A principal council must appoint a member of the council to be vice-chairman **28–22** of the council.[66] However, where a council operates executive arrangements, a member of the executive cannot be so appointed.[67] The vice-chairman, unless he resigns or becomes disqualified, holds office until immediately after the election of a chairman at the next annual meeting of the council, and during that time continues to be a member of the council notwithstanding the provisions of the Act relating to the retirement of councillors.[68]

Subject to any standing orders made by the council, anything authorised or required to be done by, to or before the chairman may be done by, to or before the vice-chairman.[69]

Quorum

A quorum of a principal council is one-quarter of the members, but if at any **28–23** time more than one-third of the members is disqualified, the quorum of the council is calculated by reference to those remaining qualified.[70]

There is no statutory provision relating to the quorum of a committee or sub-committee of a principal council; the matter will be governed by standing orders, and if these make no provision, the committee or sub-committee will fix its own quorum.[71]

Order of business

A typical order of business might be as follows: **28–24**

(a) to choose a person to preside if the chairman and vice-chairman be absent;

(b) to transact any business required by statute to be done before any other business;

(c) to approve as a correct record and sign the minutes of the last meeting of the council;

(d) to deal with business expressly required by statute to be done;

(e) to receive petitions presented by council members;

(f) to answer questions asked by residents of the area covered by the authority, pursuant to standing orders;

(g) to dispose of business remaining from the previous meeting;

(h) to receive and consider reports, minutes and recommendations from committees;

(i) to receive and consider reports from the chief executive officer;

(j) to consider notices of motion in the order in which they have been received.

[66] s.5(1).
[67] s.5(1A), inserted by Local Government Act 2000, Sched. 3, para. 3.
[68] s.5(2).
[69] s.5(3).
[70] Sched. 12, paras. 6,45.
[71] s.106.

A large part of the meeting will be taken up by item (h), reports from committees. The procedure here will usually be for the chairman of each committee to move the acceptance of the minutes of the recent meetings of that committee and its sub-committees and the adoption of the recommendations they contain. Questions can then be raised on the matters covered by the minutes to which the committee chairman will reply. Amendments to the proposals contained in the minutes may be put forward, seconded and discussed; again the committee chairman will have a right of reply. At the end of the consideration of each set of committee minutes before the council the council chairman will formally ask for the minutes to be approved: upon this resolution being passed the proposals of each committee become the decision of the council.

An exception relates to matters which have been dealt with under executive powers. Here, as the decision has already been taken by the committee, the minute relating to it comes before the council only for information. Standing orders usually provide that no discussion shall take place on "EP" items unless prior notice of, say, 24 hours has been given by the member wishing to speak.

Notices of motion (item (j)) are usually taken in the order in which they are received, and standing orders will provide that they must be delivered to the council's offices by the proposing member not less than (say) seven clear days before the meeting (but some items, usually relating to procedure, may be moved without notice). This allows time for their incorporation into the notice and agenda for the meeting. Standing orders may say that an item which falls within the province of any committee shall be referred to that committee for consideration and report, unless the council chairman allows it to be dealt with at the council meeting at which it is first brought forward.

Meetings held under executive arrangements

28–25   Executive arrangements put in place by a local authority may include provisions with respect to (a) the quorum, proceedings and location of meetings of the executive; (b) the appointment of committees of the executive; and (c) the quorum, proceedings and location of meetings of committees of the executive.[72] A member of a local authority who is not a member of the authority's executive is entitled to attend, and speak at, a meeting of the executive, or of a committee of the executive, which is held in private only if invited to do so.[73]

4   Parish and Community Councils

Holding of meetings

28–26   A parish council[74] must in every year hold an annual meeting and at least three other meetings. A community council must hold the annual meeting and "such other meetings" as the council may determine.[75]

---

[72] Local Government Act 2000, s.23, Sch. 1, para. 4.
[73] *ibid.*, para. 5.
[74] In this chapter, unless the context otherwise requires, the term "parish council" or "council" should be read as applying equally to a community council.
[75] Sched. 12, paras. 7(1),23(1),24(1).

The annual meeting of the council in a year of ordinary elections to the council must be held within 14 days after the newly elected councillors take office; in other years during the month of May.[76]

A meeting of the council may be held either within or without the council's area but must not be held in premises licensed for the sale of intoxicating liquor, except in cases where no other suitable room is available for such meeting, either free of charge or at a reasonable cost.[77]

Convening of meetings

Notice of council meetings must be given publicly by affixing a notice in some **28–27** conspicuous place,[78] and individually by leaving at or sending by post to his usual place of residence a summons to each member.[79] Three clear days' notice is necessary. Want of service of the notice does not affect the validity of the meeting.[80] The summons to each member must specify the business proposed to be transacted, and be signed by the proper officer of the council.

The chairman of the council may call an extraordinary meeting of the council at any time.[81] If the chairman refuses to call a meeting after a requisition for that purpose signed by two members of the council has been presented to him, or if without so refusing the chairman does not call a meeting within seven days after such requisition has been presented to him, any two members of the council, on that refusal or on the expiration of those seven days, as the case may be, may forthwith convene an extraordinary meeting of the council.[82]

Chairman and vice-chairman

The chairman of the council must be elected annually by the council from **28–28** among the councillors.[83] The first business at the annual meeting of the council is the election of the chairman.[84] The chairman, unless he resigns or becomes disqualified, continues in office until his successor becomes entitled to act as chairman.[85]

The council may appoint a member of the council to be vice-chairman of the council.[86] The vice-chairman, unless he resigns or becomes disqualified, holds office until immediately after the election of a chairman at the next annual meeting of the council.[87] Subject to any standing orders made by the council, anything

---

[76] Sched. 12, paras. 7(2),23(2).
[77] Sched. 12, paras. 10(1),26(1). As from a date to be appointed, paras. 10(1) and 26(1) are to be amended to read "premises which are at the time of such a meeting by, by virtue of a premises licence or temporary event notice under the Licensing Act 2003, be used for the supply of alcohol within the meaning of [s.14 of the Licensing Act 2003])." See also s.134 as to the use of a schoolroom or other room maintainable out of any rate.
[78] Sched. 12, paras. 10(2)(a),26(2)(a). See *West Ham Corporation v. Thomas* (1908) 73 J.P. 65.
[79] Sched. 12, paras. 10(2)(b),26(2)(b).
[80] Sched. 12, paras. 10(3),26(3). For "clear days" see para. 5–10.
[81] Sched. 12, paras. 9(1),25(1).
[82] Sched. 12, paras. 9(2),25(2).
[83] ss.15(1), 34(1).
[84] ss.15(2), 34(2).
[85] ss.15(4), 34(4).
[86] ss.15(6), 34(6).
[87] ss.15(7), 34(7).

authorised or required to be done by, to or before the chairman may be done by, to or before the vice-chairman.[88]

During their terms of office, the chairman and vice-chairman continue to be members of the council, notwithstanding the provisions relating to the retirement of parish councillors.[89]

Conduct of proceedings

28–29   At a meeting of a parish council the chairman of the council, if present, or in his absence the vice-chairman, presides. Should both the chairman and the vice-chairman be absent from a meeting of the council, such councillor as the members of the council present choose presides.[90]

Quorum

28–30   No business can be transacted at a meeting of a parish council unless at least one-third of the whole number of members of the council is present, provided that in no case can the quorum be less than three members.[91] If more than one-third of the members is disqualified, the quorum is calculated in relation to those remaining qualified, subject to there being a minimum of three.[92]

Voting

28–31   The mode of voting at meetings of a parish council is by show of hands, unless the council's standing orders otherwise provide, and on the requisition of any member of the council the voting on any question must be recorded so as to show whether each member present and voting gave his vote for or against that question.[93] If there is an equality of votes, the person presiding has a second or casting vote.[94]

Public Participation

28–32   Standing orders may allow a period of time to be set aside at each council meeting for questions by members of the public—but see paragraph 29–14, below, in relation to the problems which can be caused when a large number of people attend to hear debate on a controversial issue.

5   PARISH AND COMMUNITY MEETINGS[95]

28–33   Local government parishes exist in areas of the rural districts which existed before the organisational changes introduced by the 1972 Act, and where they have been

---

[88] ss.15(9), 34(9).
[89] ss.15(8), 34(8).
[90] Sched. 12, paras. 11, 27.
[91] Sched. 12, paras. 12, 28.
[92] Sched. 12, para. 45.
[93] Sched. 12, paras. 13, 29.
[94] Sched. 12, para. 39(2).
[95] In this section, the term "parish" should not be understood as necessarily applying to a "community"; the main provisions as to communities are set out in para. 28–41 below.

created after 1972 from former urban districts or boroughs. For every such parish there is a parish meeting for the purpose of discussing parish affairs and exercising any functions conferred on the meeting by any enactment.[96] The parish meeting can influence the activities of the parish council, and it provides an excellent forum if the community is faced with a matter of major controversy—for example, a proposal relating to a new road or superstore. Under the Local Government and Rating Act 1997 there was a considerable increase in the role and powers of parishes and community councils.

Holding of meetings

The parish meeting of a parish shall consist of the local government electors for   **28–34**
the parish.[97]

A parish meeting must be held annually between the first day of March and the first day of June in each year, both days inclusive. Where there is no council, the parish meeting must be held at least twice in each year. The proceedings must not commence earlier than 6 pm. Where there is a parish council, the council determines the date and time of the meetings. If there is no parish council, the chairman[98] of the parish meeting fixes the date and time of the meetings.

A parish meeting must not be held in premises licensed for the sale of intoxicating liquor, except in cases where no other suitable room is available for such meeting either free of charge or at a reasonable cost.[99]

Standing orders

If a parish has a parish council, the council may make standing orders for the   **28–35**
parish meeting; if there is no parish council, the parish meeting may, subject to the 1972 Act, regulate its own proceedings.[1]

Convening of meetings

A parish meeting may be convened by (a) the chairman of the parish council, or   **28–36**
(b) any two parish councillors for the parish or, (c) in the case of a parish not having a parish council, the chairman of the parish meeting or any person representing the parish on the district council, or (d) any six local government electors for the parish.[2]

Seven clear days' notice must be given of the meeting by posting a notice of the meeting in some conspicuous place or places in the parish and in such other manner, if any, as appears to the conveners to be desirable for giving publicity to it.[3] The notice must be signed by the person or persons convening the meeting and

---

[96] s.9(1).
[97] s.13(1).
[98] See para. 28–35 below.
[99] Sched. 12, para. 14(1)–(5). As from a date to be appointed, paras. 14(5) is to be amended to read "premises which are at the time of such a meeting by, by virtue of a premises licence or temporary event notice under the Licensing Act 2003, be used for the supply of alcohol within the meaning of [s.14 of the Licensing Act 2003])."
[1] Sched. 12, para. 20.
[2] Sched. 12, para. 15.
[3] Sched. 12, paras. 15(2),(4).

must specify the time and place of the meeting and the business to be transacted.

If the business relates to the establishment or dissolution of a parish council, or the grouping of a parish, not less than 14 days' notice is necessary.[4]

Chairman

28–37   In a parish not having a separate parish council, the parish meeting, subject to any grouping order, must at its annual assembly choose a chairman to serve until a successor is elected.[5] Qualifications and disqualifications are not expressly prescribed by statute as the parish meeting, as such, is not within the definition of a "local authority."[6] A casual vacancy must be filled by the parish meeting convened forthwith for the purpose.[7]

In a parish not having a separate parish council, the chairman of the parish meeting must preside at all assemblies of the parish meeting at which he is present.[8]

In a parish having a separate parish council, the chairman of that council, if present, must preside at a parish meeting and, in his absence, the vice-chairman (if there is one), if present, must preside.[9] If not electors for the parish, however, these persons may not vote; but they can if necessary exercise a casting vote.[10]

If the above persons are absent from an assembly of the parish meeting, the meeting may appoint a person to take the chair, and that person has, for the purpose of that meeting, the powers and authority of the chairman.[11]

Voting

28–38   Subject to the provisions of the 1972 Act, each local government elector may, at a parish meeting or at a poll consequent thereon, give one vote and no more on any question.[12]

A question to be decided by a parish meeting must, in the first instance, be decided by the majority of those present at the meeting and voting thereon, and the decision of the person presiding at the meeting as to the result of the voting is final, unless a poll is demanded.[13]

In the case of an equality of votes thereon, the person presiding at the meeting has a second or casting vote.[14]

A poll may be demanded before the conclusion of a parish meeting on any question arising at the meeting; but no poll shall be taken unless either the person presiding at the meeting consents or the poll is demanded by not less than 10, or one-third, of the local government electors present at the meeting, whichever is

---

[4] Sched. 12, para. 15(3).
[5] s.15(10).
[6] s.270.
[7] s.88(3).
[8] Sched. 12, para. 17(2).
[9] Sched. 12, para. 17(1).
[10] Sched. 12, para. 16.
[11] Sched. 12, para. 17(3).
[12] Sched. 12, para. 18(1).
[13] Sched. 12, para. 18(2).
[14] Sched. 12, para. 18(3).

the less.[15] When a poll is duly called for it will be a poll of the whole parish and must be taken by ballot under rules made by the Secretary of State.[16]

The following case illustrates not only the meaning of "any question arising at the meeting", in the paragraph of Schedule 12 of the Act referred to above, but also the general need for business at a meeting to be placed within the context of a resolution:

> A parish council called a parish meeting to consider a proposal to transfer an area of land to the county council as a public open space in perpetuity. The plaintiff wished to purchase part of this land in order to extend the runway of a civil airport which he operated. He attended the meeting and most of the discussion related to his own proposal, but he did not formally move any amendment to the resolution before the meeting, which related to the open space proposal. This latter was approved by the meeting both on a show of hands and at a poll. The plaintiff later sought an order that a poll should be taken on his own proposal, but the Court of Appeal held that the words "any question arising at the meeting" meant "any question arising for decision"; and a decision (according to Lord Denning, M.R.) could only be taken by a parish meeting either by a resolution being put to and voted on by the meeting or by an amendment to such a resolution being put to and voted on by the meeting.[17]

Minutes

Minutes of the proceedings of a parish meeting, or of a committee thereof, must **28–39** be drawn up and entered in a book provided for that purpose, and must be signed at the same or next ensuing assembly of the parish meeting or meeting of the committee, as the case may be, by the person presiding thereat, and any minute purporting to be so signed shall be received in evidence without further proof.[18]

Until the contrary is proved, a parish meeting or meeting of a committee thereof, in respect of the proceedings whereof a minute has been so made and signed, is deemed to have been duly convened and held, and all the persons present at the meeting are deemed to have been duly qualified, and where the proceedings are those of a committee the committee is deemed to have been duly constituted and to have had power to deal with the matters referred to in the minutes.[19]

It is the duty of the chairman of the parish meeting to take the minutes or to arrange for somebody else present at the meeting to take them. The clerk to the parish council may, and often does, attend and take minutes of the parish meeting, but it is not his duty to do so.

The minutes of the annual parish meeting can be signed either at the same meeting or the next assembly of the parish meeting. The person to sign the

---

[15] Sched. 12, para. 18(4).
[16] Sched. 12, para. 18(5). The rules so made are the Parish and Community Meetings (Polls) Rules 1987, S.I. 1987 No. 1 as amended by the Parish and Community Meetings (Polls) (Amendment) Rules 1987, S.I. 1987 No. 262.
[17] *Bennett v. Chappell* [1966] Ch. 391, C.A.
[18] Sched. 12, para. 19(1).
[19] Sched. 12, para. 19(2).

minutes would be the chairman at the meeting at which they are submitted to be signed. He may not necessarily be the same person who had presided at the meeting in respect of which the minutes were had.

The minutes of the parish meeting should be kept separate from those of the parish council, if any.

In the case of a parish not having a separate parish council, the district council is to provide for the custody of the minutes and other papers if the parish meeting so desires.[20]

Committees

28–40   In a parish not having a separate parish council the parish meeting may, subject to any provisions made by a grouping order and subject to such conditions as the meeting may impose, appoint a committee from among the local government electors for the parish for any purpose, but any such arrangement does not prevent the meeting from exercising those functions.[21]

Community meetings

28–41   As has been stated, the "community" as a local government area takes the place, in Wales, of the "parish" in England. In the main, what has been said above regarding parish meetings applies equally to community meetings. There are, however, slight differences between the effect of the statute in the two cases:

(a) while, in respect of parish meetings, the 1972 Act requires an annual meeting and at least one other in the year, it is provided only that a community meeting may be convened at any time.[22]

(b) The 1972 Act confers on the community meeting, as it does on the parish meeting, the right to regulate its own proceedings by standing orders, but unlike the provision in respect of parish meetings it does not provide for the community council, where there is one, to prescribe standing orders for a community meeting.[23]

(c) In the case of the community meeting, there is no provision for its dates and times to be fixed by the community meeting chairman. This is because no provision being made for an annual meeting, there is no provision for the appointment of a chairman for the year to hold office until a successor is appointed. The chairman of a community meeting is an appointment for the immediate meeting only.[24]

(d) A community meeting may be convened—

    (i) in a case where there is a community council, by the chairman of the council or by any two councillors representing the community on the council; and

    (ii) in any case, by six local government electors for the community.[25]

---

[20] s.227(2).
[21] s.108.
[22] Sched. 12, para. 30.
[23] Sched. 12, para. 36.
[24] Sched. 12, paras. 30(1),33(2).
[25] Sched. 12, para. 30(1).

(e) A parish meeting makes its own arrangements for minuting its proceedings. It may arrange for the district council to have custody of the minute book, but is under no obligation so to do. The minuting of the community meeting is the responsibility of the community council, where there is one, and otherwise of the council of the principal area (*i.e.* a county or county borough) in which the community is situated.[26]

(f) Special arrangements as to notice and procedure on a poll apply in respect of meetings where the business to be transacted includes any of the matters mentioned in section 29B(4) of the 1972 Act (*i.e.* matters concerned generally with the establishment or dissolution of a community council, the grouping of a community with another community or communities and other like items).[27]

---

[26] Sched. 12, para. 35(1).
[27] Sched. 12, para. 30(3).

CHAPTER 29

LOCAL AUTHORITIES[1] AND OTHER BODIES—ACCESS TO MEETINGS AND INFORMATION

1 INTRODUCTION AND HISTORICAL BACKGROUND

29–01 This chapter concerns itself with public rights of access to meetings, and to information, held within the sphere of local government in general and principal, parish and community councils in particular. It aims to provide the reader with a framework that will be at least sufficient as a general guide and, where it is not, to offer direction as to where more specialist information may be obtained.[2] Unsurprisingly the area is one that is subject to a dense thicket of statutory regulation and, of necessity, many of the references that point towards further learning are to legislation.

Yet whilst the area is statute-based now it was not always so. Indeed until the passing of the Local Authorities (Admission of the Press to Meetings) Act 1908, meetings of local authorities were, essentially, private affairs.[3] The 1908 Act itself was, as its name would suggest, concerned with the rights of the press and it was not until the enactment of the Public Bodies (Admission to Meetings) Act 1960 ("the 1960 Act") that the legislature turned its attention to the wider public. The statutory rights there afforded allowed for attendance at the meetings of local authorities and certain other bodies.[4] They were then extended to local authority committees by the 1972 Act.[5]

It is that Act of 1972 which still provides the bedrock for any study of this topic. Since its passing, though, the legislative framework has been subject to a number of significant reforms. The first such was effected by the Local Government (Access to Information) Act 1985.[6] That added (so far as England and Wales are concerned) a new Part VA, in the form of 11 new sections, and also a schedule to the 1972 Act; being sections 100A to 100K and Schedule 12A.[7] It considerably extended public access in the process. The sections and Schedule introduced made provision for access to the meetings and documents of principal councils, a term carefully

---

[1] As defined by the s.48 of the LGA 2000 as opposed to s.270(1) of the 1972 Act.
[2] For a truly detailed study the reader is referred to a loose-leaf such as the five volume *Encyclopedia of Local Government Law* produced by Sweet & Maxwell.
[3] *Tenby Corp. v. Mason* (1908) 6 L.G.R. 233.
[4] For those bodies to which this Act still applies, see para. 29–11 below.
[5] s.100.
[6] As in Chapter 28 ante, this Act will be referred to as "the 1985 Act."
[7] Again using the same nomenclature as in the previous chapter, these will be referred to as (for example) "section 100A of the 1972 Act."

defined,[8] along with those of and pertaining to their committees and sub-committees. They also obliged principal councils to supply the public with agenda and reports in advance of such meetings. Albeit those access rights were made, and remain, subject to certain exclusionary provisions in relation to information deemed "confidential" or "exempt".

In the new millenium the change to executive arrangements forced upon local authorities by Part II of the LGA 2000[9] has compelled re-consideration of the 1972 Act, leading to limited further amendment and more extensive secondary legislation. The reader should also bear in mind the yet more recent coming into force of the Freedom of Information Act 2000 ("the FOI") and the important, but less well known, Environmental Information Regulations 2004 ("the EIA"). The combination of the two has significantly increased the pace of change in relation to public access to information in general and within the local government arena in particular.

Although all are local authorities under the 1972 Act,[10] and share a common corporate character, it is well to remember that principal councils are a very different beast from their parish or community cousins. Indeed in statutes subsequent to the 1972 Act the term "local authority" is used frequently to refer to them alone.[11] Given it is they, rather than parish or community councils, that tend to make decisions touching upon substantive interests it is only right that they should be the focus of this chapter.

2   PRINCIPAL COUNCILS—ACCESS TO MEETINGS

Although in an electronic age access to information has grown in importance, in line with the almost exponential growth of information itself, there remains an instinctive need to attend, bear witness to and, on occasion, be heard at the meetings in which such information is discussed and founds decision. For any number of reasons, amongst them accountability, it is well that this is so. Whereas Schedule 12 to the 1972 Act tends to govern the calling and conduct of meetings it is Part VA that deals with access.   **29–02**

Section 100A of the 1972 Act provides that a meeting of a principal council[12] shall be open to the public except to the extent that they are excluded (whether during the whole or part of the proceedings) under the provisions relating to confidential[13] or exempt information.[14] By section 100E this obligation is expressly stated to include committees and sub-committees of a principal council; effectively

---

[8] See para. 28–01 ante and s.100J of the 1972 Act. . Reference to a principal council includes a reference to a joint authority, the Common Council of the City of London, the authority established by the Norfolk and Suffolk Broads Act 1988, a National Park authority, a joint board or joint committee which is constituted as a body corporate and which discharges the functions of two or more principal councils, a police authority established under s.3 of the Police Act 1996 and a combined fire authority.

[9] Again see para. 28–01 ante.

[10] 1972 Act, s.270(1).

[11] For example the LGA 2000, see note 1 supra.

[12] See note 8 above.

[13] s.100A(2)

[14] s.100A(4).

an extension of section 1 of the 1960 Act to such meetings with some modifications It is probable that the 1972 Act does not, however, cover a meeting outside the normal committee structure, *e.g.* an informal "group" meeting of a political party.

Be aware also that meetings of a local authority executive or a committee of an executive are now governed by a regime that, although similar, is distinct. As most of the important decisions taken by principal councils will now be taken by the "executive" it is well to understand it. By virtue of section 22(9) of the LGA 2000 a principal council may decide whether "executive" meetings are to be open or private, unless already determined by regulations. The Local Authorities (Executive Arrangements)(Access to Information)(England) Regulations 2000 ("the 2000 Regulations")[15] in many respects ensure that the provisions of the 1972 Act apply also to executive arrangements.

The 2000 Regulations make public access to meetings, documents and decisions where an executive, a committee of an executive or an executive member is to make a "key decision", or a matter included in the "forward plan" discussed, the general rule. A "key decision", in general, is one which is; (a) likely to result in expenditure or savings that are "significant" in relation to the budget for the service or function to which the decision relates; or (b) "significant" in terms of its effects on communities living or working in an area comprising two or more wards or electoral divisions in the principal council's area.

Whether a meeting is "executive" or no public notice must be given. Thus the time and place of the meeting must be posted at the council offices at least five clear[16] days beforehand or, if the meeting is convened at shorter notice,[17] at the time it is convened. The requirement was formerly three clear days.[18] Where an executive meeting concerns a "key decision" the 2000 Regulations impose detailed requirements for preparation and publication of a document stating, *inter alia*, that key decisions are to be made, that a forward plan containing particulars of those decisions will be prepared monthly and that this, along with relevant documents, will be made available.[19]

Exclusion

29–03   Whilst the meeting is open to the public the council shall not have the power to exclude members of the public from the meeting.[20] However whatever the type of meeting the public either may or must be excluded during an item of business whenever it is likely, in view of the nature of the business or of the proceedings, that if members of the public were present, certain information would be disclosed.[21] In general this means "confidential" or "exempt" information. The

---

[15] S.I. 2000 No. 3272 as amended. For Wales see the Local Authorities (Executive Arrangements)(Decisions, Documents and Meetings)(Wales) Regulations 2001 (S.I. 2001 No. 2290) as amended.

[16] Regulation 10 of the 2000 Regulations in respect of executive meetings and s.100A(6)(a) of the 1972 Act for others. Here the reference to "clear days" has been defined as excluding days other than working weekdays, so that Saturday and Sunday are excluded from the calculation: see *R v. Swansea City Council, ex p. Elitestone Ltd* (1993) 66 P. C.R. 422, C.A.

[17] An event both unlikely and certainly requiring real justification.

[18] Para. 4 to Sch. 12, 1972 Act.

[19] Regulation 11(2)

[20] s.100A(6)(a).

[21] s.100A(2).

distinction between the two is interesting and calls for careful consideration as and when the question arises.

"*Confidential information*" means information furnished to the council by a government department upon terms which forbid disclosure to the public and information the disclosure of which is prohibited by or under any enactment or court order.[22] Here the public must be excluded. There is no discretion. Note, though, that the statutory definition of the term is probably narrower than that at common law.

"*Exempt information*" means information exempted by description under Schedule 12A of the 1972 Act. That is more of a checklist provision than anything else. Here the council may by resolution exclude the public but do not have to. There is, then, a discretion. Hence whenever as regards a meeting as a whole or an item of business within a meeting it is likely, in view of the nature of the business or of the proceedings, that if members of the public were present there would be an exempt disclosure, as defined in section 100I and schedule 12A to the 1972 Act, the council, committee or sub-committee, as the case may be, have a choice to make and a resolution will be required.[23] The resolution must identify the proceedings or the part of the proceedings to which it applies and state the description, in terms of Schedule 12A, of the exempt information in question.

As to Schedule 12A itself the schedule is lengthy and only a much-reduced summary of its main categories is offered as follows:

1. Information relating to particular council employees or to council tenants, or to any particular applicant for or recipient of services or financial assistance from the council;
2. Information relating to the adoption, care, fostering or education of any particular child;
3. Information relating to the financial or business affairs of any individual;
4. The amount of any proposed expenditure under any particular contract for property, goods or services and the details of proposed contract terms;
5. The identity of the authority as a person offering a tender for a contract;
6. Information relating to labour relations matters;
7. Instructions to, and opinions of, counsel;
8. Information relevant to notices and orders proposed to be given or made by the council;
9. Any action relating to crime prevention, investigation or prosecution; and
10. The identity of a protected informant.

In addition, and particularly in respect of "executive" public meetings, the advice of a political adviser or assistant is also exempted.[24]

---

[22] s.100A(3).
[23] s.100A(4).
[24] Regulation 21 of the 2000 Regulations.

As noted by others elsewhere[25] it is possible that the exemptions might lead to the exclusion, by virtue of their status as a member of the public, of the very person who provided the "exempt" information. The suggestion that, where this concerns an "appeal" from an officer's decision, careful thought should be given to the exclusion of that person is endorsed. Indeed considerations of natural justice may well force the decision maker's hand in this regard.

The rights of exclusion conferred by section 100A are without prejudice to any power of exclusion to suppress or prevent disorderly conduct or other misbehaviour at a meeting.[26]

Rights of the press

29–04   In general, the press enjoys no rights of admission to meetings of a principal council over and above those enjoyed by members of the public. However the authority is required, so far as practicable, to provide duly accredited representatives of the press, attending the meeting for the purpose of reporting the proceedings, with reasonable facilities for taking their report. In addition, and unless the meeting is held in premises not belonging to the council or not connected to the telephone system, the authority is required to provide, so far as practicable, facilities by which such persons may telephone such a report at their own expense.[27]

For the avoidance of doubt so far as photography, recording or live transmission is concerned there is nothing to require a meeting of a principal council to permit the taking of any photographs of any proceedings or the use of any means to enable persons not present to see or hear any proceedings, whether at the time or later, or the making of any oral report of any proceedings as they take place.[28]

3   PRINCIPAL COUNCILS—ACCESS TO INFORMATION

General

29–05   As noted above the FOI has formally opened up great swathes of material previously denied the public. As regards information of an "environmental" nature the EIR offer a separate, mutually exclusive, regime under which rights of access are probably as broad as those provided for under the FOI and, interestingly, can be sought against a wider range bodies. There is no room here for a consideration of what is a very complicated scheme. Rather it is right to merely to note its existence, the need to be alert for "environmental" content, and that, as a result of privatisation and PPP, many private companies now performing public functions will be affected by it. For more information the reader is referred to one of the various specialist texts.[29] Instead the focus must, necessarily, be on the nut and bolt

---

[25] At page 2108 of the *Encyclopedia of Local Government Law* cited supra.
[26] s.100A(8). *See R. v. Brent Health Authority, ex p. v. Francis* [1985] 1 All E.R. 74.
[27] s.100A(6)(c). See also paras. 29–08 and 29–13.
[28] s.100A(7).
[29] Of which one of the more up to date is *Information Rights* (Philip Coppell, 2004, Sweet & Maxwell).

mechanics of information prepared for, produced by and connected with the meetings of principal councils.

As before this is to be found in Part VA of the 1972 Act. The various Part VA sections make provision for public access to a variety of such documents. Section 100H catches all of them by providing that any document directed by any provision in its fellow Part VA sections to be open to inspection shall, accordingly, be so at all reasonable hours and without payment. An exception relates to documents which are open to inspection under section 100D(1), *i.e.* those termed "background papers", where a reasonable charge may be made for the facility. Where a document is open to inspection the person making the inspection may make copies of the document or extracts or require the person having custody of the document to supply to him a photographic copy of or extract from the document. Subject, though, to payment of a reasonable fee for the privilege.[30] However nothing in the section authorises a breach of copyright unless owned by the principal council itself.[31]

Before the meeting

Under section 100B copies of the agenda for a meeting of a principal council **29–06** and copies of any report for the meeting shall be open to inspection by members of the public at the offices of the council. Subject to the same exclusionary provisions for confidential and exempt matters as apply for actual access to the meetings. Again the section extends to committees and sub-committees of a principal council.[32]

As with notices for meetings such documents shall be open to inspection at least five clear days before the meeting. This is subject to the same exception regarding convention of a meeting at shorter than five clear days' notice. There is also an exception in respect of an item added to an agenda copies of which are already open to inspection by the public.[33] Hence:

(a) Where the meeting is convened at shorter than five clear days notice, the copies of the agenda and reports shall be open to inspection from the time the meeting is convened; and

(b) Where an item is added to an agenda copies of which are open to inspection by the public copies of the item, or of the revised agenda, and copies of any report for the meeting relating to the item shall be open to inspection from the time the item is added to the agenda.

The public has no right to the agenda copies until they are available to members of the council.[34] Further an item of business may not be considered at a meeting unless either:

---

[30] s.100H(2).
[31] s.100H(3). Where the principal council own the copyright then there is, of course, no breach. Only waiver.
[32] s.100E(1).
[33] s.100B(3).
[34] s.100B(3).

(a) A copy of the agenda including the item, or a copy of the item, is open to inspection by members of the public as described above for at least five clear days before the meeting or, where the meeting is convened at shorter notice, from the time the meeting is convened; or

(b) By reason of special circumstances, which shall be specified in the minutes, the chairman of the meeting is of the opinion that the item should be considered at the meeting as a matter of urgency.[35]

Where a meeting is required by section 100A to be open to the public during the whole of the proceedings or any part of them there must be made available for the use of members of the public present at the meeting a reasonable number of copies of the agenda and of the reports for the meeting.[36]

As noted the obligation under section 100B to provide copies of reports is subject to the qualification that the proper officer[37] may, if he thinks fit, exclude from the copies provided for public inspection the whole or any part of any report which, in his "opinion", relates only to items during the discussion of which the meeting is likely not to be open to the public.[38] Again this provision raises the question of which matters do and which matters do not involve confidential or exempt information within the meaning of section 100A. It presents a potentially interesting problem. Possession of relevant documents prior to any meeting is necessarily crucial to the ability of the public to play any meaningful part in both the meeting itself and the preliminaries to it. However, statute leaves the decision very much at the officer's discretion and, indeed, within the realm of his "opinion". So any court challenge aimed at forcing production of the excised document or excised parts of a document would not only have to be expedited, given the five clear day timeframe, but also surmount a high threshold test in order to succeed.[39]

After the meeting

29–07   Section 100C of the 1972 Act provides that after a meeting of a principal council certain documents must be open to inspection by members of the public at the offices of the council until the expiration of a period of six years beginning with the date of the meeting. Those documents[40] are:

(a) The minutes or a copy of the minutes of the meeting, excluding so much of the minutes of proceedings during which the meeting was not open to the public as discloses exempt information;

(b) A copy of the agenda; and

(c) A copy of so much of any report for the meeting as relates to any item during which the meeting was open to the public.

---

[35] s.100B(4).
[36] s.100B(6).
[37] s.270.
[38] s.100B(2).
[39] *Padfield v. Minister of Agriculture* [1968] A.C. 997.
[40] Listed at s.100C(1).

Of these normally the minutes will be the most significant followed, probably, by any report. Previously minutes of meetings where merely delegated, as opposed to referred, powers were being exercised were open to inspection only on discretionary, rather than legal, basis.[41] It should be understood that the word "report" means just that; works in progress that may one day become reports to be placed before a principal council or one of its committees but have not yet been so are not open to inspection.[42]

It may be that, in consequence of the exclusion of parts of the minutes which disclose exempt information, the minutes open to inspection do not provide members of the public with a reasonably fair and coherent record of the whole or part of the proceedings. If so the proper officer shall make a written summary of the proceedings or the part, as the case may be, that provides such a record but without disclosing the exempt information. In other words the officer must do his or her best to produce a coherent account that yet gives nothing away. The summary produced must then be made available for inspection.[43]

Again the section applies to committees and sub-committees of the principal council. As noted this reverses the position whereby, prior to the passing of the 1972 Act, there was no general right of access to the minutes of such meetings except when the minutes of a committee exercising referred powers were submitted to the council for approval[44] or when access was expressly required by statute.

As regards "executive" meetings the 2000 Regulations, at Part II,[45] formalise similar requirements. They impose an obligation for a written record of the meeting, termed a "written statement", to be produced by the proper officer or person presiding after the meeting. This is the case whether the meetings are public or private, subject to the now-familiar exemptions.[46] Such statements are to contain information as to each and every executive decision reached. This is to include a record of the decision itself, the reasons for it, any alternatives considered and rejected and any conflict of interest arising. The statement must be made available for inspection by members of the public at the principal authority's offices at all reasonable hours[47] as soon as is reasonably practicable. It is to be accompanied by any relevant report, a list of the relevant "background papers" and at least one copy of the documents in that list.

Inspection of background papers

Under section 100D the public has the right to inspect background papers for **29–08** reports which have to be made available for inspection under sections 100B and 100C. Note, however, that in regard to the latter section, *i.e.* regarding minutes *etcetera*, the period during which the papers have to be made available is four years rather than six.[48]

[41] *Wilson v. Evans* [1962] 1 All E.R. 247.
[42] *Maile v. Wigan MBC* (27/05/1999) Eady J, where the issue concerned a database containing unfinished work regarding contaminated sites in the area.
[43] s.100C(1)(*b*). See also *Administrator*, July 1990, p. 28.
[44] *Williams v. Manchester Corporation* (1897) 45 W.R. 412.
[45] Regulations 3 to 6.
[46] See Regulation 21.
[47] Regulation 22(1).
[48] s.100D(2).

The proper officer[49] must prepare a list of the background papers for the report and provide at least one copy of each of the documents included in that list. These have to be available for public inspection at the offices of the council.[50] Background papers are those relating to the subject-matter of the report which; (a) disclose facts or matters on which, in the opinion of the proper officer, the report or an important part of it is based; and (b) are papers which have, in his opinion, been relied on to a material extent in preparing the report. They do not, though, include any published works.[51] Similarly in relation to "executive" meetings what constitutes a "background paper" is a matter for the individual officer concerned. Of course nothing in section 100D requires the inclusion of exempt information or authorises the disclosure of confidential information.[52]

Rights of the press

29–09   In relation to the information disclosure provisions the only additional right conferred on the press is that contained in section 100B, subsection (7) of which states that there must, on request and on payment of postage or other necessary charge for transmission, be supplied for the benefit of any newspaper:

> (i) A copy of the agenda for a meeting of the principal council or, again, of its committees or sub-committees[53];
> (ii) subject to the same exclusion of items which relate to confidential or exempt information as applies to the public's right to inspect[54] a copy of each of the reports for the meeting;
> (iii) such further statements or particulars, if any, as are necessary to indicate the nature of the items included in the agenda; and
> (iv) if the proper officer[55] thinks fit copies of any other documents supplied to members of the council in connection with any item.

This is mirrored by the 2000 Regulations in respect of executive meetings. There again the press enjoy slightly heightened rights in that copies of relevant documents must be transmitted to them on request subject to payment of any necessary charge.[56] By contrast it appears that members of the general public must attend in person.[57]

Rights of members of the council

29–10   As individuals elected through democratic franchise members of a principal council, like their slightly more exalted Westminster equivalents, have their feet in two quite distinct camps; the corporate body that is the principal council and their

---

[49] s.270.
[50] s.100D(1).
[51] s.100D(5).
[52] s.100D(4).
[53] s.100E(1).
[54] See para. 29–06.
[55] As defined by s.270.
[56] Regulation 5.
[57] Regulation 22(2).

electoral ward. Accordingly they enjoy not only particular rights to information but also, if "enjoy" is the right word, consequential dilemmas. Put simply often the needs of the authority conflict with those of an individual elector or part of the electorate.

By section 100F of the 1972 Act any document that, (a) is in the possession or under the control of a principal council and (b) contains material relating to any business to be transacted at a meeting of the council or a committee or sub-committee of the council, shall be open to inspection by any member of the council. Provided, as before, that the document does not, in the opinion of the proper officer,[58] relate to certain categories of exempt information.

The rights conferred by the section on a member of a principal council are in addition to, rather than exclusionary of, any other rights he may have apart from the section.[59] This is significant because at common law a council member *prima facie* has the right to inspect documents which are addressed to the council. That right arises naturally from the duty of the member to keep himself informed of matters which are relevant to his function as an elected representative:

> Foster parents of a child placed in the care of Birmingham District Council applied to adopt. The matter was given lengthy consideration in the course of which a councillor applied to see papers held by the council's social services committee. Of which she was not a member. The context was that, as a member of the council's housing committee, the councillor was in possession of information about the applicants which had convinced her that the adoption ought not to be approved. The councillor's request to see the papers held by the social services committee was opposed not by the council but by the prospective adoptive parents. *Held,* a councillor who is not a member of a particular committee must demonstrate a "need to know" before access to documentary material can be granted. Further the decision as to whether such a need exists is ultimately a matter for the full council but one that can be delegated.[60]

On the facts of the *Birmingham* case the House of Lords ruled that the councillor was entitled to see the files in the social services department. As a result the case is often taken as giving strong support for a member's right to full access. Yet no member has an absolute right to see documents. Mere curiosity is not sufficient[61] nor, for example, is the wish to help an individual who is in dispute with the council.[62]

If a councillor can establish a "need to know", and hence a right to access, the provisions in section 100F that relate to exempt information will offer no bar to such access. As stated the rights conferred by the section are in addition to a member's common law rights rather than exclusionary of them. There is authority, too, to the effect that once a councillor has established a "need to know" sufficient to show entitlement to papers held by, *e.g.*, a sub-committee of which he or she is not a member, then the councillor is necessarily entitled also to attend that

---

[58] s.270.
[59] s.100F(5).
[60] *R. v. City of Birmingham District Council ex p. O* [1983] 1 All E.R. 497, H.L.
[61] *R. v. Southwold Corp.* (1907) 5 L.G.R. 888.
[62] *R. v. Hampstead Borough Council* (1917) 15 L.G.R. 309.

meeting.[63] This, though, should not be pushed too far. Even if a need to know exists a councillor will not usually be entitled to attend bodies such as working parties where a need to know is outweighed by other factors, such as the likelihood that frank discussion will be inhibited.[64]

Returning from the common law to the statutory so far as "executive" matters are concerned here too members enjoy enhanced rights of access by virtue of Part IV to the 2000 Regulations. Any document in the possession or under the control of the executive containing information related to any business to be transacted at public meeting must be made available for inspection, whilst for private meetings such documentation must be made available immediately upon the meeting's conclusion.[65] Subject, as ever, to the right to avoid disclosure of specified categories of exempt information[66] or advice provided by a "political adviser or assistant".[67] Similar access rights apply in respect of the members of an overview and scrutiny committee.

Additional information to be published by principal councils

29–11   By section 100G of the 1972 Act[68–69] principal councils must maintain a register stating the name and address of each member of the council and the ward or division which he represents. This may one day be extended to include the name and address of each committee and sub-committee member. The council must also maintain a list of powers delegated to officers under statute, except where the delegation is for a period not exceeding six months.[70] Further at the office of every council must be kept a written summary of the rights to attend meetings of the principal council and its committees and sub-committees, and to inspect and copy documents.[71]

The register, the list and the summary maintained under this section must be open to inspection by the public at the offices of the council.[72]

4   ACCESS TO MEETINGS OF BODIES OTHER THAN PRINCIPAL COUNCILS

29–12   As noted the sections introduced into the 1972 Act by the 1985 Act relate to principal councils.[73] Certain other bodies, left behind by the flow of legislation

---

[63] *R. v. Hackney London Borough Council, ex p. Gamper* [1985] 1 W.L.R. 1229; *R. v. Sheffield City Council, ex p. Chadwick, The Times,* December 19, 1985.

[64] *R. v. Eden District Council, ex p. Moffatt, The Independent,* December 16, 1988.

[65] Regulation 17.

[66] 1972 Act, Sched. 12A, Pt I paras 1–6, 9, 11, 12 and 14.

[67] As appointed under s.9 of the Local Government and Housing Act 1989 or by regulations made under Sched. 1, para. 6 to the LGA 2000 (*i.e.,* a mayor's assistant).

[68–69] Subject to amendment, as from a day that remains to be appointed and, it can be assumed from that, will likely never come, by the Local Government Act 1989 Sched. 11, para. 24.

[70] s.100G(2).

[71] s.100G(3).

[72] s.100G(4).

[73] For definition, see para. 29–01 supra.

aimed at the principal organs of local government, remain regulated by the Public Bodies (Admission to Meetings) Act 1960.[74] These include:

(a) Parish or community councils, the Council of the Isles of Scilly and joint boards or joint committees which discharge the functions of any of those bodies (or of any of those bodies and those of a principal council);

(b) The parish meetings of rural parishes;

(c) The Land Authority for Wales;

(d) Health Authorities;

(e) Certain other bodies having, under the Public Works Loans Act 1875, power to levy a rate;

(f) Regional and local flood defence committees;

(g) Advisory committees established and maintained under section 12 or 13 of the Environment Act 1995; and

(h) Customer service committees maintained under section 28 of the Water Industry Act 1991.

The 1960 Act, as amended by Schedule 2, para. 6 of the 1985 Act, also applies to committees of parish and community councils.

By section 1(1) of the 1960 Act, it is provided that any meeting of a body to which the 1960 Act applies shall be open to the public.

Exclusion by resolution

The body affected may, however, by resolution exclude the public, whether **29–13** during the whole or part of the proceedings, whenever publicity would be prejudicial to the public interest by reason of: (a) the confidential nature of the business to be transacted; or (b) other special reasons stated in the resolution and arising from the nature of that business or of the proceedings.[75] The body is obliged by the 1960 Act to specifically state in the resolution the reason for its decision that the public is to be excluded. There exists the possibility of legal challenge through the administrative courts should the power to exclude be used unreasonably or improperly.

In relation to this power an affected body may treat the need to receive or consider recommendations or advice from sources other than members, committees or sub-committees of the body as a special reason why publicity would be prejudicial to the public interest. It may do so without regard to the subject or purport of the recommendations or advice.[76] By way of example:

A committee met to consider whether more hackney carriage licences should be issued to taxi drivers in the area. Forty members of the public wished to attend the meeting but there were only 14 seats available for the press, the public and those making representations to the committee. The chairman suggested to the committee that it was not practicable, given the limited

---

[74] This Act will be referred to as "the 1960 Act." Reference will also be made to Circular no. 45/75 of April 16, 1975 issued by the Department of the Environment (the "Circular").

[75] 1960 Act, s.1(2).

[76] 1960 Act, s.1(3).

seating available, to open the meeting to the public and, further, that it was desirable that those making representations should be heard in the absence of those making conflicting representations. A resolution broadly to this effect was passed. *Held* that the two reasons for the committee's deliberate decision to exclude the public amounted to "special reasons" within the meaning of section 1(2) of the 1960 Act[77] and hence the exclusion was lawful.

Necessary arrangements

29–14   Where the 1960 Act requires that a meeting or part of a meeting be open to the public then they must be given notice of both its time and place. This notice must be posted at the offices of the body or, if it has no office, at some central and conspicuous place in the area with which it is concerned three clear days at least before the meeting. Alternatively, if the meeting is convened at shorter notice, then at the time it is convened.[78] Note that the "three clear days" requirement has not been altered upwards to "five clear days" as it has with principal councils.

In addition the body shall, on request and on payment of postage or other necessary charge for transmission, supply for the benefit of any newspaper[79] a copy of the agenda for the meeting as supplied to members of the body. Subject, though, to exclusion, if the body thinks fit, of any item during which the meeting is likely not to be open to the public. Such agenda supplied to the press are to be accompanied by such further statements or particulars, if any, as are necessary to indicate the nature of the items included or, if thought fit in the case of any item, with copies of any reports or other documents supplied to members of the body in connection with the item.[80] While the statutory right to receive these documents is given only to the press it is naturally desirable that they also be distributed to members of the public who attend a meeting in person so that they may follow the proceedings.[81]

As with principal councils for so long as the meeting is open to the public the body holding it has no power to exclude members of the public. In addition, and similarly, duly accredited representatives of the press must, so far as practicable, be afforded reasonable facilities for taking their report and, unless the meeting is held in premises not belonging to the body or not connected to the telephone network, for telephoning any such report at their own expense.[82] By way of practical example "facilities" would suggest chairs and a table conveniently placed so that reporters can both hear and see what is going on.[83] The authority may in its discretion permit the taking of photographs of any proceedings, or the use of any means to enable persons to see or hear the proceedings, or the making of any oral report while the proceedings are going on.[84] There is, though, no right to such.

---

[77] *R. v. Liverpool City Council, ex p. Liverpool Taxi Fleet Operators' Association* [1975] 1 W.L.R. 701.
[78] 1960 Act, s.1(4)(*a*).
[79] See 1960 Act, s.1(7). The expression includes a news agency and any organisation systematically engaged in collecting news for sound or television broadcasts.
[80] 1960 Act, s.1(4)(*b*).
[81] App. to Circular, para. 7.
[82] 1960 Act, s.1(4)(*c*).
[83] App. to Circular, para. 8.
[84] 1960 Act, s.1(7), and App. to Circular, para. 8.

Where a body to which the 1960 Act applies resolves to turn itself into committee, the proceedings in committee are treated as forming part of the proceedings of the body at the meeting.[85]

The provisions described above are without prejudice to any power of exclusion to suppress or prevent disorderly conduct or other misbehaviour.[86] To which we now turn.

Maintenance of order

Parish council meetings tend to be informal affairs. That is to be applauded in   **29–15** so far as it aids public participation and confidence. However this positive can have a negative side; friendly informality can quickly descend into something less conducive to a well-run meeting and pose the chairman a particular problem. If feelings run high large numbers of people may attend. As debate proceeds the public may try to join in. The chairman must suppress this immediately. A particular danger is the demagogue-councillor whose words are supported by cheers from a faction within the audience. There are, though, certain steps which may be taken, and suggestions that may be followed, which may help to maintain order.

Layout of venue: The public's seating should be a good distance from the councillors. This avoids any ordinary risk that a councillor will feel threatened by their audience. However the public must still be able to hear. Hence for particular occasions the hire of audio equipment may be appropriate.

Agenda management: If the agenda includes questions from the public it is often wise to deal with these early in the meeting. If a difficult decision is to be taken by the council, and it is debated before question-time, public interruption will be difficult to control and the business at hand disadvantaged as a result.

Red herrings: The public should be reminded that the rules of debate must and will be followed. Indeed the public should probably first be reminded of what the rules of debate comprise.[87] Speakers must be allowed to deliver their argument without interruption, save for properly regulated points of order, in the time allotted. Courtesy must prevail at all times and no scurrilous or slanderous remarks will be allowed.

Minutes

By section 228 of the 1972 Act the minutes of a parish or community council   **29–16** and a parish meeting are available for inspection by electors. This same right also applies to joint authorities, police authorities and the Metropolitan Police authority and may be exercised even by a person acing as an agent for an elector.[88]

---

[85] 1960 Act, s.1(6).
[86] 1960 Act, s.1(8).
[87] *The Oxford Union Guide to Successful Public Speaking* (Hughes and Phillips) may assist.
[88] *R v. Glamorganshire County Council* [1936] 2 All E.R. 168.

CHAPTER 30

DEFAMATORY STATEMENTS

30–01 In a work of this nature it would be inappropriate to embark upon any study of the subject of defamation in depth; the proper place for such treatment is a work on tort. However, those who accept responsibility for the conduct of meetings, whether public or private, should have some awareness of the nature of defamation and the liabilities it entails.

Neither the Defamation Act 1952 nor the Defamation Act 1996 provide a definition of defamation, but one which gathers into a single phrase expressions from the dicta of various distinguished judges is offered in *Halsbury's Laws of England*[1]:

> "A defamatory statement is a statement which tends to lower a person in the estimation of right-thinking members of society generally, or to cause him to be shunned or avoided or to expose him to hatred, contempt or ridicule, or to convey an imputation on him disparaging or injurious to him in his office, profession, calling, trade or business."

Defamation is a personal matter, and a meeting, as such, can neither defame nor be defamed. A corporation, however, as it possesses legal personality, can be defamed where the words complained of reflect on the corporation and are proved damaging to its business (for example the conduct of its business or its solvency) and not just on its individual officers or members.[2] A corporation can also be guilty of defamation. A local authority[3] and a trade union (but not a political party) can sue for defamation. A meeting is not a corporation, however, and even a company meeting is not the company, but a gathering together of individuals whose deliberations control and determine the company's decisions. Although this is so, it is possible for a company or other corporation to become legally liable for statements made at a company meeting if those statements are made by a person who can be shown to have acted as its servant or agent.

When defamatory words are written or spoken of a class of persons, it is not open to a member of that class to say that the words were spoken of him unless there was something to show that the words about the class refer to him as an individual. In cases of this kind two questions must be asked: first, one of law, whether the words are capable of referring to the plaintiff; secondly, one of fact, whether reasonable people who know the plaintiff think the words refer to him.[4]

---

[1] (4th ed.), Vol. 28, para. 10.
[2] *Multigroup Bulgaria Holding AD v. Oxford Analytica Ltd* [2001] EMLR 28.
[3] See *Bognor Regis UDC v. Campion* [1972] 2 All E.R. 61, and s.221 of the Local Government Act 1972.
[4] *Knupffer v. London Express Newspaper Co. Ltd* [1944] A.C. 116, H.L.

1 LIBEL AND SLANDER

It is necessary to distinguish between the two kinds of defamation, "libel" and   **30–02**
"slander." Traditionally, and in broad terms, libel is written, and slander is spoken.
The importance of the distinction is that while libel is actionable *per se* and will
attract damages whether or not the plaintiff can show actual loss, slander, apart
from certain exceptions to be mentioned later, is actionable only upon proof of
special damage. This simple distinction between libel and slander has become
blurred, however, and is likely to be more so because of the advance of technology,
and this is important in considering the subject of defamation as affecting meetings.

Even before the 1952 Act, when the old distinction rested squarely on the
question whether the words complained of were written or only spoken, a
broadening of the definition of libel had been made in a celebrated case[5] so that it
included words recorded on the sound track of a film. Nowadays, radio, television
and video recordings will be treated as libel.

To be actionable as libel or slander a statement must defame, and must therefore
basically be untrue. If true, words cannot, in legal theory, destroy any reputation
which a person complaining of them deserves to possess. It is important to
recognise, however, that it is one thing to believe, or even to know, that words are
true, and another to prove that they are true in the strict sense required for a
defence of justification (see below). Therefore, if statements derogatory of any
person are made at a meeting, the chairman or sponsor of the meeting must
intervene and exercise control; otherwise the adverse consequences could be
incalculable.

Slanders which are actionable without proof of special damage are those
which:

(a) are calculated to disparage a person in any office, profession, calling, trade
   or business held or carried on by him at the time of the publication[6];

(b) impute that a person has committed any crime which is punishable by
   imprisonment;

(c) impute that a person is currently suffering from disease which would tend
   to exclude him from society; or

(d) impute unchastity or adultery to a woman or girl.[7]

Special damage means, in essence, that the plaintiff has suffered material or
pecuniary loss.

2 MALICE

The plaintiff does not have to prove malice unless the defendant succeeds in   **30–03**
showing that the words were published on a privileged occasion. The plaintiff may

---

[5] *Youssoupoff v. Metro-Goldwyn-Mayer Pictures Ltd* (1934) 50 T.L.R. 581, C.A.
[6] Defamation Act 1952, s.2.
[7] Slander of Women Act 1891.

defeat a plea of qualified privilege, privileged report or fair comment (defences which are discussed below[8]) by proof of express or actual malice.

Malice, in this sense, means a wrong motive which dominated the defendant at the time of the publication. Knowledge of the falsity of a statement, or a reckless disregard of whether it be true or false, gives rise to a presumption that publication was malicious, but "irrationality, stupidity or obstinacy do not constitute malice, though in an extreme case they may be some evidence of it."[9] Where malice was proved against one of three partners who were signatories to a letter admitted to be defamatory, but qualified privilege applied, liability attached only to the partner guilty of malice.[10] Similarly, where a letter was written on an occasion of qualified privilege and the assistant secretary and three members of the committee were not actuated by malice, the malice of the other seven signatories did not defeat the plea of privilege of those not actuated by malice.[11]

Where there is no evidence of malice in the words themselves, evidence may be given of connected or surrounding circumstances to show the malicious state of the defendant's mind, so that, for example, evidence may be given to show the tone or atmosphere of a meeting in order to establish that the defendant was actuated by some improper motive, such as a desire to harm the plaintiff in retaliation or spite.[12]

3 THE STATEMENT

30–04 In order to be actionable the words used must be capable of conveying to the minds of reasonable persons an imputation about the plaintiff which would bring him into hatred, ridicule or contempt, or lower him in their estimation. Mere hurt feelings are insufficient to found an action. Where the words used are not defamatory in themselves but only by reason of extrinsic circumstances, the plaintiff must prove the facts causing the words to have a defamatory meaning to those persons to whom they were published.

This is called the innuendo and, in the true sense, it must be supported by extrinsic facts which establish the special meaning and not merely by an interpretation of the words themselves, but it can include cases where the "sting" lies not so much in the words themselves as in what the ordinary man will infer from them.[13]

4 PUBLICATION

30–05 Proof of publication is an essential feature of the civil action. Publication must be to a third person.

---

[8] paras. 30–06 to 30–12.
[9] *Turner v. Metro-Goldwyn Mayer Pictures Ltd* [1950] 1 All E.R. 449, 463, *per* Lord Porter.
[10] *Meekins v. Henson and Others* [1964] 1 Q.B. 472.
[11] *Egger v. Chelmsford (Viscount)* [1965] 1 Q.B. 248.
[12] See generally on the subject of malice, *Horrocks v. Lowe* [1975] A.C. 135.
[13] *Grubb v. Bristol United Press Ltd* [1963] 1 Q.B. 309. *Lewis v. Daily Telegraph Ltd* [1964] A.C. 234.

The writer of a libel publishes it as soon as he does anything with the writing which permits it to be seen by any person other than the person defamed, so that transmitting a libel by postcard[14] or by telegram[15] is publication. Publication may also be found where the defendant knew or might have expected that a letter would be opened and read by someone other than the plaintiff as, for instance, the spouse of the plaintiff[16] or his clerk.[17] A slander is published when the words are uttered in the presence of a third person.

Any person into whose hands a libel falls is liable for publication of the libel as soon as he permits it to be seen by any person other than the person defamed, unless he can show that he neither knew nor ought to have known that the writing contained a libel.[18] Booksellers, libraries and newspaper distributors can generally escape liability under this head and this type of defence has now been made statutory by section 1 of the Defamation Act 1996. The defence is available to a person other than the author, editor or publisher (as defined in each case) if such a person can show that he took reasonable care in relation to the publication of the statement and that he did not know and had no reason to believe that what he did caused or contributed to the publication of a defamatory statement. A person shall not be considered the author, editor or publisher of a statement if he is only involved—

    (a) in printing, producing, distributing or selling printed material containing the statement;

    (b) in processing (etc.) a film or sound recording containing the statement;

    (c) in processing (etc.) any electronic medium in which the statement is recorded, or ancillary actions;

    (d) as the broadcaster of a live programme containing the statement when he had no effective control over the maker of the statement; and

    (e) as the operator (etc.) of access to a communications system by means of which the statement is transmitted by a person over whom he has no effective control.

Where the defendant authorises or intends a repetition of the defamatory words, he will be liable both for the original publication and the re-publication; for example, the making of a defamatory statement to a newspaper reporter (perhaps about the proceedings at a meeting) could cause the defendant to be liable for the subsequent publication in the newspaper. The same could apply where the chairman of a meeting encourages the reporting of defamatory remarks,[19] but not where he did not know that the remarks were being reported.[20]

---

[14] *Robinson v. Jones* (1879) 4 L.R.Ir 391.
[15] *Williamson v. Freer* (1874) L.R. 9 C.P. 393.
[16] *Theaker v. Richardson* [1962] 1 W.L.R. 151. Cf. *Huth v. Huth* [1915] 3 K.B. 32.
[17] *Delacroix v. Thevenot* (1817) 2 Stark 63; *Pullman v. Hill Co.* [1891] 1 Q.B. 524.
[18] *Vizetelly v. Mudies* [1900] Q.B. 170, C.A.
[19] *Parkes v. Prescott* (1869) L.R. 4 Ex. 169.
[20] *McWhirter v. Manning, The Times*, October, 29 and 30, 1954; and see the cases reported in nn. 41 and 50 below.

5 Defences

30–06   The following are defences to an action for defamation:

(a) Justification
(b) Fair comment
(c) Absolute or qualified privilege
(d) Offer of amends
(e) Leave and licence
(f) Limitation

These defences are considered below.

(a) Justification

30–07   The truth of the words complained of is a defence to a civil action for libel or slander.

The defendant in a civil action who pleads justification must show the truth of the words complained of, not of his own version of them.[21]

Where the plaintiff attaches an innuendo to the words, the defendant may justify them in their ordinary meaning, or in the plaintiff's meaning, or both, but he cannot set up his own innuendo and justify that.[22]

By section 5 of the Defamation Act 1952, in an action for libel or slander in respect of words containing two or more distinct charges against the plaintiff, a defence of justification shall not fail by reason only that the truth of every charge is not proved if the words not proved to be true do not materially injure the plaintiff's reputation having regard to the truth of the remaining charges.[23]

(b) Fair comment

30–08   Analogous to the defence of privilege, but of wider application and certainly of the greatest importance in judging what can be safely said at a public meeting, is the defence of fair comment on a matter of public interest. It is concerned with expressions of opinion as distinct from assertions of fact and is equally available to a private person and to a professional critic, provided always that the criticism is fair and not actuated by malice. There must be a sufficient basis of fact to warrant the making of the observation complained of if the defence is to succeed.[24]

What is a matter of public interest is a question of law and in the courts will be decided by the judge: the conduct of public officials,[25] the administration of a local authority,[26] the speeches of public people[27] and even the affairs of business which

---

[21] *Rassam v. Budge* [1893] 1 Q.B. 571, C.A.
[22] *Watkin v. Hall* (1868) L.R. 3 Q.B. 396. For the meaning of innuendo see para. 30–04.
[23] See *Polly Peck Holdings v. Trelford* [1986] Q.B. 1000.
[24] *London Artists v. Littler (and Associated Actions):* [1969] 2 All E.R. 193, C.A.
[25] *Hunt v. Stuart Newspaper Co.* [1908] 2 K.B. 309, C.A.
[26] *Purcell v. Sowler* (1877) 2 C.P.D. 215, C.A.
[27] *Odser v. Mortimer* (1873) 28 L.T. 472.

affect only a section of the public[28] have been held to be of sufficient public interest to make a fair comment on them a good defence to an action for defamation.

It will then be for the jury to decide whether the statements are statements of fact or of opinion; and, in the latter case only,[29] to determine whether or not they are "fair." Whether or not a comment is "fair" turns on whether or not the publisher of the words has expressed an opinion which could, as a matter of objective judgement, be reasonably held on the facts as proved, even if the opinion, and the comment, might be exaggerated or obstinate. By section 6 of the Defamation Act 1952, in an action for libel or slander in respect of words consisting partly of allegations of fact and partly of expressions of opinion, failure to prove the truth of some of the facts alleged will not defeat the plea if the comment is fair having regard to the remaining facts which are proved to be true.

It has been held that the fact that the writer of a defamatory letter to the press was fictitious and that a false address was given did not defeat the defence of fair comment; provided that there was no malice and the letter did not exceed the limits of fair comment on a matter of public interest, the defence was open to the publishers of the letter. Furthermore, there is no obligation on the part of newspaper proprietors to satisfy themselves as to the bona fides of their correspondents.[30]

In all cases where "fair comment" is adopted as a defence, the defence will fail if it can be proved that the comment was made maliciously.[31] The fact that the writer, at the time he wrote, honestly believed in the truth of the charges he was making, will be no defence to an action, if such charges be made recklessly, unreasonably, and without any foundation in fact.[32]

(c) Privilege

The administration of justice, the business of government and private and commercial relationships would be gravely handicapped if every occasion of publication of words to which exception might be taken were liable to give rise to an action, and certain occasions are held, by common law or by statute, to be covered by absolute or qualified privilege.   **30–09**

A defendant who admits publication but proves that the occasion was absolutely privileged is relieved of all liability. If the occasion was one of qualified privilege, the defendant is liable only if he acted maliciously—as where he knew of the falsity of the words used or used them without their being relevant to the occasion.[33]

Absolute privilege. The following statements are protected by absolute privilege: **30–10**

    (1) Statements made in the course of parliamentary proceedings.

---

[28] *South Hetton Coal Co. v. North Eastern News Association* [1894] 1 Q.B. 133.
[29] A defence of "fair *information* on a matter of public interest" does not exist: *Blackshaw v. Lord* [1984] Q.B. 1, C.A.
[30] *Lyon Lyon v. Daily Telegraph Ltd* [1943] K.B. 746.
[31] *Joynt v. Cycle Trade Publishing Co.* [1904] 2 K.B. 292.
[32] *Campbell v. Spottiswoode* (1863) 3 B. S. 769, 32 L.J.Q.B. 185. See also *Telnikoff v. Matusevitch* [1992] 2 A.C. 343.
[33] See para. 30–03.

(2) Statements made in the ordinary course of any proceedings before any court or tribunal recognised by law.

(3) Fair and accurate reports of judicial proceedings.[34]

(4) Statements covered by s.10 of the Parliamentary Commissioner Act 1967 and s.32 of the Local Government Act 1974 (relating to reports by an ombudsman).

(5) Statements made by one officer of state to another in the course of their official duties.

Absolute privilege is not likely to apply to meetings the subject of this book, so it is not proposed to deal with the subject in detail.

30–11   *Qualified privilege.* Qualified privilege is, at common law, extended to any occasion where the person making the statement has an interest, or a legal, social or moral duty, to make the statement to the person to whom it is made, provided that the person to whom it is made has a corresponding interest or duty to receive it.[35] Effectively, the law recognises the interest or duty to make the statement and protects the person making the statement, unless there is malice on his part. The interest referred to in the definition does not include mere curiosity or political opinion, and the occasions upon which a public meeting will be privileged are rare,[36] for all the recipients of a statement made at such a meeting can seldom have a common interest with the person making the statement.

Whether any particular occasion is one of qualified privilege will depend upon all the circumstances, but, speaking generally, a communication made to a private meeting about matters which are the concern of the meeting will be privileged.

It has been held that "a legal duty is one imposed by the common law or created by statute." It is for the judge to decide what is a moral or social duty, but a fair test would appear to be the duty recognised by people of ordinary intelligence and moral principle:

> The managing director of a company, in response to an inquiry from the company's correspondents in Japan regarding another person, reported in terms of a defamatory nature as to the subject of the inquiry. The occasion was held to be privileged even though the statement was dictated to a clerk and was copied into the letter and cable books of the company.[37] The same would apply to dictation to a typist and to people taking photocopies, provided this was in the usual course of business.[38]

> Where a confidential letter was sent by one interested person to another interested person making charges injurious to the professional character of a third person in the management of certain concerns, the occasion was held to be privileged.[39] Statements made before or to governing bodies are similarly privileged, but privilege would be lost where, for example, a complaint about

---

[34] Defamation Act 1996, s.14.

[35] *Adam v. Ward* [1917] A.C. 309.

[36] *Plummer v. Charman* [1862] 1 W.L.R. 146. See also *Watts v. Times Newspapers* [1996] 1 All E.R. 152.

[37] *Edmonson v. Birch Co. Ltd* [1907] 1 K.B. 371, C.A.

[38] *Bryanston Finance Ltd v. De Vries* [1975] Q.B. 703.

[39] *McDougall v. Claridge* [1808] 1 Camp. N.P. 267.

an officer or an organisation is addressed not to the governing committee but to all members of the association.[40]

Unnecessary publication will, in other words, rebut the presumption of privilege. Thus, it was held that the privilege was destroyed where a letter was published in the magazine of a voluntary association which was on sale to the public.[41]

"A man ought not to be protected if he publishes what is in fact untrue of someone else when there is no occasion for his doing so or when there is no occasion for his publishing it to the person to whom he in fact publishes it."[42]

In another example:

A shareholder of a railway company summoned a meeting of shareholders at which he invited people other than shareholders, including reporters for the press, to attend. At the meeting comments of a defamatory nature were made against one of the directors, relating to the affairs of the company. In subsequent proceedings to recover damages it was held that the shareholder had a right to bring before the meeting a matter that was of interest to the shareholders, but in view of the fact that other persons besides shareholders were invited to attend, and as it was publicly stated that representatives of the press would be there, the occasion was not privileged.[43]

Where, however, reporters were present at a meeting in accordance with custom, and a member made untrue statements of a defamatory nature against an employee, bona fide, without malice, and believing them to be true, privilege was not lost as the member had the right to say what he felt was true on a matter of interest to the general body of members, and the fact that reporters were present did not alter the position; had the member specially invited the press, the report would not have been privileged.[44]

A matter may cease to be covered by privilege after the circumstances affording the initial protection no longer apply.[45]

Qualified privilege extends to meetings of members of public companies, so as to protect persons making a statement in good faith and in pursuance of a duty or interest to make the statement to persons who have a corresponding duty or interest to receive it. The statement must not be made with malice. The privilege also extends to reports circulated to the members, subject, of course, to their fulfilling these requirements.[46] For example:

A solicitor, acting for shareholders of a company, printed and distributed to them, but to no one else, a circular which reflected upon the promoters and

---

[40] *Martin v. Strong* (1836) 5 A. E. 535; 6 L.J.K.B. 48.
[41] *Cutler v. McPhail* [1962] 2 Q.B. 292.
[42] *Adam v. Ward* [1917] A.C. 321.
[43] *Parsons v. Surgey* (1864) 4 F. F. 247.
[44] *Pittard v. Oliver* [1891] 1 Q.B. 474, C.A.; and see *Sharman v. Merritt and Hatcher Ltd* (1916) 32 T.L.R. 360 *Cf. Purcell v. Sowler* (1877) 2 C.P.D. 215, C.A.
[45] *R. v. Lancashire County Council Police Committee* [1980] 1 Q.B. 603.
[46] *Lawless v. Anglo-Egyptian Cotton Co.* (1869) L.R. 4 Q.B. 262, 38 L.J.Q.B. 129.

directors of the company and invited shareholders to meet and discuss the position and take measures to protect their common interests. The Court of Appeal was of the opinion that the circular on the face of it appeared to be of a privileged description.[47]

Privilege also extends to statements made at meetings of directors, provided they act *bona fide* and in the interests of the company. Communications made in the proper following up of board meetings are usually covered by qualified privilege provided they are made on a "need to know" basis.[48]

Similarly, letters written to the Stock Exchange, the Department of Trade or the Take-over Panel about the conduct of a company's affairs (including the conduct of meetings) would be privileged.

Qualified privilege will cover statements made at meetings of local authorities and their committees but will probably not extend to informal groupings such as party caucus meetings and meetings of officers. It also arises in two areas covered by statute:

(1) Section 10 of the Defamation Act 1952 provides that a defamatory statement published by or on behalf of a candidate in any election to a local government authority or to Parliament shall not be deemed to be published on a privileged occasion on the ground that it is material to a question in issue in the election, whether or not the person by whom it is published is qualified to vote in the election. Other defences, such as fair comment, remain of course available in respect of matters published at elections.

(2) Under section 100H of the Local Government Act 1972, where any accessible document for a meeting of a principal council or its committees and sub-committees is supplied to or open to inspection by a member of the public or is supplied for the benefit of any newspaper, the publication of any defamatory matter in the document is covered by qualified privilege. "Accessible documents" mean the agenda, reports and background paper for a local authority meeting, as discussed in Chapter 29.

It should again be emphasised that a defence of qualified privilege can only succeed in the absence of malice; the burden of proving malice is on the plaintiff.

Media reports

30–12   Qualified privilege is, by section 15 of the Defamation Act 1996, given to the publication of any such report or other matter as is mentioned in the Schedule to the Act unless the publication is proved to be made with malice.[49] The medium of publication includes newspapers, radio, television and all forms of broadcasting.

---

[47] *Quartz Hill Gold Mining Co. v. Beall* (1882) 20 Ch.D. 501, 51 L.J. Ch. 874.
[48] *Watt v. Longsdon* [1930] 1 K.B. 130.
[49] Defamation Act 1996, s.15(1).

Reports having qualified privilege are divided into two groups: those in the first group are privileged without explanation or contradiction; those in the second group are privileged subject to explanation or contradiction.

In defamation proceedings in respect of the publication of a report or other statement mentioned in Part II, there is no defence under the section if the plaintiff shows that the defendant:

    (a) was requested by him to publish in a suitable manner a reasonable letter or statement by way of explanation or contradiction, and

    (b) refused or neglected to do so.

For this purpose "in a suitable manner" means in the same manner as the publication complained of or in a manner that is adequate and reasonable in the circumstances.[50] The section does not apply to the publication to the public, or a section of the public, of matter which is not of public concern and the publication of which is not for the public benefit.[51] No privilege attaches to the publication of any matter the publication of which is prohibited by law.

Three types of report contained in the group listed in Part II of the Schedule to the Defamation Act 1996 are of particular importance in the context of meetings:

    (i) Paragraph 11 provides that the qualified privilege conferred by the section shall extend to a fair and accurate report of the proceedings at any public meeting or sitting in the United Kingdom of (among others) a local authority or local authority committee, a person appointed by a local authority to hold a local enquiry in pursuance of any statutory provision and any other tribunal, board, committee or body constituted by or under any statutory provision.

        For example, a newspaper published a fair and accurate report of an agenda paper supplied for the use of councillors at a borough council meeting which was open to the public. The agenda paper contained a committee report which imputed incompetence to the superintendent of a public cemetery. It was held that the report dealt with a matter of public concern, and that its publication was for the public benefit and therefore privileged.[52]

    (ii) Paragraph 12 covers a fair and accurate report of proceedings at any public meeting held in a member state of the European Union. Here, "public meeting" means a meeting *bona fide* and lawfully held for a lawful purpose and for the furtherance or discussion of a matter of public concern, whether admission to the meeting is general or restricted.

    (iii) Paragraph 13 covers a fair and accurate report of proceedings at a general meeting of a UK public company.

        However, the report must confine itself to matters in which the public have an interest: a report in a financial paper of a company meeting included verbatim the chairman's speech, in which accusations were

---

[50] *ibid.*, s.15(2).
[51] *ibid.*, s.15(3).
[52] *Sharman v. Merritt and Hatcher Ltd* (1916) 32 T.L.R. 360.

made against the cashier of the company which were of a defamatory nature and, furthermore, were unfounded. The newspaper was held liable in damages as the chairman in his reference to the cashier was not discussing matters in which the public was interested, and the publication was not for the public benefit.[53]

Apart from the absolute or qualified privilege granted by statute to certain types of report, privilege would only attach to a publication in a newspaper where it was proved that it was the duty of the defendant to publish the report in the interests of society generally, which in turn had a legitimate interest in receiving it.[54]

(d) Offer of amends

30–13   Sections 2–4 of the Defamation Act 1996 are designed to enable a person who publishes a statement alleged to be defamatory of another to make amends instead of paying damages in defamation proceedings. They provide as follows:

The offer of amends may be general or "qualified"—*i.e.* in relation to a specific defamatory meaning. It must be in writing, must be expressed to be an offer for the purposes of section 2, and must state whether the offer is a qualified offer.

The making of an offer consists of making a suitable correction and sufficient apology; the person making the statement must publish the correction and apology in a "reasonable and practicable manner" and pay to the aggrieved party such compensation (if any) and costs as are agreed or determined to be payable.

An offer may not be made by a person who has served a defence in relation to the statement complained of. An offer of amends under the section can be withdrawn before it is accepted.

The aggrieved person cannot, after accepting the offer, bring or continue defamation proceedings against the maker(s) of the statement but he is entitled to enforce the offer and the court will enable him to do so.

Section 4 provides that if an offer is duly made and not accepted then the fact of the offer shall be a defence to defamation proceedings against the offeror by the person aggrieved. There is no defence available to the person who made the statement if that person knew or had reason to believe that the statement complained of:

(a) referred to the aggrieved party or was likely to be understood as referring to him, and

(b) was both false and defamatory of that party;

but it shall be presumed until the contrary is shown that he did not know and had no reason to believe that was the case.

(e) Leave and licence

30–14   It is a defence[55] to an action for the defendant to plead and prove that the plantiff has authorised or assented to the publication of the words complained of.

---

[53] *Ponsford v. Financial Times Ltd* (1900) 16 T.L.R. 248.

[54] *Allbutt v. General Council of Medical Education* (1889) 23 Q.B.D. 400 and *Loutchansky v. Times Newspapers Ltd* [2001] EWCA Civ 1805

[55] *Moore v. News of the World Ltd* [1972] All E.R. 913, C.A.

(f) Limitation

The time limit applicable to actions is one year from the date on which the cause **30–15** of action accrues); however the court may disapply this time limit if it considers it is inequitable.[56]

---

[56] Defamation Act 1996, s.5.

INDEX